3 3014 00087 0487

British and Irish architectural history

British and Irish architectural history

a bibliography
and guide to
sources
of information

Ruth H Kamen

The Architectural Press: London

Framingham State College
Framingham, Massachusetts

First published in 1981 by The Architectural Press Ltd,
9 Queen Anne's Gate, London SW1H 9BY

© Ruth H. Kamen 1981

British Library Cataloguing in Publication Data

Kamen, Ruth
   British and Irish architectural history.
   1. Architecture—Great Britain—Bibliography
   I. Title
   016.720'941   Z5944'941
    ISBN 0 85139 077 3

All rights reserved. No part of this publication may be
reproduced, stored in a retrieval system or transmitted, in
any form or by any means, electronic, mechanical,
photocopying, recording or otherwise, without the prior
permission of the publishers. Such permission, if granted,
is subject to a fee depending on the nature of the use.

Book and typographic design by
Peter Rea ARCA FSTD
Archetype Visual Studies London

Text filmset in VIP Imprint
9/9pt regular and bold; track 1 spacing; unjustified
Index set in 7/8pt regular

Printed in Great Britain by Mackays of Chatham

Contents

Z
5944
G7
K34
1981b

Foreword

Until now the forest of architectural history has never been systematically charted. The explorer plunged in, took his chance, and sometimes went wildly astray. One example will make the point. In 1901 the reputable scholars Inigo Triggs and Henry Tanner published their *Some authentic works of Inigo Jones*; it is now known that over 60% of the buildings they attributed to Jones were not in fact his work at all.

In the last 40 years pioneers—Summerson, Pevsner, Colvin, Harris chief among them—have introduced a meticulously detailed scholarship, and wrought a revolution in technique and method. The subject is now a true discipline, with a new generation of trained researchers mapping in detail the areas colonised by these explorers. The forest has been marked out, its broad configurations and vantage points established, its trails blazed, and its swamps and seemingly impenetrable thickets at least signposted.

But until the present book there has not been a reliable bird's eye view of the whole terrain. Of course a map doesn't tell you everything; it simply shows where to start and the direction it is best to move in. And this is essential, not just for already expert researchers (though they will find much useful detail here), but for an altogether wider public too.

Society has come increasingly to see that architecture is not its own self-contained world, of aesthetics, of design and technical skills, but the physical fabric which gives form to all our lives age by age. The built environment and those who have contributed to it, bit by bit, at whatever scale, have lessons for the social and economic historian, the conservationist, the planner, the biographer, as well as for the architect himself and the historian of his work. Here is a town (and country) trail for them.

The unending enquiries to the Royal Institute of British Architects' British Architectural Library make crystal clear the range of approaches to the history of architecture, and the diversity of reasons for them. Here I must declare an interest. Ruth Kamen is a colleague of mine. Her book is founded on the solid experience of eight years as Head of our Information Services. Like all good information workers she has a passionate pertinacity; she dislikes (indeed, spurns) the very possibility of being beaten by queries.

All of us whose work involves the constant use of reference material are sharply aware of the regrettable tendency to put together, with scissors and paste, collages of sources and titles simply lifted from existing works. *British and Irish architectural history* is different in kind from these merely parasitical compilations. Everything cited in it has been examined or checked by its compiler. The result will make my work life, and that of everyone wise enough to keep a copy at his desk side, appreciably easier.

David Dean
Director of Library Services
British Architectural Library

Acknowledgement

The research, compilation and publication of this bibliography and guide have been made possible with the help of grants from the Interbuild Fund and the Building Centre Trust.

British and Irish architectural history: a bibliography and guide to sources of information is intended as an aid to reference and research. The descriptions of books, periodicals and periodical articles, indexes and abstracts, collections, organisations and services are designed to assist students, scholars, researchers, teachers in schools and universities, librarians, local historians, picture researchers and the general public in identifying and using the tools and sources available when seeking information about British and Irish architecture. While the guide includes 870 annotated entries, such a work can never hope to be fully comprehensive. The entries therefore form a highly selective and even subjective list, based largely on the collective experience of the staff at the RIBA's British Architectural Library in answering three types of query. The first type is architect oriented. Having only the name of an architect, the enquirer wishes further information, often as minimal as birth and death dates, sometimes more exhaustive such as a complete list of the architect's work with corresponding bibliographic references. The second type of query is building oriented. Knowing the name or location of a building, the enquirer wants to find out when it was built, who built it, and whether there are any descriptions, drawings, plans or illustrations of it. The third type concerns building types and periods or styles, and it is in response to such enquiries that the selective bibliography is included in this guide.

This guide is a very modest starting point, which for the most part omits several categories of sources which could prove valuable indeed, but which, because of their specific nature, fall outside the scope of a general guide. Categories which have been excluded are works devoted to individual architects, works of a regional or local character (with the occasional exception of London), and works on specific buildings. While this guide will not answer the question 'What information is there on the Houses of Parliament?', it will indicate where and how to find out.

The items selected for inclusion were chosen for a variety of reasons; sometimes because they are 'standard' works or the 'best' books, sometimes because they are the 'only' books, and definitive works have yet to appear. In some cases both scholarly and introductory texts have been included, to cater for the needs of different users. Many of the entries are included simply because they themselves provide good lists of references for further reading. If users of this guide also use the bibliographies in the books noted here, then many of the items omitted in this list will not altogether be missed. The printed library catalogues: Avery (no 4); Department of the Environment

(no 18); Harvard (no 29); and the Royal Institute of British Architects (no 45), serve as comprehensive bibliographies of all the subjects covered in this guide. The bibliographies and printed catalogues are particularly useful when trying to identify or locate contemporary source books for a particular period, construction detail or method, building type, etc, as such publications are generally excluded from this guide. An attempt has been made to select references which are available in the average modern library, or through the interlibrary loan service. Most of the items have been personally inspected and are held by the British Architectural Library. Some older and more obscure items have been included when they were thought to be too important and useful to ignore and, with the increasing issue of reprints, may become more widely available. Reprint and microform editions are indicated when I was aware of them, but no special effort was made to record these. Many of the items cited are in serious need of up-dating, but until superseded, remain very useful and are included for this reason.

Criteria for inclusion in the sections on societies, institutions and organisations (5.2) and on sources of architectural photographs, slides and films (6.2) were far less stringent than for the bibliographical sections. Listed here are not only the major architectural collections and archives, but also more specialist and fringe bodies. Thus organisations concerned with business records find a place as they can sometimes advise on the archives or history of an architectural practice or building firm; general register offices and genealogical societies are listed to aid anyone trying to trace dates of birth or death or the descendants of a particular architect; church, theatre, transport, horticultural, furniture and other specialist societies are listed because although not primarily architectural, their records or corporate knowledge may be helpful when trying to find out about particular buildings, building types or details; open-air and other museums are included where vernacular and other buildings or parts of buildings can be studied; and some organisations without collections or information services are included, either for the purpose of explaining their role (eg in preservation) or to bring their activities to the attention of the architectural enthusiast who might wish to support their aims or participate in their programmes.

It is difficult to indicate a precise cut-off date for entries appearing in the guide. New items were added and annotations amended as late as the final weeks of preparation of the manuscript in May 1980; a limited number of additions and amendments have been inserted at proof stage. Some items which were not yet published have also been included when they have come to my attention.

In order to improve the usefulness of future editions of this guide, the author and the publishers welcome all suggestions and additions. Corrections will be most welcome.

Acknowledgement is due to all those organisations and individuals who have completed the questionnaires and to the many authors, compilers and editors of reference works on which I have so much relied. I hope that their inclusion in this guide will indicate my indebtedness. Special thanks are due to Philippa Lewis for providing information on photographic collections and to my colleagues at the British Architectural Library for their suggestions, advice, encouragement and patience. Above all I should like to express my gratitude to all those who have visited, telephoned or written to the British Architectural Library asking 'How do I find out about . . . ?' or 'Is there any information on . . . ?' – it is they who have prompted me to write this book and it is to them I dedicate it. I hope it goes some way towards answering their questions.

Ruth H. Kamen
British Architectural Library
Royal Institute of British Architects
66 Portland Place
London W1N 4AD

August 1981

How to use the guide

General information

The guide is arranged in seven main sections and within each section the entries are arranged alphabetically by author, or corporate body. Anonymous works are entered alphabetically by title. Each entry is prefixed by an item number; references within the text and from the index are to these numbers, not to page numbers. Each entry is intended to be listed only once, under what appears to be the most appropriate heading. The disadvantages of this scheme are hopefully counter-balanced by the index and cross-references.

There are three points of entry to the guide:
1. By broad subject areas, which are set out on the contents page. To facilitate a subject approach, many sections include lists of cross-references to useful entries elsewhere in the guide and the index includes subjects.
2. By author or corporate body, by consulting the index.
3. By title, by consulting the index.

The arrangement

The first section of the guide, **1 How to find out: guides to the literature**, includes publications which describe or list sources such as topographical collections, archives, maps and books. Some of the items are 'how to' books which provide guidance on what material is available and how to approach and use it; others are merely bibliographies or directories.

The second section of the guide, **2 How to find out about architects and buildings: published sources**, is in two parts. The first includes biographical dictionaries, encyclopaedias, directories, surveys, and indexes, while the second describes indexes to research and theses.

In most of the publications listed in this section one can look up either the name of an architect or the name of a building, or in some cases both. Some publications span the whole of architectural history, while others may be limited to a particular period or even year. In order to make it possible to scan the entries to ascertain quickly which items will be useful when searching for information on, for example, an architect working in the 1930s or an eighteenth-century building, each entry is coded, following the bibliographical description, as follows:

archts   Indicates that it is possible to look up the names of architects in the item described

bldgs   Indicates that it is possible to look up the names of buildings (sometimes indirectly under location) in the item described

prehist/ med   Useful for the period from prehistory to medieval

ren/ neoclas   Useful for the period from renaissance to neoclassic

19/20c   Useful for the nineteenth and/or twentieth centuries

For example, Colvin's *Biographical dictionary of British architects* is coded 'archts, bldgs; ren/neoclas', which indicates that in this publication it is possible to look up the names of architects (fairly obvious from the title) as well as the names of buildings (not at all obvious from the title) and that it is useful for the period roughly from the renaissance to the neoclassic.

Depending on the publication, the information found for any architect or building will range from a full biography or description to just a note of an architect's dates or references to other publications or sources. If one is just searching for some general information about a well-known figure or famous building then the major biographical dictionaries (Colvin, Harvey, etc) and guides (*Buildings of England, Shell*, etc) will probably provide the information, but if trying to find 'everything' about a particular architect or building or if trying to locate details of more obscure persons or buildings, then a wider range of publications may have to be consulted.

The third section, **3 How to find out about architects and buildings: unpublished sources**, provides descriptions of catalogues, indexes and other unpublished sources in the British Architectural Library which either provide information about an architect (eg the RIBA Nomination Papers often provide biographical details) or a building (eg the Goodhart-Rendel index gives the name of the architect for each church listed) or serve as a starting point to where information will be found (eg the 'Grey Books' index provides references to periodical articles). Each item is coded as in the previous section. References to additional unpublished sources are indicated at the end of this section.

The fourth section, **4 How to find out about architects and buildings: periodicals and periodical indexes**, is divided into four parts. The first includes publications which either list or describe journals which are currently being published or have been published which devote themselves either exclusively or substantially to architecture; the second includes those publications which provide a library location in Britain for a particular journal; the third lists some of the more important, mainly nineteenth-century, journals of value to the architectural historian; the fourth is a list of periodical indexes.

The fifth section, **5 Societies, institutions and organisations**, begins with a list of published directories to societies. This is followed by a description of relevant societies, etc which provides for each, where applicable, the following information: name, address, date of founding, collections/library, enquiry services and conditions of use, hours, publications and activities.

The sixth section, **6 Photographs, slides and films**, begins with descriptions of publications useful to picture researchers, lecturers, etc. This is followed by a guide to collections of architectural photographs and slides.

The seventh section, **7 British and Irish architectural history: a selective bibliography**, is intended as a basic list of books. The section begins with general books on architectural history, including dictionaries of terms, then lists books on the various periods and styles, the history of building construction, details and decoration and concludes with sections devoted to various building types.

At the end of each section references are provided to items elsewhere in the book which relate to that section, whether monographs, bibliographies, catalogues, periodicals, organisations or photographic collections. For example, if trying to locate information on theatres, besides the books on theatres listed in section 7.11 Building types: recreational, the reader will be referred to items described elsewhere, such as directories of theatre research resources, periodical indexes in which it is possible to trace articles on theatres, library catalogues which will indicate additional material on the subject, collections of photographs of theatre buildings and organisations with an interest in or information about theatres. Thus each section is designed to serve as a mini-guide to sources of information on the subject.

One of the most difficult problems encountered in compiling this guide was deciding into which section a particular title should be placed, eg John Harvey's *Perpendicular style* could as easily have been placed in 7.9 Building types: ecclesiastical as in 7.2 Renaissance to neoclassic. Cross-references have therefore been provided and it is hoped that the index will direct the user to the relevant material.

Abbreviations used

BAL	British Architectural Library
Bibl	bibliography/bibliographical
c	circa
cm	centimetres
dept	department
ed	edition
enl	enlarged
GB	Great Britain
GLC	Greater London Council
HMSO	Her/His Majesty's Stationery Office
in	inches
incl	including
m	million
mm	millimetres
mss	manuscripts
n.d.	no date
n.p.	no place
orig	originally
p/pp	page, pages
PSA	Property Services Agency
pt/pts	part, parts
publ	published
ref/refs	reference, references
repr	reprinted
rev	revised
RIBA	Royal Institute of British Architects
suppl	supplement
UDC	Universal decimal classification
UK	United Kingdom
vol/vols	volume, volumes

Introduction

This section includes publications which describe or list sources, such as topographical collections, archives, maps and books. Some of the items are 'how to' books which provide guidance on what material is available and how to approach and use it, others are merely bibliographies or directories.

Many publications often cited as sources of information have been omitted, not because they do not provide information, but because the more specialist publications generally cover the same ground and more. Thus, for example, the *British humanities index*, the *Art index* and the *Architectural index* are not included because the *Architectural periodicals index* (and its predecessors) and the *Avery periodicals index* will probably have indexed the same architectural journals in greater depth.

For information on the resources, and guides to the resources of specific institutions, Section 5.2: Guide to societies, institutions and organisations should be consulted.

Ancient monuments and historic buildings.   1
    Government publications sectional list,
    no 27. London: HMSO. Annual.
        Lists the guides to ancient monuments and
        historic buildings in England, Wales and
        Scotland published by the Department of the
        Environment as well as the publications of the
        Royal Commissions on Ancient and Historic
        Monuments and Constructions.

Architectural periodicals index. Vol 1, no   2
    1– ; Aug/Dec 1972– . London: British
    Architectural Library, 1973– .
        An index of selected articles in some 300
        periodicals from all over the world on
        architecture and related subjects. The fields
        covered in the *API* include architecture and
        allied arts, constructional technology, design and
        environmental studies, landscape, planning, and
        relevant research. In all these fields articles on
        both current practice and historical aspects are
        included. In planning the stress is on actual
        schemes, conservation and urban history rather
        than on pure theory and research, or its
        sociological aspects. In construction and
        building technology proprietary product
        information and highly technical material
        written for other disciplines such as civil or
        mechanical engineering, surveying etc are not

indexed. Nor in professional practice are statistics or case law covered. In areas such as interiors, decoration, painting, sculpture, furniture, landscaping and the like, the criterion is normally the involvement of, or the direct significance of the work to, the architect. As to form, book reviews, letters and news items are generally omitted but obituaries of architects (though not simply notices of death) are included.

Issued four times a year, the fourth issue cumulates all material included in the three previous issues, as well as articles indexed in the fourth quarter. It is an analytical index arranged alphabetically by subject. General articles about an architect and his work (but not articles on specific projects) are entered under the heading Architects: GB, which is further subdivided alphabetically by the name of the architect or architectural practice. The cumulative issue (and from 1978 the quarterly issues) also includes a names index which provides access to articles on specific projects of an architect, as well as to general articles on him. To locate references to a specific building, the approach is by subject (building type), subdivided by country (eg GB), town, then name of project. From 1978 the cumulative edition includes a topographical and building names index.

Continues the *Comprehensive index to architectural periodicals* (46) and the *RIBA Annual review of periodical articles* (47).

Armstrong, Norma, E. S.   3
Local collections in Scotland. Glasgow:
    Scottish Library Association, 1977. 174pp.
    (Scottish library studies, no 5).
        The second section is a directory of resources
        with a subject index.

Avery Architectural Library   4
Catalog of the Avery Memorial
    Architectural Library of Columbia
    University. 2nd ed, enl Boston (Mass): G. K. Hall,
    1968. 19 vols. 1st suppl 1973. 4 vols. 2nd suppl 1975.
    4 vols. 3rd suppl 1977. 3 vols. 4th suppl 1979. 3 vols.
    (further supplements in progress).
        A union catalogue representing author, subject

subject/*continued*
(and selectively, title) entries for books and
periodicals in the Avery Library, and other
volumes primarily on sculpture and painting in
the Columbia University Library system.
Entries are arranged in one alphabetical
sequence. Material on an architect is located
under his surname. Material on a specific project
of an architect is entered indirectly under
location (eg London. Buckingham Palace). The
Avery Library's drawings collection is entered
under the heading 'Architectural drawings',
beneath which material is sub-arranged
alphabetically by architect's surname, or if
anonymous, by title.

Avery Architectural Library 5
An index to architectural periodicals.
2nd ed. Boston (Mass): G. K. Hall, 1973. 15
vols. First suppl 1975. 1 vol. Second suppl 1977. 1
vol. Third suppl 1979. 1 vol (further supplements in
progress).
A periodicals index, begun in 1934, with
world-wide coverage of architectural periodicals
(excluding those in non-western alphabets), with
the major American and some European
architectural periodicals back-indexed to their
beginning date. This is a dictionary catalogue,
arranged in one alphabetical sequence, which
can be approached by name of architect,
building type, location, name of building, or
subject. When searching by location, it is useful
to note that while some information is indexed
under country (eg England), it is more usually
entered under the proper name of the town,
village, etc.

Baggs, A. P. and **Gee**, E. A. 6
Copy books. York: Institute of Advanced
Architectural Studies, 1964. 32pp.
A bibliography of pattern books and craftsmen's
handbooks up to the mid-nineteenth century.
The books noted in this list in general give a
series of measured plans, elevations and details
which can be copied by other architects and
craftsmen. Also included are books used by
craftsmen during their work. The books are
listed in chronological order within the following
groups: (1) continental precursors; (2) architects'
designs; (3) craftsmen's text books; (4) special
studies; (5) gothic exemplars; (6) foreign
exemplars; (7) modern facsimiles.

Baggs, A. P. 7
'Pattern books and vernacular architecture
before 1790', in *Vernacular architecture*,
vol 3, 1972, pp 22–23.
A list of eleven popular handbooks and six books
of design published in Britain between 1724 and
1788 which may be considered to have
influenced vernacular architecture. Not a
complete listing, but supplemented by a short
bibliography and a note of other sources.

Barley, M. W. 8
A guide to British topographical collections,
by M. W. Barley; with contributions by P.
D. A. Harvey and Julia E. Poole. London: Council
for British Archaeology, 1974. 159pp.
Describes briefly those collections of
topographical illustrations (drawings, prints and
photographs) to be found in public repositories,
and also in a few private collections, in Britain.

British Tourist Authority 9
Town trails and urban walks. 2nd ed.
London: British Tourist Authority, 1976.
52pp. Bibl p50.
Trails are listed in England, Isle of Man,
Scotland and Wales, alphabetically by place
name within counties or regions. Each trail is
numbered and an index of places appears at the
end. The trails are identified by symbols which
indicate when they have an architectural theme,
are of general interest, focus on historical
features, are concerned with industrial
archaeology etc. *See also* 23.

The British Transport Historical Records 10
collection: a provisional guide.
[London]: Public Record Office, 1977. 13pp.
The records of the various private companies
and other bodies engaged in the transport
industry were taken over by the British
Transport Commission in 1948 following the
nationalisation of transport under the Transport
Act 1947. This guide deals with those records
and others transferred subsequently by the
various nationalised undertakings. Includes a
brief note of other sources of material for
transport history. For a discussion of the
usefulness of these records *see* 43.

Carrick, Neville 11
How to find out about the arts: a guide to
sources of information. Oxford:
Pergamon Press, 1965. 164pp. (The Commonwealth
and international library, libraries and technical
information division).
Includes architecture. Format similar to item 51.

Colvin, H. M. 12
English architectural history: a guide to
sources. 2nd ed. Shalfleet Manor (Isle of
Wight): Pinhorns, 1976. 23pp. (Pinhorns handbooks,
1).
Refers to sources of records and original
documents. Contents include: royal buildings;
public buildings; churches; domestic
architecture; architects and craftsmen; drawings
and topographical views; architectural journals.
Based on an article by the author entitled
'Architectural history and its records' (*Archives*,
vol 2, 1955, pp 300–311). For Scottish
architectural history *see* 20.

Cossons, Neil   13
The BP book of industrial archaeology.
> Newton Abbot: David and Charles, 1975.
> 496pp. Bibl pp 476–488.
>> A detailed introduction with appendices listing museums of industry and industrial archaeological organisations.

Coulson, Anthony J.   14
A bibliography of design in Britain,
> **1851–1970**. London: Design Council, 1979.
> 299pp.
>> Contents include table of important dates, sections on 'Fostering design' (developments in education; official bodies, professional organisations and sponsors; international exhibitions; museums and collections), 'Design and designers' (theories of design and craftsmanship; general chronological studies, periods and tendencies; important designers; colour, ornament and pattern; technical, social and economic factors), 'Areas of design activity' (interior design; furniture design etc) 'Journals', 'Bibliographies, indexes, abstracts and catalogues'. The 'Subject finder' provides an index of sections, subjects and some important individuals, but *not* an index of authors or of all individuals named. The bibliography excludes most aspects of architecture, town and country planning and civil engineering.

Courtauld Institute of Art, University of London   15
Annual bibliography of the history of
> **British art**. Vols 1–6, 1934–1946/8.
> Cambridge: Cambridge University Press, 1936–56.
> 8 vols. Reprinted, New York: Johnson, 1970. 5 vols.
>> Classified bibliography with an index at the end of each volume. Indexes some 160 periodicals, as well as including books. Covers architecture, painting, sculpture, the graphic arts and the applied arts. Primarily concerned with the history of art, but writings on modern art and living artists are included. A list of periodicals searched appears in each volume. Each volume contains an index. An index to publications of the 1930s and '40s, a period not well-served by the Avery, Harvard or RIBA indexes.

Currer-Briggs, Noel, *editor*   16
A handbook of British family history: a
> **guide to methods and sources.**, 2nd rev
> ed. Saffron Walden: Family History Services, 1979.
> 88pp. Bibl refs pp 86–88.
>> An introductory booklet to the type of material available for tracing ancestry. Includes a list of record offices and libraries in Great Britain and Eire. No index.

Day, Alan Edwin   17
Archaeology: a reference handbook.
> London: Clive Bingley, 1978. 319pp.
>> Contains 639 annotated entries in alphabetical order covering bibliographies, encyclopaedias, atlases, gazetteers, dictionaries, standard works, societies and journals relevant to the study of British archaeology. Index.

Department of the Environment Library   18
Catalogues of the United Kingdom
> **Department of the Environment**
> **Library**. Boston (Mass): G. K. Hall, 1977. 15 vols.
>> Formed by the amalgamation of the Library of the Ministry of Housing and Local Government and the Library of the Ministry of Transport, the Department of the Environment is one of the largest collections of its kind in the world. Approximately 250,000 books, pamphlets and government reports, and some 2,500 current periodicals provide rich source material on all subjects pertaining to the environment.
>> The catalogues of the library contain approximately 580,000 bibliographic entries offering access by author and by subject. Major subject areas covered by the literature include social and environmental planning; roads, traffic and transport; countryside and recreation; housing and local government; new towns, water, sewerage and public hygiene; and the built environment. The collection is particularly strong in post-war planning material. The scope of the collection ranges from early-nineteenth century local government reports to recent economic, parliamentary, statistical, scientific and technical information.
>> The catalogues are divided into five parts: author and classified sequences covering books, reports, surveys, and published and semi-published material of all kinds; author and classified sequences of abstracts of periodical articles; and an extensive alphabetical subject index to the revised Library of Congress classification used in the two classified sequences.

Dobai, Johannes   19
Die Kunstliteratur des Klassizismus und
> **der Romantik in England**. Bern: Benteli,
> 1974–77. 3 vols.
>> Vol 1 (1974) covers the period 1700–1750. Includes chapters on Palladian architectural publications, building dictionaries and architectural treatises, writings of the leading architects, pattern books, a few further sources to architectural changes in taste and landscape gardening.
>> Vol 2 (1975) covers the period 1750–1790. Includes chapters on general works of illustration and theory (writings on building projects, building techniques and building

building/*continued*
types), archaeological architectural publications,
Sir William Chambers, various publications of
the leading architects of the time, pattern books
and landscape gardening.

Vol 3 (1977) covers the period 1790–1840.
Includes chapters on theoretical and general
publications and writings, writings on building
technique and practice, architectural theory and
architectural history, pattern books, Sir John
Soane, Augustus Welby Northmore Pugin and
landscape gardening.

An extremely comprehensive work. There
are introductory bibliographies in each volume
as well as extensive bibliographies appended to
each chapter. No index, which makes it rather
difficult to use.

Dunbar, John G.   20
**'Source materials for Scottish architectural
history'**, in *Art libraries journal*, vol 4, no
3, Autumn 1979, pp 17–26.

A short guide to the main printed and
documentary source materials that are available
for the study of Scottish architectural history.
The general arrangement of the text follows that
adopted by H. M. Colvin in his *Guide to the
sources of English architectural history* (12).
Contents include: royal buildings; public
buildings; churches; domestic architecture;
architects and craftsmen; architectural drawings
and photographs, topographical views, etc; and
standard works of reference, journals, etc. This
is a revised version of a pamphlet published by
the Scottish Georgian Society under the same
title in 1969.

Emmison, F. G.   21
Archives and local history. 2nd ed.
Chichester: Phillimore, 1974. 112pp.

The starting point is around 1538 and the
emphasis is almost wholly on local records in
local repositories. Gives a detailed account of all
the main groups of local records, county,
borough, ecclesiastical, parish, estate, and
family. Within each of these sections there are
notes on the kind of information which can be
got from the classes most commonly used:
quarter sessions records, railway plans, borough
court books, wills, inventories, bishops'
visitation books, parish registers, vestry books,
overseers of the poor accounts, settlement
papers, guardians' minutes, charity and school
minutes, non-conformist accounts, manor court
rolls, and household accounts.

Georgian Group   22
**Recommended books on Georgian
architecture and decoration**. London:
The Georgian Group, 1965. 23pp. (Georgian
pamphlet, 5).

An annotated list of books which are considered
likely to prove most useful to the general reader
as an introduction. Contents: books of a general

nature; biographies of architects; books on
particular places; books on particular types of
buildings; books on particular architectural
features; dictionaries. In need of up-dating.

Goodey, Brian   23
**Urban walks and town trails: origins,
principles and sources**. Birmingham:
University of Birmingham, Centre for Urban and
Regional Studies, Dec 1974. 118pp. (Research
memorandum, 40).

This book is particularly useful for its complete
list of town trails in Britain up to December 1,
1974. Supersedes the author's *Urban trails: a
preliminary list of trails and sources*, Working
paper 29, Nov 1974. *See also* 9.

Guide to the literature of art history. Edited   24
by Etta Arntzen and Robert Rainwater.
Chicago: American Library Association; London: Art
Book Company, 1980. 635pp.

An authoritative annotated bibliography divided
into four sections: general reference sources
(bibliographies, directories, dictionaries and
encyclopaedias); general primary and secondary
sources; the particular arts (including
architecture); serials (periodicals and series).
Developed from Mary W. Chamberlin, *Guide to
art reference books* (Chicago: American Library
Association, 1959).

Guildhall Library   25
**London buildings and sites: a guide for
researchers in Guildhall Library**.
London: Corporation of London, 1976. 21pp.

Explains the sources available to the researcher
under the following headings: street names,
numbers and signs; the owner (title deeds,
freeholders); the occupier (street directories,
census returns and the 1695 inhabitants list,
electoral registers, rate and land tax assessments,
famous occupiers); descriptions of property
(general surveys, Noble Collection, periodicals
and newspapers, parish and ward histories, etc,
insurance valuations, estate archives,
inventories, property sale catalogues, building
regulations, planning and redevelopment);
illustrations (plans, maps, other surveys);
Medieval and Roman topography (Corporation
of London Records Office, Public Record
Office, secondary sources, archaeological
evidence).

Harley, John Brian   26
**Historian's guide to Ordnance Survey
maps**. London: National Council of Social
Service, 1964. 51pp.

Deals with the various editions of the smaller
scale OS maps as well as the larger town plans,
which are particularly important to the urban
historian. The survey includes maps for
Scotland and Wales as well as England.

Harley, John Brian   27
Maps for the local historian: a guide to the
  British sources. London: National
Council of Social Service, 1972. 86pp, 8 plates.
Bibl postscript, pp 77–86.
      Separate chapters deal with town plans, estate,
    enclosure and communication maps and county
    maps. Treatment is confined to Great Britain
    and the time span is from the origin of maps to
    approximately mid-nineteenth century.
    Ordnance Survey maps are not included. Useful
    aid to locating or interpreting particular groups
    of maps and plans. No index.

Harris, John   28
'Sources for architectural history in
  England'. (Reprint from *Journal of the*
Society of Architectural Historians, vol 24, no 4, Dec
1965, pp 297–300).
      Includes: private domestic architecture,
    manuscript documentation, drawings, engraved
    and printed sources, modern publications and
    photographs, royal buildings, secular and
    ecclesiastical public buildings.

Harvard University. Graduate School of   29
Design.
  Catalog of the Library of the Graduate
  School of Design, Harvard University. Boston
(Mass): G. K. Hall, 1968. 44 vols. 1st suppl 1970. 2
vols. 2nd suppl 1974. 5 vols 3rd suppl 1979. 3 vols
(further supplements in progress).
      A catalogue representing subject, author and
    title entries for books, pamphlets, theses and
    periodical articles covering the fields of
    architecture, landscape architecture and urban
    planning. Entries are arranged in one
    alphabetical sequence. Material on an architect is
    located under his surname. Material on a specific
    project of an architect is entered indirectly under
    location (eg London. Buckingham Palace).

Harvey, John H.   30
'Architectural archives', in *Archives*, vol 2,
  no 2, 1954, pp 117–122.
      Describes the nature and significance to the
    historian of two distinct types of architectural
    archives: records of all kinds produced by
    professional architects in the course of their work
    and all documents which throw light upon the
    production of buildings.

Harvey, John H.   31
Sources for the history of houses. London:
  British Records Association, 1974. 61pp.
  (Archives and the user, 3).
      Intended for the ordinary occupier of a house of
    some age (built before 1850), this pamphlet gives
    guidance on how to find out when a house was

built and when subsequently altered or enlarged,
who built, enlarged or altered it, who have been
the actual occupiers, and with what events of
interest it can be associated.

Hudson, Kenneth   32
Industrial archaeology: a new introduction.
  3rd ed. London: John Baker, 1976. 240pp. Bibl pp
  210–25.
      Useful primarily for the five page list of local
    societies carrying out research, recording,
    publicity and political action within the field of
    industrial archaeology, as well as for the chapters
    on building materials and recording, publication
    and documentation.

Humphreys, Arthur L.   33
A handbook to county bibliography, being
  a bibliography of bibliographies relating to the
  county towns of Great Britain and Ireland.
  Folkestone: Dawson, 1917 (1974 reprint). 501pp.
  Originally published: London: A. L. Humphreys.
      A detailed and still invaluable guide. The 6,000
    bibliographies are arranged under counties,
    A–Z, the general works being followed by those
    on the individual towns and villages. The entries
    include manuscript and periodical sources. Full
    bibliographical details are given. Detailed index
    of authors, personal names, places and subjects.

Industrial archaeologists' guide, 1971–73.   34
  Edited by Neil Cossons and Kenneth
  Hudson. Newton Abbot: David and Charles, 1971.
  210pp.
      Basically a guide to what industrial archaeology
    is, what sites there are, and how to go about
    preserving them, it provides information on
    societies and organisations, useful addresses and
    a bibliography. Needs up-dating, but still useful.

Iredale, David   35
Discovering local history. 2nd ed. Aylesbury:
  Shire Publications, 1977. 64pp.
      An introductory booklet to the type of material
    available (maps, estate papers, town books,
    church archives, business and government
    records, etc). Includes a list of some record
    repositories in Britain. Index.

Iredale, David   36
Discovering your old house. 2nd ed.
  Aylesbury: Shire Publications, 1977. 64pp. Revised
  title of *This old house*.
      An introductory booklet, by an archivist. Mostly
    provides documentary clues and a list of record
    repositories in Great Britain. Also deals with
    plan and style, with illustrations and references.
    Index.

Iredale, David   37
**Local history research and writing: a
manual for local history writers**. London:
Elmfield Press, 1974. 225pp. Bibl pp 203–213.
    Has chapters devoted to houses, industrial
archaeology, archives, maps, estate papers, town
books, church archives, quarter sessions,
business records and government records.
Appendix 1: Some useful addresses for
fieldworkers. Appendix 2: Some record
repositories in Britain.

Keen, Michael E., *compiler*   38
**A bibliography of the trade directories of
the British Isles, in the National Art Library**.
London: Victoria and Albert Museum, 1979. 121pp.
    In the first part of the bibliography the 889
directories are alphabetically arranged under the
name of the country, county, city, town, or
district of the British Isles covered by the
collection. Every entry is then sub-divided
alphabetically under publisher, compiler, or
book-title. The second section consists of an
index in which authors, compilers, publishers or
names of publications are linked numerically to
the entries. Excludes directories of particular
trades or professions. *See also* 40.

Mullins, Edward L. C.   39
**Texts and calendars: an analytical guide to
serial publications**.London: Royal Historical
Society, 1958. 674pp. (Royal Historical Society.
Guides and handbooks, 7).
    A guide to the publications of the county record
societies which covers texts (transcriptions of
documents) and calendars (abstracts of
documents) for English and Welsh history issued
by the various Record Commissions, the Public
Record Office and local authorities and record
societies. The index enables individual places,
persons and types of document to be located in
the volume.

Norton, J. E.   40
**Guide to the national and provincial
directories of England and Wales, excluding
London, published before 1856**. London: Royal
Historical Society, 1950, 241pp. (Royal Historical
Society. Guides and handbooks, 5).
    Includes 878 numbered entries (English,
national, chronologically arranged; English,
local by counties A–Z, then chronologically;
Welsh chronologically). Locations for each
directory are given. Excludes directories of
particular trades or professions. Index. *See also*
38. For London one should refer to Goss, C. W.
F. *The London directories 1677–1855* (London:
Archer, 1932), a detailed bibliography of
London directories with analyses of contents and
locations of copies.

The Open University   41
**Arts: a third level course: History of
architecture and design 1890–1939: Project
guide**. Prepared by Stephen Bayley, Charlotte and
Tim Benton, Tony Coulson, Colin Cunningham and
Elizabeth Deighton, for the Course Team. [Milton
Keynes]: Open University, [1976?]. 20pp.
    An extremely useful guide to how to find out,
covering study resources, dating architecture
(maps, Kelly's and other street directories, title
deeds or contracts proving ownership,
inventories or surveys, new materials or
structural techniques, contemporary
documents), how to answer ten basic questions
(who designed it?, who commissioned it?, who
approved its design?, who paid for it?, what
materials were used in the construction?, what
was it designed for?, who arranged the contracts
or agreements?, who now controls any of these
people?, who is the present owner?), the subject
in its time (local newspapers, local collections,
back files of magazines and journals). The
project bibliography includes libraries, museums
and archives, biographical sources, and technical
literature. There is an advanced recommended
reading list including some British periodicals
published during the period 1890–1939.

Owen, Dorothy M.   42
**The records of the established church in
England, excluding parochial records**. London:
British Records Association, 1970. 64pp. (Archives
and the user, 1).
    Describes the records and their location by
diocese. Index.

Harris, Henry   43
**'British Transport Historical Records and
their value to the architectural historian'**, in
Architectural history, vol 2, 1959, pp 50–62.
    With the exception of the Public Record Office,
British Transport Historical Records form the
largest single record collection relating to
architecture in this country in the 19th century.
Includes canals, river navigation, docks and
harbours as well as railways. This article
illustrates the usefulness of these archives for
architectural history. Since the publication of
this article, the British Transport Historical
Records have been transferred to the Public
Record Office which has available a provisional
guide to the material, *see* 10.

**RILA (International repertory of the
literature of art/Répertoire
international de la littérature de l'art)**. Vol 1– ;   44
1975– . Williamstown (Mass): RILA; London:
RILA/British Center, 1975– .
    An initial demonstration issue appeared in 1973
and was followed by regular semi-annual
publication starting in 1975. Includes abstracts
and detailed indexing of current publications

(books, journals, newspaper articles, essays in *Festschriften*, congress reports and symposium proceedings, exhibition catalogues and dissertations) in all fields of art from about the 4th century. The *Architectural periodicals index* (*see* 2) covers more journals, but for anyone tracing book reviews and publications other than periodical articles, *RILA* is most useful. The arrangement is: reference works, general works, medieval art, renaissance and baroque art, modern art. Under each period division there is a section on architecture. The detailed author-subject index, includes all names of persons and places (buildings and places are listed by city or province and country).

A five-year *Cumulative index*, merging into one alphabetical listing of the contents of vols 1–5, 1975–1979 (10 issues) is due late 1981. The index serves as a reference work in itself, including names of all persons and places, patrons, critics, historians, architectural and manufacturing firms mentioned in the more than 30,000 citations published in vols 1–5. Persons are identified with brief descriptions of nationality, profession, and dates, wherever possible. The index contains a separate alphabetical listing of authors for all five volumes.

Royal Institute of British Architects. Library 45
Catalogue of the library. London: Royal
  Institute of British Architects, 1937–38.
  2 vols. Reprinted, London: Dawsons of Pall Mall.
    Vol 1 is an author catalogue of books and manuscripts in the collection. Vol 2 contains a classified index and an alphabetical subject index; it enables the reader to locate material on a given subject and shows that subject in conjunction with broader and related subjects. Sufficient information is given (author's name and date) in vol 2 to enable books to be identified and their author entries found, if necessary, with full information in vol 1. Works on specific buildings will be found under the appropriate building type, usually with references from the place in the topographical classification. Individual biographies are listed in the classified sequence under '92: biography'. Books written by (and in some cases about) architects will be found in vol 1. The *Catalogue* is continued by lists in the *RIBA Journal* until January 1946, then by the classified accessions list in the *Library bulletin* (1946–72) quarterly, not cumulated (*see* 49), and from 1973 as a quarterly, duplicated *Accessions list*.

Royal Institute of British Architects. Library 46
**Comprehensive index to architectural
  periodicals, 1956–70**. London: World
  Microfilms, 1971. 20 reels of 16mm film.
    Reproduces all the cards in the Library's Periodicals subject index (*see* 164) for the years 1956–70. All architectural subjects are covered. General articles about an architect and his work

(but not articles on specific projects) are entered under the heading 'Architects: GB', which is further subdivided alphabetically by surname. Specific buildings are sought under the appropriate building type, subdivided by country, then town. Includes an alphabetical subject index to headings. Continued by the *Architectural periodicals index* (see 2).

Royal Institute of British Architects. Library 47
RIBA Annual review of periodical articles.
  Vol 1–vol 7, 1965/66–1971/72. London: RIBA,
  1966–1973.
    A printed, classified (UDC) index which provides a selective list of index entries for periodical articles. A large proportion of the index is devoted to building types. The entries identify buildings and record their architects' names. Includes an alphabetical list of the main subject headings used. Gathers together the index entries for articles from the *RIBA Library bulletin* (*see* 49) into one annual volume. Continued by the *Architectural periodicals index* (*see* 2) 1972 onwards.

Royal Institute of British Architects. Library 48
RIBA Booklist. London: RIBA Publications
  Ltd, 1969–. Annual.
    Compiled by the Professional Literature Committee of the RIBA as a general guide to the literature for school of architecture librarians, practitioners and students. A priced, un-annotated subject list of about 500 items covering information sources, dictionaries and encyclo-paedias, history of architecture, building construction and practice, landscape and planning. Material on building types and the work of individual architects has hitherto been excluded, but from the 1980/81 list, works on individual architects are listed. Continues the *RIBA basic list of books and technical reference list*.

Royal Institute of British Architects. Library 49
RIBA Library bulletin. Vol 1, no 1–vol 26, no
  4, Nov 1946–July 1972. London: RIBA, 1947–1973.
    A printed classified (UDC) index which appeared quarterly, listing books added to the library and a separate selective list of index entries for periodical articles. A large proportion of the index is devoted to building types. The entries identify buildings and record their architects' names. From 1966 the periodical index entries were cumulated in the *RIBA Annual review of periodical articles* (*see* 47).

**'Early printed books in the RIBA Library.
Short title list'**, in *RIBA Library bulletin*, vol 3(3), May 1949–vol 5(2), Feb 1951.
In seven parts each starting on the inside front cover:

cover:/*continued*
vol 3(3).   I 1478–1600
vol 3(4).   1478–1600;   II 1601–1700
vol 4(1).   1601–1700;   III 1701–1750
vol 4(4).   1701–1750;   IV 1751–1800
vol 5(1).   1751–1800;   V 1801–1830
vol 5(2).   1801–1830.

A complete descriptive catalogue of the British Architectural Library's Early Works Collection (books published up to and including 1840) is being prepared for publication.

Sheehy, Eugene P., *compiler*   50
Guide to reference books. 9th ed. Chicago: American Library Association, 1976. 1,040pp. *Supplement*. Chicago: American Library Association, 1980. 305pp.
> An authoritative bibliographical tool which is useful for finding details of reference books which may help in obtaining information.

Smith, D. L.   51
How to find out in architecture and building: a guide to sources of information. Oxford: Pergamon Press, 1967. 232pp. (The Commonwealth and international library, library and information division).
> Contents include: 1. Careers and training, 2. The organisation of knowledge and use of libraries, 3. Bibliographies, indexes and abstracts, 4. Dictionaries and encyclopaedias, 5. Periodicals, 6. Directories, institutions, and special libraries, 7. Books and pamphlets on building, 8. Books and pamphlets on town and country planning, 9. Books and pamphlets on architecture: general and history, 10. Books and pamphlets on architecture: building types and details. It is aimed at the student of architecture and concentrates on modern study and practice. Needs up-dating.

Smith, John F., *compiler*   52
A critical bibliography of building conservation: historic towns, buildings, their furnishings and fittings. Compiled at the Institute of Advanced Architectural Studies, University of York. London: Mansell, 1978. c 250pp.
> Compiled from a large variety of sources including books, periodicals, papers and reports, the bibliography covers all aspects of the conservation of historic towns, buildings and their contents, with particular emphasis on the practical problems encountered in conservation work. It also covers background history, details of techniques (including case histories), information related to the work of specialist consultants. Some 2,250 entries are arranged under broad subject headings, then in order of descending elements, ie towns, buildings, parts of buildings, contents. Each entry includes a brief note on the contents and, where necessary,

its possible relevance to the user's requirements. Contents: history, philosophy and attitudes to conservation; legislation; towns and villages (history and analysis, conservation, case studies); buildings (history of building construction, building types, general problems of repair and conservation, the fabric, furnishings and fittings, installations, materials, special requirements); historical gardens and landscapes; tourism; archaeology in conservation (archaeology and industrial archaeology); the organisation of conservation (general considerations, training, surveys, inspections and recording, photography and photogrammetry, economics and the financing of conservation, public participation, amenity societies and pressure groups); conservation abroad; bibliographies, directories and dictionaries of conservation, and advisory and grant-giving bodies; author and place indexes.

Stanley-Morgan, R.   53
'Architectural library facilities in the provinces', in *RIBA Journal*, 3rd series, vol 70, no 1, Jan 1963, pp 24–29.
> Mainly for current practice and in need of up-dating.

Storey, Richard and **Madden**, Lionel   54
Primary sources for Victorian studies: a guide to the location and use of unpublished materials. London: Phillimore, 1977. 81pp.
> Aims to provide a short introductory guide for students to the identification and use of collections of primary source materials. Information is given both about the main types of collection in Britain (Historical Manuscripts Commission and the National Register of Archives, national repositories and local repositories), followed by a brief survey of the sources of information about primary materials in a number of subject areas (including architecture and the visual arts, education, religious history, transport, visual sources, etc). The final section discusses practical questions concerning the use of unpublished materials. Bibliographical references are given to guides and other reference and background works cited. Selective index.

Sutcliffe, Anthony R.   55
The history of modern town planning: a bibliographic guide. Birmingham: Centre for Urban and Regional Studies, University of Birmingham, 1977. 112pp. (Research memorandum, 57).
> A critical review of the current study of the history of town planning. Introductory essay on the identity, motivations and methods of planning historians. Annotated bibliography of

656 items. An expanded version, published as *The history of urban and regional planning: an annotated bibliography* (London: Mansell, 1981, 284pp), includes more than 1,300 references in eight subject sections: 1. Planning history: definitions, methods and objectives, 2. Encyclopaedias, bibliographies and guides of relevance to planning history, 3. General studies of planning as a movement, 4. General studies of planning history in individual countries, 5. Planning in individual cities, 6. Individual planners, designers and theorists, 7. Themes in nineteenth-century planning, 8. Aspects of urban and regional planning.

Upcott, William   56
A bibliographical account of the principal works relating to English topography. [1st ed reprinted]; with a new introduction by Jack Simmons. Wakefield: E P Publishing, 1978. 416pp. Facsimile reprint. Originally published in three volumes; London: W. Upcott, 1818.

While there are other bibliographies to the literature of English local history, this one provides a detailed analysis of each work it lists, enumerating all its component parts, in text and plates. Index of places (including names of buildings). Index of names.

Urban history yearbook. Leicester: Leicester   57
University Press, 1974–. Annual.

The yearbook contains a 'Current bibliography of urban history' which aims to provide comprehensive coverage of all books published in Britain and listed in the *British national bibliography* for the period 1 August–31 July preceding publication of the yearbook. Other English language books, particularly those published in the United States, Canada and Australia are included. A large number of periodicals is scanned. The bibliography is arranged in classified order, with cross-references provided. An index of towns concludes the section. Continues *Urban history newsletter*, nos 1–20 (Leicester: Urban History Group, 1963–73).

Walford, A. J., *editor*   58
Guide to reference material.
Vol 1: *Science and technology*. 3rd ed. 1973. 615pp. 4th ed. 1980. 697pp.
Vol 2: *Social and historical sciences, philosophy and religion*. 3rd ed. 1975. 647pp.
Vol 3: *Generalities, languages, the arts and literature*. 3rd ed. 1977. 710pp.
London: Library Association.

Useful for finding details of reference books which may help in obtaining information. Vol 1 includes building, vol 2 includes biography, history, atlases and maps, guide books, economics, and vol 3 includes encyclopaedias,

reference books and architecture as well as a cumulated subject index to the third edition, vols 1–3. The 4th ed. published as *Walford's guide to reference material*.

For other entries relating to this section see items in:

2.1 Biographical dictionaries, encyclopaedias, directories, surveys and indexes
64 Avery Architectural Library. *Avery obituary index*.
68 *A bibliography of Leicestershire churches*.
96 Hall. *A bibliography on vernacular architecture*.
97 Harris. *Catalogue of British drawings for architecture, decoration, sculpture and landscape gardening 1550–1900 in American collections*.
98 Harris. *A country house index*.
101 Historical Manuscripts Commission. *Architectural history and the fine and applied arts: sources in the National Register of Archives*.
107 Kelly's local London, provincial and other directories.
108 Kenyon. *Castles, town defences, and artillery fortifications in Britain: a bibliography, 1945–74*.
113 Michelmore. *Current bibliography of vernacular architecture (1970–1976)*.
127 Royal Institute of British Architects, Drawings Collection. *Catalogue of the Drawings Collection of the RIBA*.
131 Sharp. *Sources of modern architecture: a critical bibliography*.
137 Victoria and Albert Museum. *Topographical index to measured drawings of architecture which have appeared in the principal architectural publications*.
144 Wodehouse. *British architects, 1840–1976*.

5.2 Guide to societies, institutions and organisations
223 Architectural Association. (Publications).
236 British Architectural Library. (Publications).
241 British Library, Reference Division. (Publications).
242 British Museum, Department of Prints and Drawings. (Publications).
246 British Theatre Institute. (Publications).
254 Catholic Record Society. (Publications).
264 Council for British Archaeology. (Publications).
273 Department of Finance, Works Division Library. (Publications).
274 Department of Health and Social Security. (Publications).
275 Department of the Environment and Transport, Library. (Publications).
276 Department of the Environment, Directorate of Ancient Monuments and Historic Buildings (England). (Publications).
280 Design and Industries Association. (Publications).
284 Ecclesiological Society. (Publications).
285 Edinburgh City Libraries. (Publications).
296 Greater London Council. (Greater London History Library).
297 Guildhall Library. (Publications).

(Publications)./*continued*
311 Institution of Civil Engineers (Publications).
314 Irish Architectural Record Association. (Publications).
319 Lambeth Palace Library. (Publications).
332 National Library of Scotland. (Special catalogues).
350 Property Services Agency. (Publications).
352 Public Record Office. (Publications).
355 The Queen's University of Belfast, Architecture and Planning Information Service. (Publications).
364 Royal Commission on Historical Manuscripts (and National Register of Archives). (Publications).
370 Royal Horticultural Society. (Publications).
374 Royal Institution of Chartered Surveyors. (Publications).
383 Science Museum Library. (Publications).
387 Scottish Record Office. (Publications).
389 Sir John Soane's Museum. (Publications).
400 Society of Genealogists. (Publications).
402 Standing Conference for Local History. (Publications).
415 Victoria and Albert Museum Library. (Publications).
416 Victoria and Albert Museum, Department of Prints and Drawings and Paintings. (Publications).
423 William Morris Gallery. (Publications).

7.1 General
526 Watkin. *The rise of architectural history.*

7.3 Renaissance to neoclassic
552 Cruickshank. *London: the art of Georgian building.*

7.10 Building types: industrial and commercial
806 Farries. *Researching a county's windmill history: Essex.*
808 Lindsey. *Windmills: a bibliographical guide.*

7.11 Building types: recreational
827 Stoddard. *Theatre and cinema architecture: a guide to information sources.*

7.15 Landscape and planning
855 *The Garden: a celebration of 1,000 years of British gardening.*

Biographical dictionaries, encyclopaedias, directories, surveys and indexes

This section includes biographical dictionaries, encyclopaedias, directories, surveys, bibliographies and indexes. In most of the publications listed in this section one can look up either the name of an architect or the name of a building, or in some cases both. Some publications span the whole of architectural history, while others may be limited to a particular period or even year. In order to make it possible to scan the entries to ascertain quickly which items will be useful when searching for information on, for example, an architect working in the 1930s or an eighteenth-century building, each entry is coded, following the bibliographical description, as follows:

archts Indicates that it is possible to look up the names of architects in the item described

bldgs Indicates that it is possible to look up the names of buildings (sometimes indirectly under location) in the item described

prehist/ med Useful for the period from prehistory to medieval

ren/ neoclas Useful for the period from renaissance to neoclassic

19/20c Useful for the nineteenth and/or twentieth centuries

For example, Colvin's *Biographical dictionary of British architects* is coded '**archts, bldgs; ren/neoclas**', which indicates that in this publication it is possible to look up the names of architects (fairly obvious from the title) as well as the names of buildings (not at all obvious from the title) and that it is useful for the period roughly from renaissance to the neoclassic.

Depending on the publication, the information found for any architect or building will range from a full biography or description to just a note of an architect's dates or references to other publications or sources. If one is just searching for some general information about a well-known figure or famous building then the major biographical dictionaries (Colvin, Harvey, etc) and guides (Buildings of England, Shell, etc) will probably provide the information, but if trying to find 'everything' about a particular architect or building or if trying to locate details of more obscure persons or buildings, then a wider range of publications may have to be consulted.

Allgemeines Lexikon der bildenden   59
**Künstler von der Antike bis zur
Gegenwart** . . . Leipzig: Seeman, 1907–50. 37 vols.
Spine title: Thieme-Becker Künstler-Lexikon.
archts; prehist/med, ren/neoclas, 19/20c
> In German. The most comprehensive dictionary in existence of painters and engravers, including some architects and sculptors. Living persons are included. The signed articles, arranged alphabetically, give biographical data and good bibliographies. Continued by Vollmer (139). A new German edition is in preparation. An English translation, the *International dictionary of artists*, in 55 volumes has been advertised by the International Translations Publishing Company. Volume 1 has been published, but no evidence of ongoing work on the project can be detected.

Architect's, engineer's and building-trades'   60
**directory: a business book of reference
for the various industries concerned with the
arts of construction. 1868.** London: Wyman, 1868.
832pp.
archts; 19/20c
> One section lists architects, and indicates whether an architect is a fellow or associate of the RIBA. The length of entry varies greatly. Names and addresses are always given, and sometimes a list of work completed and under construction is also included. Additional sections list builders, engineers, surveyors, etc.

The Architect's valuator and directory of   61
architects, etc. Manchester: William
Osborn, 1890.
archts; 19/20c
> Directory of architects belonging to the recognised Institutes and Associations of the United Kingdom . . . India, etc. No copy was seen.

Architectural Association   62
Brown book series, sessions 1859 to 1918.
> London: The Association. 57 vols in 12.
> **archts; 19/20c**
>> Includes, for each annual session, names and addresses of members, and date of election. In alphabetical order, within session.

2.1 Biographical dictionaries, encyclopaedias, directories, surveys and indexes

Architectural Publication Society   63
The dictionary of architecture with
  illustrations. Edited by W. Papworth. London:
  Richards, 1852–92. Reprinted, New York: DaCapo,
  1969. 8 vols. Microfiche, Pine Plains (NY): Earl M.
  Coleman.
  archts, bldgs; prehist/med, ren/neoclas, 19/20c
      Includes architects of all nationalities dead by
      the time of compilation. Great variation in the
      length of biographies. Some include
      bibliographies. The value of its biographies is
      reduced now that Colvin's dictionary (78) has
      appeared in its second edition. Often good
      entries on the architecture of a place entered
      under the name of the town, giving names of
      buildings, architects, dates, and sometimes cost
      and bibliographical references. Includes lengthy
      essays on architectural forms and subjects,
      definitions and explanations of terms. Remains
      an important work.
        Related to it is the Society's *Detached essays
      and illustrations issued during the years 1848–52*.
      London: Richards, 1853.
        A typescript *Index to A P S Dictionary*,
      compiled in 1944 by Dorothy Stroud for the
      National Buildings Record (108pp) is held by
      the British Architectural Library. It is divided
      into two sections, firstly London buildings (pp
      1–28) listed by name of building or street,
      followed by a section on buildings in the
      provinces, arranged by place. For each entry the
      name of the architect is provided. Reference to
      the entry for the architect in the *Dictionary* often
      provides additional information and
      bibliographical references (such as to an
      illustrated article in the *Builder*). The index does
      not include the great architects on whom
      standard works have been written, such as
      Wren, Adam or Nash.

Avery Architectural Library   64
Avery obituary index of architects. 2nd ed.
  Boston (Mass): G. K. Hall, 1980. 530pp.
  archts; 19/20c
      Worldwide coverage, though with the emphasis
      on American architects. Gives birth and death
      dates and bibliographical references. Many
      obituaries in the *Builder* (from 1843) the *RIBA
      Journal* and *Transactions* (from 1865) are
      included. Principally covers the period from the
      nineteenth century onwards. The index is
      primarily concerned with architects, but
      eminent art historians, archaeologists, and town
      planners are represented as well. The obituaries
      of artists included until 1960 are no longer
      recorded, hence the *Obituary index* is no longer
      entitled as was the first edition, published in
      1963, the *Avery obituary index of architects and
      artists*. This new edition contains over 17,000
      entries.

Beard, Geoffrey   65
Georgian craftsmen and their work.
  London: Country Life, 1966. 207pp.
  Bibl pp 190–198.
  archts, bldgs; ren/neoclas
      Gives details, in monograph form, about the life
      and work of 18th-century craftsmen, and in
      particular those who decorated in various ways
      the large country houses. Includes plasterers,
      wood-carvers and workers in metal. Appendix 1:
      Selected list of craftsmen of the Georgian period
      (pp 161–182), arranged by craft, and within
      each craft, alphabetically, giving dates of
      activity, place of work followed by date, when
      known, and the evidence for the statement. The
      lists do not overlap the existing dictionaries of
      Colvin (79), Croft-Murray (654) or Gunnis (95).
      A revised and expanded select list of craftsmen,
      arranged alphabetically by craftsman's surname,
      appears in Geoffrey Beard's *Craftsmen and
      interior decoration in England, 1660–1820*
      (Edinburgh: J. Bartholomew and Son, 1981,
      pp 241–296). Alphabetical index.

Bell, S. P., *compiler*   66
A biographical index of British engineers in
  the 19th century. New York, London: Garland,
  1975, 246pp. (Garland reference library of social
  science, 5).
  archts; 19/20c
      An index to obituary notices of some 3,500
      British engineers who died on or before 1900.
      The 24 journals scanned include the *Civil
      engineer and architect's journal* (1837–1868) and
      the *Proceedings of the Institution of Civil
      Engineers* (from 1837). Included are not only all
      branches of engineering proper, but also of
      persons whose activities connected them closely
      with engineering, such as architects. Each entry
      gives names, dates, and specialist field, followed
      by references.

Bennett, J. D.   6
Leicestershire architects, 1700–1850.
  Leicester: Leicester Museums, 1968. [70pp.]
  Bibl pp [8–9].
  archts; ren/neoclas, 19/20c
      A biographical dictionary of architects who were
      living and working in Leicestershire during the
      18th and first half of the 19th centuries. Entries
      generally consist of three parts: an account of the
      architect's life; a chronological list of buildings
      designed, with dates and comments; and special
      sources of information. Work done outside the
      county has been included where known. Of the
      48 architects listed, 18 do not appear in Colvin.
      No index.

A Bibliography of Leicestershire churches.   68
Part 1: The periodical sources. Edited by
David Parsons. [Leicester]: Department of Adult
Education, University of Leicester in association with
Leicestershire Libraries and Information Service,
1978. 60pp.
bldgs; prehist/med, ren/neoclas, 19/20c
This is the first instalment of an intended
three-part compilation of sources for the
architectural history and archaeology of parish
churches in Leicestershire. It deals with articles,
notes and passing references in the periodical
literature from the middle of the nineteenth
century. Parts 2 and 3 are expected to cover the
references in printed books and unpublished
documents respectively. The criteria for
inclusion are that a building should be a
structurally independent church or chapel of the
Church of England or of a former monastic
house, either in use or with identifiable
upstanding remains. Vanished churches for
which there is only documentary evidence and
chapels forming part of another building are not
included. Twenty-seven journals have been
searched for references, including the *Builder*,
the *Church builder* and the *Ecclesiologist*. The
method of search has been to rely on cumulative
or volume indexes where these are available and
appear to be reliable. In cases where indexes are
non-existent or obviously rudimentary, each
volume has been searched page by page. Defunct
journals have been searched from the first issue
to the end of the sequence; journals still current
have been searched up to the issue for 1974, with
the exception of the *Builder* when the search
ended with vol 113 (1917) when the section
'Church Building News' dies out. Entries are
alphabetically by place followed by the name of
the church and then the references. Pieces
illustrated with diagrams or plates are indicated
by an asterisk.

Biographical dictionary of British   69
   gardeners.
   archts, bldgs; ren/neoclas, 19/20c
An A–Z listing, including landscape gardeners
and architects involved in landscape. Contains
over 500 biographies of gardeners from the
sixteenth century to the present, with about
1,000 illustrations (portraits, prints and
photographs). First published as a series in
House and garden (1971, Sept–1979, March,
addenda 1979, April–1980, April), then, revised
and expanded, as *British gardeners: a
biographical dictionary*, by Miles Hadfield,
Robert Harling and Leonie Highton (London:
Zwemmer in association with Condé Nast, 1980,
320pp). The latter includes indexes to people
and places referred to in the text.

Brett, C. E. B., *compiler*   70
**Buildings in the town and parish of Saint
   Helier.** Compiled for the National Trust for Jersey,
   April 1976–October 1977. [n.p.]: Ulster Architectural
   Heritage Society and National Trust for Jersey, 1977.
   84pp. Bibl p 8.
bldgs; prehist/med, ren/neoclas, 19/20c
An inventory. Index to buildings.

Briggs, Martin S.   71
**Everyman's concise encyclopaedia of
   architecture.** London: Dent, 1959. 372pp.
   (Everyman's reference library).
archts; ren/neoclas, 19/20c
Has short biographical entries on British
architects, and sometimes includes
bibliographical references. Arranged
alphabetically.

Buildings of England, *series*. Founding editor,   72
   Sir Nikolaus Pevsner. Harmondsworth:
   Penguin Books, 1951– . 46 vols.
archts, bldgs; prehist/med, ren/neoclas, 19/20c
A complete and invaluable county by county
survey in guide book form which covers in detail
the whole of England's architectural heritage,
from prehistory to the present. Architects are
listed in the index of artists in each volume.
There is an index of places in most volumes.
'Further reading' is indicated at the end of the
introduction in most volumes. Glossaries.
Revised editions are in progress. The volumes
listed below are by Sir Nikolaus Pevsner unless
otherwise noted:
*Bedfordshire and the County of Huntingdon and
   Peterborough.* 1968.
Berkshire. 1966.
Buckinghamshire. 1960.
Cambridgeshire. 2nd ed, 1970.
Cheshire, (with Edward Hubbard). 1971.
Cornwall. 2nd ed. Revised by Enid Radcliffe.
   1970.
Cumberland and Westmorland. 1967.
Derbyshire. 2nd ed. Revised by Elizabeth
   Williamson. 1978.
North Devon. 1952. (soon to be revised)
South Devon. 1952. (soon to be revised)
Dorset, (with John Newman). 1972.
County Durham. 1953. (soon to be revised; due
   1982)
Essex. 2nd ed. Revised by Enid Radcliffe. 1965.
Gloucestershire: The Cotswolds. 2nd ed. Revised
   by David Verey. 1979.
Gloucestershire: The Vale and the Forest of Dean.
   2nd ed. Revised by David Verey. 1977.
Hampshire, (with D. Lloyd). 1967.
Herefordshire. 1963.
Hertfordshire. 2nd ed. Revised by Bridget
   Cherry. 1977.
North East and East Kent. 2nd ed. Revised by
   John Newman. 1977.

2.1 Biographical dictionaries, encyclopaedias, directories, surveys and indexes

1977./continued
West Kent and the Weald. 2nd ed. Revised by
   John Newman. 1977.
North Lancashire. 1969.
South Lancashire. 1969.
Leicestershire and Rutland. 1960. (soon to be
   revised)
Lincolnshire, (with John Harris). 1964.
London I: The Cities of London and Westminster.
   2nd ed. Revised by Bridget Cherry. 1973.
*London II: Except the Cities of London and
   Westminster.* 1952. (soon to be revised; will
   incorporate *Middlesex*; due 1982)
Middlesex. 1951.
North-East Norfolk and Norwich. 1962.
North-West and South Norfolk. 1962.
Northamptonshire. 2nd ed. Revised by Bridget
   Cherry. 1973.
Northumberland, (with Ian A. Richmond). 1957.
Nottinghamshire. 2nd ed. Revised by Elizabeth
   Williamson. 1979.
Oxfordshire, (with Jennifer Sherwood). 1974.
Shropshire. 1958.
Somerset, North and Bristol. 1958.
Somerset, South and West. 1958.
Staffordshire. 1974.
Suffolk. 2nd ed. Revised by Enid Radcliffe. 1974.
Surrey, (with Ian Nairn). 1965.
Warwickshire, (with A. Wedgwood). 1966.
Wiltshire. 2nd ed. Revised by Bridget Cherry.
   1975.
Worcestershire. 1968.
Yorkshire: The East Riding. 1972.
Yorkshire: The North Riding. 1966.
Yorkshire: The West Riding. 2nd ed. Revised by
   Enid Radcliffe. 1967.
      The Buildings of England Office, Penguin
Books, 536 King's Road, London SW10 0UH,
tel (01) 351 2393, maintains the documentation
used in the preparation of these volumes (*see*
250).

Buildings of Ireland, *series.* Harmondsworth: 73
   Penguin Books, 1979– .
archts, bldgs; prehist/med, ren/neoclas, 19/20c
   This series follows the pattern of Sir Nikolaus
   Pevsner's *Buildings of England* series, but differs
   in excluding prehistoric remains. When
   completed it will provide a comprehensive
   architectural guide to the thirty-two counties of
   Ireland, from the early Christian period to the
   present day. The nine-volume series will devote
   two volumes to each of the four historic
   provinces of Ulster, Munster, Leinster, and
   Connaught, with a separate single volume on
   Dublin city and county.

   *North West Ulster: the counties of Londonderry,
   Donegal, Fermanagh, and Tyrone*, by Alistair
   Rowan. 1979.

Buildings of Scotland, *series.* Harmondsworth: 74
   Penguin Books, 1978– .
archts, bldgs; prehist/med, ren/neoclas, 19/20c
   This series follows the pattern of Sir Nikolaus
   Pevsner's *Buildings of England* series. It is
   planned to cover Scotland in ten volumes.

   Lothian, except Edinburgh, by Colin McWilliam.
   The medieval churches, by Christopher Wilson,
   1978.

Buildings of Wales, *series.* Harmondsworth: 75
   Penguin Books, 1979– .
archts, bldgs; prehist/med, ren/neoclas, 19/20c
   This series follows the pattern of Sir Nikolaus
   Pevsner's *Buildings of England* series. It is
   planned to cover Wales in six volumes.

   *Powys (Montgomeryshire, Radnorshire,
   Breconshire)*, by Richard Haslam. 1979.

Burke's guide to country houses, *series.*   76
   General editor, Hugh
   Montgomery-Massingberd. London: Burke's
   Peerage, 1978– .
archts, bldgs; ren/neoclas, 19/20c
   A projected series of ten volumes covering the
   British Isles which will form an encyclopaedic
   dictionary of over 10,000 houses, standing and
   demolished.

   Vol 1: *Ireland*, (1978) by Mark Bence-Jones
   covers nearly 2,000 Irish country houses. It
   includes houses owned by families appearing in
   Burke's genealogical series and other properties of
   significance. Each entry includes architectural
   commentary, history and devolution of each
   property, notes of interest concerning the
   gardens, family anecdotes, plus bibliographic
   references of note. More than half the buildings
   are illustrated. Vol 1 was reprinted in 1980 with
   an index and author's addenda and corrigenda.
   Vol 2: *Herefordshire, Shropshire, Warwickshire,
   Worcestershire*, (1980) by Peter Reid, appears
   under the new series title, *Burke's and Savills'
   guide to country houses.* It covers over 600 houses.

Clarke, Basil F. L.   77
Church builders of the nineteenth century:
   a study of the gothic revival in England. A reprint
   with new preface, corrections and annotations by the
   author. Orig publ 1938. Newton Abbot: David and
   Charles, 1969. 296pp.
archts, bldgs; 19/20c
   Appendix 1: Some nineteenth-century architects
   and their churches. Includes name, dates,
   biographical notes, and a selective list of their
   work. Appendix 2: Some towns and their
   churches. Index and bibliographical footnotes.

Colvin, Howard   78
A biographical dictionary of British
    architects, 1600–1840. London: J. Murray, 1978.
    1056pp.
    archts, bldgs; ren/neoclas
        This authoritative work of reference for the
        history of British architecture contains
        biographies of every significant architect
        practising in England, Scotland and Wales, the
        major part of whose actual career falls within the
        limiting dates. It supersedes the corresponding
        biographical entries in the *Dictionary of the
        Architectural Publication Society*, the *Dictionary
        of national biography* and Howard Colvin's
        *Biographical dictionary of English architects,
        1660–1840*. Every building of importance whose
        architect can be identified is listed, with details
        of date of erection and demolition, style and
        references to published descriptions. Besides
        providing an authoritative list of each architect's
        work in chronological order the book gives,
        whenever possible, a brief assessment of his
        place in British architectural history and some
        idea of the aesthetic quality of his work. Nearly
        all books by architects published in Britain
        between 1600 and 1840 are listed under their
        authors, and there are full indexes of persons and
        buildings, the latter making it possible to find
        out which architect designed or altered a
        particular building. Includes a succinct history
        of the architectural profession.

Colvin, Howard, *general editor*   79
The history of the King's works.
    Vols 1 and 2: *The middle ages*, by R. Allen Brown, H.
    M. Colvin and A. J. Taylor. London: HMSO, 1963. 2
    vols plus slip-case containing 4 plans.
    Vol 3: *1485–1660* (Part 1), by H. M. Colvin, D. R.
    Ransome and John Summerson. London: HMSO,
    1975, 469pp.
    Vol 5: *1660–1782*, by H. M. Colvin, J. Mordaunt
    Crook, Kerry Downes and John Newman. London:
    HMSO, 1976. 535pp. Bibl refs.
    Vol 6: *1782–1851*, by J. Mordaunt Crook and M. H.
    Port. London: HMSO, 1973. 744pp.
    archts, bldgs; prehist/med, ren/neoclas, 19/20c
        The standard history of royal buildings in
        Britain from the era of Offa's Dyke to the
        establishment of the Victorian Office of Works in
        1851. Covers in detail the King's houses, castles,
        palaces, tombs and monuments, royal chapels
        and public buildings undertaken by the Office of
        Works, such as the buildings of Westminster and
        Whitehall. Index to vols 1 and 2 in vol 2. Indexes
        in vols 3, 5 and 6.
        Essential reference work for the history of the
        civil, military and ecclesiastical buildings erected
        under royal authority.

Committee for the Survey of the Memorials   80
    of Greater London
Survey of London. London, 1900– .
    archts, bldgs; prehist/med, ren/neoclas, 19/20c
        Originally issued jointly by the Committee for
        the Survey of the Memorials of Greater London
        and the London County Council, now issued by
        the Greater London Council (published for the
        Greater London Council by the Athlone Press of
        the University of London). The purpose of the
        Survey of London is to provide a comprehensive
        history and description of London's building
        fabric. Each volume examines a particular area,
        usually one or part of one of the ancient parishes.
        The general topographical and architectural
        history is discussed, and selected individual
        buildings, including many now demolished, are
        fully described. The historical and architectural
        texts are based on detailed research and
        inspection. Each volume is fully illustrated with
        photographs, prints, maps and measured
        drawings.
        The following is a list of the volumes so far
        published:
        1   *Bromley-by-Bow*. 1900.
        2   *Chelsea*. Part 1. 1900.
        3   *St Giles-in-the-Fields*. Part 1 (Lincoln's Inn
            Fields). 1912.
        4   *Chelsea*. Part 2. 1913.
        5   *St Giles-in-the-Fields*. Part 2. 1914.
        6   *Hammersmith*. 1915.
        7   *Chelsea*. Part 3 (The Old Church). 1921.
        8   *St Leonard, Shoreditch*. 1922.
        9   *St Helen, Bishopsgate*. Part 1. 1924.
        10 *St Margaret, Westminster*. Part 1. 1926.
        11 *Chelsea*. Part 4 (The Royal Hospital). 1927.
        12 *All Hallows, Barking-by-the-Tower*. Part 1 (The
            Parish Church). 1929.
        13 *St Margaret, Westminster*. Part 2
            (Neighbourhood of Whitehall, vol 1). 1930.
        14 *St Margaret, Westminster*, Part 3
            (Neighbourhood of Whitehall, vol 2). 1931.
        15 *All Hallows, Barking-by-the-Tower*. Part 2. 1934.
        16 *St Martin-in-the-Fields*. Part 1 (Charing Cross).
            1935.
        17 *St Pancras*. Part 1 (Village of Highgate). 1936.
        18 *St Martin-in-the-Fields*. Part 2 (The Strand).
            1937.
        19 *St Pancras*. Part 2 (Old St Pancras and Kentish
            Town). 1938.
        20 *St Martin-in-the-Fields*. Part 3 (Trafalgar Square
            and neighbourhood). 1940.
        21 *St Pancras*. Part 3 (Tottenham Court Road and
            neighbourhood). 1949.
        22 *St Saviour and Christ Church, Southwark*
            (Bankside). 1950.
        23 *St Mary, Lambeth*. Part 1 (South Bank and
            Vauxhall). 1951.
        24 *St Pancras*. Part 4 (King's Cross
            neighbourhood). 1952.

2.1 Biographical dictionaries, encyclopaedias, directories, surveys and indexes

1952./continued

25 *St George the Martyr and St Mary Newington, Southwark* (St George's Fields). 1955.
26 *St Mary, Lambeth.* Part 2 (Southern Area). 1956.
27 *Christ Church and All Saints* (Spitalfields and Mile End New Town). 1957.
28 *Hackney.* Part 1 (Brooke House). 1960.
29, 30 *St James, Westminster,* Part 1 (South of Piccadilly). 1960.
31, 32 *St James, Westminster.* Part 2 (North of Piccadilly). 1963.
33, 34 *St Anne, Soho.* 1966.
35 *The Theatre Royal, Drury Lane, and The Royal Opera House, Covent Garden.* 1970.
36 *The Parish of St Paul, Covent Garden.* 1970.
37 *Northern Kensington.* 1973.
38 *The Museums Area of South Kensington and Westminster.* 1975.
39 *The Grosvenor Estate in Mayfair.* Part 1 (General history). 1977.
40 *The Grosvenor Estate in Mayfair.* Part 2 (The buildings). 1980.

Contemporary architects. Edited by Muriel   81
Emanuel. London: Macmillan; New York: St Martins Press, 1980. 1104pp.
archts; 19/20c
Provides detailed information on about 675 architects and architectural partnerships of international reputation. Each entry includes: a biography, a complete list of constructed works and projects, a signed evaluative essay, a commentary on his own work and ideas by the architect, a representative illustration of the person's work and a bibliography of books/articles by and about the entrant. For the purposes of this book, the meaning of the word 'contemporary' has been extended to include not only currently active individuals, but also those who have been important to the profession from the beginnings of the modern movement.

The Contractors', merchants', and estate   82
managers' compendium and catalogue. Edited by John Edward Sears. 14th annual issue. London: Compendium Publishing and Advertising Company, 1900. 485pp.
archts; 19/20c
Includes a list of architects, giving names and addresses, and indicating whether the architect is a fellow or associate of the RIBA or a member of the Society of Architects. Arranged in alphabetical sequences under the following headings: London, individual English counties, Scotland and Wales.

Department of the Environment. Directorate   83
of Ancient Monuments and Historic Buildings
Lists of buildings of special architectural or historic interest. 1946– .
bldgs; prehist/med, ren/neoclas, 19/20c
Local lists are received by the main public reference libraries throughout the country. Lists cover England, Wales and Northern Ireland.

The information given is very variable, but the Information Department of the Directorate at 25 Savile Row, London SW1 (tel 01 734 6010, ext 139), holds complete lists and can provide further information as to the grade of listing and why the building has been listed. A set can be inspected at the National Monuments Record, 23 Savile Row and at the British Architectural Library, 66 Portland Place, London, W1N 4AD. For Scotland *see* 130.

The Dictionary of national biography . . .   84
London: Oxford University Press, 1885– .
archts; prehist/med, ren/neoclas, 19/20c
Includes only those dead at the time of compilation. Originally included biographies of noteworthy inhabitants of the British Isles, and the colonies; but from 1941–50 includes only those who for a significant period of their lives were British subjects. Signed biographies arranged in alphabetical order, with bibliographies at the foot of each contribution.

The main dictionary, published 1885–1900, was completed (to 1900) by the issue of a supplement, 22 vols in all.

The twentieth-century dictionary, of which seven decennial volumes have so far appeared, brings the work up to 1970, as follows:
1901–1911. (1912)
1912–1921, with a cumulative index covering 1901–1921. (1927)
1922–1930, with a cumulative index covering 1901–1930. (1937)
1931–1940, with a cumulative index covering 1901–1940. (1949)
1941–1950, with a cumulative index covering 1904–1950. (1959)
1951–1960, with a cumulative index covering 1901–1960. (1971)
1961–1970, with a cumulative index covering 1961–1970. (1981).

The Compact edition of the *Dictionary of national biography* (London: Oxford University Press, 1975) reproduces the entries of the first 28 vols in the series in 2 vols. The entries from the decennial supplements have been reordered into one alphabetical sequence and there is a single index for all 28 vols.

Directory of official architects and 85
  planners. 1967–1973/4. London: G.
  Godwin, 1967–74.
  archts; 19/20c
    This annual publication includes names,
    addresses and telephone numbers of staff in
    architecture, planning, surveying and related
    departments of local authorities, statutory
    authorities, major commercial companies,
    churches, universities, public corporations,
    hospitals and central government. Arranged by
    type of body, and sub-arranged by location.
    Continues *Official architecture and planning year
    book (1956–66)*. Continued by *Directory of
    official architecture and planning (1974/5–)* (86).

Directory of official architecture and 86
  planning. 1974/5– . London: G. Godwin,
  1974– .
  archts; 19/20c
    See 85 above.

Linden, Peter, *editor* 87
Dictionary of land surveyors and local
  cartographers of Great Britain and Ireland,
  1550–1850. Compiled from a variety of sources by
  Francis Steer and others. Supplement. Compiled by
  Ian Adams and others. Folkestone: Dawson,
  1975–1979. 4 vols.
  archts; ren/neoclas, 19/20c
    A characteristic entry is in five parts: name,
    dates of birth, death and activity, area, class of
    map (or equivalent specialism), and additional
    detail (eg address, alternative occupation,
    collaboration and partnerships, family history,
    education and training, bibliography), if any.
    Most, though not all, whose alternative
    occupation is given as architect will be found in
    Colvin's *Dictionary* and are so noted. The
    general index, in vol 3, under the heading
    'architect' refers to 115 entries. The index in the
    supplement refers to 62 entries. There are also
    topographical indexes.

Gazetteer of pre-1914 theatres. 88
  archts, bldgs; prehist/med,
  ren/neoclas, 19/20c
    This gazetteer, which is not yet published, is
    being edited by Christopher Brereton, 68
    Thorpwood Avenue, London SE 26. The
    gazetteer contains details of all theatres and
    music halls built (or adapted permanently from
    buildings built for other purposes) for the
    presentation of shows by professional performers
    to paying audiences in England, Ireland,
    Scotland, Wales, the Channel Islands and the
    Isle of Man from Roman times to 1914. It does
    not include details of assembly rooms, cinemas,
    concert halls, night clubs, or town halls, even if
    they have been used fairly regularly for theatrical
    purposes.

The gazetteer will consist of a list, in
alphabetical order of names of towns, of all
existing and demolished theatres and music
halls. The architecture of existing theatres and
music halls will be described briefly, and even if
not used currently for theatrical purposes, brief
technical details will be given: dates of opening,
closing and alteration; names of architects;
descriptions of exterior and interior; capacity;
state of fabric and decoration; and notes on the
potential for improvement. Each building will be
listed under the last theatrical name and there
will be cross references in the index to theatre
and music hall names to any other names used
for the same building. An index of architects and
builders will consist of brief details of the work
carried out by over 700 architects and builders.
Details of birth and death will be given if they
are readily located.

Gordon, Esme 89
The Royal Scottish Academy of Painting,
  Sculpture and Architecture, 1826–1976.
  Edinburgh: Charles Skilton, 1976. 272pp. Bibl
  pp264–266.
  archts; 19/20c
    The bibliography and appendices to this work
    contain valuable data. Included are complete
    lists of members through the years, both
    honorary and professional. *See also* Royal
    Scottish Academy (129).

Gradidge, R. 90
Check list of architects, 1820–1939. London:
  Victorian Society, 1969. 21 leaves.
  archts; 19/20c
    A list giving birth and death dates, and
    indicating if the person is a major artist. Includes
    artists and engineers who were also architects.
    The list serves the purpose of indicating
    architects whose work should be looked at
    carefully before alterations. Arranged in three
    alphabetical sequences: those born before 1800,
    those born between 1800 and 1850, and those
    born after 1850.

Graves, Algernon 91
A dictionary of artists who have exhibited
  works in the principal London exhibitions from
  1760 to 1893. 3rd ed, with additions and corrections.
  London: Henry Graves, 1901. 314pp. Reprinted,
  Bath: Kingsmead, 1969; New York: B. Franklin,
  1970.
  archts; ren/neoclas, 19/20c
    Indexes the drawings (including architectural
    drawings). Lists over 25,000 artists exhibiting
    with the titles of their works and dates exhibited.

2.1 Biographical dictionaries, encyclopaedias, directories, surveys and indexes

Graves, Algernon   92
**The Royal Academy of Arts: a complete
    dictionary of contributors and their work, from
    its foundation in 1769 to 1904**. London: Graves and
Bell, 1905–06. 8 vols. Reprinted, Wakefield: S. R.
Publishers; Bath: Kingsmead, 1970. New York:
B. Frankin, 1972, 8 vols in 4.
archts; ren/neoclas, 19/20c
> Indexes the works (including architectural
> drawings) exhibited at the Royal Academy from
> its institution in 1769 to 1904. This work is very
> inaccurate and the original catalogues should be
> consulted whenever possible. Lists all artists
> exhibiting with the titles of their works, dates
> exhibited and addresses. *See also* 119.

Graves, Algernon   93
**The Society of Artists of Great Britain
    1760–1791. The Free Society of Artists 1761–1783.
    A complete dictionary of contributors and their
    work from the foundation of the societies to
    1791**. London: George Bell & Sons and Algernon
Graves, 1907. Reprinted, Calne: Hilmarton Manor
Press. 354pp.
archts; ren/neoclas
> Architectural drawings were exhibited at the
> Royal Academy from its institution in 1769
> onwards, and for some years previously at the
> Society of Artists and the Free Society of Artists.
> This publication indexes the exhibits at the latter
> two societies. Index.

Gray, A. Stuart   94
**Edwardian architecture: a biographical
    dictionary**. London: Duckworth, due 1981. c 400pp.
archts, bldgs; 19/20c
> Covering the period 1901–1910. A biographical
> dictionary of some 300 architects, sculptors and
> mural painters. The index lists principal works
> of the architects treated.

Gunnis, Rupert   95
Dictionary of British sculptors, 1660–1851.
New rev ed. London: Abbey Library, 1968. 514pp.
archts, bldgs; ren/neoclas
> The most complete work of its kind, with more
> than 1,700 entries. Bibliographical references are
> given to source material, authoritative works, etc
> (including notices in the *Gentleman's magazine*).
> Index of places, index of names.

Hall, *Sir* Robert de Zouche   96
A bibliography on vernacular architecture.
Newton Abbot: David and Charles, 1972. 191pp.
bldgs; prehist/med, ren/neoclas
> The entries run to the end of 1970 and are
> classified to cover general, regional and local

studies; rural and urban buildings; construction
techniques and building materials; and essential
references on the social and economic
background to the study of vernacular
architecture. Much of the material is compiled
from normally inaccessible local periodicals.
Author index. Continued by D. J. H.
Michelmore, *Current bibliography of vernacular
architecture (1970–1976)* (113).

Harris, John   9
**Catalogue of British drawings for
    architecture, decoration, sculpture and
    landscape gardening 1550–1900 in American
    collections**. Upper Saddle River (NJ): Gregg Press,
1971. 355pp.
archts, bldgs; ren/neoclas, 19/20c
> An A–Z listing by architect of drawings in
> American public and private collections. Full
> descriptive entries, some including
> bibliographical references. Well illustrated.
> Index includes subjects, names and places.

Harris, John   9
A country house index. 2nd ed. Shalfleet
Manor (Isle of Wight): Pinhorns, 1979. 45pp.
bldgs; ren/neoclas, 19/20c
> An index to over 2,000 country houses
> illustrated in 107 books of country views
> published between 1715 and 1872, together with
> a list of British country house guides and country
> house art collection catalogues for the period
> 1726–1880.

Harvey, John   9
**English mediaeval architects; a
    biographical dictionary down to 1550, including
    master masons, carpenters, carvers, building
    contractors, and others responsible for design**.
London: Batsford, 1954. Microfiche, London:
Architectural Press. 412pp.
archts, bldgs; prehist/med
> Includes: 1. those architects who practised in
> England and Wales, whether native or foreign;
> 2. natives, or presumed natives of England and
> Wales, or of English descent, who worked as
> architects elsewhere. The alphabetically
> arranged biographical dictionary gives data on
> the professional careers of about 1,300
> architects, indicating wages paid; appended to
> each entry are numerous references to the source
> material listed on pp xiii–xxiii. Appendices:
> portraits; tables of remuneration.
> Topographical, county and chronological
> indexes. A subject index of buildings, and a
> general index. Essential work in its field.

Matje, Gerd and **Pehnt**, W., *editors*   100
Encyclopaedia of modern architecture.
London: Thames and Hudson, 1963. 336pp. Bibl
p 327. (World of art library: general).
archts; 19/20c
> A survey from 1850 to modern times, with a
> six-page section on Great Britain as well as
> entries for notable British architects of the 20th
> century, including short essays on architects of
> the modern movement. Bibliographical
> references are given at the foot of each essay.

Historical Manuscripts Commission   101
Architectural history and the fine and
   applied arts: sources in the National Register of
   Archives. Compiled by T. W. M. Jaine and Brenda
   Weeden. London: National Register of Archives,
   1969–1974. 5 vols.
   archts, bldgs; ren/neoclas, 19/20c
> The lists, compiled by the National Register of
> Archives, cover the holdings of a number of
> institutions, including the RIBA. Each entry
> consists of a summary description of the mss
> arranged in alphabetical sequence under the
> name of the architect, artist, collector or place to
> which they refer. Includes short biographical
> introductions to persons. *See also 364.*

The Industrial archaeology of the British   102
   Isles, *series*. General editor, Keith
   Falconer. London: Batsford, 1976– .
   bldgs; 19/20c
> This series, now called *The Batsford guide to the
> industrial archaeology of the British Isles*, will
> cover all the major industrial monuments and
> sites in the British Isles. Each volume is arranged
> in gazetteer form. So far two volumes have been
> published on the industrial archaeology of
> Scotland 1. *The Lowlands and Borders* (1976) and
> 2. *The Highlands and Islands* (1977), both by
> John R. Hume, and volumes on *The Industrial
> archaeology of the West Midlands* by Fred Brook
> (1977), *The Industrial archaeology of South-east
> England: Kent, Surrey, East Sussex, West Sussex*
> by A. J. Haselfoot (1978), *The Industrial
> archaeology of East Anglia; Cambridgeshire,
> Essex, Norfolk, Suffolk* by David Alderton and
> John Booker (1980) and *The Industrial
> archaeology of Central Southern England: Avon
> County, Gloucestershire, Somerset, Wiltshire* by
> C. A. and R. A. Buchanan (1980). Also
> published by Batsford, but not specifically in
> this series, is a *Guide to England's industrial
> heritage* by Keith Falconer (1980) a county by
> county alphabetical gazetteer to the most
> important industrial monuments and sites which
> includes an index listing the sites by industry.

Industrial archaeology of the British Isles,   103
   series. Edited by E. R. R. Green. Newton
   Abbot: David and Charles, 1965– .
   bldgs; 19/20c
> An industry by industry survey of industrial
> archaeology, covering the British Isles region by
> region with associated volumes examining
> smaller areas in greater detail. The last quarter
> or third of each volume is a gazetteer,
> alphabetically arranged place by place, with
> details of the visible remains to be found there.
> Volumes include notes and references. So far the
> following volumes have been published:
> *Cornwall*, A. C. Todd and Peter Laws. 1972.
> *Derbyshire*, Frank Nixon. 1969.
> *East Midlands*, David M. Smith. 1965.
> *Galloway*, Ian Donnachie. 1971.
> *Hertfordshire*, W. Branch Johnson. 1970.
> *Isle of Man*, T. A. Bawden and others. 1972.
> *Lake Counties*, J. D. Marshall and Michael
> Davies-Shiel. 2nd ed. Beckermet: Michael
> Moon, 1977.
> *Lancashire*, Owen Ashmore. 1969.
> *North East England*. 2 vols, Frank Atkinson.
> 1974.
> *The Peak District*, Helen Harris. 1971.
> *Scotland*, John Butt. 1977.
> *Southern England*, Kenneth Hudson. 1965.
> *The Tamar Valley*, Frank Booker. Rev ed 1971.
> *Wales*, D. Morgan Rees. 1975.
>
> Associated volumes:
> *Bristol Region*, Angus Buchanan and Neil
> Cossons. 1969.
> *Dartmoor*, Helen Harris. 1968.
> *Gloucestershire woollen mills*, Jennifer Tann.
> 1967.
> *Stone blocks and iron rails*, Bertram Baxter. 1966.
> *Techniques of industrial archaeology*, J. P. M.
> Pannell. 1974.

Institute of Registered Architects   104
Official year book and list of members.
   1972– . London: Waltham Advertising, 1972– .
   archts; 19/20c
> Includes names and addresses of personal
> members and practices. Personal members are
> arranged alphabetically, practices geographically
> by the location of the office.

Jamilly, Edward   105
'Anglo-Jewish architects, and architecture
   in the 18th and 19th centuries.' [1954?] Reprint
   from *The Transactions of the Jewish Historical Society
   of England*. Vol 18, pp 127–141.
   archts; ren/neoclas, 19/20c
> Ten short biographical notes are included.

2.1 Biographical dictionaries, encyclopaedias, directories, surveys and indexes

Johnson, Jane, *compiler* 106
Works exhibited at the Royal Society of British Artists, 1824–1893 and at the New English Art Club, 1888–1917. Clopton: Antique Collector's Club, 1975. 2 vols. (An Antique Collector's Club research project).
archts; 19/20c
> An alphabetical list of exhibitors which includes a full list of works exhibited at the Suffolk Street Galleries of the Royal Society of British Artists. No index.

Kelly's local London, provincial and other 107
directories.
archs; bldgs; 19/20c
> The earlier ones in particular often give, under the name of the building, the name of the architect and who paid for the building. In the case of churches, many details of fittings may be given, and for houses, the name of the owner. A guide to the current directories, giving the date when each was begun, is *Current British directories: a guide to the directories published in Great Britain, Ireland, the British Commonwealth and South Africa* (Beckenham: CBD Research. First published 1953. Frequency: every three years). *See also* 38 and 40.

Kenyon, J. R. 108
Castles, town defences, and artillery fortifications in Britain: a bibliography, 1945–74. London: Council for British Archaeology, 1978. 76pp. (Council for British Archaeology, Research report, 25).
bldgs; prehist/med
> Britain, in the context of this bibliography, comprises England, Wales, Scotland, the Isle of Man, the Scilly Isles and the Channel Islands.
> The bibliography is divided into two parts. The first, which is devoted entirely to general works on Britain and its constituent countries, is subdivided into three categories: books and pamphlets, periodical articles, and miscellaneous. Examples of the latter are articles published in *Festschriften* and conference proceedings. The second, which deals with items on specific sites and areas within counties, is divided by country, county, and then alphabetically under the name of each site. An article covering a number of sites in a particular county will be found under that county heading, but before the listing of individual defence works. The appendix, a select bibliography for 1975 and 1976, is subdivided in a like manner. While not all guidebooks to castles and forts are included, the bibliography does list all Department of the Environment ancient monuments guides, and several other authoritative publications, including those published by the National Trust. The majority of the material listed can be found in the library of the Society of Antiquaries.

Linstrum, Derek 10
West Yorkshire architects and architecture. London: Lund Humphries, 1978. 399pp.
archts, bldgs; ren/neoclas, 19/20c
> A detailed study of the architecture in West Yorkshire with chapters devoted to different building types (estates and country houses, middle-class housing, working-class housing, churches, buildings for education, theatres and music halls, mills, warehouses and exchanges, markets and market-halls and municipal buildings). Includes a select biographical list of Yorkshire architects (1550–1900) who worked in West Yorkshire (pp 369–386). Index of persons. Index of places.

List of the fellows and members of the 11
Royal Institute of British Architects, the Institution of Civil Engineers, the Architectural Association, the promoters of the Architectural Publication Society and the Institution of Mechanical Engineers of Birmingham.
pp iii–xvi. From John Weale, publ. *Catalogue of books on the subjects of architecture, engineering, etc.* 1854.
archts; 19/20c
> A list giving names and addresses, and indicating to which society each person belongs. Arranged alphabetically.

Loeber, Rolf 11
'A biographical dictionary of engineers in Ireland, 1600–1730', in *The Irish sword, the Journal of the Military History Society of Ireland.*
archts; ren/neoclas
> According to a note in the *Irish Georgian Society Newsletter*, 1977, this dictionary will be published in instalments in *The Irish sword* as much of it deals with fortifications. Some (or all?) of it appears in vol 22 (1977).

Loeber, Rolf 11
A biographical dictionary of Irish architects, 1600–1730. London: J. Murray, due 1981. c112pp.
archts, bldgs; ren/neoclas
> The dictionary includes 97 architects. Bibliographical notes are provided for each entry. Index of names and places.

Michelmore, D. J. H., *editor* 11
Current bibliography of vernacular architecture, vol 1 (1970–1976). York: Vernacular Architecture Group, 1979. 40pp.
bldgs; prehist/med, ren/neoclas
> Contains 660 cross-referenced entries citing publications from 1970 to 1976. A continuation of Sir Robert de Zouche Hall's *Bibliography on vernacular architecture (see 96)*. Includes some

earlier entries not included in the previous book. Index of the current serial publications and collected essays which have provided entries for the bibliography, index of authors, and index of places (arranged by historic counties). The *Current bibliography of vernacular architecture* is to be issued as an occasional publication by the Vernacular Architecture Group.

Musgrave, *Sir* William, *compiler*　　　114
Obituary prior to 1800 (as far as relates to England, Scotland and Ireland). Compiled by Sir William Musgrave . . . and entitled by him 'a general nomenclator and obituary, with reference to the books where the persons are mentioned and where some account of their character is to be found'. Edited by Sir G. J. Armytage. London: Harleian Society, 1899–1901. 6 vols. (Harleian Society publications, 44–49).
　archts; ren/neoclas
　　A finding list of mainly eighteenth-century obituaries contained in about 90 works, manuscripts, collections, etc. The great majority of the works indexed are in the British Museum. Brief entries: name, description, date of death, place of residence, source of information. An invaluable supplement to the *Dictionary of national biography*. A copy is held at the Guildhall Library (297).

Obituaries from *The Times*. Compiler Frank　　115
C. Roberts. Reading: Newspaper Archive Developments, 1975– .
　archts; 19/20c
　　Volumes so far cover the years 1951–1960, 1961–1970 and 1971–1975. Each volume reprints a selection of obituaries and includes an index of all names appearing in the obituary column for the years covered. The volumes for 1961–1970 and 1971–1975 also include an index to the fields of activity (eg art and architecture) of persons whose obituaries have been reprinted.

Pevsner, *Sir* Nikolaus, **Fleming**, John and　　116
Honour, Hugh
A dictionary of architecture. Rev and enl ed. London: Allen Lane, 1975. 556pp.
　archts; prehist/med, ren/neoclas, 19/20c
　　An excellent one vol dictionary which includes short biographical entries on British architects with selected bibliographies. Arranged alphabetically. A revised edition has appeared as *The Penguin dictionary of architecture*, 3rd ed, Harmondsworth: Penguin Books, 1980. The third edition does not include bibliographic references.

The Register of architects. Vol 1– ; 1933– .　　117
London: Architects' Registration Council of the United Kingdom, 1933– . Annual.
　archts; 19/20c
　　Includes name, address, and date of registration. Arranged alphabetically. Under the Architects' (Registration) Acts 1931 to 1969, it is an offence for any person in the United Kingdom to practice under any style or title containing the word 'architect' if his name is not on the register of the Architects' Registration Council of the United Kingdom (ARCUK). *See also* 222.

Richards, *Sir* J. M., *editor*　　118
Who's who in architecture from 1400 to the present day. London: Weidenfeld and Nicolson, 1977. 368pp.
　archts; ren/neoclas, 19/20c
　　A dictionary of 500 architects from the renaissance to the present day throughout the world. The entries are arranged alphabetically. Fifty major architects are covered at greater length by a leading specialist or scholar of the period. Shorter entries provide factual information about the life and work of the other 450 architects, together with such engineers, town planners and landscape architects as have made a significant contribution to the development of architecture.

Royal Academy　　119
Royal Academy exhibitors, 1905–1970: a dictionary of artists and their work in the summer exhibitions of the Royal Academy of Arts. Wakefield: EP Publishing, 1973– . Vol 1: A–Car; Vol 2: Cas–D; Vol 3: E–Har; Vol 4: Hart–Lawl.
　archts; 19/20c
　　See also 92.

Royal Commission on Historical Monuments (England)　　120
Inventories (including reports). London: HMSO, 1910– . Microfiche of *Inventories* 1910–1979. Cambridge (Eng): Chadwyck-Healey; Teaneck (NJ): Somerset House.
　archts, bldgs; prehist/med, ren/neoclas
　　The *Inventories* of the Royal Commissions on Historical Monuments form the most detailed published record of buildings and their contents, monuments and archaeological remains in England, Scotland and Wales. The original terms of reference required that all buildings and monuments from the earliest times to 1700 should be included. In 1921 the date limit of 1700 was extended to 1714 and in 1946 the Commissioners were granted a discretionary extension to 1850, and in 1963 all date limits to the Commissioners' discretionary powers were removed.

2.1 Biographical dictionaries, encyclopaedias, directories, surveys and indexes

removed./*continued*

The general arrangement of the *Inventories* is an historical introduction, a list of buildings recommended for preservation and the illustrated inventory of the buildings and monuments inspected. The inventory is arranged in parishes, each parish being divided into: prehistoric monuments and earthworks, Roman monuments and earthworks, ecclesiastical buildings and monuments, secular buildings and monuments, and unclassified monuments. Following the inventory are glossaries of heraldic, archaeological and architectural terms and a detailed index by name and by subject.

Inventories published so far:
Buckinghamshire (2 vols, 1912–13).
Cambridgeshire (2 vols, 1968–72).
City of Cambridge (2 parts, 1959).
Dorset (5 vols, 1952–1975).
Essex (4 vols, 1916–23).
Gloucestershire (1977–).
Herefordshire (3 vols, 1931–34).
Hertfordshire (1910).
Huntingdonshire (1926).
London (5 vols, 1924–30).
Middlesex (1937).
Northamptonshire (3 vols, 1975–81).
City of Oxford (1939).
City of Salisbury (1980–).
Town of Stamford (1977).
Westmorland (1936).
City of York (5 vols, 1962–81).

Royal Commission on the Ancient and   121
Historical Monuments in Wales
Inventories (including reports). London: HMSO, 1911– . Microfiche of *Inventories* 1910–1979. Cambridge (Eng): Chadwyck-Healey; Teaneck (NJ): Somerset House.
  archts, bldgs; prehist/med, ren/neoclas
For a description of the *Inventories* see 120.

Inventories published so far:
Anglesey (1937).
Caernarvonshire (3 vols, 1956–64).
Carmarthen (1917).
Denbigh (1914).
Flint (1912).
Glamorgan (1976–).
Merioneth (1921).
Montgomery (1911).
Pembroke (1925).
Radnor (1913).

Royal Commission on the Ancient and   122
Historical Monuments of Scotland
Inventories (including reports). Edinburgh: HMSO, 1911– . Microfiche of *Inventories* 1911–1979. Cambridge (Eng): Chadwyck-Healey; Teaneck (NJ): Somerset House.
  archts, bldgs; prehist/med, ren/neoclas
For a description of the *Inventories* see 120.

Inventories published so far:
Argyll (3 vols, 1971–80).
County of Berwick (1915, rev issue).
Caithness (1911).
County of Dumfries (1920).
East Lothian (1924).
City of Edinburgh (1951).
Counties of Fife, Kinross and Clackmannan (1933).
Galloway (2 vols, 1912–14).
Lanarkshire (1978).
Midlothian and West Lothian (1929).
Orkney and Shetland (3 vols, 1946).
Outer Hebrides, Skye and the small isles (1928).
Peebleshire (2 vols, 1967).
Roxburghshire (2 vols, 1956).
Selkirkshire (1957).
Stirlingshire (1963).
Sutherland (1911).

Royal Institute of British Architects   12
The RIBA directory. 1966/67–1972. London: RIBA, 1966–71. 6 vols.
  archts; 19/20c
Gives a name, address, date of election and type of membership for personal members, and names and addresses of practices, with a list of the partners in each practice. Personal members are arranged alphabetically, and practices geographically by the location of the office, with an alphabetical index. Supersedes the *Kalendar* (126) and superseded by the *RIBA directory of members* (124) and the *RIBA directory of practices* (125).

Royal Institute of British Architects   12·
RIBA directory of members. 1974– . London: RIBA, 1973– Annual.
  archts; 19/20c
Includes name, address, date of election and telephone number. Arranged in alphabetical order. Supersedes the *RIBA directory* (123) and the *Kalendar* (126).

Royal Institute of British Architects   12·
RIBA directory of practices. 1972– . London: RIBA, 1971– .
  archts; 19/20c
Includes names of practices, addresses, prizes and commendations awarded, brief lists of work completed, and the names and qualifications of partners. Practices listed geographically by the location of the office, with an alphaetical index. Supersedes the *RIBA directory* (123).

Royal Institute of British Architects   12·
The Kalendar. 1886/87–1965/66. London: RIBA, 1886–1965. 74 vols.
  archts; 19/20c
Gives name, address, date of election and type of membership. Arrangement: 1. from

1886/87–1951/52 arranged alphabetically in a number of sequences (eg Fellow, Associate, Licentiate); 2. from 1952/52–1965/66 arranged in one alphabetical sequence. Superseded by the *RIBA directory* (123) and then the *RIBA directory of members* (124).

Royal Institute of British Architects. 127
Drawings Collection.
Catalogue of the Drawings Collection of the Royal Institute of British Architects. Farnborough (Hants): Gregg International, 1969– .
archts; ren/neoclas, 19/20c
> The main series of the *Catalogue* is being published in c21 vols, arranged under architects A–Z (eg vol 1: A), with a number of separate monographs and the final volume as a cumulative index of persons, places and subjects. Under each architect is given a short biography and bibliography; the drawings, identified (by place), unidentified (by subject) and topographical (by country), with full descriptive details including stage of realization, provenance, literary references and exhibitions. To date (Aug 1981), seven volumes covering A–S, and separate volumes on *Colen Campbell, Gentilhâtre, Inigo Jones and John Webb, Edwin Lutyens, J. B. Papworth, the Pugin family, Alfred Stevens, Visentini, C. F. A. Voysey* and the *Wyatt family* have been published. Volumes covering T–Z, *Palladio*, and the *Scott family* are to be published shortly. Each volume contains an index of names (owners, provenance etc) and places. An index of drawings held (if any) of architects not yet covered by a published catalogue or acquired since the appropriate volume was published can be found by contacting the Drawings Collection (237). A cumulative index volume will complete the series and supplementary volumes will be published. The Drawings Collection maintains subject and topographical indexes to the drawings. The original drawings catalogued in the separate volumes on individual architects are to be published in a microfilm edition by World Microfilms.

Royal Institute of British Architects. Library 128
Index of architects of several countries and many periods (except English mediaeval) in nearly 60 old and new selected indexes and indexed specialist works . . . London: RIBA, 1956. 66pp. Mimeographed.
archts; ren/neoclas, 19/20c
> References are to some 60 indexes, architectural histories, biographies and guidebooks. Includes: 1. only those architects dead at the time of compilation (1954); 2. non-architects who have done architectural work; 3. references to non-architectural work by architects (eg stained glass windows). Nearly 4,000 names arranged A–Z. List of sources.

The Royal Scottish Academy, 1826–1916, a complete list of the exhibited works by Raeburn and by academicians, associates and hon members, giving details of those works in public galleries. Orig publ 1917. Bath: Kingsmead Reprints, 1975. 485pp. 129
archts, bldgs; ren/neoclas, 19/20c
> Contains an alphabetical list of members, catalogue of exhibited works and indexes to lenders, donors and bequeathers of exhibited works, place names and important architectural subjects. *See also* 89.

Scottish Development Department 130
Lists of buildings of architectural or historic interest. Edinburgh, 1970– .
bldgs; prehist/med, ren/neoclas, 19/20c
> The information given is very variable, but always includes grade of listing and often includes a description of the building, references and notes. Sets are held in Scotland and by the British Architectural Library.

Sharp, Dennis 131
Sources of modern architecture: a critical bibliography. 2nd ed. St Albans: Granada, 1981. 192pp.
archts; 19/20c
> A revised and expanded version of *Sources of modern architecture: a bibliography* (Architectural Association, paper no 2, London: Lund Humphries for the Architectural Association, 1967). The first and major section is on individual architects and a few influential critics and painters. This section is arranged alphabetically. Each entry includes a short biographical note, a list of books and articles by the person, a list of books and monographs on the person by other writers, and then periodical articles on the individual. The coverage is international. Individuals specifically connected with Britain include: M. H. Baillie Scott, Serge Chermayeff, Wells Coates, Connell, Ward and Lucas, E. Maxwell Fry, Walter Gropius, W. R. Lethaby, Berthold Lubetkin, Charles Rennie Mackintosh, Erich Mendelsohn, Hermann Muthesius, P. Morton Shand, R. Norman Shaw, Peter and Alison Smithson, C. F. A. Voysey, Philip Webb and F. R. S. Yorke. The second section, a subject bibliography, is devoted to general works on modern architecture and theory. The third, concerned with national trends, is arranged alphabetically by country (United Kingdom, p 173). The fourth section is a select list of architectural periodicals, mainly those concerned with developments in the modern movement. Index of architects and authors.

2.1 Biographical dictionaries, encyclopaedias, directories, surveys and indexes

Shell Guides, *series*. London: Faber and Faber, 132
1935– .
bldgs; prehist/med, ren/neoclas, 19/20c
Buckinghamshire, by Bruce Watkin. 1981.
Gazetteers, originally edited by John Betjeman
and John Piper.
Cornwall, by John Betjeman. 1964.
Derbyshire, by Henry Thorold. 1972.
Devon, by Ann Jellicoe and Roger Mayne. 1975.
Dorset, by Michael Pitt-Rivers. 1966.
County Durham, by Henry Thorold. 1980.
Essex, by Norman Scarfe. 1968.
Gloucestershire, by Anthony West and David
Verey. 2nd ed 1952.
Herefordshire, by David Verey. 1955.
Isle of Wight, by Pennethorne Hughes. 1967.
Kent, by Pennethorne Hughes. 1969.
Leicestershire, by W. G. Hoskins. 1970.
Lincolnshire, by Jack Yates and Henry Thorold.
1965.
Norfolk, by Wilhelmine Harrod and C. L. S.
Linnell. 1957.
Northamptonshire, by Juliet Smith. 1968.
Northumberland, by Thomas Sharp. 3rd ed
1969.
Oxfordshire, by John Piper. 1938.
Rutland, by W. G. Hoskins. 1963.
Shropshire, by Michael Moulder. 2nd ed 1973.
Staffordshire, by Henry Thorold. 1978.
Suffolk, by Norman Scarfe. 3rd ed 1976.
Surrey, by Bruce Watkin. 1977.
East Sussex, by William S. Mitchell. 1978.
Mid Wales, by David Verey. 1960.
Mid Western Wales, by Vyvyan Rees. 1971.
North Wales, by Elisabeth Beazley and Lionel
Brett. 1971.
South West Wales, by Vyvyan Rees. 2nd ed 1976.
Warwickshire, by Douglas Hickman. 1979.
Wiltshire, by J. H. Cheetham and John Piper.
3rd ed 1968.

The Shell Guide to Wales. Introduction by 133
Wynford Vaughan-Thomas.
Gazetteer by Alun Llewellyn. London: Michael
Joseph, 1969. 360pp. Bibl pp 353–354.
bldgs; prehist/med, ren/neoclas, 19/20c
The Shell Guide to Ireland. By Lord Killanin and
Michael V. Duignan. London: Ebury Press, 1962.
486pp. Bibl pp 476–478.
The new Shell Guide to Scotland. [New ed]; edited
by Donald Lamond Macnie and Moray McLaren.
London: Ebury Press, 1977. 479pp. Bibl pp 462–464.

Society of Architects 134
Year book. 1899–1924/25. London: Society of
Architects 1899–1925. Annual vols.
archts; 19/20c
Includes names and addresses of members and
date of election. Arranged alphabetically in three
sequences: Fellows, Members, Licentiates.
Supersedes the *List of members . . .* (1892–1898).
Ceased publication when the Society was
absorbed by the RIBA.

Spain, Geoffrey and **Dromgoole**, Nicholas, 13.
compilers
'Theatre architects in the British Isles', in
*Architectural history, Journal of the Society of
Architectural Historians of Great Britain*, vol 13, 1970,
pp 77–89.
archts, bldgs; 19/20c
Entries for 15 architects providing a
chronological list of their works with references
for each when known. The list is compiled from
the *Builder* (tenders, building notes, obituaries),
Pevsner's *Buildings of England* series, Colvin's
*Biographical dictionary of English architects,
1600–1840* (1954) and the *Architectural review*.
Following the entries for individual architects
are chronological lists of theatres for which the
architect is unknown, theatres in the greater
London area and theatres outside London with
the names of their architects. References are
provided. Completed by an index of city theatres
outside London.

Thieme-Becker Künstler-Lexikon *see Allgemeines
Lexikon* (59) and Vollmer (139).

Ulster Architectural Heritage Society 13(
**Historic buildings, groups of buildings,
areas of architectural importance**. . . . Belfast:
Ulster Architectural Heritage Society, 1968– .
bldgs; prehist/med, ren/neoclas, 19/20c
The separate volumes of lists each cover various
areas in Ulster. The information provided for
each building varies but often includes a
description, date, name of architect and
references. These unofficial lists are being
complemented by the official lists, compiled
since 1969 on an extra statutory basis, but now
(since the Planning Order in Council of 1973)
given statutory force, in the course of
preparation by the Historic Buildings Council
and the Department of the Environment (*see*
279).
Lists and surveys:
1 *Queen's University area of Belfast*. Rev ed 1975.
2 *Lisburn*. 1969.
3 *Banbridge*. 1969.
4 *Portaferry and Strangford*. 1969.
5 *Antrim and Ballymena*. 1970.
6 *Downpatrick*. 1970.
7 *City of Derry*. 1970.
8 *Town of Monaghen*. 1970.
9 *West Antrim*. 1970.
10 *Craigavon*. 1969. *Lurgan and Portadown*. 1969.
11 *Joy Street area of Belfast*. 1971.
12 *Dungannon and Cookstown*. 1971.
13 *Glens of Antrim*. 1972.
14 *North Antrim*. 1972.
15 *Coleraine and Portstewart*. 1972.
16 *Enniskellen*. 1973.
17 *Towns and villages of East Down*. 1973
18 *Towns and villages of Mid Down*. 1974.

19 *Island of Rathlin*. 1974.
20 *Mourne*. 1975.
21 *North Derry*. 1975.
22 *Donaghadee and Portpatrick*. 1977.
23 *Carrickfergus*. 1978.
24 *Town of Cavan*. 1978.
25 *Raithfriland and Hilltown*. 1979.

Victoria and Albert Museum   137
Topographical index to measured drawings
of architecture which have appeared in the
principal architectural publications. London:
HMSO, 1908. 68pp.
bldgs; prehist/med, ren/neoclas, 19/20c
      The index has been compiled from the following
      sketch books: *Abbey Square Sketch book* (vols
      1–111), *Architectural Association Sketch book*
      (1867–1906), *Edinburgh Architectural*
      Association Sketch book (1875–1894), *Glasgow*
      Architectural Association Sketch book
      (1885–1894), *John o' Gaunt Sketch book*
      (1874–1883), *Liverpool University School of*
      Architecture Sketch book (1906), *Spring Gardens*
      Sketch book (1866–1883), and from the following
      periodicals: *Architect* (1869–1905), *Architectural*
      review (1896–1904), *British architect*
      (1874–1904), *Builder* (1880–1905), *Building*
      news (1871–1905). The entries (by place)
      provide the name of the building, the name of
      the draughtsman and an indication of which
      detail is illustrated (eg tower, window, plan, etc).

The Victoria history of the counties of   138
England. Edited by H. A. Doubleday and
W. Page (latterly, R. B. Pugh, currently C. R.
Elrington). London: Constable (then St. Catherine
Press and now Oxford University Press for the
Institute of Historical Research, University of
London), 1901– .
bldgs; prehist/med, ren/neoclas, 19/20c
      The *VCH*, as it is popularly called, is an
      historical encyclopaedia of the English counties,
      covering most aspects of English life. The
      'counties of England' are not the modern ones
      created by the Local Government Act, 1972, but
      the historic counties as they were constituted up
      to March 1974. The respective counties form
      'sets' and for each set there are several volumes.
      Each county 'set' is loosely divided into 'general'
      volumes (covering, for example, prehistory, the
      history of transport, economic life, sport,
      administration, and parliamentary
      constituencies, as well as a translation of the
      county section of Domesday book with a
      commentary upon it) and 'topographical'
      volumes (dealing with each city, town and village
      in the county).
            Only Northumberland and Westmorland
      have still to be attempted, but not all counties
      are completed. *The Victoria history of the counties*
      of England: general introduction (London: Oxford
      University Press for the Institute of Historical

Research, University of London) is a conspectus
of the volumes up to and including 1970, plus a
bibliographical survey, list of contents, and
indexes of titles and authors of all articles.

Volumes published to date:
General introduction (1970).
Bedfordshire: 1 (1904); 2 (1908); 3 (1912); index
(1914); (complete).
Berkshire: 1 (1906); 2 (1907); 3 (1923); 4 (1924);
index (1927); (complete).
Buckinghamshire: 1 (1905); 2 (1908); 3 (1925);
4 (1927); index (1928); (complete).
Cambridgeshire and the Isle of Ely: 1 (1938);
2 (1948); 3 (the city and university of Cambridge,
(1959); 4 (1953); index to vols I–IV (1960);
5 (1973); 6 (1978); 7 (1978).
Cheshire: 2 (1979); 3 (1980).
Cornwall: 1 (1906); 2 pts 5 and 8 (1924).
Cumberland: 1 (1901); 2 (1905).
Derbyshire: 1 (1905); 2 (1907).
Devonshire: 1 (1906).
Dorset: 2 (1908); 3 with index vols 2–3 (1968).
Durham: 1 (1905); 2 (1907); 3 (1928).
Essex: 1 (1903); 2 (1907); 3 Roman Essex with
index vols 1–3 (1963); 4 (1956); 5 (1966);
bibliography (1959); 7 (1978).
Gloucestershire: 1 (1980); 2 (1907); 6 (1965);
7 (1980); 8 (1968); 10 (1972); 11 (1976).
Hampshire and the Isle of Wight: 1 (1900);
2 (1903); 3 (1908); 4 (1911); 5 (1912); index
(1914).
Herefordshire: 1 (1908).
Hertfordshire: 1 (1902); 2 (1908); 3 (1912);
4 (1914); index (1923).
Huntingdonshire: 1 (1926); 2 (1932); 3 (1936);
index (1938).
Kent: 1 (1908); 2 (1926); 3 (1932).
Lancashire: 1 (1906); 2 (1908); 3 (1907); 4 (1911);
5 (1911); 6 (1911); 7 (1912); 8 (1914).
Leicestershire: 1 (1907); 2 (1954); 3 (1955);
4 (1958); 5 (1964).
Lincolnshire: 2 (1906).
London: 1 (1909).
Middlesex: 1 (1969); 2 (1911); 3 (1962); 4 (1971);
5 (1976); 6 (1980).
Norfolk: 1 (1901); 2 (1906).
Northamptonshire: 1 (1902); 2 (1906); 3 (1930);
4 (1937).
Nottinghamshire: 1 (1906); 2 (1910).
Oxfordshire: 1 (1939); 2 (1907); 3 (University of
Oxford, 1954); 4 (1979); 5 (1957); 6 (1959);
7 (1962); 8 (1964); 9 (1969); 10 (1972).
Rutland: 1 (1908); 2 (1935); index (1936).
Shropshire: 1 (1908); 3 (1979); 8 (1968).
Somerset: 1 (1906); 2 (1911); 3 (1974); 4 (1978).
Staffordshire: 1 (1908); 2 (1967); 3 (1970);
4 (1958); 5 (1959); 6 (1970); 8 (1963); 17 (1976).
Suffolk: 1 (1911); 2 (1907).
Surrey: 1 (1902); 2 (1905); 3 (1911); 4 (1912);
index (1914).
Sussex: 1 (1905); 2 (1907); 3 (1935); 4 (1953);
5 pt 1 (1980); 7 (1940); 9 (1937).

2.1 Biographical dictionaries, encyclopaedias, directories, surveys and indexes

(1937)./*continued*
Warwickshire: 1 (1904); 2 (1908); 3 (1945);
4 (1947); 5 (1949); 6 (1951); index to vols 1–6.
(1955); 7 (1964); 8 (1969).
Wiltshire: 1 pt 1 (1957); 2 (1955); 3 (1956);
4 (1959); 5 (1957); 6 (1962); 7 (1953); 8 (1965);
9 (1970); 10 (1975); 11 (1980).
Worcestershire: 1 (1901); 2 (1906); 3 (1913);
4 (1924); index (1926).
Yorkshire (general): 1 (1907); 2 (1912); 3 (1913);
index (1925).
Yorkshire East Riding: 1 (1970); 2 (1974);
3 (1976); 4 (1979).
Yorkshire North Riding: 1 (1914); 2 (1923); index
(1925).
Yorkshire City of York: 1 (1961); (complete).

W. R. Dawson, Cannon House, Folkestone,
Kent are engaged upon a continuing programme
of photographic facsimile reprints.

Vollmer, Hans.   139
**Allgemeines Lexikon der bildenden
   Künstler des XX. Jahrhunderts** . . . Leipzig:
Seeman, 1953–62. 6 vols.
   archts; 19/20c
      In German. Supplements *Allgemeines Lexikon*
      (59), though entries on the same person can
      appear in both works. Concerned with
      twentieth-century, and some nineteenth-century
      artists. The signed articles give biographical data
      and bibliographies. The main alphabetical
      sequence runs from vols 1–5, and a separate
      sequence of supplementary articles is included in
      vols 5–6.

Ware, Dora   140
A short dictionary of British architects.
London: Allen and Unwin, 1967. 312pp.
   archts, bldgs; prehist/med, ren/neoclas, 19/20c
      Biographical dictionary of a representative
      selection in terms of period, style, fame and
      achievements of British architects from the
      middle ages to the present. Entries are brief,
      giving basic biographical data and lists of works
      and writings. No bibliography. Arranged
      alphabetically. Index of persons. Index of places,
      in which names of buildings appear under city or
      town; country houses directly under name. New
      edition in preparation.

**Who was who . . .: a companion to 'Who's   141
   who', containing the biographies of
   those who died during the period** . . . Vol 1
(1897–1915)– . London: A. and C. Black, 1935– .
   archts; 19/20c
      The entries are generally as they last appeared in
      Who's who, with the date of death added, and, in
      some cases, additional information to bring them
      up to date. Arranged alphabetically.

**Who's who; an annual biographical   142
   dictionary. 1849–** . London: A. and C.
Black, 1849– .
   archts; 19/20c
      Gives biographical sketches of 'eminent living
      persons of both sexes, in all parts of the civilized
      world'. Arranged alphabetically, though in its
      early days mainly lists of names under various
      headings without any individual biographical
      details.

**Who's who in architecture, giving brief   143
   biographies and other useful
   particulars of architects practising in the United
   Kingdom**. London: Technical Journals, 1914.
338pp. London: Architectural Press, 1923. 407pp.
London: Architectural Press, 1926. 460pp.
   archts; 19/20c
      Gives a succinct account of all the most notable
      men in the profession, and includes a list of the
      names and addresses of architects practising in
      the United Kingdom in 1914, 1923, and 1926.
      Arranged alphabetically.

Wodehouse, Lawrence   144
**British architects, 1840–1976: a guide to
   information sources**. Detroit: Gale Research, 1978.
353pp. (Art and architecture information guide
series, vol 8). (Gale information guide library).
   archts, bldgs; 19/20c
      Contains two parts, the first consists of notations
      on 354 publications on British architecture,
      including the whole of Ireland, towns, cities,
      geographic areas and building types, and the
      second part a selected annotated biographical
      bibliography of 288 architects or firms of
      architects. General index and building index.

For other entries relating to this section see items in:

1.   **How to find out: guides to the literature**
      2 *Architectural periodicals index.*
      4 Avery Architectural Library. *Catalog.*
      5 Avery Architectural Library. *An index to
         architectural periodicals.*
      15 Courtauld Institute of Art, University of
          London. *Annual bibliography of the history of
          British art.*
      18 Department of the Environment Library.
          Catalogues.
      19 Dobai. *Die Kunstliteratur des Klassizismus und
          der Romantik in England.*
      29 Harvard University, Graduate School of Design
          Catalog of the Library.
      44 *RILA.*
      45 Royal Institute of British Architects, Library.
          Catalogue.
      46 Royal Institute of British Architects, Library.
          *Comprehensive index to architectural periodicals,
          1956–70.*

■■■■■ **2.2**

Indexes to research and theses

This section gives details of sources which enable a researcher to discover unpublished theses or identify contacts which are potentially useful, but because difficult to trace, are often ignored. Lists of theses completed will indicate where work has been done and is unpublished.

Academic theses are usually kept by university or college libraries, but can often be borrowed through inter-library loan.

It may be of interest to anyone trying to locate a copy of a particular thesis that the British Library Lending Division can make available the majority of British theses. The Lending Division's arrangements, which now cover thirty-two British universities and over 3,500 theses per annum, provide the following services to libraries: 1. loan of a microfilm or hard copy; 2. retention of the microfilm, or retention of the hard copy. They also have all University Microfilm dissertations from 1870, and are thus able to lend American theses. As only member libraries can borrow from the British Library Lending Division, individuals should apply to their own library.

Registers of research index the researchers, institutions and the topics which are currently being worked on. Registers of current research, such as that of the Society of Architectural Historians, are valuable as a means not only of finding out what research is in progress so that duplication can be avoided, but of tracing people who are involved in research projects, who will usually be aware of the latest developments in their subjects.

Most entries are coded as in the previous section (see introduction to section 2.1 for fuller explanation):

archts	Indicates that it is possible to look up the names of architects in the item described
bldgs	Indicates that it is possible to look up the names of buildings (sometimes indirectly under location) in the item described
prehist/ med	Useful for the period from prehistory to medieval
ren/ neoclas	Useful for the period from renaissance to neoclassic
19/20c	Useful for the nineteenth and/or twentieth centuries

2.2 Indexes to research and theses

Archaeological theses in progress in British   145
   universities. Produced by the London
Institute of Archaeology in conjunction with the
Council for British Archaeology. London: Institute of
Archaeology, 1977. 28pp. Annual supplements.

ASLIB   146
Index to theses accepted for higher degrees
   in the universities of Great Britain and Ireland
   and the Council for National Academic Awards.
   Vol 1, 1950/51– . London: Aslib, 1953– . Annual.
   archts, bldgs
      Contains author and subject indexes. Vol 26,
      1975–76 contained 17 entries for architecture,
      with about one quarter of these relating to the
      history of British architecture.
         Abstracts of theses accepted for higher degrees
      by the Universities of Great Britain and Ireland
      and the Council for National Academic Awards is
      issued on microfiche from vol 26, 1977 of the
      Index to theses.

'British and German-language theses   147
   compiled from material collected by
   the Courtauld Institute and the Zentral Institut
   für Kunstgeschichte in Munich', in *Burlington
magazine* and in *Kunstchronik*. Appears annually,
month varies.
   archts, bldgs
      Covers all the arts, including architecture.
      Theses listed are newly begun, completed and
      re-titled and besides British universities,
      includes those from West German universities
      and institutes, German institutes in Florence
      and Rome and from Swiss and Austrian
      universities and institutes. The list in the
      Burlington magazine is arranged (from 1976
      onwards) by subject while that in *Kunstchronik* is
      arranged by institution. The *Burlington magazine*
      entries give title, author's name, name of
      supervisor, town, and level of thesis. For more
      precise information on the author's institutional
      affiliation it is necessary to consult the fuller list
      in *Kunstchronik*. Architecture appears under the
      following headings: Architecture (general);
      Urbanism and landscape architecture; Mediaeval
      architecture; Renaissance/Baroque: Modern
      architecture; as well as sections for the artists of
      each period, including architects.
         A similar listing for American theses is
      provided by the College Art Association,
      formerly in the *Art journal*.

Comprehensive dissertation index. Ann   148
   Arbor (Mich): University Microfilms,
   1973–.
   archts, bldgs
      Composed of 32 subject volumes and five author
      volumes covering the entire output of United
      States doctoral dissertations, plus a large

proportion of Canadian ones, as well as some
others, from 1861 to 1972. Subject access is via
keywords from titles, arranged within major and
minor basic subject categories. Supplemented
annually since 1973. In 1979 the *Comprehensive
dissertation 5-year cumulation, 1973–1977* was
published, listing doctoral dissertations accepted
by North American universities between 1973
and 1977, indexed by subject and by author,
with full bibliographic data (19 vols or
microfiche).
      University Microfilms also provides subject
catalogues, eg *Architecture; The arts; Fine arts;
Civil engineering; Regional and city planning* and
Books on demand: Architecture, which list,
alphabetically by author, recent North American
doctoral dissertations.
      University Microfilms also offers Datrix II,
a computer search and retrieval system for
dissertations and theses in the *Comprehensive
dissertation database*.
      Full text copies of dissertations and theses
can be purchased in 35mm microfilm,
microfiche, or xerographic form.

Dissertation abstracts international: 149
   abstracts of dissertations and
   monographs in microform. Ann Arbor (Mich):
University Microfilms; London: University
Microfilms International, vol 12, 1952– . Monthly
and quarterly. Vols 1–11, 1938–51, as *Microfilm
abstracts*. Author index, 1956.
   archts, bldgs
      A compilation of abstracts of doctoral and
post-doctoral dissertations submitted to
University Microfilms by co-operating
institutions. Beginning with vol 27, no 1, 1966,
in two separate sections: A. The humanities and
social sciences, and B. The sciences and
engineering. These are issued monthly.
Beginning with vol 37, no 1, 1976, a third
section has been added: C. European abstracts.
Section C is issued quarterly and covers
dissertations in all disciplines successfully
submitted for doctoral and post-doctoral degrees
in Western Europe, although some Eastern
European material is included. Entries are
grouped by subjects covering the branches of the
humanities and of the sciences with their
relevant sub-groups. Each entry comprises the
following information: title of the dissertation in
the original language, author's name, year and
awarding institution (followed by the country
code). Whenever possible or appropriate, the
information also includes: translation of title into
English, degree awarded, language of the full
dissertation text if not in English and University
Microfilms order number when full text copies
are available on demand. The bibliographic
description is followed by a brief abstract,
generally supplied by the author. Each issue has
author and keyword-in-title indexes. Annual
cumulative index.

Two additional abstracting services are available: *Master abstracts*, a quarterly publication, providing abstracts of masters theses, and *Research abstracts*, begun in 1976, which provides abstracts of published research other than doctoral dissertations and masters theses.

Institute of Historical Research 150
History theses, 1901–70: historical research for higher degrees in the universities of the United Kingdom. Compiled by P. M. Jacobs. London: University of London, Institute of Historical Research, 1976, 456pp.
Subject index includes references to architecture, housing and house-building, manor houses, etc.

Institute of Historical Research 151
Historical research for university degrees in the United Kingdom. London: University of London, Institute of Historical Research. Annual.
Supplements the above publication. Issued in two parts. Part 1: Theses completed (in year past). Part 2: Theses in progress. Issued in May for the current year. The general arrangement is by period divisions, subdivided by subject. The subject section on education, the arts and sciences includes architecture.

Open University 152
A305: History of architecture and design 1890–1939. Student project titles 1975–1979. [Milton Keynes: Open University, 1981.] 113pp. Mimeographed (further lists in progress).
archts, bldgs; 19/20c
A list of projects arranged by town (or subject), giving the title of the building or project, name of architect/s, dates of building, student name and number and whether the project is held by the Open University. Cross-references from names of architects. The Open University has an expanding archive of research projects in the field of architecture and design covering the period from c1850 to c1950. The projects are researched by students taking the University's course on the history of architecture and design 1890–1939. Each year a selection is made of the most interesting work for retention in the University Library, either on microfiche or in the original. The topics cover a wide range of subjects and provide a valuable source of detailed information culled from both national and local records and which is not readily available elsewhere. *Bona fide* students are welcome to make use of the archive by arrangement with The Librarian, Jenny Lee Library, The Open University, Walton Hall, Milton Keynes MK7 6AA. A duplicate set of the microfiche archive has been deposited in the British Architectural Library.

Research in British universities, polytechnics and colleges. Boston Spa: 153 British Library, Lending Division, RBUPC Office, 1979– . Annual. Vol 1: Physical sciences. Vol 2: Biological sciences. Vol 3: Social sciences.
archts, bldgs; prehist/med, ren/neoclas, 19/20c
A register of current research in British academic institutions.
The main sequence in each volume of *RBUPC* is arranged in broad subject order. Within each subject group arrangement is alphabetical by institution. The subject groups and the names of institutions are listed in the preliminary sections of each volume. Volume 1, subject group B, covers architecture and building science.
All research in progress in a given department is listed together. The name and address of the department and the name of the head of department are also provided. The projects within the department are in alphabetical order of research team with sponsors and dates of project duration where appropgcate. Departments are cross-referenced where a proportion of the research is more relevant to another subject group.
Separate name and keyword indexes are supplied in each volume. Keywords include names of architects, buildings, places, building types, periods, styles, materials etc, when they feature in the title of the project.
Supersedes *Scientific research in British universities and colleges*.

Retrospective index to theses of Great Britain and Ireland, 1716–1950. Roger R. 154 Bilboul, editor, Francis L. Kent, associate editor. Santa Barbara: ABC-Clio; Oxford: EBC-Clio. 5 vols. Vol 1: Social sciences and humanities. 1975. 393pp.
archts, bldgs
Vol 1 lists 13 entries under Architecture: Great Britain and 3 under Architecture: Ireland, but additional entries will be found under Archaeology and antiquities as well as under specific building types, towns, etc. The main subject listing is supplemented by an author-title index.

Royal Institute of British Architects 155
Prizes and scholarships in the Royal Institute of British Architects. London: The Institute, 1967. 14pp. Mimeographed.
A list, organised by the name of the RIBA prize, which provides the name of the author and title and date of the prize essay. Author index. Many of the essays are on historical subjects.

Society of Architectural Historians of Great Britain   156
    Research register. (Title varies). Keele: The Society, 1967– .
    archts, bldgs; prehist/med, ren/neoclas, 19/20c
        A list issued at irregular intervals of completed, unpublished writings and works in progress. Includes a section 'The work of individual architects', which is arranged alphabetically by the architect's surname. Other sections include: theory; periods of architecture; national architecture; architecture of the British Isles; types of buildings (eg ecclesiastical, public, domestic); building; architectural elements and components; architectural decoration; landscape gardens and parks; planning; the architectural profession; and bibliographies, indexes, etc.

        Each list incorporates relevant entries from previous lists. From 1979 arrangements have been made for future numbers to be published jointly by the Society and the John Rylands University Library of Manchester. Further information from Dr F. Taylor, FSA, Register of Research, Society of Architectural Historians of Great Britain, The John Rylands University Library of Manchester, Oxford Road, Manchester M13 9PP. It succeeds *Unpublished theses and work in progress in British institutions relating to the history of architecture*: Pt 1 in *Architectural history*, vol 2, 1959: and Pt 2, in *Architectural history*, vol 8, 1965. *Research register, list no 5, Autumn 1980* was published in 1981.

University of Birmingham: Centre for Urban and Regional Studies   157
    A first list of UK students' theses and dissertations on planning and urban and regional studies. Compiled by A. J. Veal and W. K. Duesbury. Birmingham: The Centre, 1976. 245pp. (Research memorandum no 55).
        Entries are arranged by institution and chronologically (mainly from the late 1960s, some from 1930s) within each institution. Includes 3,752 entries. Includes two indexes, one referring to subjects and one to place names. These have been based entirely on titles, so while many theses will contain case-studies of particular areas, unless the name of the area appears in the title, it will not appear in the index. Only a small proportion of the entries will be of interest to architectural historians, eg industrial buildings of historic significance or historic town centres; some are listed in the subject index under 'historic' or under 'conservation'.

Urban history yearbook. Leicester: Leicester   158
University Press, 1974– . Annual.
    bldgs
        The *Yearbook* contains a section 'Research in urban history' which is in two parts: 1. Survey of recent work and 2. Register of research. The Register of research is based chiefly on replies given to enquiries directed to individual researchers or their supervisors but also draws to some extent on other listings, notably the *Theses supplements* of the *Bulletin of the Institute of Historical Research* and the lists prepared annually under the auspices of the Conference of Heads of Departments of Geography in British Universities, and from two comparable lists prepared by the Institute of British Geographers: Historical Geography Research Group, *Register of research in historical geography*; Urban Geography Study Group, *Register of members' research interest*. An index to place-names and themes is provided at the end. Continues *Urban history newsletter*, nos 1–20 (Leicester: Urban History Group, 1963–73).

For other items relating to this section see:

This section concentrates on unpublished secondary sources in the British Architectural Library. Additional sources can be located by using the publications detailed in section 1: How to find out: guides to the literature and by consulting section 5: Societies, institutions and organisations. Descriptions of the unpublished sources, indexes and catalogues of particular societies, institutions and organisations are provided in section 5.1. References to these entries are given at the end of this section.

Most entries are coded as in section 2 (see introduction to section 2.1 for fuller explanation):

archts   Indicates that it is possible to look up the names of architects in the item described

bldgs   Indicates that it is possible to look up the names of buildings (sometimes indirectly under location) in the item described

prehist/   Useful for the period from prehistory to
med   medieval

ren/   Useful for the period from renaissance to
neoclas   neoclassic

19/20c   Useful for the nineteenth and/or twentieth centuries

Competitions held in the British Isles since   159
    the War. London: Royal Institute of
    British Architects, 1965. 25pp.
    archts, bldgs; 19/20c
      A mimeographed list of competitions from 1945 to 1965 giving the name of the competition, date the result was published, premiums, names of assessors, names of winners and number of entries.

British Architectural Library. Author   160
    catalogue.
    archts
      Card catalogue in which there are entries in one alphabetical sequence for individual and corporate authors, organisations, government departments, etc, titles (mainly for books published since 1972) and series for the books, pamphlets, some manuscripts and typescripts in the library. Items written by an architect will be found under his name.

British Architectural Library. Classified   161
    catalogues. [UDC] Two sequences:
    [–1955]; [1956–].
    archts, bldgs; prehist/med, ren/neoclas, 19/20c
      A card catalogue. Books, occasional chapters in books, manuscripts, and other material about an architect have cards in the biographical sequence (92s), in the latest classified catalogue. This sequence is subdivided alphabetically by the surname of the architect. Biographical dictionaries are listed in the beginning of the sequence.

      For books on buildings one must consult the alphabetical subject index to the classified catalogues. One looks under the subject (general building type) in the alphabetical subject index which gives the class-number, then in both classified indexes under that number. For books on a given subject in a stated place or period, one looks up each subsidiary item in the alphabetical index and finds its number in the class sections following that of the main subject – in the first case in round brackets, eg (42.1), in the second beginning .03. . . .

      For all books on a given country or place, whatever the subject, one looks under the name of the place in the alphabetical subject index, then in the latest classified index under the topographical number (91 followed by the number), where cards for general works are followed by references to all subjects bearing on the place (except where too numerous to be detailed).

British Architectural Library. Biography   162
    files.
    archts; ren/neoclas, 19/20c
      The British Architectural Library Periodicals Names Index (165) also includes a card for each of the c9000 biography files.

      Principally includes British architects, but also some designers, architectural critics and foreign architects. The amount of information supplied varies greatly. Some files include bibliographical references. Many files include correspondence which may indicate who is undertaking, or has undertaken, research on a specific architect.

British Architectural Library. Grey books   163
    index.
archts, bldgs; 19/20c

> Divided into two separate sequences:
> 1900–1919, 1920–1974. Provides references to
> illustrated periodical articles on works by RIBA
> members.
>
> 1 *Index of buildings illustrated in principal
> journals, 1900–1919.*
> 1 vol, looseleaf.
> Part one is arranged in alphabetical order by
> building type, with specific buildings
> sub-arranged alphabetically by architect's
> surname within each building type. Part two is
> an alphabetical index of architects' names, giving
> references to building types in part one.
> Citations are only to the volume number of the
> periodical, not to the actual page number, as is
> also the case with the earlier entries in the
> sequences below. Country houses in Britain are
> not included. Includes reference to *Academy
> architecture*, the *Architect, Building news*, the
> *British architect*, the *Architectural review* and the
> *Builder*.
> 2 *Index of RIBA members' work, as illustrated in
> the professional press, 1920–1974.*
> 145 vols, looseleaf.
> In two sections. In the first, entries are arranged
> alphabetically by architects' names, and then
> sub-arranged by location. In the second, the
> entries are arranged alphabetically by building
> type, and then sub-arranged by location. The
> number of periodicals indexed increased over the
> years. Discontinued when the Periodicals names
> index (165) began.

British Architectural Library. Periodicals   164
    subject index.
archts, bldgs; prehist/med, ren/neoclas, 19/20c

> Card catalogue. Divided into two sequences:
> 1934–1971 and 1972– .
>
> General articles about an architect and his
> work (but not articles on specific projects) are
> entered under the heading Architects: GB,
> which is further subdivided alphabetically by
> surname.
>
> Specific buildings are sought under the
> appropriate building type, subdivided by
> country, then town.
>
> An alphabetical subject index to the
> headings is on cards. The subject headings will
> be published as *API keywords* in late 1981.
> The index for the period 1956–1972 is
> available on microfilm from World Microfilms
> (*see* 46).
> From 1972 the index has been published as
> the *Architectural periodicals index* (*see* 2).

British Architectural Library. Periodicals   165
    names index.
archts; prehist/med, ren/neoclas, 19/20c

> A card catalogue in which material is entered
> under the name of an architect, architectural
> practice, author and institutions, and filed in the
> following order after each name:
> 1 Obituaries – includes references to obituaries
> in the *Builder* from 1843 to date, and in other
> architectural journals from 1974 onwards.
> 2 Biography files – the existence of a biography
> file is noted (*see* 162).
> 3 Articles by or about an architect – cards for
> these articles have been included from 1974
> onwards.
> 4 Articles on specific buildings designed by an
> architect – cards for these articles have been
> included from 1974 onwards and are arranged in
> subject order by building type.

British Architectural Library. Periodicals   166
    topographical index. 1974– .
bldgs; prehist/med, ren/neoclas, 19/20c

> This is a card index to periodical articles on
> specific places arranged by country and then
> town. London is further subdivided by borough.
> From 1974 to 1977 general articles on countries
> with no more specific place designation are given
> cross-references to the appropriate subject
> headings in the Periodicals subject index (164),
> but from 1978 the full citations are included.
>
> Within each specific topographical heading
> the filing arrangement is as follows:
> 1 General articles on the place (chronologically
> arranged).
> 2 Unnamed projects arranged alphabetically by
> building type.
> 3 Named projects arranged alphabetically by
> name.

British Architectural Library. Drawings   167
    collection catalogue.
archts, bldgs; prehist/med, ren/neoclas, 19/20c

> The card catalogue includes both those drawings
> in the published catalogue (127), where there is
> generally more detail, and those acquired since
> the various volumes went to press. It also
> contains (on blue cards) the location of some
> architectural drawings in other collections.
>
> The main catalogue entry is under the name
> of the architect with references from both place
> and subject.
>
> For a description of the collections *see* 237.

Goodhart-Rendel index of   168
    **nineteenth-century churches and their
    architects.**
archts, bldgs; 19/20c

> This card index to churches in England,
> Scotland and Wales was compiled by the late

H. S. Goodhart-Rendel, PPRIBA. It is based on various sources, including the records of the Incorporated Church Building Society. There are two sequences of cards, one of churches arranged alphabetically under the architect's name, and the other of churches arranged by county. The only information given is the name of the architect or architectural practice, and the name and date of the church. No bibliographical references are provided.

Two sets exist, one at the British Architectural Library and the other at the National Monuments Record (365).

Kendrick, *Sir* Thomas, *compiler* 169
Nineteenth-century stained glass: a copy of the index . . . now in the Library of the Royal Institute of British Architects. Photocopy. 2 vols.
bldgs; ren/neoclas, 19/20c

Vol 1 includes an alphabetical list of glass-painters, chronological list of windows, 1525–1880, various notes and bibliography. Many references to the *Builder*. Vol 2 is a topographical index (by county, then town), including England, Wales, Scotland and Ireland.

Duplicate photocopies are held by the GLC Historic Buildings Division and the Victoria and Albert Museum.

Roberts, H. V. Molesworth 170
Index to old English country houses and some Welsh, Scottish and Irish. [BAL] [n.d.]
bldgs; ren/neoclas, 19/20c

This is a typescript index to country houses and some town houses and other buildings in monograph articles in standard works in the British Architectural Library. The works indexed include: Britton, *Architectural antiquities of Great Britain*; Belcher and Macartney, *Later renaissance architecture in England*; Tipping, *English homes of the early renaissance*; Knyff and Kip; Latham and Tipping; *Vitruvius Britannicus; Vitruvius Scoticus*.

RIBA Competitions. [Typewritten list of competitions.] [n.d.] [41pp.]
bldgs; 19/20c 171

A chronological list of competitions from 1884–1967, of which the competition conditions are held in the British Architectural Library. Within each year, competitions are listed by place and then by name of competition.

Royal Institute of British Architects.
Membership index, 1834–1886.
archts; 19/20c 172

A card index of members giving dates and class of membership, addresses and posts held in the RIBA.

Royal Institute of British Architects. 173
Nomination papers of RIBA members.
1834– .
archts; 19/20c

The amount of information provided varies greatly, but always includes the name and address and sometimes includes details of architectural training and works executed.

In order to consult the Nomination Papers, the following information must first be provided: the name of the member; the type of nomination held (Fellow, Associate, Licentiate); and the year of election. This information can be found in the RIBA *Kalendars* (later *Directories*) (123, 124, 126) or the RIBA Membership Index, 1834–1886 (172).

Simo, Melanie, *compiler* 174
An index of country houses in The Gardener's magazine (1826–1843), ed J. C. Loudon. With additional references from The Architectural magazine (1834–1838) and The Gardener's gazette (1841), also edited by J. C. Loudon. Compiled 25 April 1975. [10pp.]
Photocopied typescript.
archts, bldgs; 19/20c

A selective, not exhaustive index. Most references include information on the architecture, landscape gardening, arboriculture, or general maintenance of the country house or grounds.

For other items relating to this section see:

Council./*continued*
297 Guildhall Library.
298 Hampstead Garden Suburb Archives.
311 Institution of Civil Engineers.
314 Irish Architectural Record Association.
317 Ironbridge Gorge Museum Trust.
322 Liturgy Commission of the Roman Catholic
    Bishops' Conference of England and Wales,
    Department of Art and Architecture,
    Conservation Sub-Committee.
323 London Topographical Society.
326 Moated Site Research Group.
328 Museum of London.
331 National Institute for Physical Planning and
    Construction Research (An Foras Forbartha).
332 National Library of Scotland.
333 National Library of Wales.
335 National Museum of Antiquities of Scotland.
337 National Record of Industrial Monuments.
338 National Register of Archives (Scotland).
339 National Trust Archive.
344 North Hertfordshire District Council, Planning
    Department.
345 North Hertfordshire District Council Museums
    Services, First Garden City Museum.
352 Public Record Office.
353 Public Record Office of Northern Ireland.
356 Railway and Canal Historical Society.
359 Registry of Business Names.
361 Royal Academy of Arts Library.
364 Royal Commission on Historical Manuscripts
    (and National Register of Archives).
365 Royal Commission on Historical Monuments
    (England) including the National Monuments
    Record.
366 Royal Commission on the Ancient and
    Historical Monuments of Scotland including the
    National Monuments Record of Scotland.
367 Royal Commission on Ancient and Historical
    Monuments in Wales including the National
    Monuments Record for Wales.
376 Royal Society for the Encouragement of Arts,
    Manufactures and Commerce.
378 Royal Town Planning Institute.
383 Science Museum Library.
387 Scottish Record Office.
389 Sir John Soane's Museum.
394 Society for the Protection of Ancient Buildings.
396 Society of Antiquaries of London.
400 Society of Genealogists.
404 Theatre Museum.
409 Transport Trust.
414 Vernacular Architecture Group.
415 Victoria and Albert Museum Library.
416 Victoria and Albert Museum. Department of
    Prints and Drawings and Paintings.
417 Victorian Society.
418 Weald and Downland Open Air Museum.

.1

Lists and guides to periodicals

In order to discover which journals are currently being
published or have been published which devote
themselves either exclusively or substantially to
architecture, the following are useful.

Adams, Maurice B.   175
Architectural journalism', in *RIBA Journal*,
9 March, 1907, pp 313–326.
Includes a brief history of architectural journals
as well as a list of American, Colonial and foreign
architectural periodicals, with their terms of
subscription in England.

Jenkins, Frank   176
**Nineteenth-century architectural
periodicals'**, in John Summerson, ed, *Concerning
architecture*. London: Allen Lane, 1968, pp 153–160.
Discusses the different characteristics of British
architectural journals.

Roberts, Helene E.   177
**British art periodicals of the eighteenth and
nineteenth centuries'**, in *Victorian periodicals
newsletter*, (Bloomington: Indiana University), no 9,
July 1970, 55pp. (Reprinted, Ann Arbor: University
Microfilms).
An exhaustive checklist of 317 periodicals
published between 1774 and 1899 which (a)
devote themselves principally to the subjects of
art and architecture, (b) cover a more general
subject field, but deal with the arts for at least a
third of their contents, (c) contain illustrations of
sufficient number and quality for them to be of
interest in themselves, regardless of the text, or
(d) concern themselves with the artistic aspects
of subjects peripheral to art. A chronological
table of art periodicals indicates the journals
published for each year from 1774–1899. This is
a particularly valuable feature, as it enables the
researcher who knows the date of a building or
event, to identify those contemporary journals
which might have commented on it. Index of
editors.

For other entries relating to this section see:

14 Coulson. *A bibliography of design in Britain,
1851–1970.*
24 *Guide to the literature of art history.*
25 Guildhall Library. *London buildings and sites: a
guide for researchers in Guildhall Library.*
41 Open University. *Arts: . . . history of architecture
and design 1890–1939: project guide.*
131 Sharp. *Sources of modern architecture.*
208 *House's guide to the construction industry.*

4.2

Location guides to periodicals

In order to find a library location in Britain for a particular
periodical, the searcher should refer to the following.

British Union catalogue of periodicals: a   178
**record of the periodicals of the world,
from the seventeenth century to the present day,
in British libraries**. Ed for the Council of the British
Union-Catalogue of Periodicals by James D. Stewart,
with Muriel E. Hammond and Erwin Saenger.
London: Butterworth, 1955–58. 4 vols.
Lists more than 140,000 titles contained in about
440 libraries with indication of holdings. All
periodicals are entered under their earliest
known names, followed by particulars of all
changes of name in chronological sequence.
References are given from all later names to the
original name. Periodicals issued by an
organisation are entered under the name of the
organisation unless the title is specific in itself.
Records titles up to 1950.

——**Supplement to 1960**. London: Butterworth, 1962.
991pp.
Includes entries for new periodicals reported as
first appearing since publication of the main
volumes, some expanded or amended entries,
and some entries for earlier volumes not
previously reported.

——**Incorporating the World list of scientific
periodicals. New periodical titles**. London:
Butterworths, 1964–1980. Quarterly; annual

annual/*continued*
cumulation. Cumulative issues for 1960–68,
1969–73.
> Aims to list periodicals and serials which began
> in or after 1960, changed title, began a new
> series, or ceased publication.

**Serials in the British Library: together with
locations and holdings of other British and Irish
libraries.** No 1 (June 1981)– . London: British
Library, Bibliographic Services Division, 1981– .
Quarterly; annual cumulation (microfiche).
> Continues *British union–catalogue of periodicals:
> new periodical titles*. Records, in a single
> alphabetical sequence, serial titles newly
> acquired by the various departments of the
> British Library and a small number of other
> major libraries.

Bullock, Graham R., *compiler*　　　　179
**Union list of periodicals on art and related
　　subject fields.** Art Libraries Society, 1978. 303pp.
> Lists holdings of more than 1,500 periodical
> titles in fifty-five libraries in the UK, including
> the relevant periodical holdings of the Victoria
> and Albert Museum (current titles only) and the
> British Library Lending Division. Subjects
> covered include art, design, fashion, architecture
> and photography; holdings are given for
> annuals, and for microform and hard-copy
> reprints. For every title a maximum of ten
> locations is given, with priority listing for the
> British Library and national library holdings
> where these occur, and with other holdings
> selected according to their degree of
> completeness and with the intention of
> specifying holdings in as many geographical
> regions as possible. New edition in preparation.

4.3

Some of the most important periodicals

Whereas any architectural journal is likely to cover work in
Britain, the following entries concentrate primarily on
those important early magazines which existed prior to
systematic, cumulative indexes such as the Avery *Index* (5)
and the indexes of the British Architectural Library (46,
47, 49, 163–166) came into being. The indexes and pages
of these early magazines may be fruitfully searched. The
journals of the local historical and archaeological societies
also provide a valuable source of information, but are not
dealt with here.

Academy architecture and annual　　　　180
　　architectural review. vol 1–62,
　　1889–1931.
> Continued later as an occasional supplement to
> the *Architectural review*.
> *Academy architecture* is available on microfilm
> from University Microfilms International.
> This comprehensive annual (later

bi-annual) pictorial survey of important projects
and buildings usually reproduced the architect's
original drawings together with photographs of
the completed buildings.
> Classified index to vols 1–21; 1889–1902.
> For an index to the work of RIBA members
> illustrated in *Academy architecture* from 1900 *see*
> 163.

Annals of the fine arts. London. vol 1–5,　　181
　　no 1–17, 1816–20. Edited by James Elmes.
Quarterly.
> Each number contains several lengthy essays on
> aesthetics, art history or biography, followed by
> a section of reviews of books and prints, and
> news from England and abroad.

The Architect. London. Jan 1869–Jan 1980.　　182
Title varies:
The Architect. vol 1–49, Jan 1869–5 May 1893.
The Architect and contract reporter. vol 49–100,
12 May 1893–Dec 1918.
The Architect. vol 101–115, 3 Jan 1919–12 March
1926.
Architect and building news. vol 115–234 [vol 6, no 7].
19 March 1926–7 Jan 1971.
The Architect. vol 121–126, Feb 1971–Jan 1980.
19 March 1926 united with *The Building news and
engineering journal* (*see* 189) to form the *Architect and
building news*.
Weekly, then 1971 on monthly.

> For an index to measured drawings in *The
> Architect* (1869–1905) *see* 137.
> For an index to the work of RIBA members
> illustrated in *The Architect* from 1900 *see* 163.
> For a selection of plates from *The Architect*
> *see* 574.

The Architects' journal. London. vol 49– , 5　　183
March 1919– .
Title varies:
The Builders' journal. vol 1–3, 12 Feb 1895–1 July
1896.
The Builders' journal and architectural review. vol 3–4,
8 July–4 Nov 1896.
The Builders' journal and architectural record. vol
4–23, 11 Nov 1896–16 May 1906.
The Builders' journal and architectural engineer. vol
23–31, 23 May 1906–30 March 1910.
The Architects' and builders' journal. vol 31–49, April
1910–Feb 1919.
Weekly.
> *The Architects' journal* (from 1924) is available on
> microfilm from University Microfilms
> International.
> The offices of Architectural Press hold
> many of the photographs used in *The Architects'
> journal* (*see* 434).

Architectural magazine and journal of   184
  **improvement in architecture, building
  and furnishing, etc**. vol 1–5, March 1834–38.
(Reprint, 1973). Edited by J. C. Loudon. Monthly.
> *The Architectural magazine* is available on
> microfilm from University Microfilms
> International.
>> *The Architectural magazine* was the first
> periodical in either Britain or America devoted
> to architecture. It reported on important
> buildings in the UK and abroad, but has few
> illustrations.
>> Vol 5 contains an index in three parts to vols
> 1–5: subjects, books reviewed or noted,
> engravings. It is not particularly easy to
> approach from the name of an architect.
>> For an index of country houses *see* 174.

Architectural review. London. vol 1–, Nov   185
  1896– . Monthly.
Began as magazine issue of *The Builders' journal*,
July–Nov 1896, then independently.
> *The Architectural review* is available on
> microfilm from University Microfilms
> International.
>> More concerned with architectural criticism
> than with technical information.
>> For an index to measured drawings in
> *Architectural review* (1896–1904) *see* 137.
>> For an index to the work of RIBA members
> illustrated in *Architectural review* from 1900 *see*
> 163.
>> The offices of Architectural Press hold
> many of the photographs used in the
> *Architectural review* (*see* 434).

The British architect. Manchester, London.   186
  vol 1–89, 2 Jan 1874–April 1919. Weekly,
then monthly.
Absorbed by *The Builder*, 16 May 1919.
> *The British architect* will be available on
> microfilm from University Microfilms
> International.
>> Attempted to reduce the dominance of
> London as a focus of architectural fashion by
> calling in Scotland and the North of England.
> No periodic indexes.
>> For an index to measured drawings in *The
> British architect* (1874–1904) *see* 137.
>> For an index to the work of RIBA members
> illustrated in *The British architect* from 1900 *see*
> 163.
>> For a selection of plates from *The British
> architect see* 572.

British competitions in architecture.   187
  London: London County
Council/Academy Architecture. vol 1, part 1,
no 1–vol [4], parts 41–42, [1905–1914].
> Each part treats a single competition.

The Builder. London. vol 1, no 1–vol 110,   188
  no 6406, Dec 1842–Feb 1966.
Changed title to *Building*, vol 110, no 6407, March
1966. Incorporated *The British architect* and
Architecture. Weekly. First issue preceded by sample
copy dated Dec 1842.
> *The Builder* is available on microfilm from
> Kraus Reprint and from University Microfilms
> International.
>> The most comprehensive and influential
> architectural periodical of the nineteenth
> century, profusely illustrated with pictures of
> contemporary buildings.
>> For a selection of plates from *The Builder*
> *see* 572.

Indexes.

Each volume of *The Builder* has an index which
was compiled at the end of the year or half year.
These indexes are of some help to the
researcher, but they have certain disadvantages:
1. the methods of indexing frequently change so
that topics under one heading in one volume
may be under a completely different heading in
the next; 2. the coverage of material varies
considerably; 3. even at their most thorough the
indexes fail to record many items, eg names and
places mentioned within articles, small news
items and details of tenders reported, or they
record them under a heading which is not
obvious to the modern reader.

Bound volumes of yearly and half-yearly
indexes to *The Builder* (not cumulative):
vol 1–51, 1843–1886;
vol 52–87, 1887–1904;
vol 88–127, 1905–1924;
vol 128–181, 1925–1951.

For partial indexes to *The Builder, see* the
following items:
  63 Architectural Publications Society. *The
     dictionary of architecture*. Entries often
     provide references to *The Builder*.
  64 Avery Architectural Library. *Avery
     obituary index*.
  68 *A Bibliography of Leicestershire churches*.
     Indexes Leicestershire churches in *The
     Builder* to 1917.
 127 Royal Institute of British Architects,
     Drawings Collection. *Catalogue of the
     Drawings Collection of the RIBA*. The
     biographies include references to *Builder*
     obituaries and the literary references given
     for the drawings often provide *Builder*
     citations.
 135 Spain. *Theatre architects in the British Isles*.
 137 Victoria and Albert Museum.
     *Topographical index to measured drawings of
     architecture which have appeared in the
     principal architectural publications*. Indexes
     The Builder from 1880–1905.

Framingham State College
Framingham, Massachusetts

4.3 Some of the most important periodicals

1880–1905./*continued*

163 British Architectural Library. Grey books index. Indexes the work of RIBA members illustrated in *The Builder* from 1900.
165 British Architectural Library. Periodicals names index. The BAL has indexed obituaries in *The Builder*, mainly for architects, from the beginning of the journal to the present. One set is interfiled in the Periodicals names index and another is kept at the Drawings Collection.
169 Kendrick. *Nineteenth-century stained glass.*
250 Buildings of England Office. Ferriday index of Victorian church restorations.
279 Department of the Environment for Northern Ireland, Historic Monuments and Buildings Branch. Holds Hugh Dixon's index to Irish architects, with many references to *The Builder*.
296 Greater London Council. The Survey of London Office has a card index to London, except the City, for *The Builder* from 1842–1892 (architects; artists, builders, engineers, and craftsmen; topographical; subject). The British Architectural Library holds photocopies of the entries for architects from the GLC's index (in three bound volumes).
297 Guildhall Library. The Library has indexed all obituaries in *The Builder*, regardless of occupation. The Library's periodicals index to the City's architecture contains references mainly to *The Builder*. Articles and illustrations have both been indexed and well cross-referenced with entries for buildings, streets and architects. At present, *The Builder* has been indexed up to the 1940s, but it is progressing rapidly.
833 Seaborne. *The English school.* Appendices of elementary day schools and middle-class schools illustrated in *The Builder*, 1843–70.

Index to Victorian architectural competitions. Dr Roger H. Harper, Department of Architecture, University of Sheffield, The Arts Tower, Sheffield S10 2TN, is compiling an index to all competitions mentioned in *The Builder*. The index currently covers the period 1860–1900, but will expand to cover the period 1843–1900. It is in four parts: 1. by place; 2. by name of architect; 3. by building type; 4. chronologically.

Building news. vol 3–130, 2 Jan 1857–12   189
March 1926. Weekly.
Merged in *The Architect* (*see* 182) on 19 March 1926.
Formerly:
The Freehold land times. vol 1, no 1–no 20, 1854.
The Land and building news. vol 1, no 21–vol 2, no 44, 1 Jan 1855–27 Dec 1856.
Title varies:
Building news, 1857–1859.
Building news and architectural review, 1860–1862.

Building news and engineering journal, 1863–1926.
Important contemporary picture source for the Victorian period.
For an index to measured drawings in *Building news* (1871–1905) *see* 137.
For an index to the work of RIBA member illustrated in *Building news* from 1900 *see* 163.
For a selection of plates from *Building news see* 572.
For an index to middle-class schools illustrated in *Building news* before 1870 *see* 833.

The Church builder. London. vol 1–72, Jan   19
1862–Oct 1916. A quarterly journal of church extension in England and Wales.
Published in connection with the Incorporated Church Building Society. Its main purpose was to set down in a popular form the expansion of the church in connection with building. A large amount of space was devoted to reporting the Society's operations by providing descriptions and illustrations of newly-built or restored churches to which the Society had contributed its funds. The section which makes the periodical fundamental to the history of church architecture during the period is formed by the pages at the end of each number which list the newly-built churches with the date of their consecration, record the name of the architect and give a brief outline of the main features of the building. Similar lists are also included for mission halls, chapels and church schools, and for churches which had been restored and enlarged. Well illustrated.
For an index to Leicestershire churches in *The Church builder see* 68.
For an index to Victorian church restorations in *The Church builder see* 250.

The Civil engineer and architect's journal.   19
London. vol 1–31, 1837–May 1868.
Monthly, weekly. Supersedes *The Architect and building operative.*
Particularly valuable as a source of information on nineteenth-century buildings and building techniques. Included the listing of buildings completed or erecting. Well illustrated.
Obituaries have been indexed in Bell, *A biographical index of British engineers in the 19th century* (*see* 66).

Country life. vol 13– , 1907– . London.   19
Weekly. Continues *Country life illustrated*, vol 1–12, 1897–1902.
Cumulative indexes issued periodically to the country houses, eg cumulative index to vols 1–152 (bound in vol 152).
The Guildhall Library has analytical entries for all London articles (one page or more) as part of their general London Catalogue (*see* 297).
The offices of *Country life* are also a massive photographic archive with an index to their negatives (*see* 445).

Ecclesiologist. vol 1–3, Nov 1841–Sept 1844;   193
new series, vol 1–26, Jan 1845–Dec 1868.
Monthly, bi-monthly.
> The well known instrument of the reform
> movement in the Anglican church, which
> prominently became the instrument of the
> gothic revival. Founded in 1838 as the
> Cambridge Camden Society, the name changed
> in 1846 to Ecclesiological, late Cambridge
> Camden Society, and in 1856 to the
> Ecclesiological Society.
>> The British Architectural Library has a 2
>> vol manuscript index.
>> For an index to Leicestershire churches in
>> the *Ecclesiologist see* 68.

Gentleman's magazine. Jan 1731–Sept 1907.   194
> The *Gentleman's magazine* is available
> on microfilm from University Microfilms
> International.
>> Indexes:
>> 1–20, 1–50, 1–56. 1787–1818.
>> *An index to the biographical and obituary
>> notices in the Gentleman's magazine, 1731–1780.*
>> London: British Record Society, 1866–91.
>> (Index Society publications, no 15). This has
>> single-line entries: name, residence, year and
>> volume number of the magazine.

The Irish builder. vol 9– , Jan 1867– .   195
> Formerly *The Dublin builder*, vol 1–8, 15
> Jan 1859–15 Dec 1866.
>> In addition to the retrospective or antiquarian
>> articles on buildings, carries full notices, often
>> illustrated, of contemporary buildings.

Royal Institute of British Architects.   196
Journal.
Formerly:
Transactions. vol 1–34, 1835/36–1883/84.
Transactions (new series). vol 1–8, 1885–92 (vol
    3–25, 1850/53–1874/75 as *Papers read*; vol
    26–28, 1875/76–1877/78, as *Sessional
    papers*).
Proceedings. 1878/79–1883/84.
Proceedings (new series). vol 1–9, 1885–93. 31 vols of
> Notices of meetings, annual reports and
> papers read, bound under title *RIBA
> proceedings*, cover the years 1834–1877/78.
> The official designation *Proceedings* was not
> used until 1878.
Journal (3rd series). vol 1– , Nov 1893– . Formed by
> the amalgamation of the *Proceedings* and the
> *Transactions.*
> The *Transactions and proceedings*, 1835–93, are
> available on microfilm from World Microfilms.
> The *RIBA Journal* is available on microfilm
> from University Microfilms International.
>> A major source of RIBA history. Reports of
>> papers read at RIBA meetings and publication of

official notices. A history of the *Journal* by
Edward Carter, appears in J. A. Gotch, ed, *The
growth and work of the Royal Institute of British
Architects, 1834–1934.* London: RIBA, 1934, pp
141–156.

The Studio. An illustrated magazine of fine   197
and applied art. vol 1–166, April
1893–1963. American edition: *International Studio.*
vol 1–99, 1897–1931.
> *The Studio* is available on microfilm from
> University Microfilms International.
>> An important journal for the new
>> tendencies in art and a particularly valuable
>> source for Arts and Crafts architects.
> *General index to The Studio, vols 1–42.*
> London: Sims and Reed, 1979. First published
> 1902 and 1909. Arranged in two sections:
> volumes 1–21 (1893–1901) and volumes 22–42
> (1901–1908). In the first section there is a
> general index, index of artists and illustrations,
> index of reviews, index of prize competitions. In
> the second section there is an index of articles,
> index of artists, classified index of illustrations,
> index of prize competitions, index of reviews.
>> *The Studio: a bibliography: the first fifty
>> years, 1893–1943.* London: Sims and Reed,
>> 1978. 142 pp. A bibliography of the separate
>> publications issued by the London office of *The
>> Studio.* Subject, title and general indexes.

■ **4.4**

Periodical indexes and abstracts

**For published indexes and abstracts see the
following entries:**

1945–74./continued

113 Michelmore. *Current bibliography of vernacular architecture (1970–1976).*
137 Victoria and Albert Museum. *Topographical index to measured drawings.*
264 Council for British Archaeology. (Publications).
274 Department of Health and Social Security. (Publications).
275 Departments of the Environment and Transport, Library. (Publications).
350 Property Services Agency. (Publications).
374 Royal Institution of Chartered Surveyors. (Publications).

For unpublished indexes see the following:

163 British Architectural Library. *Grey books index.*
164 British Architectural Library. *Periodicals subject index.*
165 British Architectural Library. *Periodicals names index.*
166 British Architectural Library. *Periodicals topographical index.*
250 Buildings of England Office. *Ferriday Index of Victorian church restorations.*
290 The Garden History Society.
297 Guildhall Library.
414 Vernacular Architecture Group.

Societies, institutions and organisations

.1

Published directories to societies, institutions and organisations

In order to discover which societies, institutions and organisations exist which devote themselves either exclusively or substantially to architecture or might be of relevance for a particular area of architectural study (eg if researching *pubs* one might want to contact *brewery organisations*), the directories listed in this section are useful.

Whereas the guide provided in section 5.2 is extensive, it cannot be comprehensive; and much of the information is liable to become out of date with time. Many of the directories listed here are published annually, or at frequent intervals, and the latest editions should therefore be consulted for current addresses, telephone numbers, etc.

In addition to the societies etc described in section 5.2, the researcher may wish, depending on the nature of the search, to contact the following:

● County record offices, (listed in 207).
They often hold much architectural material, representing the work of national and local architects, in the form of estate and parish records and deposits of other papers.
● County archaeological or historical societies, (listed in 204).
● Local archaeological societies.
A list is available from the Council for British Archaeology (*see* 264).
● Local history societies, (listed in 205).
● Local history collections in public libraries, (listed in 212).
● Local architecture and/or planning departments, (listed in 86).
Their records, either as client or planning controller, may be of value.
● Local amenity societies.
A list is available from the Civic Trust (*see* 260).
● The owners of the building.
In some cases documents and drawings may be in their possession, particularly in the case of cathedrals, churches, colleges and country houses.
● The architect, if still living (*see* 117 and 123).
● The architectural practice, if still in existence (*see* 124).

ARLIS Directory of members. ARLIS.   198
    Annual.
       Incorporates a directory of member libraries of ARLIS (the Art Libraries Society), their collections and services.

ASLIB Directory: a guide to sources of   199
    information in Great Britain and Ireland.
    Vol 1: Information sources in science, technology and commerce. Edited by Ellen M. Codlin. 4th ed. 1977. 634pp.
    Vol 2: Information sources in the social sciences, medicine and the humanities. Edited by Ellen M. Codlin. 4th ed. 1980. 871pp.
    London: Aslib.
       Entries typically give the address and essential details of library service. Arranged alphabetically by name of organisation with an alphabetical subject index. Together, the volumes include over 6,500 organisations, from the very large to the very small: professional and amateur, institutional and voluntary, learned and academic, commercial and scientific, research, service, governmental, producers of data, statistics and abstracts, experts in specialised technologies, crafts, arts and sports, repositories of vast collections of books and documents and holders of small special collections.

The Building Centre and CIRIA guide to   200
    sources of information. 3rd ed. London: Building Centre Group and CIRIA, 1979. 89pp. Supplement, 1981.
       First published 1970 as the *CIRIA guide to sources of information in the construction industry*. Lists and describes organisations and associations, their libraries and information services, which are relevant to the building industry. Fourth edition is due to be published in 1982.

Civic Trust   201
Environmental directory: national and
    regional organisations of interest to those
    concerned with amenity and the environment.
    5th ed. London: The Trust, 1981.
       Organisations listed include government departments and agencies, voluntary societies, professional institutions and trade associations. Addresses and telephone numbers are given, with a brief outline of the function of each organisation and the services available. Includes about 300 organisations.

5.1 Published directories to societies, institutions and organisations

Conservation sourcebook, for conservators, 202
**craftsmen and those who have historic
objects in their care**. London: Crafts Advisory
Committee, 1979. 358pp. Supplement, 1980.
 A guide to more than 250 organisations in
England, Scotland and Wales whose work is
directly concerned with conservation, or who,
through their other interests, are able to offer
help or information to conservators, craftsmen
or owners. A wide range of organisations is
listed, including government departments,
professional, research and scientific institutions,
trade organisations, learned societies and those
established for the amateur or the enthusiast for
historic objects. Each entry outlines the aims and
activities of the organisation and includes a list of
services offered. Sections deal with archaeology,
industrial archaeology, buildings, ecclesiastical
buildings, building materials, etc. There is a
subject index which also includes names of
organisations. Intended to be a regularly
up-dated publication. A supplement, noting
changes of address and personnel, was published
by the Crafts Council in 1980.
 The Conservation Section of the Crafts
Council (formerly the Crafts Advisory Council),
12 Waterloo Place, London SW1Y 4AU, tel
01–930 4811, provides an information service for
conservation. They operate a conservation
register providing detailed information on
specialist conservation workshops and are
co-ordinating the establishment of a national
Conservation Craft Skills Register for Buildings
on a regional basis. For Scotland, a similar
register and advisory service is available from the
Conservation Bureau of the Scottish
Development Agency, 102 Telford Road,
Edinburgh EH4 2NP, tel Edinburgh (031) 343
1911.

Councils, Committees and boards: a 203
**handbook of advisory, consultative,
executive and similar bodies in British public
life**. Edited by I. G. Anderson. Beckenham: CBD
Research Ltd, 1970– .
 Covers England, Scotland, Wales and Northern
Ireland. Limited to national or regional bodies.
Arranged in four parts: 1. alphabetical directory;
2. abbreviations index; 3. index of chairmen; and
4. subject index. Entries provide address and
telephone number of secretariat, name of
chairman and name of secretary, as well as aims,
publications etc. Frequency: every two or three
years. Fourth edition published 1980.

Directory of British associations and 204
associations in Ireland. Edited by G. P.
Henderson and S. P. A. Henderson. Beckenham:
CBD Research Ltd, 1965– .
 An alphabetical list of over 8,000 associations.
The subject index can be used to trace names of
relevant associations. Entries include titles of
publications, names of executives and related
international organisations and numbers of
members both inside and outside the UK. There
is an abbreviations index, making it possible to
trace an organisation when only an acronym is
known. The editors (CBD Research Ltd, 154
High Street, Beckenham, Kent, tel 01–650
7745) are willing to attempt to trace details of
any association not listed, or whose details have
become out of date since publication.
Frequency: every two or three years. Sixth
edition published 1980.

The Environment: sources of information 20
for teachers. Prepared by the Department
of Education and Science from material originally
compiled by Peter S. Berry, Director of the
Conservation Trust. London: HMSO, 1979. 132pp.
 A guide to national and regional organisations
concerned with the environment which provides
brief descriptions of each organisation, with an
indication of the resources it is able to offer
schools and/or colleges and activities such as
conferences, courses, the provision of speakers
or careers information. There is a subject index
which identifies organisations concerned with
ancient and historic monuments, archaeology,
architecture and design, buildings, the built
environment, churches, gardens, housing,
industrial archaeology, landscape, etc. It is
planned to publish revised editions every two
years.

Guide to government department and other 20
libraries. 24th ed. London: British
Library, Science Reference Library, 1980. 95pp.
 Of particular interest are the sections covering
national libraries, transport engineering,
building and architecture, the environment
(town and country planning, etc), arts and
design, photography and history. Information
provided for each organisation: name, address,
telephone, librarian, stock and subject coverage,
services, availability, hours, loans and
publications. Index. Previous edition published
as *Guide to government department and other
libraries and information bureaux*, 1978.

Historical Manuscripts Commission 20
**Record repositories in Great Britain: a
geographical directory**. 6th ed. London: HMSO,
1979. 35pp. Bibl pp 31–32.
 A guide to where record material may be found
in this country and what organisations will help
one to approach and use it. The main types of
repository listed are: 1. national record offices
and libraries, 2. local record offices and libraries,
3. university libraries and archives and 4. special
libraries and archives. Index.
 'Archives and manuscript collections in the

United Kingdom: a supplementary list' in
Archives, vol 14, no 63, Spring 1980, pp
163–177, is the first of supplementary lists to
Record repositories in Great Britain, 6th ed.

House's guide to the construction industry. 208
London: House Information Services,
1978– .
Previously *House's guide to the building industry*
(1970, 1972, 1974) and *Construction industry UK*
(1976) it continues *Redland guide to the
recommendations, regulations and statutory and
advisory bodies of the construction industry.*
Particularly valuable for the alphabetical
directory to over 400 professional, trade,
technical and official organisations, as well as
government departments and related offices.
The classified subject directory can be used to
trace names of relevant organisations. Entries
give functions, addresses, personnel and
services. A separate section includes a list of all
local authorities in Great Britain and Ireland.
The chapter on information and communication
provides a book-list for architects as well as a
listing of current periodicals with their
addresses. Frequency: every two or three years.
*House's guide to the construction industry,
1981–82*, 8th ed, was published in 1981.

Howard, Diana, *compiler* 209
**Directory of theatre research resources in
Great Britain**. London: Arts Council of Great
Britain, 1979.

Howard, Diana, *compiler* 210
**Directory of theatre research resources in
Greater London**. London: Commission for a British
Theatre Institute, 1974, 26pp. Amendments. 1978.
7pp.
In five parts: 1 Associations and institutes;
2 Museums; 3 Private collections; 4 Public
libraries; 5 Record offices. For each organisation
the following information is provided: address,
nearest station, name of person in charge, hours,
description of contents, catalogues and services.

The Libraries, museums and art galleries 211
yearbook, 1978–79. Edited by Adrian
Brink. Cambridge (Eng): James Clark, 1981. [272
pp.]
Full descriptive entries are given for the British
Library, public libraries, special libraries,
museums, art galleries and stately homes in the
UK, Channel Islands, Isle of Man and the
Republic of Ireland. There is a combined index
for the volume which includes general subjects,
special collections and the names of individual
institutions. The next edition is due to be
published in 1982.

Library Association. Reference, Special and 212
Information Section.
Library resources in East Anglia. 1974.
Library resources in the East Midlands. 2nd ed.
1979.
**Library resources in London and South East
England**. 2nd ed. 1979.
Library resources in the North East. 1978.
Library resources in the North West. 1980.
**Library resources in South West England and
the Channel Isles**. 2nd ed. 1978.
Library resources in Wales. 1975.
**Library resources in Yorkshire and
Humberside**. 4th ed. 1980.
Library resources in the West Midlands. 3rd ed.
1977.
London: Library Association. Reference, Special and
Information Section.
This series of pamphlets provides details of
libraries in each region, including for each:
name, address, telephone number, name and
designation of officer in charge of library, date
founded, conditions of admission, times when
open, number of books, number of periodicals,
other materials (eg films, slides, prints, mss),
main subjects, special subjects or departments,
publications and services. Each pamphlet has a
topographical index and a subject index.
The Library Association also publishes
*Libraries in the United Kingdom and the Republic
of Ireland* (9th ed, 1981) which includes
addresses and telephone numbers of central
libraries and branches, university libraries,
polytechnic libraries and selected national
government and special libraries.
The Scottish Library Association publishes
Library resources in Scotland, 1980–81 (Glasgow:
Scottish Library Association, 1981, 149 pp).

Royal Institute of British Architects 213
**Schools of architecture recognised by
the RIBA**. London: RIBA Publications. Annual.
Provides full name, address and telephone
number as well as descriptions of each school.
The libraries of the schools of architecture
(details are not given) often have outstanding
architectural collections, and in some cases are
available to the general public for reference use.
A list of the schools of architecture is also given
in the *RIBA directory of members* (*see* 124).

Smith, Stuart B. 214
**Industrial archaeology: a directory of local
organisations**. Compiled by Stuart B. Smith,
Alastair Penfold and Patrick Delaney. London:
Phillimore in association with the Association for
Industrial Archaeology, 1979. 40pp.
A list of 85 industrial archaeological societies.
Entries generally provide the names and
addresses of the secretary and editor of each
society, lists of publications and sometimes a
brief description of the organisation.

5.1 Published directories to societies, institutions and organisations

---

Standing Conference for Local History   215
Directory of national organisations.
London: Standing Conference for Local History,
1978, 10pp. (Information for local historians, no 1).
Gives the names, dates of formation, addresses,
telephone numbers and brief descriptions of
national organisations which local historians may
wish to consult.

Standing Conference for Local History   216
Local history societies in England and
Wales: a list. London: Standing Conference for
Local History, 1978. 34pp. (Information for local
historians, no 3).
A list of local organisations which are concerned
either exclusively or in large measure, with the
promotion of local history. Excludes local
archaeological and civic societies and branches of
the Historical Association. Societies are listed
under counties.

For other entries relating to this section see items in:

5.2

Guide to societies, institutions and organisations

Not all the societies, institutions and organisations listed in
this section are sources of information or advice. Many of
the bodies listed, particularly the government advisory
committees, have strictly limited functions which do not
include the answering of enquiries either about their own
activities or on subjects within their fields of interest.
However, as such organisations often play an important
role, it seemed worthwhile including them for two reasons:

firstly to explain their functions; and secondly to prevent
researchers wasting their time approaching such
organisations for information or advice.

Entries are arranged in alphabetical order. The
address is usually that of the main office. Where the
address for enquiries differs this is indicated. Regional and
branch offices are mentioned where appropriate.
Telephone numbers are given wherever possible. STD
codes should be checked in cases of doubt. The hours of
service are indicated, but visitors are encouraged to verify
this information, particularly during holidays or between
terms for academic libraries. Each entry gives a brief
description of the organisation, with an indication of the
resources it is able to offer. An attempt has been made to
define an organisation's ability to answer enquiries. This
should be particularly noted. The majority of entries have
been derived from questionnaire responses. Some were
more complete than others.

The organisations listed span a range of interests, in
some cases touching only marginally on architecture. They
also vary widely in the resources they command, from
large government departments with specialised staff to
voluntary bodies, perhaps run in their members' spare
time. It is important to bear this in mind when writing to
them. Most of the smaller organisations do not have the
facilities to handle many enquiries. Some receive a large
number of letters asking for information in such general
terms that they find it impossible to send a helpful reply.

It will help organisations to give the best possible
service if these points are observed:
• Make sure you are contacting the appropriate
organisation.
• Make your enquiry as specific as possible.
• Indicate the purpose of your enquiry.
• Include return postage, preferably on a stamped,
self-addressed label.
• Allow a reasonable time for reply.

Societies, institutions and organisations in addition to
those listed below are indicated in the introduction and
directories in section 5.1. Since much of the information
given in this section is liable to become out of date with
time, the most recent editions of the directories listed in
section 5.1 should be consulted for current addresses,
telephone numbers, etc.

Advisory Board for Redundant Churches   21
Fielden House
Little College Street
London SW1P 3SH
tel 01–222 9603/4

Founded 1969

Aims:
Statutory body established by the Pastoral
Measure 1968 to give information and advice to
Church Commissioners on historic and
architectural qualities of redundant and
potentially redundant Anglican churches.
Considers all redundant churches for which
demolition, structural alteration to fit them for
alternative uses, or preservation in the interests
of the nation and the Church of England may be
proposed.

Collections/Library:
Files containing architectural descriptions and photographs of the redundant or potentially redundant churches about which the Church Commissioners have consulted the Board, together with relevant correspondence, draft schemes and Statutory Instruments. The individual files, which now number about 900, are alphabetically arranged under the 42 dioceses. The files contain confidential material and can only be made available by arrangement for inspection on the premises by suitably qualified persons approved by the Secretary.

Enquiry services and conditions of use:
Application to consult the files can be made in person, by post and by telephone and will be considered by the Secretary.

Hours:
By appointment.

Publications:
Annual report.

An Foras Forbartha *see* 331: National Institute for Physical Planning and Construction Research.

Ancient Monuments Board for England   218
    Fortress House
    Savile Row
    London W1X 2HE
    tel 01–734 6010 ext 157

Founded 1913

Aims:
To advise the Secretary of State for the Environment on the preservation of monuments and when they are in danger of destruction or damage.

Collections/Library:
None.

Enquiry services:
None.

Publications:
Annual report (published by HMSO).
Principles of publication in rescue archaeology.

Ancient Monuments Board for Scotland   219
    Argyle House
    Lady Lawson Street
    Edinburgh EH3 8JN
    tel Edinburgh (031) 229 9321 ext 218

Founded 1913

Aims:
To advise the Secretary of State for Scotland on the preservation of monuments and when they are in danger of destruction or damage.

Collections/Library:
None.

Enquiry services:
None.

Publications:
Annual report (published by HMSO).

Ancient Monuments Board for Wales   220
    Government Buildings
    Ty-Glas, Llanishen
    Cardiff CF4 5UP
    tel Cardiff (0222) 753271 ext 2257

Founded 1913

Aims:
To advise the Secretary of State for Wales on the preservation of monuments and when they are in danger of destruction or damage.

Collections/Library:
None.

Enquiry services:
None.

Publications:
Annual report (published by HMSO).

Ancient Monuments Society   221
    St Andrew-by-the-Wardrobe
    Queen Victoria Street
    London EC4V 5DE
    tel 01–236 3934

Founded 1924

Aims:
To encourage the study and conservation of ancient monuments, historic buildings, and examples of fine old craftsmanship.

Collections/Library:
The Society is establishing a collection of historic architectural postcards. The collection so far numbers about 2,000, the majority dating from the turn of the century. Indexed by place.

Enquiry services and conditions of use:
Postcard collection may be consulted by appointment.

Publications:
Transactions of the Ancient Monuments Society (annual). A list of offprints for sale is available from the Society.

5.2 Guide to societies, institutions and organisations

Society./*continued*
Newsletter (2 per year).
A list of members appears in the *Transactions*,
vol 22, pp 130–186, plus supplement in Winter
Newsletter, 1976.
I. M. Angus-Butterworth. 'The early history of
the Society', in *Transactions of the Ancient
Monuments Society*, New Series 20, 1975, pp
49–84.

Activities:
Casework.
Lectures.
Walks, visits.

Archaeological Survey *see 279*: Department of
the Environment for Northern Ireland, Historic
Monuments and Buildings Branch, Archaeological
Survey.

Architects' Registration Council of the   222
United Kingdom (ARCUK)
73 Hallam Street
London W1N 6EE
tel 01–580 5861/2

Founded 1931

Aims:
Legal protection of the style 'architect'; the
maintenance of a register of all persons entitled
to practise in the UK under any style containing
the word 'architect'; the determination of
qualifications needed for registration, including
the recognition of examinations; the
maintenance of standards of professional
discipline; the award of grants to needy students;
and promotion of architectural research. The
Architects' (Registration) Act does not apply to
the Channel Islands, the Isle of Man or the
Republic of Ireland. Landscape and naval
architects are not covered by the Act.

Collections/Library:
Registration records.

Enquiry services and conditions of use:
For architects on the Register, they can usually
answer questions on where an architect trained,
date of birth, etc.

Hours:
Mon–Fri 9.00–17.00

Publications:
Annual report.
Register of architects (annual). (*see* 117).

Architectural Association   223
34–36 Bedford Square
London WC1B 3ES
tel 01–636 0974

Founded 1847

Aims:
The objects of the Association are to promote
and afford facilities for the study of architecture
and to further these objects by any of the
following methods: (1) the establishment and
carrying on of a school of architecture; (2) the
founding of scholarships and the giving of
prizes; (3) the provision of lectures and classes;
(4) the formation of a library (and museum); (5)
the organisation of discussion of architectural
and cognate matters and the promotion of publi
interest in the progress of architecture; (6) the
organisation of visits to works and buildings; (7)
the production and circulation of periodicals an
other publications.

Collections/Library:
The library contains 24,000 volumes, classified
by UDC, with author and classified catalogues
and indexes to subjects, architects and places.
Subject specialisations are architecture, plannin
and building. The technical collection contains
5,000 technical articles, pamphlets and trade
catalogues, classified by CI/SfB with a subject
index. The collection includes 30,000 general
periodical articles arranged by subject, with a
subject index.
Slide Library (*see* 433).
Video-Audio Library of the AA
Communications Unit.

Enquiry services and conditions of use:
Available to members only. Applicants for
membership should be proposed by two
members (although Council can override this
condition). Every member should be studying o
practising architecture or one of the arts/science
associated therewith. Applicants have to be over
18 years of age; employed by the Architectural
Association; a student of the AA School of
Architecture or a member of staff.
        Personal, postal and telephone enquiries
accepted from members.

Hours:
Mon–Fri 10.00–18.00 during term
Mon–Fri 10.00–17.00 during vacation
Closed for part of some vacations.

Publications:
Architectural Association and School of
Architecture publications:
AA Quarterly.
AA Notes.
AA Papers.
AA Cahiers.
Exhibition catalogues.
The Architectural Association.
AA School Publications.
AA School annual prospectus.
Events lists.

The Architectural Association, 1847–1947, by Sir
John Summerson (1947).
Architectural Association. *Brown book series*,
sessions 1859 to 1918 (*see* 62).

Library publications:
Introduction to the Library (annual).
Annual report.
AA Library bibliographies series.
Index to AA Journal 1945–1974 (typescript).
Periodicals and serials in the AA Library (at
intervals).
Architectural Association Library. *Catalogue of
the books in the Library of the Architectural
Association.* London: Langley and Son, 1895.
180pp.

Activities:
Exhibitions, open to the public.
Lectures, open to the public.
Bookshop.

rchitectural Heritage Fund *see* 260: Civic
Trust

rkwright Society   224
c/o Tawney House
Matlock
Derbyshire
tel Matlock (0629) 3809

Aims:
To promote the conservation of buildings and
machinery of industrial archaeological and
historical interest, the preservation of Richard
Arkwright's buildings in Cromford, and the
publication of material and lectures on
Arkwright's influence in the industrial
revolution.

rt Workers' Guild   225
6 Queen Square
London WC1N 3AR
tel 01–837 3474

Founded 1884

Aims:
To advance education in all visual arts and crafts
and to foster high standards of design and
craftsmanship.

Collections/Library:
The library, largely built up through gifts by
guildsmen, is mainly concerned with the Guild
and the work of its members.

Enquiry services and conditions of use:
Information service available to all serious
enquirers.

Publications:
Annual report.
H. J. L. J. Massé, *The Art-Workers' Guild,
1884–1934.* Oxford: Shakespeare Head, 1935.
Includes a list of members for each year from
1884–1934 and an alphabetical index of
members for the same period. The list gives the
dates elected, resigned and died and the
profession of each member.

Activities:
Conferences.
Meetings.
Visits and excursions.

Association for Industrial Archaeology   226
The Wharfage
Ironbridge, Telford
Salop TF8 7AW
tel Ironbridge (095 245) 3522

Founded 1973

Aims:
To promote the study of industrial archaeology
and to encourage approved standards of
recording, research, publication and
conservation. To assist and support regional and
specialist survey research groups and bodies
involved in the preservation of industrial
monuments and to represent the interests of
industrial archaeology at a national level. To
hold conferences and seminars and to publish
the results of research. Co-operation with other
organisations having related functions is an
essential element of Association policy.

Collections/Library:
None.

Enquiry services:
Enquiries should be addressed to the Secretary.

Publications:
Bulletin (six times a year).
Industrial archaeology review (three times a year,
in conjunction with Oxford University Press).
*Industrial archaeology: a directory of local
organisations* (*see* 214).

Activities:
Annual conference in September of each year.
Seminars, often jointly with other organisations,
from time to time.

Association for Studies in the Conservation   227
of Historic Buildings
The Institute of Archaeology
31–34 Gordon Square
London WC1H 0PY
tel 01–387 6052

01–387 6052/*continued*
Hon Secretary, James Elliott
6 Woodland Place
Bathwick Hill
Bath, Avon BA2 6EH
tel Bath (0225) 4576

Founded 1968

Aims:
To keep its members informed of all aspects of
the conservation of historic buildings by
providing a forum for meetings, lectures and
discussions and arranging visits to buildings and
places of interest. Membership is by invitation
and is open to individuals or bodies who are
professionally engaged in work relating to the
conservation of historic buildings.

Enquiry services:
Enquiries should be addressed to the Hon
Secretary.

Publications:
Newsletter.
Transactions.

Activities:
Not less than five meetings are held annually, in
addition to one or more visits in this country and
a study tour abroad.

Association for the Protection of Rural Scotland   228
20 Falkland Avenue
Newton Mearns
Renfrewshire G77 5DR
tel (041) 639 2069

Aims:
Set up with similar aims to those of the Council
for the Protection of Rural England (267) and
the Council for the Protection of Rural Wales
(268).

Collections/Library:
None.

Enquiry services:
Postal and telephone enquiries only.

Hours:
Mon–Fri 9.00–17.00

Publications:
Annual report.

Association of Art Historians   229
c/o Dr Charles Avery, Hon Secretary
Department of Architecture and Sculpture
Victoria and Albert Museum
South Kensington
London SW7 2RL
tel 01–589 6371

Founded 1974

Aims:
The advancement of the study of the history of
art; to enable art historians working in often
widely differing fields to meet each other socially
and professionally and to exchange ideas and
information.

Collections/Library:
None.

Enquiry services:
None.

Publications:
Art history (quarterly journal).
Bulletin (twice yearly).

Activities:
Annual conference.
Special conferences.

Association of Genealogists and Record Agents   230
c/o Mrs Mary Gandy, Hon Secretary
80 Pollard Road
London N20
tel 01–368 3530

Founded 1968

Aims:
An association of genealogists and record agents

Enquiry services:
Broadly speaking the genealogist directs research
while the record agent undertakes it. The
genealogist acts as a consultant, settling a line of
enquiry, initiating, supervising and participating
in the work it entails. He then reports and
suggests possible lines of further research. The
record agent's work lies in searching specific
records for particular information which may be
required by a genealogist, historian or
biographer. Many members of the Association
act in both these capacities. Their fees vary to
some extent and are a matter for negotiation.
Having chosen a genealogist or record agent
from the list of members, the enquirer should
send a preliminary letter setting out the problem
and stating clearly the known facts, particularly
dates and places of birth, marriage and death,
together with some indication of occupation. A
stamped label, or, from abroad, international
reply coupons, should be enclosed.

Publications:
List of members.

Avoncroft Museum of Buildings   231
Stoke Heath
Bromsgrove B60 4JR
tel Bromsgrove (0527) 31886/31363

Aims:
An open air museum established to rescue
buildings from destruction. Encourages
restoration of ancient and interesting buildings
in situ wherever possible. When this approach
has been impossible, buildings have been
dismantled and moved to the museum's 10-acre
site, repaired and re-erected.

Collections/Library:
A 14th-century aisled hall, the 14th-century roof
of the Guesten Hall of Worcester Cathedral, a
15th-century merchant's house, a 16th-century
inn, a cruck-framed barn, a granary and a
windmill, both built about 1800.

Hours:
Museum: March–Nov, daily 10.30–17.30

Publications:
Leaflets about the museum and its education
service.
Teaching pack.
Postcards, slide sets, information leaflets.
List of publications available.

Activities:
Courses and conferences.

Beamish North of England Open Air   232
Museum
Beamish Hall
Beamish, Nr Stanley
Co Durham
tel Stanley (0207) 33580/6

Founded 1971

Aims:
The studying, collecting, preserving and
exhibition of buildings, machinery, objects and
information illustrating the development of
industry and the way of life in the North East of
England. Beamish was England's first open air
museum.

Collections/Library:
Reference library of books, periodicals, trade
catalogues and maps. Indexes. Collection of
more than 12,000 photographic negatives on all
aspects of regional material. Specialises in
agriculture, industry and local history. The
museum is divided into separate areas: railway
area; farm; rebuilt colliery; furnished cottages
and shops; transport depot; Victorian pub.

Enquiry services and conditions of use:
Personal, postal and telephone enquiries
accepted.

Hours:
Mon–Fri 8.30–17.00
Museum: April–Sept, daily 10.00–18.00;
Oct–March, Tues–Sun 10.00–17.00

Publications:
Annual report, *Beamish.*
Guides.
Newsletters.
Monographs.

Biggar Museum Trust   233
Gladstone Court Museum
Biggar ML12 6DN
tel Biggar (0899) 20005

Founded 1968

Aims:
To preserve and document all aspects of local
history.

Collections/Library:
Local history collection, housed in indoor street
museum. Open air museum, begun in 1975,
currently contains a 17th-century farmhouse and
an 1839 gas works.
   The archive/library contains local
architects' plans from the mid-1830s, but no
index is yet available.

Enquiry services and conditions of use:
Personal and postal enquiries accepted.

Hours:
Daily 10.00–12.30; 14.00–17.00

Publications:
Guides.
Newsletters.
Monographs.

Black Country Museum Trust Ltd   234
Black Country Museum
Tipton Road
Dudley
West Midlands DY1 4SQ
tel Dudley (021 557) 9643

Founded 1975

Aims:
The preservation of Black Country history
through the development of an open air
museum.

5.2 Guide to societies, institutions and organisations

museum./*continued*
Collections/Library:
Museum collections cover all aspects of the
industrial and social history of the Black
Country, with particular emphasis on
19th-century domestic and industrial
architecture. There is a library of books, journals
and manufacturers' sample books. Records of all
buildings moved and researched.

Enquiry services and conditions of use:
Personal and postal enquiries accepted.

Hours:
Daily (except Sat) 10.00–16.00

Publications:
Friends newsletter: *Contact* (bi-monthly).
School leaflets.

Brick Development Association   235
Woodside House
Winkfield
Windsor SL4 2DP
tel Winkfield Row (034 47) 5651

Founded 1969

Aims:
Promotes the use of clay and calcium silicate
bricks through technical literature, exhibitions,
films, etc. It is also the recognised structural
advisory centre for building and engineering
bricks.

Collections/Library:
Mainly technical. Some historical material.

Enquiry services and conditions of use:
Personal, postal and telephone enquiries
accepted.

Hours:
Mon–Fri 9.00–17.00

Publications:
A list of publications is available on request.

British Architectural Library   236
Royal Institute of British Architects
66 Portland Place
London W1N 4AD
tel 01–580 5533

Founded 1834

Aims:
The Royal Institute of British Architects was
founded in 1834 for the general advancement of
civil architecture and for promoting and
facilitating the knowledge of the various arts and
sciences connected therewith. The Library exists
to further these aims.

Collections/Library:
In addition to more than 100,000 books, the
British Architectural Library has extensive
collections of pamphlets, periodicals,
manuscripts, photographs and ephemera. The
collections cover architecture of all periods and
all countries; theory, design, building types,
interiors, environment, planning, landscape
architecture, construction, building methods
and materials.
• Books and pamphlets. The book collection
includes recently published titles as well as rare
volumes. There are a number of special
collections: the Early Works comprise some
3,500 books published before 1841 and a full
bibliographic catalogue is being prepared for
publication. This collection is rich in the classic
British works of the 17th and 18th centuries.
Amongst the 19th-century books there are good
collections of cottage architecture, Pugin,
lithograph platebooks and the great Victorian
texts. The Handley-Read collection consists of
some 1,350 titles dealing mainly with late
19th-century architecture, furniture and design.
The key International modern movement works
of the first thirty years or so of this century are
particularly well represented.
• Reference sources. The Library stocks a large
collection of reference sources to help in finding
facts or tracing published material.
• Periodicals. The large periodical collection
(about 1,200 periodical titles, more than 600
current, from 60 countries) includes all the
major architectural magazines.
• Manuscripts. The manuscript collection
constitutes an important collection of the papers
of architects, designers, builders, craftsmen,
tradesmen and architectural historians. It
consists of more than 200,000 documents,
ranging in date from the 17th century to the
present day.
      The types of document in the collection
include personal correspondence, diaries,
manuscripts of published and unpublished
works, ledgers and journals, office
correspondence files, letter-books, project files,
contracts, specifications of works, and minutes
of meetings, and a number of groups relate
closely to drawings in the Drawings Collection.
Among the host of those represented in the
collection are Sir Herbert Baker, the Barry
family, J. F. Bentley, Sir William Chambers,
C. R. Cockerell, William Burges, Sir Ninian
Comper, the Dance family, Erno Goldfinger,
W. R. Lethaby, Sir Edwin Lutyens, Sir Edward
Maufe, John Nash, A. W. N. Pugin, Thomas
Rickman, the Scott family (including Sir George
Gilbert Scott, George Gilbert Scott junior and
Sir Giles Gilbert Scott), Norman Shaw, Sir
Robert Smirke, Sydney Smirke, Sir Raymond
Unwin, Lewis Vulliamy, Sir Christopher Wren
and the Wyatt family.

Organisations represented include the Architects Club, the London Architectural Society, the Ecclesiological Society and the Design and Industries Association.

Amongst the multitude of buildings that feature in the collection are Somerset House, Dorchester House, Westonbirt House, the Houses of Parliament, Greenwich Hospital, the Horse Guards, Winchester Palace, Nash's London buildings – particularly in Regent Street and Regent's Park – the Brighton Pavilion, Westminster Abbey, Westminster Cathedral and St Paul's Cathedral. The collection is a prime source also of information on the many churches that were built or restored during the 19th century in Britain.

Some of the manuscripts have been listed by the Historical Manuscripts Commission (*see* 101). Many of those listed have been published by World Microfilms. A catalogue of the entire collection is now being compiled, but will not be completed for some years. A topographical and names index (on cards) and lists are available for consultation.
• Photographs. The Library has some 60,000 photographs including a fine collection of modern British architecture and many fine portraits of architects. Searches can be undertaken for photographs of works by specific architects or of specific buildings, but not subject searches. A names index (on cards) is available for consultation.
• Indexes and catalogues (*see* section 3).
• Drawings (*see* 237).

Enquiry services and conditions of use:
The Library is freely open to any member of the public. There is no admission fee, no formality of joining, and no reader's ticket is required. A general information service is provided and personal, postal and telephone enquiries are accepted. Lengthy and comprehensive searches can sometimes be undertaken, but a charge must be made for this service. Estimates will be provided in advance. The collection is primarily reference only; a loan section is available for RIBA members and inter-library lending. Bibliographical, photocopying and photographic services are available.

Hours:
Mon 10.00–17.00
Tues–Thurs 10.00–20.00
Fri 10.00–19.00
Sat 10.00–13.30
Closed public holidays and during August. During the August closing the staff will make every effort to deal with urgent phone calls and written requests.

Publications:
Guide to the British Architectural Library (a series of information sheets) includes a list of Library publications.

World Microfilms is engaged in a publication programme of items from the collection. Series include:
Microfilmed Collection of Rare Books, 35 reels of 35 mm positive microfilm (section 1: English pattern books; section 2: Cottage architecture; section 3: Country houses and palaces; section 4: Ancient civilisation; section 5: Architectural treatises and works on perspective. Unpublished Manuscripts, 16 reels of 35 mm positive microfilm.

For publications described elsewhere in this guide *see* items 45, 46, 47, 48, 49, 127, 128, 164.

British Architectural Library: Drawings Collection   237
21 Portman Square
London W1H 9HF
tel 01–580 5533

Founded 1834

Collections/Library:
The Drawings Collection, the largest collection of British architectural drawings in the world, dates from the foundation of the Institute in 1834. During the early years members presented their drawings for use as exemplars. Many of these were measured drawings and sketches of both classical and gothic buildings that furnished design precedents for those articled pupils unable to afford the expense of travelling to the original buildings. Other drawings, such as the collection of 17th and early 18th-century stage designs presented by an amateur architect, Sir John Drummond Stewart in 1835, were splendid examples of both design and draughtsmanship. By 1872, drawings were collected so as to form a record of an architect's work and in this way, in due course, the very comprehensive collections of drawings by, for example, J. B. Papworth, William Burn, Anthony Salvin, William Burges, Alfred Waterhouse, Sir Edwin Lutyens, C. F. A. Voysey and the architectural families of the Wyatts, Pugins and Scotts, were formed. Drawings by Palladio bought by Inigo Jones in 1615 and afterwards acquired by Lord Burlington are (together with Jones' and Burlington's own drawings) also in the Collection. In all, there are something like a quarter of a million drawings mostly, though not entirely, British. Chronologically the Collection ranges from a single later 15th-century drawing for a turreted tower to the hundreds of drawings for Foster Associates' building at Ipswich.

Indexes and catalogues (*see* 167).

Enquiry services and conditions of use:
The Drawings Collection is freely open to any member of the public. There is no admission

5.2 Guide to societies, institutions and organisations

admission/*continued*
fee, no formality of joining, and no reader's
ticket is required. Postal and telephone enquiries
accepted. Personal callers by appointment.
    Photographs of any drawing in the
Collection can be made by the BAL's authorised
photographer. The BAL holds negatives of
many of the drawings. Permission for
reproduction has to be requested.

Hours:
Mon−Fri 10.00−13.00 (by appointment)
Closed public holidays and during August.

Publications:
*Catalogue of the Drawings Collection of the Royal
Institute of British Architects.* Farnborough
(Hants): Gregg International, 1969− . (*see* 127).

World Microfilms is engaged in a publication
programme of drawings from the collection.
    A list of publications for sale is available
from the Drawings Collection.

Guide to the British Architectural Library (a
series of information sheets) includes
information about the Drawings Collection.

Activities:
Exhibitions. The Heinz Gallery provides a
changing programme of exhibitions of
architectural interest, including the work of
contemporary architects (both English and
foreign) and historical exhibitions devoted to a
particular architect, period or theme. Original
drawings from the Collection and elsewhere,
photographs, paintings, models and other
material may be included. A catalogue usually
accompanies the exhibition, and catalogues from
some past exhibitions are available at the gallery
desk. Entrance is free. The gallery is open
Mon−Fri 11.00−17.00 and Sat 10.00−13.00. It is
closed on public holidays.

British Centre of the International Theatre Institute 238

44/48 Earlham Street
London WC2H 9LA
tel 01−836 1477

Founded 1978

Aims:
The International Theatre Institute provides a
worldwide network of centres whose aims are to
encourage and promote international exchange
and collaboration between practitioners in the
performing arts.

Collections/Library:
Current and recent issues of theatre journals,
which may be consulted by prior arrangement.

Enquiry services and conditions of use:
Personal (by appointment), postal and telephone
enquiries accepted. There is a subscription
scheme available for theatre practitioners,
theatre groups and organisations.

Publications:
Annual report.
British theatrelog (quarterly).
International theatrelog (quarterly).
Weekly information column, 'ITI News',
published in *The Stage and television today.*
*Theatre London: an authoritative guide book to
London theatres.* (London: London Transport
Executive, 1980).

British Film Institute 239

127 Charing Cross Road
London WC2H 0EA
tel 01−437 4355

Founded 1933

Aims:
Development of the art of the film and of the
public appreciation of it.

Collections/Library:
Library of books, periodicals, etc, including
information on cinemas.

Enquiry services and conditions of use:
Personal, postal and telephone enquiries
accepted. Contact Library Services.

Hours:
Tues, Thurs, Fri 11.00−18.00
Wed 11.00−21.00

Publications:
British national film catalogue (1963−) (quarterly:
annual cumulation). Records all films and
videocassettes made available for non-theatrical
loan in Britain. The non-fiction entries are
arranged by subject (UDC). Entries include:
title; distributor(s); terms of distribution; year of
release in the UK; production company and
sponsor (where applicable); technical data
(running time, gauge etc); language version(s);
main production credits; and a synopsis giving a
concise summary of each film's contents.
Subject/title index, list of distributors' addresses
and telephone numbers and an addenda listing
changes in distribution, withdrawn titles, etc. In
addition to cumulating the information in the
quarterly issues the annual volume contains a
production index, which provides a full
alphabetical record of sponsors, directors,
scriptwriters, etc, associated with all the films
listed, and an alphabetical listing of British
production companies' addresses.
Film bulletin (monthly).
Sight and sound (quarterly).

British Institute of Interior Design 240

22/24 South Street
Ilkeston
Derbyshire DE7 5QE
tel Ilkeston (0602) 329781

Founded 1899

Aims:
A professional organisation of interior designers
which exists to foster the following objectives: to
encourage public awareness and appreciation of
the interior environment; to promote excellence
of interior design in the public interest; to assist
in the educational development of designers and
potential designers, both in Britain and overseas,
to uphold the ethics of the profession as
expressed by the Institute's Code of Professional
Conduct; to represent the legitimate interests of
the qualified professional designer.

Collections/Library:
The Institute maintains a library of about 400
titles. A list of books available for loan is
published. The library is housed at Dewsbury
and Bailey Technical and Art College,
Cambridge Street, Batley, Yorkshire.

Enquiry services and conditions of use:
Postal enquiries should be addressed to
J. Chisem FBID, Hon Librarian BIID, 449
Leeds Road, Huddersfield, Yorks HD2.

Publications:
Annual report.
Year book.
Bulletin.
Newsletters.
Prospectus.

British Library: Reference Division 241

Great Russell Street
London WC1B 3DG
tel 01–636 1544

Founded 1753 (British Museum); 1973 (British
Library)

Collections/Library:
Comprises the former library departments of the
British Museum (including the Science
Reference Library). The collections cover all
fields of human knowledge. As a copyright
library, the Department of Printed Books
receives a copy of every work published in the
United Kingdom and the Republic of Ireland.

The Department of Printed Books includes
periodicals and books, maps (charts, plans and
topographical views and the largest extant
collection of Ordnance Survey material) and
official publications.

The Newspaper Library, Colindale Ave,

London NW9 5HE (tel 01–200 5515) holds
London newspapers and journals from 1801
onwards, English provincial, Scottish and Irish
newspapers from about 1700 onwards. (Hours:
Mon–Sat 10.00–17.00). The Burnley collection
of pre-1800 English newspapers is in the Great
Russell Street building.

The Science Reference Library, 25
Southampton Buildings, London WC2A 1AW
(tel 01–405 8721) covers all branches of
engineering and industrial technologies and
holds the most comprehensive collection of
patent specifications in the UK. (Hours:
Mon–Fri 9.30–21.00; Sat 10.00–13.00).

Manuscripts (hand-written books and
documents, including maps) are looked after by
the Department of Manuscripts. (Hours:
Mon–Sat 10.00–16.45).

Enquiry services and conditions of use:
The library services in the Great Russell Street
(British Museum) building are tailored to meet
the requirements of those conducting research,
usually of a long term nature and which cannot
be carried out elsewhere. Admission may be
refused if the reader's requirements can be more
conveniently met in another type of library.
Admission is not granted to students reading for
first degrees at British or overseas universities,
nor are persons normally admitted who are
under 21 years of age. These restrictions do not
apply to the Science Reference Library. Leaflets
about the services in the Great Russell Street
building, *viz* the Reading Room and North
Library; and the Students Room of the
Department of Manuscripts are available from
the British Library.

Hours:

	Reading room	Map library	Official publications library
Mon	9.00–17.00	9.30–16.30	9.30–16.45
Tues	9.00–21.00	9.30–16.30	9.30–20.45
Wed	9.00–21.00	9.30–16.30	9.30–20.45
Thur	9.00–21.00	9.30–16.30	9.30–20.45
Fri	9.00–17.00	9.30–16.30	9.30–16.45
Sat	9.00–17.00	9.30–16.30	9.30–16.45

All departments closed Dec 24–26, Jan 1, Good
Friday and the first Monday in May.

Publications:
British Library general catalogue of printed books
(to 1975), London: Clive Bingley, 1979– .
General catalogue of printed books (to 1970).
—*Five-year supplement* (1971–1975).
Short title catalogue (to 1600).
Catalogue of 15th century books.
Catalogue of printed maps, charts and plans (16
vols, complete to the end of 1964).
—*Ten-year supplement (1965–1974).*
Catalogue of the manuscript maps, charts, and

5.2 Guide to societies, institutions and organisations

charts, and/continued
plans, and of the topographical drawings (3 vols,
originally printed 1844–1861).
Catalogue of the newspaper collections in the
British Library (8 vols, 1975).
Subject index of books published before 1880 (4
vols, 1928–1948).
—Subject index 1881–1960, 1961–70 (in
preparation).
Guides for readers.
List of publications available.

British Museum: Department of Prints and   242
Drawings
Great Russell Street
London WC1B 3DG
tel 01–636 1555

Founded 1753

Collections/Library:
A very large collection of engravings and
drawings, and a few photographs, some of which
relate to British architecture. Generally
speaking, the collection is classified by artists
and there is no subject index other than an
incomplete blue strip index to topographical
drawings in the collection. There are series of
prints kept topographically. The English series is
large, but random in its contents. The strongest
area is the topography of London where there is
the Crace collection, the Potter collection of
North London topography and the Crowle
extra-illustrated Pennant's *London.*

Enquiry services and conditions of use:
A leaflet describing the regulations for admission
to the Print Room and use of the collection is
available from the Museum. Photographs can be
ordered of any item in the collection, but
permission for reproduction has to be requested.

Hours:
Mon–Fri 10.00–13.00; 14.15–16.00
Sat 10.00–12.30

Publications:
Catalogue of the Crace Collection, 1878.
Benjamin Stone. *National Photographic Record*
(the British Museum's photographs are almost
all entered).

British Railways Board   243
British Rail Board Headquarters
Melbury House
Melbury Terrace
London NW1 6JU
tel 01–262 3232

British Rail, Eastern Region
British Railways Board
Hudson House
York YO1 1HP
tel York (0904) 53022

British Rail, London Midland Region
Stephenson House
67/87 Hampstead Road
London NW1 2PP
tel 01–387 9400

British Rail, Scottish Region
Buchanan House
58 Port Dundas Road
Glasgow G4 0HG
tel Glasgow (041) 332 9811

British Rail, Southern Region
Southern House
Wellesley Grove
East Croydon
Surrey
tel 01–686 3422

British Rail, Western Region
Chief Architects Department
CP 163
Paddington Station
London W2
tel 01–773 7000

Collections/Library:
There is no single location of drawings and
photographs of railway buildings, nor is
there general public access to records since
they are not used as historical documents,
but are in fact working documents in day to
day use. Generally records are held in plan
rooms belonging to the regional and
divisional civil engineers, some by the
regional architects and some in the British
Rail Property Board regional offices. It
therefore requires some knowledge of the
system to track down quickly any sources of
information. Generally speaking, if a
building or structure is operational, there
will invariably be drawings of it somewhere.
The office of the Chief Architect, British
Rail Board Headquarters, keeps a schedule,
updated regularly, of their listed buildings
and this information is made available to the
Historic Buildings Council, the Science
Museum, National Railway Museum, the
Transport Trust, the Victorian Society and
SAVE. They are in the process of ensuring
that the list is backed up by drawings,
photographs and historic details of each
entry.

Enquiry services and conditions of use:
It is suggested that any requests from
serious enquirers are directed to the office
of the Chief Architect, British Rail Board
Headquarters, where they can either
provide the information or make the
necessary arrangements to see documents.

British Society of Master Glass Painters   244
6 Queen Square
London WC1 2AR
tel 01–693 6574

Founded 1921

Aims:
To advance the art of stained glass and promote
its scholarly study. Its scope has subsequently
been extended to cover all forms of decorative
glass used in architecture.

Collections/Library:
The library is presently housed at Hetleys,
Beresford Avenue, Wembley, Middlesex.

Enquiry services and conditions of use:
Postal and telephone enquiries accepted.

Publications:
Journal (annual).
Newsletter (2 per year).
Directory (every 5 years).

Activities:
Exhibitions.
Events, lectures.

British Theatre Association   245
9 Fitzroy Square
London W1P 6AE
tel 01–387 2666

Founded 1919

Aims:
To assist the development of the art of the
theatre and to promote a right relation between
drama and the life of the community.

Collections/Library:
The library contains over 250,000 books as well
as a collection of press cuttings, play
programmes, costume designs and other theatre
documentation. While most of the information
relates to drama, there is also some information
on theatre buildings.

Enquiry services and conditions of use:
The library and information service is available
to members.

Hours:
Mon–Fri 10.00–17.00 (Wed to 19.00)
Closed August.

British Theatre Institute   246
Diana Howard, Hon Secretary
30–36 Clareville Street
London SW7 5AW
tel 01–370 4154 or Secretary (02774) 57464

Founded 1975

Aims:
To press for the creation and proper funding of a
professional institute for the theatre.

Publications:
*Bibliography of theatre and stage design: a selected
list of books and articles published 1960 to 1970.*
Compiled by D. F. Cheshire. 1974.
Fortnightly paper.
British theatre directory (in association with John
Orford Publications).
*Directory of theatre research resources in Great
Britain. (see* 208).
*Directory of theatre research resources in Greater
London. (see* 209).
London theatres and music halls. (see 819).
Single sheet study guides.
List of publications available on request.

British Tourist Authority   247
239 Old Marylebone Road
London NW1 5QT
tel 01–262 0141 ext 46

Founded 1969

Aims:
To be responsible for promoting tourism to
Great Britain from overseas; to encourage the
provision and improvement of tourist amenities
in Great Britain as a whole, and to advise
ministers and public bodies on matters affecting
tourism in Great Britain as a whole.

Collections/Library:
The Tourist Information Library holds detailed
information on all subjects of tourist interest
within Britain, eg local guides, museums,
historic houses, castles and gardens. The
collection, started in 1946/47 under the Travel
Association of Great Britain and Ireland,
consists of 3,750 files and 2,000 books. There are
title and classified subject catalogues of books
and subject and geographical indexes to files.
Includes a photograph library of black and white
and coloured negatives and transparencies, (*see*
442).

Enquiry services and conditions of use:
The BTA deals with all enquiries within the
scope of their collection but is unable to
undertake research and compilation tasks.
Personal callers by appointment with the
Librarian. Postal and telephone enquiries
accepted.

Hours:
Mon–Fri 9.30–17.30

5.2 Guide to societies, institutions and organisations

9.39–17.30/*continued*
Publications:
Annual report.
Town trails and urban walks (*see* 9).
A wide range of tourist promotion and
information publications and brochures.
A guide to the BTA's Tourist Information
Library.
*List of books added to the Tourist Information
Library* (6 per year).

British Transport Historical Records *see* 352:
Public Record Office

British Waterways Board 248
Melbury House
Melbury Terrace
London NW1 6JX
tel 01–262 6711

Founded 1963

Aims:
To provide services and facilities on the
commercial and cruising waterways owned or
managed by them. The Board's system
comprises some 2,000 miles of canals and river
navigations (mainly in England, but including
several in Scotland and Wales), together with
their associated reservoirs, docks, warehouses
and other installations and facilities about 345 of
which are scheduled as ancient monuments or
listed as being of special architectural or historic
interest. The British Waterways Board is the
successor to the Docks and Inland Waterways
Executive of the former British Transport
Commission.

Collections/Library:
By agreement with the Transport Trust (*see*
409), a limited number of press cuttings,
periodicals and other printed material, mainly
concerned with restoration, is passed on to their
library at the University of Surrey, Guildford.

Enquiry service:
Personal, postal and telephone enquiries
accepted.

Hours:
Mon–Fri 9.00–17.30

Publications:
Annual report (published by HMSO).
Information sheets.
Posters.
Postcards.
Slides (on waterway architecture).
Canal architecture in Britain, by Frances Pratt.
A catalogue of publications is available on
request.

Activities:
The Board runs the Waterways Museum, Stoke
Bruerne, Nr Towcester, Northants NN12 7SE
(tel Northampton (0604) 862229) where many
maps, drawings and relics of canal life are
housed in an historical canalside granary. The
Waterways Board can provide a leaflet about the
museum.

Building Conservation Trust 24
39 Hampton Court Palace
East Molesey, Surrey KT8 9BS
tel 01–943 2277

Founded 1977

Aims:
The Building Conservation Trust aims to
promote the proper conservation, alteration, use
and maintenance of buildings of all types and
ages. It encourages the sympathetic conservation
of our architectural heritage and the employment
of professional expertise and craft skills and the
correct use of materials and products. In this
way it supplements and extends the activities of
many bodies working in the field of preservation
and improvement of the built environment.

Collections/Library:
A research library is in the process of being
formed at Hampton Court Palace. A permanent
exhibition will be opened at Hampton Court
Palace in 1982.

Enquiry services and conditions of use:
An information service will be established on a
'paid for' basis.

Hours:
To be announced.

Publications:
Newsletter (quarterly).

Buildings of England Office 250
Penguin Books
536 King's Road
London SW10 0UH
tel 01–351 2393

Aims:
To publish and continuously revise the *Buildings
of England* series, founding editor: Sir Nikolaus
Pevsner.

Collections/Library:
The collections include the notes,
correspondence and documentation used in the
preparation of the volumes. They also hold Peter
Ferriday's *Index of Victorian Church
Restorations*, a manuscript card index in three
drawers, organised topographically. It includes

references to the *Builder, Church builder*, etc. They are in the process of compiling detailed indexes by building type, details, etc, to the individual volumes of the *Buildings of England*. More than 13 volumes have been indexed.

Enquiry services:
None.

Publications:
Buildings of England, series. (*see* 72).

Business Archives Council   251

Denmark House
15 Tooley Street
London Bridge
London SE1 2PN
tel 01–407 6110

Founded 1934

Aims:
To provide advice for owners of business records of historical importance, to encourage businessmen to preserve their records of historical interest, to advise individual companies on modern records management and to encourage and facilitate the study of business history.

Collections/Library:
The Council has a comprehensive library of business histories for use by members. It includes sections on all areas of industry and commerce.

Enquiry services and conditions of use:
Personal, postal and telephone enquiries accepted.

Hours:
Mon–Fri 9.30–15.30

Publications:
Annual report.
Business archives (annual journal).
Newsletter (quarterly).
Broadsheets.
Prospectus.

Activities:
Courses, meetings, exhibitions and conferences.

Business Archives Council of Scotland   252

City Archives Office
PO Box 27
City Chambers
Glasgow G2 1DU

Secretary
Loanhead Transport Limited
Boghouse, Brookfield
Johnstone PA5 8UD
tel Johnstone (0505) 21555

Founded 1959

Aims:
To promote the preservation of archives which bear upon the history of commercial and industrial enterprise and of economic relationships generally; to encourage the study of such archives; and to collect information which will promote these aims.
To accept responsibility at discretion for archives which cannot otherwise be rescued from oblivion.
To undertake such publications as may further the objects of the Council.
To co-ordinate its activities with those of the Business Archives Council (*see* 251).
To establish a fund or funds to enable the objects of the Council to be carried out.

Enquiry services:
The Council does not hold records but is prepared to assist enquirers by directing them to deposit sources.

Hours:
Mon–Fri 9.15–16.45

Publications:
The Council is a co-subscriber to the periodical *Scottish industrial history*, which is published three times a year, on average. It contains articles and lists of records deposited in the period prior to publication.

Cathedrals Advisory Committee   253

83 London Wall
London EC2M 5NA
tel 01–638 0971/2

Founded 1949

Aims:
To offer advice and technical information to Deans or Provosts and Cathedral Chapters on all matters relating to the architecture, furnishing and conservation of Anglican cathedrals in England.

Collections/Library:
See Council for Places of Worship (265).

Enquiry services:
See Council for Places of Worship (265).

Activities:
The Committee meets regularly to discuss cases referred for its consideration and advice.
Organises a triennial Cathedral Architects Conference.
Organises site visits to consider alterations to cathedral fabric and furnishing.

5.2 Guide to societies, institutions and organisations

Catholic Record Society   254
c/o 114 Mount Street
London W1Y 6AH

Founded 1904

Aims:
Promotes the study of post-Reformation
Catholic history in England and Wales.

Collections/Library:
Non-indexed 'County Files' of local Catholic
history containing much factual information on
early Catholic chapels, churches and
mass-centres, but with architectural or art
information rather haphazardly collected. A fair
proportion of parish histories. Small collection of
early Catholic periodicals, magazines and
Diocesan directories, at present neither
catalogued nor indexed, but which might
contain a good deal of information on the
19th-century building and furnishing of Catholic
churches. A good deal of unexplored
biographical information on Catholic architects
and craftsmen, particularly of the 17th and 18th
centuries, is scattered through their publications.

Enquiry services and conditions of use:
Personal (after an appointment by post) and
postal enquiries accepted.

Publications:
Annual report.
Recusant history (twice yearly journal).
Monographs.
The Catholic Record Society, 1904–1972: a
descriptive catalogue of its publications with a
subject index of their contents.

Cement and Concrete Association   255
Wexham Springs
Slough SL3 6PL
tel Fulmer (395) 2727

Founded 1935

Aims:
To encourage and promote a high standard of
concrete design and construction.

Collections/Library:
The main subjects covered by the library are
concrete technology and concrete product data
literature, but the history of concrete structures
is also included.

Enquiry services and conditions of use:
Personal, postal and telephone enquiries
accepted.

Hours:
Mon–Fri 9.00–17.00

Centre for Industrial Archaeology,
Kingston Polytechnic *see* 409: Transport Trust

Centre for the History of Technology,
Science and Society *see* 337: National Record
of Industrial Monuments

Charles Rennie Mackintosh Society   256
Queen's Cross
870 Garscube Road
Glasgow G2
tel Glasgow (041) 946 6600
or Killearn (0360) 50595
(Secretary's home telephone)

Founded 1973

Aims:
To foster interest in and conserve the buildings
and artefacts designed by Mackintosh and his
associates. To build up a collection of Charles
Rennie Mackintosh reference material.

Collections/Library:
Small collection of books and journals referring
to Charles Rennie Mackintosh. Press cuttings
since 1973.

Enquiry services and conditions of use:
The Society tries to answer general enquiries
and is particularly interested in arranging for
parties of students and others to see Mackintosh
buildings. Personal, postal and telephone
enquiries accepted.

Hours:
Mon, Tues and Thurs 12.00–17.30
Sun 14.30–17.30

Publications:
Newsletter (quarterly).

Activities:
Photographic exhibitions.
Tape-slide programmes.
Lectures, dicussions.
Study weekends for members.
Tours for members (eg Barcelona, Vienna etc).

Chiltern Open Air Museum   257
Newland Park
Goreland's Lane
Chalfont St Giles, Bucks.
tel Chalfont St Giles (02407) 71117

Aims:
An open air museum of vernacular buildings
which is devoted to demonstrating the growth
and development, from earliest times to the
present, of human settlement in the Chiltern
Hills.

Collections/Library:
When the museum opened in 1981, five buildings had been re-erected on the site: a thatched, cruck-framed barn from Arborfield; a reconstruction of an iron-age hut; a 19th-century cart shed from Didcot; a 19th-century baker's granary from Wing; and a farm granary from Rossway. A brick toll house and a chair-making factory from High Wycombe have been started. Several other buildings are awaiting reconstruction.

Hours:
Museum: May–Sept, Sun and bank holidays 14.00–17.30

Church Commissioners for England 258
1 Millbank
London SW1P 3JZ
tel 01–222 7010

Founded 1948

Aims:
To manage efficiently the historic endowments of the Church of England. To carry out administrative and quasi-judicial functions in connection with the reorganisation of pastoral supervision and the future of redundant churches. Established by the uniting of Queen Anne's Bounty (1704) and the Ecclesiastical Commissioners (1836), under the Church Commissioners Measure 1947.

Collections/Library:
In some cases the medieval fabric rolls and other documents connected with the history of the buildings of collegiate and some former monastic churches are now in the possession of the Church Commissioners.
Records of the Commissioners for Building New Churches under the Act of 1818 are preserved by the Church Commissioners (*see* 306 and 319), and the Commissioners' printed reports were issued as Parliamentary Papers between 1821 and 1856. Most of the new churches were in the suburbs of London or in the industrial towns of the Midlands and North. A complete list appears in M. H. Port, *Six hundred new churches* (1961) (*see* 793), and for London in Gerald Lawrence Carr, *The Commissioners' churches of London* (1976) (*see* 758).

Hours:
Mon–Fri 9.00–17.00

Publications:
Annual report.
Parsonage houses – a guide to their improvement and replacement. 1975.
G. F. A. Best, *Temporal pillars* (Cambridge, 1964). The standard source for the history of the Church Commissioners.

C. E. Welch. 'The Records of the Church Commissioners' in *Journal of the Society of Archivists* (vol 1, 1955).
E. J. Robinson. 'The Records of the Church Commissioners' in *Journal of the Society of Archivists* (vol 3, 1968).

The Cinema Theatre Association 259
c/o Marcus Eavis, Hon Secretary
123b Central Road
Worcester Park
Surrey KT4 8DU

Founded 1967

Aims:
To promote interest in and to provide an organisation for those already interested in the history, architecture and technical equipment of film exhibition. Purpose built cinemas are the primary concern, although the Association encompasses buildings adapted from other uses, such as live theatres and music halls.

Collections/Library:
The Cinema Theatre Association archive, currently stored in a theatre in south London, mainly consists of photographs, programmes, tickets, newscuttings, and other printed ephemera of cinemas (and some legitimate theatres) existing and disappeared. The Association is just starting a collection of larger items such as seating, cinema café plate, etc. The archive also contains the results of research by members of the Association into their local cinemas.

Enquiry services and conditions of use:
The Archivist should be contacted, care of the Hon Secretary, for permission to use the archive and will also help with research as far as possible. Personal visits and postal enquiries accepted.

Hours:
The Association is voluntary so visits to the archive have to be either in the evenings or on Sundays.

Publications:
Bulletin (6 per year to members). Carries news of cinema developments (openings, closures, conversions) throughout the country; also feature articles on cinema histories – construction, architecture, technical details of projection and stage facilities, chronological development.
Directory of cinemas. Compiled by Keith Skone and Malcolm Gilden. 1980.
Photographs.
Books.

Activities:
Regular visits to cinemas and theatres which give

give/*continued*
members the opportunity to inspect particular
buildings in detail. Most visits in the London
area, but many now being organised in
provincial locations. Usually seven or eight visits
per year. Always held on Sundays and generally
at least two properties visited.
Occasional lectures, slide evenings and social
events.

Civic Trust   260
17 Carlton House Terrace
London SW1Y 5AW
tel 01–930 0914

Associate Trusts:

Civic Trust for the North East
34/5 Saddler Street
Durham DH1 3NU
tel Durham (0385) 61 182

Civic Trust for the North West
56 Oxford Street
Manchester M1 6EU
tel Manchester (061) 236 7464

Scottish Civic Trust
24 George Square
Glasgow G2 1EF
tel Glasgow (041) 221 1466/7

Civic Trust for Wales/Treftadaeth Cymru
Welcome House
Llandaff
Cardiff CF5 2YZ
tel Cardiff (0222) 567701

Founded 1957

Aims:
Voluntary organisation founded to raise
environment standards. Encourages quality in
architecture and town planning and the
preservation of buildings of architectural or
historic merit. Supports and advises over 1,300
local amenity societies. Provided the UK
Secretariat for European Architectural Heritage
Year. Administers the Architectural Heritage
Fund, which provdes loan capital to local
building preservation trusts; on behalf of the
Historic Buildings Council, government grant
aid to non-outstanding conservation areas; and
also on behalf of the Department of the
Environment, the work of the Heritage
Education Group.

Collections/Library:
Reference library:
        Approximately 4,500 books and pamphlets
covering conservation, planning, architecture,
roads and transport, and planning legislation.
        Periodicals, trade literature, annual reports,
conference material relating to the environment.

A unique collection of local amenity society
publications. (It is a requirement of registration
that each society sends its publications.)
        The main collection and society collection
have separate author catalogues; the former also
has a limited subject catalogue. In addition there
is an information index to the information files.

Slide and photographic collection:
        An extensive colour slide and black and
white photographic collection on similar topics
to the book stock, including all schemes that
have received Civic Trust Awards and
commendations since 1959.
        Arranged by subject matter; no catalogue.
        Slides and photographs are for reference
and loan. Up-to-date charges for loan and
purchase are available from the library.

Films and an exhibition are available for hire.

Enquiry services and conditions of use:
Postal enquiries preferred. Personal callers by
appointment only.

Hours:
Mon–Fri 9.30–12.30 and 14.00–17.30

Publications:
A catalogue of publications and visual aids is
available from the Civic Trust, including a list o
more than 700 local amenity societies registered
with the Trust.
Environmental directory gives details of about
300 organisations (*see* 201).
Heritage centres. A list of existing centres and
embryo centres is available on request.
Heritage outlook: the journal of the Civic Trust
(formerly *Civic Trust news*) (six per year).

Committee for Environmental   26
Conservation (CoEnCo)
29 Greville Street
London EC1N 8AX
tel 01–242 9647

Founded 1969

Aims:
A national coalition of UK non-governmental
organisations (NGOs) focusing on major
environmental problems, including those of the
built environment. It is a central agency
designed to promote concerted action by NGOs
and make representations to government and
other bodies on their behalf. Its members
include the Ancient Monuments Society, Civic
Trust, Council for British Archaeology,
Georgian Group, National Trust and National
Trust for Scotland, Royal Society of Arts,
Society for the Protection of Ancient Buildings,
Town and Country Planning Association and
the Victorian Society.

Collections/Library:
None.

Enquiry services:
Postal enquiries only.

Hours:
Mon–Fri 9.30–16.00

Publications:
Annual report (includes a list of publications).

Commonwealth War Graves Commission   262
2 Marlow Road
Maidenhead, Berkshire SL6 7DX
tel Maidenhead (0628) 34221

Founded 1917

Aims:
Established as the Imperial War Graves
Commission; assumed its present title in 1960.
Provides for the permanent marking and care of
the graves of members of the Commonwealth
Forces who died in the 1914–1918 and
1939–1945 Wars. Builds memorials to those who
have no known grave and keeps records and
registers, including, after the Second World
War, a record of the civilian war dead.

Collections/Library:
Photographic and documentary archives.
The Commission has compiled cemetery and
memorial registers for the two World Wars.
Civilian war dead register for the Second World
War.

Enquiry services and conditions of use:
The enquiries dept will trace a particular grave
or memorial commemoration location, given as
much as possible of the following data about the
casualty: full name, rank, unit, date of death,
number, age, home town, place of death. In
most cases the Commission is able to supply, for
a small fee and given sufficient time, black and
white photographs of individual graves or names
on memorials, as well as general views of
cemeteries and memorials. Personal, postal and
telephone enquiries accepted.

Hours:
Mon–Fri 8.30–12.30; 13.30–17.00

Publications:
Annual report.
Philip Longworth, *The unending vigil: a history of
the Commonwealth War Graves Commission
1917–1967.* Constable, 1967.
Their name liveth. A series of books containing
photographs and descriptions of war cemeteries
and memorials of both World Wars (Methuen
and HMSO).

Companies House *see* 359: Registry of
Business Names

Conway Library *see* 446: Courtauld Institute
of Art, Conway Library

Corporation of Trinity House   263
Trinity House
Tower Hill
London EC3N 4DH
tel 01–480 6601 Public Relations Officer, ext 231

Founded 1514

Aims:
Trinity House has three main functions: it is the
general lighthouse authority for England, Wales,
the Channel Islands and Gibraltar; it is the
principal pilotage authority in the UK; it is a
charitable body.

Enquiry services and conditions of use:
All enquiries to be addressed to the Public
Relations Officer.

Publications:
Flash (half-yearly journal).
The Trinity House Gazette (bi-monthly tabloid).

Council for British Archaeology   264
112 Kennington Road
London SE11 6RE
tel 01–582 0494

Founded 1944

Aims:
The Council for British Archaeology replaced
the Congress of Archaeological Societies, a body
formed during the 19th century to represent
national and county archaeological societies. The
Council co-ordinates archaeological activities in
the British Isles, promotes research in
archaeology, and the preservation of ancient
monuments and historic buildings. The Council
is one of the bodies to whom all applications to
demolish listed buildings are submitted
statutorily.

Collections/Library:
None.

Enquiry service:
General archaeological enquiries: careers,
courses, digs.

Publications:
Annual report.
*Archaeological bibliography for Great Britain and
Ireland* (annual). 1946–72 available on

5.2 Guide to societies, institutions and organisations

available on/*continued*
microfiche, with printed introductory handlist
and cumulated index, from Oxford Microform
Publications.
Archaeology in Britain (annual).
Archaeology of Lincoln.
Archaeology of York.
British archaeological abstracts (semi-annual);
available on microfiche from Oxford Microform
Publications.
Historic buildings and planning policies, by David
Peace. (1979).
Newsletter and calendar of excavations (monthly,
March–Jan).
Research report series.
A catalogue of publications is available on
request.

Council for Places of Worship   265
From March 1981,
Council for the Care of Churches
83 London Wall
London EC2M 5NA
tel 01–638 0971/2

Founded 1921

Aims:
Co-ordination of the work of the 42 Diocesan
Advisory Committees. Provision of advice and
information on all aspects of the fabric and
furnishing of Church of England parish
churches and chapels, including conservation
and maintenance. Encouragement of
contemporary architects and craftsmen.
Provision of advice on the layout of new
churches and the re-arrangement of existing
churches. The Council has the statutory
function of advising on merits of churches which
may be affected by pastoral reorganisation. On
March 1, 1981 it reverted to its former title, the
Council for the Care of Churches.

Collections/Library:
Reference collection of c12,000 volumes and 112
periodical titles, including annual reports of
Friends of Cathedrals. About 15,000 survey files
on individual parish churches and cathedrals,
with illustrations, early postcards, photographs,
guide books, press cuttings, correspondence,
etc. The library collects information on artists
and craftsmen involved in church work,
maintains files on construction and conservation
work and special collections on wall-paintings,
spires and sculptured crosses. It can provide
information on ecclesiastical art and architecture
(including church furnishings), ecclesiology,
conservation of works of art in churches, with
particular reference to the churches and
cathedrals of the Church of England. Anyone
engaged in researching the history of a particular
Anglican church will benefit by a visit to the
library. There is a card catalogue (dictionary
catalogue) to the collection. The library of the

late Canon Basil Clarke, which includes a
collection of twentieth-century postcards and a
unique series of manuscript notebooks annotated
with details of church architects, restorers and
builders, has recently been acquired.

The slide collection contains 4,500 slides for loan
(a catalogue of the slides is available for sale).
Churches and cathedrals are arranged by county

Enquiry services and conditions of use:
Postal and telephone enquiries accepted.
Personal callers preferably by prior
appointment. Available to the public.

Hours:
Mon–Fri 10.00–13.00; 14.00–17.30

Publications:
Newsletter (annual). From 1981 entitled
Churchscape.
Series of technical publications.
Writing a church guide.
List of publications available from the Council.

Council for Small Industries in Rural Areas   26
(CoSIRA)
Queen's House
Fish Row
Salisbury, Wilts SP1 1EX
tel Salisbury (0722) 24411

Founded 1921

Aims:
CoSIRA is charged with improving the
prosperity of small businesses in the
countryside, particularly in specified rural areas
where the population is declining or which are in
other ways disadvantaged or deprived. About
10,000 small firms are already being helped by
means of advice, training and finance. Building,
equipment and working capital loans approved
annually amount to some £5,000,000. CoSIRA
is an agency of the Development Commission
whose main objective is to regenerate the rural
areas of England and to create viable and
prosperous communities.

Enquiry service:
Professional consultancy, advisory and training
services are available on a wide range of subjects
some of which are related to architecture, such a
thatching.
Personal, postal and telephone enquiries
accepted.

Publications:
Craft workshops in the countryside (annual).
List of publications available from the Council.
Includes: *Wrought ironwork, Decorative
ironwork, The Thatcher's craft.* Select list of
books and information sources on trades, crafts
and small industries in rural areas.

Council for the Care of Churches *see* 265:
Council for Places of Worship

Council for the Protection of Rural England   267
4 Hobart Place
London SW1W 0HY
tel 01–235 9481

Founded 1926

Aims:
To organise concerted action to improve, protect
and preserve the rural scenery and amenities of
the English countryside, its towns and villages,
and to act as a centre for furnishing or procuring
advice and information. It also seeks to educate
public opinion and to take such action as may be
necessary to ensure the promotion of these aims.
There are branches in most counties. The
equivalent body in Scotland is the Association
for the Protection of Rural Scotland (*se*. 228).

Collections/Library:
There is a reference library. Collections of
photographs and slides. No catalogue.

Enquiry services and conditions of use:
Information service on rural matters affecting
countryside planning and on other organisations
dealing with specific aspects of conservation.
Personal callers (preferably by appointment),
postal and telephone enquiries accepted.

Hours:
Mon–Fri 9.30–17.30

Publications:
Annual report.
Background, a monthly digest of press and
parliamentary matters.
Bulletin (quarterly).
Printed reports.

Council for the Protection of Rural Wales   268
14 Broad Street
Welshpool
Powys SY21 7SD
tel Welshpool (0938) 2525

Founded 1928

Aims:
To organise concerted action to secure the
protection and improvement of rural scenery
and of the amenities of the countryside and
towns and villages in Wales and
Monmouthshire.
To act as a centre for furnishing or procuring
advice and information upon any matters
affecting such protection and improvement.
To arouse, form and educate opinion in order to
ensure the promotion of the aforesaid objects.

Collections/Library:
Collection of and lists of, publications and
reports relevant to countryside, planning and
conservation. Slides.

Enquiry services and conditions of use:
Personal, postal and telephone enquiries
accepted.

Hours:
Normal office hours.

Publications:
Annual report.
Newsletters.

Activities:
Seminars, conferences, meetings.

Courtauld Institute of Art, Book Library   269
University of London
20 Portman Square
London W1H 0BE
tel 01–935 9292 ext 14

Founded 1933

Aims:
To provide a library of books, exhibition
catalogues and periodicals for the Institute's
registered students and teaching staff.

Collections/Library:
The scope of the collection is the European fine
arts and architecture from the Early Christian
period. Of the more than 80,000 books,
approximately 2,500 are on British architecture.
Of the nearly 200 periodical titles received, 12
are architectural, though there are many dead
files in addition.

Enquiry services and conditions of use:
Regular access to books and periodicals, and
book loans, are restricted to students and staff of
the Institute. Other enquirers may be given
access to material not available elsewhere in
London, but must in the first place apply to the
Institute's librarians.

Hours:
Mon–Fri 9.30–19.00 during term
Mon–Fri 10.00–18.00 during vacations
Closed throughout August.

Courtauld Institute of Art, Conway Library
see 446: Courtauld Institute of Art, Conway
Library

Crown Estate Commissioners   270
13–15 Carlton House Terrace
London SW1Y 5AH
tel 01–214 6000

5.2 Guide to societies, institutions and organisations

01–214 6000/*continued*
Founded 1956

Aims:
On behalf of the Crown, to manage and turn to
account land and other property, rights and
interests; and to hold such of the property, rights
and interests under their management as for any
reason cannot be vested in the Crown, or can
more conveniently be vested in the
Commissioners. The Crown Estate
Commissioners are successors to the
Commissioners of Crown Lands (constituted
under the Crown Lands Acts 1829 to 1843),
which were successors to the Commissioners of
Woods.

Collections/Library:
The records are important for building
developments on royal estates such as Regent's
Park.

Enquiry services and conditions of use:
Postal and telephone enquiries accepted. Letters
to The Secretary, Crown Estate Commissioners,
Crown Estate Office. Tel numbers for enquiries
01–214 6439 or 214 6561.

Hours:
Mon–Fri 9.00–17.00

Publications:
Annual report (published by HMSO).
R. B. Pugh, *The Crown Estate* (HMSO, 1960).

Activities:
The Crown Estate Commissioners administer
the hereditary Land Revenue of the Crown. The
Estate includes properties in England, Wales and
Scotland, Windsor Great Park, and most of the
foreshore and seabed round the coast of the
United Kingdom.

Decorative Arts Society 1890–1914 271
c/o The Keeper of Applied Art
Royal Pavilion
Art Gallery and Museum
Brighton, Sussex BN1 1UE
tel Brighton (0273) 603005

Founded 1975

Aims:
A registered charity established to encourage an
interest in, and research into, the decorative arts
in Europe, America and Great Britain from 1890
to 1914. The term 'decorative arts' is used in the
broadest sense; it includes such areas as
architecture, interior and industrial design,
fashions and textiles, theatre, ballet and film
design and the graphic arts.

Publications:
Journal (annual).

Department of Education and Science 272
Elizabeth House
York Road
London SE1 7PH
tel 01–928 9222

Aims (in present context):
Carries out improvements in the standards of
design of state schools. Research into the
development of educational buildings generally.

Collections/Library:
Material relating to the work of the Department.

Enquiry services and conditions of use:
Mainly for official use, but may sometimes be
used for reference by *bona-fide* research workers.

Publications:
Building bulletins.
Handbooks.
Pamphlets.
School standards.

Department of Finance, Works Division 273
Library
Room 1408
Churchill House
Victoria Square
Belfast BT1 4QW
tel Belfast (0232) 34343 extns 441, 338

Founded 1956

Aims:
The Department of Finance, Works Division, is
responsible for the design, construction and
maintenance of buildings for Northern Ireland
Departments, Police Authority, Post Office and
the Northern Ireland Office of the United
Kingdom government. The library provides a
service for the professional, technical and
administrative staff of the Department of
Finance engaged in the design and maintenance
of public buildings and works.

Collections/Library:
The library collections cover all aspects of
building and engineering and comprise about
1,000 books, 50 journal titles, 600 slides and 100
photographs.

Enquiry services and conditions of use:
Personal, postal and telephone enquiries
accepted.

Hours:
Mon–Fri 8.30–17.00

Publications:
Library bulletin consisting of abstracts of new
books and library activities.

Department of Health and Social Security   274
Euston Tower
286 Euston Road
London NW1 3DN
tel 01–388 1188
Architectural Division extns 359, 321, 293
Engineering Division extns 333, 223, 225
Library ext 206

Aims:
Carries out research into the design and
construction of health buildings.

Collections/Library:
Material relating to the work of the Department,
ie architectural, engineering and related aspects
of buildings for the health and social services.
The Health Buildings Library holds a
collection, begun in 1960 and terminated in
1973, of about 1,000 monochrome slides and
5,000 colour transparencies of hospital
buildings. A subject index to the collection is
held in the library. Loans are made to *bona fide*
researchers only. Copy prints are not available.
Access to the collection is by prior appointment
only.

Enquiry services and conditions of use:
Normally for staff of health and local authorities.
The Health Buildings Library is primarily for
the use of officers of the department.

Hours:
Mon–Fri 9.00–17.00

Publications:
Hospital abstracts.
Hospital building bulletins.
Hospital building notes.
Hospital equipment notes.
Hospital/Health service design notes.
Hospital technical memoranda.
Local authority building notes and design guides.

Departments of the Environment and   275
Transport Library
Headquarters:
2 Marsham Street
London SW1P 3EB
tel 01–212 4847/8/50 (General enquiries)
    01–212 4844 (Headquarters Library)
    01–212 4842 (Chief Librarian)

Branches:
Architects Sub-Library,
Becket House
Lambeth Palace Road
London SE1 7ER
tel 01–928 7855 ext 513

Countryside Commission Library
John Dower House

Crescent Place
Cheltenham
Gloucestershire GL50 3RA
tel Cheltenham (0242) 21381

Directorate of Ancient Monuments and Historic
Buildings Library (*see* 276)
Fortress House
23 Savile Row
London W1X 2HE
tel 01–734 6010 ext 323

St Christopher House Sub-Library (Transport
Engineering)
Room G/44
Southwark Street
London SE1 0TE
tel 01–928 7999 ext 2891

Central Water Planning Unit Library
Reading Bridge House
Reading
Berkshire RG1 8PS
tel Reading (0734) 57551

Aims:
The Department of the Environment has a wide
range of responsibilities, all concerned with the
physical environment.

Collections/Library:
Over 200,000 books, pamphlets, memoranda etc
and more than 2,500 periodical titles. Collections
cover housing; local government; regional
planning; town and country planning; new and
expanded towns; roads; traffic; transport (road,
railway, inland waterways, etc); environmental
pollution; water supply; sewage; countryside;
sport and recreation; ports. There are special
collections of development and structure plans;
local acts (from 1780); Ministry of Housing and
Local Government circulars (from 1848).

For slide and photograph collections *see* 448 and
449.

Enquiry services and conditions of use:
Open to accredited researchers and professional
staff of local authorities and of new towns by
appointment on written application.

Hours:
Mon–Fri 10.00–17.00

Publications:
DOE/DTp Annual list of publications.
DOE/DTp Library bulletin (fortnightly).
DOE/DTp Register of research.
Department of the Environment Library.
Catalogues. (*see* 18).
Department publications can be obtained from
the DOE/DTp South Ruislip Sub-Library,
Building 6, Victoria Road, South Ruislip,
Middlesex HA4 0NZ, tel 01–845 7788.

**Department of the Environment.
Directorate of Ancient Monuments and
Historic Buildings (England)**
 23 Savile Row
 London W1X 2HE
 tel 01–734 6010 Library: ext 323

276

Aims:
The Directorate of Ancient Monuments and
Historic Buildings of the Department of the
Environment is the official body in England
responsible for conserving historic and
man-made features of the land. In Wales and
Scotland similar functions are carried out by the
Welsh and Scottish Offices (*see* 420 and 385) and
appropriate branches of the Department of the
Environment on behalf of the respective
Secretaries of State.
 The Department of the Environment
compiles lists of buildings of special architectural
or historical interest as a guide for local planning
authorities. Such lists are prepared by the
Department's investigators of historic buildings
in accordance with standards of quality, age, and
interest recommended by the Historic Buildings
Councils and approved by the Secretary of State.
Listed buildings are classified into Grades I, II*
and II to indicate their relative importance. A
listed building may not be demolished or altered
without the consent of the local planning
authority. Over 200,000 buildings throughout
England are now listed and some 18,000 more
are added each year. They range from the
earliest survivors to examples of
twentieth-century architecture, and cover every
type, domestic, industrial, ornamental etc. In
practice all buildings surviving almost intact
from before 1700 are listed. There is more
selection for buildings of 1700 to 1800 and still
greater selection for buildings of 1830 to 1914,
which tend to be the works of principal
architects of the period or industrial buildings.
There are over 100 post-1914 listed buildings,
some of which are examples of the Modern
Movement.
 The Ancient Monuments Acts empower
the Secretary of State to protect and preserve
outstanding monuments and, with the
guidance of the Ancient Monuments Board, to
schedule those whose preservation is of
national importance.
 In addition to individual buildings of
architectural or historical interest, whole
districts can be designated as legally protected
conservation areas.

Collections/Library:
The Ancient Monuments Branch (23 Savile
Row) maintains a small library (books etc on
archaeology, architecture, county histories,
historic buildings and monuments, local
history and a special collection of books and
prints dealing with topography, architecture
and buildings of London – the Mayson Beeton
Collection), which is open to the public,

Mon–Fri 9.30–16.30. For additional
collections and enquiry services *see* Royal
Commission on Historical Monuments
(England) incorporating the National
Monuments Record (365) and Departments of
the Environment and Transport Library (275)

Publications:
A full list of Department of the Environment
guides can be found in Government
Publications: Sectional List 27: *Ancient
monuments and historic buildings* (*see* 1).

*Department of the Environment Mayson Beeton
collection: guide to a collection of topographical
prints of London and the home counties from
1420–1930.* Compiled by Dorothy Parsons.
(Occasional paper no 1). London: Department
of the Environment, Directorate of Ancient
Monuments and Historic Buildings Library,
1974, 75pp. This is an index to the Mayson
Beeton collection of prints which is held in the
Library of the Directorate of Ancient
Monuments and Historic Buildings. The
collection consists of over 1,000 volumes,
mainly on London topography, architecture
and archaeology, and between three to four
thousand prints which include views,
elevations and social scenes of London. The
prints are filed topographically by location,
title and date. The guide lists the headings
used in identifying each print, eg Buckingham
Palace, and the location of the print. The guide
is arranged in two sections, a title index and a
subject index.

**Department of the Environment, Historic
Buildings Bureau** *see* 299: Historic Buildings
Bureau

**Department of the Environment. Property
Services Agency** *see* 350: Property Services
Agency

**Department of the Environment. Regional
offices concerned with listed buildings
casework.**
 East Midlands Regional Office
 Department of the Environment
 Cranbrook House
 Cranbrook Street
 Nottingham NG1 1EY
 tel Nottingham (0602) 46121

277

  Area: Derbyshire, Leicestershire, Lincolnshire,
  Northamptonshire, Nottinghamshire

 Greater London Area
 Department of the Environment
 25 Savile Row
 London W1X 2BT
 tel 01–734 6010

Area: Greater London

Northern Regional Office
Department of the Environment
Wellbar House
Gallow Gate
Newcastle upon Tyne NE1 4TU
tel Newcastle upon Tyne (0632) 27575

    Area: Cleveland, Cumbria, Durham,
    Northumberland, Tyne and Wear

North West Regional Office
Department of the Environment
Sunley Buildings
Piccadilly Plaza
Manchester M1 4AX
tel Manchester (061) 832 9111

    Area: Cheshire, Lancashire, Greater
    Manchester, Merseyside

South East and East Anglia
Department of the Environment
Charles House
375 Kensington High Street
London S14 8QH
tel 01–603 3444

    Area: Bedfordshire, Berkshire,
    Buckinghamshire, Cambridge, Essex,
    Hampshire, Hertfordshire, Isle of Wight, Kent,
    Norfolk, Oxfordshire, East and West Suffolk,
    Surrey, East and West Sussex

South West Regional Office
Department of the Environment
Croomsgate House
Rupert Street
Bristol BS1 2QN
tel Bristol (0272) 297201

    Area: Avon, Cornwall, Devon, Dorset,
    Gloucestershire, Somerset, Wiltshire

West Midland Regional Office
Department of the Environment
Fiveways House
Islington Row
Birmingham 15
tel Birmingham (012) 643 8191

    Area: Hereford and Worcester, Salop,
    Staffordshire, Warwickshire, West Midlands

Yorkshire and Humberside Regional Office
Department of the Environment
City House
Leeds LS1 4JD
tel Leeds (0532) 38232

    Area: Humberside, Yorkshire (North, South
    and West)

Department of the Environment for Northern Ireland

278

Parliament Buildings
Stormont
Belfast BT4 3SS
tel Belfast (0232) 63210

Aims:
Responsible for housing, planning,
comprehensive development and the listing and
preservation of historic buildings and ancient
monuments.

Department of the Environment for Northern Ireland, Historic Monuments and Buildings Branch

279

Archaeological Survey
66 Balmoral Avenue
Belfast BT9 6NY
tel Belfast (0232) 661621

Historic Monuments and Buildings Branch
1 Connsbrook Avenue
Holywood Road
Belfast BT4 1EH
tel Belfast (0232) 653251/4
(For listing, grant-aid and conservation areas)

Founded 1951

Aims:
The branch of government dealing with the
recording, protection and presentation of
historic monuments and objects of
archaeological or historic interest in Northern
Ireland. Its activities include a county-by-county
archaeological and architectural survey for
publication; listing buildings of special
architectural or historic interest (since 1973);
scheduling important monuments; conservation
and presentation of monuments; excavation of
threatened sites; and maintenance of a
comprehensive record.

Collections/Library:
Building records, descriptions, drawings and
photographs are stored at Balmoral Avenue,
indexed by subjects and locations. They are
gathered partly for the county volumes and
partly as rescue recordings of threatened
buildings which may be included in later
inventories. The Survey office holds an *Index of
Architects* (begun 1969) made by Hugh Dixon,
first as research assistant to Dr A. Rowan for the
Buildings of Ireland series, then as Fellow of the
Institute of Irish Studies, Queen's University,
and lately as Senior Inspector in the Branch.
When possible the Survey acquires or borrows
for copying, collections of photographs
(archaeological, antiquarian, topographical and
architectural). For example, the part-set of
photographs taken by Dr Rowan for the
Buildings of Ireland: North West Ulster came by
agreement with Queen's University from the
Institute of Irish Studies.

Studies./*continued*

Enquiry services and conditions of use:
In the first instance enquiries should be made to
the Historic Monuments and Buildings Branch,
1 Connsbrook Avenue, where reference to other
collections (local museums, the Public Record
Office of Northern Ireland, private collections)
may be made.

Publications:
List of publications available.

Activities:
The Branch has a close association with the
Ulster Archaeological Society, whose annual
volume, *Ulster journal of archaeology*, contains
much architectural material. It also maintains a
close association with the Ulster Architectural
Heritage Society.

Design and Industries Association 280
2 Carlton House Terrace
London SW1Y 5AL
tel 01–940 4925

Founded 1915

Aims:
The DIA was set up by a group of architects,
designers, industrialists and retailers, to
encourage government, industry, educationalists
and the consumer to improve design standards.
Its ideas were adopted by government and later
led to the forming of the Design Council and the
opening of the Design Centre. The DIA is a
voluntary, independent pressure group whose
membership is open to everyone—companies,
educational establishments and individuals.

Collections/Library:
Some DIA archives are held at the British
Architectural Library (*see* 236) and listed in the
National Register of Archives list (*see below*).

Enquiry services:
Postal or telephone enquiries should be
addressed to the Secretary, Mrs Nell
Chamberlain, 17 Lawn Crescent, Kew Gardens,
Surrey TW9 3NR, tel 01–940 4925.

Publications:
Yearbook with a list of members and reports of
the year's activities.
Various booklets, leaflets or pamphlets on design
matters are published from time to time.
Regular newsletters and press releases are
circulated to members and the media.
Noel Carrington, *Industrial Design in Britain*
(London: Allen and Unwin, 1977) deals with the
history of the DIA between 1915 and 1945.
*Index to the printed and manuscript material
concerning the Design and Industries Association*
(London: Historical Manuscripts Commission,
1972).

Activities:
The DIA organises, promotes or sponsors
overseas study tours, conferences, seminars,
talks and visits. Regular lunchtime talks, evening
meetings and one-day seminars are held in
London and in the regions.

Design History Society 28
c/o Secretary, Penny Sparke
Dept of Art History
Faculty of Art and Design
Brighton Polytechnic
Grand Parade
Brighton, Sussex BN2 2JY
tel Brighton (0273) 604141

Founded 1977

Aims:
To promote interest in design history studies; to
help organise an annual conference in design; to
help research projects in the subject; to help
publish papers and research material in design
history.

Collections/Library:
The Society is compiling a list of unpublished
research projects in design history, from
educational sources, museums and private
individuals. A register of research was published
in the Design History Society *Newsletter* (no 9,
Nov 1980, pp 19–33, with additions and
amendments in no 10, Feb 1981, pp 41–42). No
library or collections.

Publications:
Newsletter (quarterly).
Conference proceedings.
The Society aims to secure the publication of
papers on design history presented by members
at conferences and meetings.

Activities:
Meetings.
Annual conference.

Doctor Williams's Library 28
14 Gordon Square
London WC1H 0AG
tel 01–387 3727

Founded 1729

Collections/Library:
Mainly, but not exclusively, nonconformist. The
collections do not relate specifically to
nonconformist architecture or architects,
although such information may be found here.

Hours:
Mon, Wed, Fri 10.00–17.00
Tues and Thurs 10.00–18.30

Ecclesiastical Architects' and Surveyors' Association   283

c/o The Hon Secretary
32/34 Mosley Street
Newcastle upon Tyne NE1 1DF
tel Newcastle upon Tyne (0632) 23884

Founded 1872

Aims:
Founded in 1872 as the association of 'Surveyors of Ecclesiastical Dilapidations' when the Ecclesiastical Dilapidations Acts 1871–72 introduced a new system of inspection of dilapidations and settlement of claims for these, supplementing the Gilbert Acts of 1776 onwards, and bringing in Queen Anne's Bounty as a central authority. The name was modified to its present form in 1953 to embrace the widening activities of the Association's membership. Membership of the Association includes Diocesan Surveyors holding appointments under the Repair to Benefice Buildings Measure 1972 and its precursors the Ecclesiastical Dilapidations Measures 1923–1951 and Acts 1871–72; architects and surveyors appointed to cathedrals and cathedral official residences under the Cathedrals Measure 1963; those holding appointments as church architects having under their practices care and repair of churches; members of the official architects' and surveyors' staffs of the Church Commissioners engaged on the provision or care of episcopal houses, parsonage houses or churches; also those known to have knowledge and experience of church architecture and the conservation of historic buildings, or the design and construction and the conservation of historic buildings, or the design and construction of new churches, clergy houses, and other church buildings. It is the aim of the Association to serve as a forum for architects and surveyors professionally engaged in work relating to church property in its widest aspects and belonging to any Christian denomination. Among its membership there is a fairly high proportion of architects specialising in conservation work on churches.

Enquiry services and conditions of use:
The Association is not administratively equipped to deal with matters other than for its own members.

Publications:
Occasional papers
Regular newsletters, reports, etc.
Ecclesiastical Architects' and Surveyors Association centenary booklet 1972, includes a short account of the history of Ecclesiastical Dilapidations, as well as the work of the Association.

Ecclesiological Society   284

S. C. Humphrey, Hon Secretary
1 Cornish House
Otto Street
London SE17 3PE

Founded 1839

Aims:
Founded in 1839 as the Cambridge Camden Society, its aims were to exercise vigilance over the design and fittings of new churches, to preserve and restore existing medieval churches, and to introduce the spirit of Catholic worship into the Anglican liturgy. In 1846 it changed its name to the Ecclesiological, late Cambridge Camden Society, and in 1856 to the Ecclesiological Society, which was dissolved and resurrected as the St Paul's Ecclesiological Society, which was reorganised in 1937, resuming the name Ecclesiological Society.

Collections/Library:
Lantern slide collection.
Some early archives of the Society are to be found in the British Architectural Library (*see* 236).

Publications:
The Ecclesiologist, 1841–1868 (*see* 193).
Newsletter. No 1, Sept 1980 includes the first part of a list of all the Society's publications from its foundation in 1839. The first list includes all the books and booklets published since 1942, but excludes occasional papers, which will be treated separately in a later newsletter.
S. C. Humphrey, *Primary sources for the architectural history of Anglican churches in the nineteenth century* (1981).
James F. White, *The Cambridge movement: the ecclesiologists and the gothic revival* (Cambridge University Press, 1962). An account of the work of the Cambridge Camden Society and its successors, which includes a list of the Society's publications from 1839–1864 (*see* 797).

Activities:
Visits.

Edinburgh City Libraries   285

Central Library
George IV Bridge
Edinburgh EH1 1EG
tel Edinburgh (031) 225 5584

Founded 1890

Aims:
Public library.

Collections/Library:
There are three subject departments with

departments with/*continued*
relevant architectural sources; in addition
material on allied subjects such as transportation
is available in Central Home Reading and
Central Reference.

The Fine Art Library holds about 35,000
books covering art and architecture, about 2,000
colour transparencies and over 3,000
illustrations for loan. There are subject,
transparency and prints and illustrations
indexes.

The Edinburgh Room holds about 450
plans and elevations, about 1,450 maps, about
8,000 photographs, 8,000 prints, 4,000 colour
transparencies and 4,000 lantern slides. There
are subject, transparency and prints indexes.

The Scottish Library holds 1,000 prints,
1,000 photographs, 750 colour transparencies
and 280 lantern slides. There are transparency
and prints indexes.

Enquiry services and conditions of use:
Personal, postal and telephone enquiries
accepted.

Hours:
Mon–Fri 9.00–21.00
Sat   9.00–13.00

Publications:
*The Edinburgh scene: catalogue of prints and
drawings in the Edinburgh Room, Central Public
Library.* 1951.
Historical slide pack 1: *Daniell's views in Scotland.*

First Garden City Museum *see* 345: North
Hertfordshire District Council Museums
Services, First Garden City Museum

Fortress Study Group   286
c/o David Barnes, Hon Secretary
24 Walters Road
Hoo, Rochester, Kent ME3 9JR

Founded 1975

Aims:
To co-ordinate the study of all aspects of
fortifications and their armaments, especially
works constructed to mount or resist artillery; to
publish a journal devoted to this subject; to
encourage and co-ordinate the recording of such
works in the UK; to maintain a library of
references on this subject for the use of
members; to offer expert advice on a consultancy
basis to official or private organisations involved
in the restoration or preservation of works of
fortifications, and to campaign for the
preservation, protection, and recording of such
works; to organise group visits to interesting
fortifications in the UK and abroad; and to
co-operate with societies in other countries
having similar aims.

Collections/Library:
The address of the librarian of the Fortress
Study Group, Mr J. R. Kenyon, is National
Museum of Wales, Cardiff CF1 3NP. The
library is still in its infancy and consists of some
120 items, mainly on artillery fortifications.

Publications:
Casemate (newsletter).
Fort (annual journal).
Members' list.

Activities:
Annual conference.

Friends Historical Society   287
Friends House
Euston Road
London NW1 2BJ
tel 01–387 3601

Founded 1903

Aims:
Publishes original material from the records of
the Society of Friends and articles on Quaker
history.

Collections/Library:
See 360: Religious Society of Friends.

Friends of Friendless Churches   288
12 Edwardes Square
London W8 6HG
tel 01–602 6267

Founded 1957

Aims:
Preservation of churches and chapels of
architectural or historic interest which are
threatened with collapse or demolition and
which fall outside the scope or policy of other
organisations.

Collections/Library:
Books on churches, guide books, files of
correspondence, photographs and
transparencies. No catalogues or indexes.

Enquiry services and conditions of use:
Personal callers by appointment.

Hours:
Mon–Fri (normal office hours)

Publications:
Annual report.
Interim report.
Appeal leaflets.

urniture History Society   289
Department of Furniture and Woodwork
Victoria and Albert Museum
South Kensington
London SW7 2RL
tel Secretary (Mrs T. Ingram) 01–741 1461

Founded 1964

Aims:
To study furniture of all periods, places and
kinds, to increase knowledge and appreciation of
it, and to assist in the preservation of furniture
and of its records.

Collections/Library:
None.

Publications:
Annual report.
Furniture history (annual journal).
Newsletter (quarterly).
*Medieval furniture in England, France and the
Netherlands*, by Dr P. Eames.
The Hardwick Inventories of 1601, by Dr L. O. J.
Boynton.
Printed furniture designs before 1650, by Simon
Jervis.
*A Dictionary of English furniture makers
1660—1840* (in preparation).

Activities:
Annual conference.
Annual symposium.
Visits to collections of notable furniture.
Overseas visits.

The Garden History Society   290
No official premises
c/o Mrs Mavis Batey, Hon Secretary
12 Charlbury Road
Oxford
tel Oxford (0865) 55543 (private)

Founded 1965

Aims:
To bring together those who are interested in the
various aspects of garden history (horticulture,
landscape design, architecture, forestry and
related subjects), and to publish research in the
subject. To index relevant historical material and
to work in conjunction with other bodies to
preserve and advise on the restoration of historic
gardens. Membership is open to anyone
interested in garden history. Members include
architects, botanists, landscape architects,
foresters, art historians, archaeologists and
garden-lovers.

Collections/Library:
A small collection of books is housed at Bath
University.
A collection of photographs is housed at the
National Monuments Record (*see* 365).
An index of garden literature (including
19th-century and current periodical articles) is
maintained by the Society's librarian, Mr Ray
Desmond, 79 Ennerdale Road, Kew,
Richmond, Surrey.
A register of current research in garden history is
kept by R. Holden, 3 Merrick Square, The
Borough, London SE1 4JB. It is published
occasionally in *Garden history* (vol 4, no 1,
Spring 1976, no 2, Summer 1976, vol 6, no 1,
Spring 1978).
A slide lecture entitled 'A history of gardening in
Britain' is available on loan from R. Bisgro, Dept
of Agriculture and Horticulture, University of
Reading, Earley Gate, Reading, Berks.
A slide and photograph collection is held by Dr
D. N. Truscott, 3 Bulstrode Gardens,
Cambridge CB3 0EN.

Enquiry Services:
Postal enquiries only.

Publications:
Garden history (quarterly), vol 1, 1972– .
Newsletter (1966–1972, 1981–).
Occasional paper: no 1 (1969), no 2 (1970).

Activities:
Visits are arranged to gardens of historic interest
in Britain and abroad.
There is an annual spring symposium on some
aspect of garden history, eg Victorian gardens in
1977 and the treatment of the surroundings of
historic buildings in 1975.
The AGM is held each summer in a different
part of the country during a residential weekend
with lectures and garden visits.
Winter lectures are held in London.
The Society gives advice on the restoration of
historic gardens and helps with conservation
studies.
The Society is preparing a list of historic gardens
county by county, indicating their present
condition.

General Register Office   291
St Catherine's House
10 Kingsway
London WC2B 6JP
tel 01–242 0262

Founded 1837

Collections/Library:
Holds indexes to records of births, deaths and
marriages in England and Wales from 1837;
overseas by consular returns since 1849. They
are records of separate events and are not linked
together in families.

5.2 Guide to societies, institutions and organisations

families,/*continued*
Enquiry services and conditions of use:
Anyone wishing to trace a specific event may
well be able to do so by writing to the Registrar
General or, rather more cheaply, by spending
half an hour or so in the search rooms at St
Catherine's House where the indexes may be
searched free of charge. Fruitless searching can
be reduced if one first obtains from family
sources and documents as much information as
possible about the events being sought. The
registers themselves are not open to inspection.
Information from them is supplied in the form
of certified copies of entries which can normally
be issued within 48 hours if applied for in person
or seven to ten days if the matter is arranged by
post. No information from the records is given
over the telephone.

Hours:
Mon–Fri 8.30–16.30

Publications:
Leaflets:
Personal searches at the General Register Office.
*Summary of registers and records in the custody of
the Registrar General.*
*Records available at the General Register Office:
brief notes for visitors.*
*Information about the issue of birth, marriage and
death certificates.*
*Postal applications for certificates of events which
occurred in Scotland, Northern Ireland and the
Irish Republic.*

General Register Office (Ireland)   292
Custom House
Dublin 1
tel Dublin 742961

Collections/Library:
Registers of births, deaths and marriages,
registered in all Ireland on and after 1st January
1864 to 31st December 1921, and in Ireland
(exclusive of the six north eastern counties) from
that date. Registration of marriages other than
those celebrated by Catholic clergy began on 1st
April 1845.

Enquiry services and conditions of use:
Searches are made for entries of births, deaths or
marriages when the information supplied is
sufficient to enable the entries to be identified (if
found). Names in full and the approximate date
and place of the event should be stated. In the
case of a birth, the names of the parents,
including the mother's maiden surname, are
required. General searches are not undertaken
by the office staff, but by the applicant or
someone acting on his behalf.

Hours:
Mon–Fri 9.30–17.00

General Register Office (Northern Ireland)   29
Oxford House
49/55 Chichester Street
Belfast BT1 4HL
tel Belfast (0232) 35211

Collections/Library:
Holds index to births, deaths and marriages
from 1922 to date. Registers of birth and death
occurring in Northern Ireland from 1864 to
date. Registers of marriages from 1922 to date.
Marriage registers from 1864 (Roman Catholic)
and from 1845 for other marriages are held by
District Registrars.

Enquiry services and conditions of use:
Personal, postal and telephone enquiries
accepted.
Certified copies of entries in the register are
supplied on payment of the stated fees.

Hours:
Mon–Fri 9.30–15.30

General Register Office for Scotland   29
New Register House
Edinburgh EH1 3YT
tel Edinburgh (031) 556 3952 ext 24

Founded 1855

Collections/Library:
Holds parish registers of Church of Scotland,
1553–1844 (very few indexes available).
Registers of births, deaths and marriages, 1855
to date (annual indexes available).

Enquiry services and conditions of use:
Particular searches are made for entries of birth,
deaths or marriages only if sufficient identifying
information is supplied. General searches are no
undertaken by the office staff but by the
applicant or someone acting on his behalf. Ther
is limited accommodation in the search rooms
and fees are payable. Telephone enquirers are
invited to write.

Hours:
Mon–Thurs 9.30–16.30
Fri   9.30–16.00

Publications:
Ancestry leaflet.
Table of fees.
Pamphlet on history and functions of the
department.

The Georgian Group   29
2 Chester Street
London SW1X 7BB
tel 01–235 3081

Founded 1937

Aims:
The Georgian Group was founded in order to awaken and direct public opinion to the need to protect the nation's steadily diminishing Georgian heritage, and by means of action in parliament and in the press to rescue from demolition squares, terraces, and individual buildings of beauty and importance. It should be noted that the word 'Georgian' was adopted for convenience only: broadly speaking, all buildings designed in the classical manner come within the scope of the Group's activities. The formal objects of the Group are: (1) to awaken public interest in and public appreciation of Georgian architecture and town planning; (2) to afford advice to owners and public authorities in regard to the preservation and repair of Georgian buildings and the uses to which they can, if necessary, be adapted; (3) to save from destruction or disfigurement Georgian squares, terraces, streets and individual buildings of special architectural merit; and (4) to ensure, when an area is replanned, that Georgian buildings are not wantonly destroyed and that new buildings harmonise with the old. The Group depends on the subscriptions of its members to finance its work. The Group is one of the bodies to whom all applications to demolish listed buildings are submitted statutorily.

Collections/Library:
The Group holds casework files, some of which contain photographs, slides, plans, and other documentation about specific buildings.

Enquiry services:
Anything related to the work of the Group.

Hours:
Mon–Fri 9.30–17.30

Publications:
Annual report.
The Georgian Group News.

Activities:
Casework.
Visits, conferences and lectures are usually for members only.

Gladstone Court Museum *see* 233: Biggar Museum Trust, Gladstone Court Museum

---

Greater London Council   296
    County Hall
    London SE1 7PB

The architectural history resources comprise:

Historic Buildings Division (Architect's Dept): tel 01–633 5891.
The department maintains case files, with research notes mainly on listed buildings which have been the subject of planning applications.

The Division holds an index of London almshouses and an index of timber-framed buildings in London.

Drawings made for the *Survey of London* volumes are kept in the Division. They include many not yet published.

Survey of London (Director General's Dept): tel 01–633 5881 or 5852
The research team has built up mountains of notes and information, but little that has not been put into the published volumes (*see* 80). The Survey office has a card index to the *Builder* (1843–1892) for London buildings (excluding the City). In addition to the entries by architect (photocopies of which are held in the British Architectural Library), there are two drawers of artists, builders, engineers and craftsmen, 18 drawers of topographical entries (divided into districts: Lambeth, Southwark, etc) and one drawer of subjects.

Photograph Library:
tel 01–633 3255
Contains over 250,000 photographs of schools, housing estates, transport, parks, bridges, public buildings, private houses, etc. There is a large topographical section. The library is fully catalogued, but there are no printed lists of subjects which can be issued. Duplicate copies can be borrowed and sale copies can be ordered. By appointment only.

Print Collection:
tel 01–633 7193
A topographical collection, classified by area. Subject and artist indexes.

Greater London Record Office:
tel 01–633 6851
The London Section is responsible for the official records of the London County Council and its predecessors, dating from 1570, as well as for those of the Greater London Council, while the Middlesex Section has custody of the records of the Middlesex County Council and the Middlesex Sessions dating from 1549.

Greater London History Library:
tel 01–633 7132
A special library of works on the history and topography of London and on local government and the many subjects on which the Council's work impinges. It is particularly rich in books on architecture and town planning. Book stock of some 90,000 volumes. In addition to the current author and classified subject catalogues on cards,

5.2 Guide to societies, institutions and organisations

cards,/*continued*
there is a printed catalogue of the topographical books (published in 1939) which still forms a useful bibliography. The library is open to the public for reference purposes, Mon–Fri 9.15–17.00.

Guildhall Library   297
Aldermanbury
London EC2P 2EJ
tel 01–606 3030

Founded 1824

Aims:
British history and topography, with particular emphasis on London.

Collection/Library:
Printed Books Section:
The collection covers all aspects of London as well as English topography, including unique collections of London and provincial directories and poll books, long, usually complete files of historical, bibliographical, commercial periodicals and annuals, and proceedings of local societies. Complete file of Commons sessional papers from 1835, with many earlier papers. The library maintains an index to the City's architecture, mainly from the *Builder*, plus other journals. Articles and illustrations have both been indexed and well cross-referenced with entries for buildings, streets and architects. A card index to obituaries from the *Builder* is also maintained. The emphasis of this index is on the 19th century and all names are recorded regardless of occupation (which is not noted). The library has a typescript index to the Apprenticeship Records in the Public Record Office 1710–1774 which often makes it possible to identify the offices and workshops in which individual architects and craftsmen were trained.

Manuscripts Section:
Extensive estate records (13th to 20th centuries), notably those of Christ's Hospital School, the diocese of London, the Dean and Chapter of St Paul's Cathedral, and the London livery companies; including surveys, plans, building accounts, manorial court rolls, and title deeds relating to property in the City of London and its environs and the Home Counties. Records of City of London property companies (19th to 20th centuries), including registers of leases, reports, valuations, correspondence etc relating to alterations to property. Administrative records of the diocese of London, including faculty registers and papers (17th–20th centuries), original and copy conveyances (14th–20th centuries), and visitation returns (16th–20th centuries), throwing light on the design, construction and maintenance of parish churches throughout the diocese. Records of City-based insurance companies (some with

business covering the whole country) (17th to 20th centuries), including fire policy registers describing buildings insured, with details of fittings, construction materials and function. Rate books (16th to 20th centuries) compiled by street and precinct. Personnel and administrative records of the Carpenters', Masons', Plaisterers' (ie Plasterers'), Tylers' and Bricklayers', and Paviors' companies of London (15th to 20th centuries), including biographical details of members and minutes and reports relating to the supervision of their activities and materials used. Surveys of sites of City property destroyed in the Great Fire of London made by Peter Mills and John Oliver (1666–72). Business papers of the Adam brothers (1754–1807). Rough note, account and estimate book of Thomas Wood (fl 1705–46), builder (1735–37).

Print Room:
Approximately 30,000 prints and drawings and 30,000 maps and plans relating chiefly to London and its environs, 15th–20th centuries. Also some items relating to property of certain City of London institutions in other parts of the kingdom including N. Ireland. Special collections include the Baddeley Collection (90 pen and ink drawings by R. Randall of buildings in Cripplegate Ward); Chadwyck Healey Collection (437 drawings by J. Crowther of livery halls, inns of court and buildings threatened with demolition at the end of the 19th century); E. Borough Johnson Collection (68 drawings of war damaged buildings); Sydney Jones Collection (c 110 pencil drawings of London streets and buildings, 1909–1942). Also approximately 14,000 photographs, mainly of streets and buildings in central London; approximately 10,000 portraits; 1,600 slides; 1,500 trade cards; playbills; etc. The majority of the items appear in the department's card catalogue. Most choice items feature in *Selected prints and drawings in Guildhall Library*, pts 1–111.

Enquiry service and conditions of use:
Personal, postal and telephone enquiries accepted.
The Guildhall Library is a public library and open to all.

Hours:
Mon–Sat 9.30–17.00 (Mon–Fri in Print Room)

Publications:
Guildhall studies in London history (half yearly journal).
A list of books printed in the British Isles and English books printed abroad before 1701 in Guildhall Library. 2 vols.
Facsimiles of London prints, including Hogarth's *Industry and Idleness* series, and a portfolio of 18th-century engravings of the City of London.

Facsimiles of London maps including Ogilby and Morgan's large-scale survey of the City of London, 1676 (20 sheets) and Morgan's survey of London, Westminster and Southwark, 1682 (16 sheets). Other large scale surveys forthcoming.

Handlists of parish registers, vestry minutes, churchwarden accounts, and London rate assessments and inhabitants lists. Guides to the records of the City of London Guilds and Livery Companies in preparation.

Medieval Guildhall of London, by Caroline Barron.

London buildings and sites: a guide for researchers in Guildhall Library (see 25).

Guide to genealogical sources in Guildhall Library. 2nd ed. 1979.

A Guide to records at Guildhall, by P. E. Jones and R. Smith, 1951.

Guide to the London collections. 1978.

Activities:
Occasional exhibitions.

Hampstead Garden Suburb Archives 298
c/o The Archivist
Hampstead Garden Suburb Institute
Central Square
London NW11 7BN

Collections/Library:
Comprehensive drawings coverage of the development of Hampstead Garden Suburb with plans submitted for approval to the Hampstead Garden Suburb Trust. Major examples of work by Sir Edwin Lutyens, Barry Parker and Raymond Unwin, M. H. Baillie Scott, C. M. Crickmer, Herbert Welch, Michael Bunney, G. L. Sutcliffe, J. C. S. Soutar, C. Cowles-Voysey, and many other major Edwardian domestic architects. Collection of photographs showing the development of the suburb; collection of documents, books and memorabilia relating to the founder – Dame Henrietta Barnett; minutes and documents relating to the Hampstead Garden Suburb Trust.

Enquiry services and conditions of use:
Enquiries to the archivist.

Hours:
By appointment with the archivist, Mrs Grafton-Green (tel 01–499 9040).

Publications:
Hampstead Garden Suburb, 1907–1977: a history (1977).
Hampstead Garden Suburb: the care and appreciation of its architectural heritage (1977).

Historic Buildings Bureau 299
Department of the Environment
25 Savile Row
London W1X 2BT
tel 01–734 6010

Historic Buildings Bureau for Scotland
Scottish Development Department
New St Andrews House
St James' Centre
Edinburgh EH1 3TA
tel Edinburgh (031) 556 8400 ext 5003 or 5414

Historic Buildings Bureau for Wales
Welsh Office
Estates Division
New Building
Cathays Park
Cardiff CF1 2NQ
tel Cardiff (0222) 82 5111 ext 3873

Founded c1954

Aims:
To assist in the preservation of historic buildings by finding new uses and users for historic buildings available for sale or lease.

Collections/Library:
None.

Enquiry services and conditions of use:
Personal, postal and telephone enquiries accepted.

Hours:
Normal office hours.

Publications:
List of historic buildings for sale or to be let (quarterly). One list for England and Wales, separate list for Scotland. Lists of statutorily listed buildings on the market for disposal which have been referred to the Bureaux. At the present time these lists are issued free of charge to the public upon application. Brief details are given in the first instance. The Bureaux act in an introductory capacity only and do not participate in negotiations.

Historic Buildings Council for England 300
25 Savile Row
London W1X 2BT
tel 01–734 6010 ext 400

Founded 1953

Aims:
To advise the Secretary of State for the Environment on the making of grants towards the repair or maintenance of buildings of outstanding historic or architectural interest and similarly towards the preservation or

5.2 Guide to societies, institutions and organisations

preservation or/*continued*
enhancement of the character or appearance of
outstanding conservation areas. To advise the
Secretary of State on the listing of buildings of
special architectural or historic interest.

Collections/Library:
None.

Enquiry services:
None.

Publications:
Annual report (published by HMSO).

Historic Buildings Council for Northern Ireland   301

Department of the Environment for Northern
Ireland
1 Connsbrook Avenue
Belfast BT4 1EH
tel Belfast (0232) 653251

Founded 1973

Aims:
To advise the Department of the Environment
for Northern Ireland on the listing of buildings
of outstanding architectural or historic interest;
the designating of conservation areas; the
making of grants or loans for the preservation of
listed buildings; the provision of financial
assistance for works in conservation areas; and
general matters relating to the preservation of
historic buildings and conservation areas.

Collections/Library:
None.

Enquiry services:
None.

Publications:
Annual report (published by HMSO, Belfast).

Historic Buildings Council for Scotland   302

25 Drumsheugh Gardens
Edinburgh EH3 7RN
tel Edinburgh (031) 226 3611–4

Founded 1953

Aims:
To advise the Secretary of State for Scotland on
the making of grants towards the repair or
maintenance of buildings of outstanding historic
or architectural interest and similarly towards
the preservation or enhancement of the character
or appearance of outstanding conservation areas.
To advise the Secretary of State on the listing of
buildings of special architectural or historic
interest.

Collections/Library:
None.

Enquiry services:
None.

Publications:
Annual report (published by HMSO).

Historic Buildings Council for Wales   303

Crown Buildings
Cathays Park
Cardiff CF1 3NQ
tel Cardiff (0222) 82 3160/3163

Founded 1953

Aims:
To advise the Secretary of State for Wales on the
making of grants towards the repair or
maintenance of buildings of outstanding historic
or architectural interest and similarly towards
the preservation or enhancement of the character
or appearance of conservation areas. To advise
the Secretary of State on the listing of buildings
of special architectural or historic interest.

Collections/Library:
None.

Enquiry services:
None.

Publications:
Annual report (published by HMSO).

Historic Churches Preservation Trust   304

Fulham Palace
London SW6 6EA
tel 01–736 3054

Founded 1952

Aims:
The Trust is an independent
non-denominational and non-political
organisation whose main purpose is to raise
funds with which to augment the efforts of
parishioners in preserving the historic churches
of which for the time being they are guardians.
The Trust does not operate in Ireland or Wales.
For Scotland *see* 384.

Collections/Library:
None.

Enquiry services:
None.

Publications:
Annual report.

Activities:
The Trust, with the expert assistance of
well-qualified architects, enquires fully into the
technicalities of the churches which they help.

Historic Houses Association   305
  10 Charles II Street
  London SW1Y 4AA
  tel 01–839 5345

  Founded 1973

  Aims:
  An association representing the owners and
  guardians of over 800 historic houses, parks,
  gardens and places of interest (and their
  associated contents) in private ownership,
  throughout Great Britain, formed to promote
  and safeguard their legitimate interests so far as
  they are consistent with the interests of the
  nation.

  Collections/Library:
  Library.

  Enquiry services and conditions of use:
  Information service available to all serious
  enquirers.

  Publications:
  Annual report.
  Journal.
  Newsletter.
  List of members.
  Conference reports.

  Activities:
  Conferences.
  Meetings.
  Research.
  Exhibitions.
  Seminars.

Historical Manuscripts Commission *see* 364:
Royal Commission on Historical Manuscripts

History of Planning Group *see* 349: Planning
History Group

Incorporated Church Building Society   306
  St Matthew's Chapel
  24 Great Peter Street
  London SW1P 2BU
  tel 01–222 0892

  Founded 1818

  Aims:
  To provide financial assistance towards the
  building, enlarging and repair of churches and
  chapels in England and Wales.

  Collections/Library:
  It has contributed towards the erection,
  alteration and repair of churches in every part of

England and Wales and has preserved its records
from the date of its foundation. Every church
assisted is represented by a docket or file
containing correspondence and a certificate of
completion of the work. Those files relating to
building, enlarging and alteration of seating
generally contain plans and elevations as well.
Lewis's *Topographical dictionary* (1831)
mentions all the grants made up to the date of its
publication.
    The Society's records from 1818 to c1850
are at Lambeth Palace Library (*see* 319), from
1850 to the turn of the century they are in store
and from then on they are at the above address.

Enquiry services and conditions of use:
Personal and telephone enquiries accepted.

Hours:
Mon–Fri 9.30–17.30

Publications:
Annual report.
Fifty modern churches. 1947.
Sixty post-war churches. 1956.

Industrial Buildings Preservation Trust   307
  12/13 Henrietta Street
  London WC2E 8LH
  tel 01–836 1894

  Aims:
  To preserve industrial buildings of particular
  historical or environmental significance, and to
  find new uses for them.

Institute for the Study of Worship and   308
Religious Architecture: A centre for liturgical,
architectural and socio-religious research
  University of Birmingham
  Birmingham B15 2TT
  tel Birmingham (021) 472 1301

  Founded 1962

  Aims:
  To promote and provide facilities for research
  into the relationship between worship and
  architecture, in terms both of the history of these
  two subjects and of contemporary building.
  While its main concern is with Christian forms
  of all denominations, its programme is not
  confined to these, but seeks to advance the study
  of all types of worship in conjunction with their
  architectural setting. As the work of the Institute
  has developed, there has been an increasing
  concern with the sociological aspects of the
  relationship between liturgy and architecture.

  Collections/Library:
  Small seminar library with card index. Main
  items on liturgy and architecture, etc are housed
  in the University Library and also in the library
  of the Barber Institute.

Institute./*continued*
Enquiry services and conditions of use:
Personal, postal and telephone enquiries
accepted.

Hours:
Mon–Fri 9.00–17.00

Publications:
Research bulletin (annual).
A list of publications is available.

Institute of Advanced Architectural Studies,   309
University of York
King's Manor
York YO1 2EP
tel York (0904) 59861 ext 832

Founded 1949

Aims:
The Institute offers an annual programme in
mid-career education for the professions allied to
building, of seminars, conferences, short
courses, etc, usually from one to ten days in
length, as well as a one year course in
Conservation Studies. Higher degree students
are also accepted. It has an architectural
practice, the York University Design Unit, a
Research Section, Photogrammetric Unit and
Building Science Research Unit.

Collections/Library:
The collections of the library aim to serve the
literature needs of the staff and
mid-career/post-graduate students of the
Institute. Areas of special provision are:
architectural and building history and the
conservation of monuments and sites, together
with topics which recur frequently in courses or
research projects at the Institute, such as
housing. The stock includes 12,000 books and
pamphlets, about 80 current periodical titles and
about 100 dead titles. There is a slide collection
of about 10,000 2×2 in slides and about 600
$3\frac{1}{4} \times 3\frac{1}{4}$ in slides and a collection of about 3,000
photographs. There are author and classified
(UDC) card catalogues, plus an A–Z index for
the bookstock and periodicals. There is a
separate finding list on cards for photographs.
The slides are not catalogued, the sequence
acting as its own record.

Enquiry services and conditions of use:
Primarily for the staff and students, but books
are loaned to members of the local community
with a genuine interest, on registering with the
librarian.
Personal, postal and telephone enquiries are
accepted.

Hours:
Mon–Fri 9.00–17.15

Publications:
*Conservation studies in York: the first eight years,
1972–1980: a list in order of author, followed by a
list grouped by subject* (1980). Theses are
arranged under the following subjects: principle
and education; management and practice;
history (biography, localities); building types;
materials; problems; and fittings and equipment
Occasional bibliographies, eg on architectural
conservation.

Activities:
In late 1979 the Institute commenced a two year
research project on the conservation of gardens
and parks of historic interest in the United
Kingdom. The first part of the project is an
investigation of suitable methods by which a
comprehensive survey might be carried out. The
object of a comprehensive survey would be to
identify and describe gardens and parks of
historic interest of all kinds, and to build up an
inventory of them together with accompanying
details and illustrations. It is intended that the
inventory should eventually become an
important source of information for all who are
engaged in the study and conservation of historic
gardens and parks. Peter Goodchild is
co-ordinating the trial survey.

Institute of Archaeology   31
University of London
31–34 Gordon Square
London WC1H 0PY
tel 01–387 6052

Founded 1937

Aims:
To provide courses leading to First Degrees and
Higher Degrees of the University of London in
Archaeology, and to carry out archaeological
research, including research on the environment
and technology of early peoples, and to act as a
centre for various organisations connected with
work in this field. First and Higher Degree
courses on Archaeological Conservation are also
offered, which include some instruction in the
care of historic buildings.

Collections/Library:
The library contains small sections of
architectural history, one general and one
specifically on British architectural history.
Some books on building techniques are held
both in the main library and in the Conservation
Department.

Enquiry services and conditions of use:
Limited. Personal (for serious enquiries), postal
(with stamped, addressed envelopes), and
telephone (simple bibliographic enquiries only).

Hours:
Term: Mon–Fri 10.00–20.45; Sat 10.00–16.45
Vacation: Mon–Fri 10.00–17.30
Sat 10.00–16.45. Closed on Saturdays during
summer vacation.

Publications:
Annual report.
Bulletin.
Occasional papers.
*Archaeological theses in progress in British
Universities.* Produced by the London Institute
of Archaeology in conjunction with the Council
for British Archaeology (1977–) (*see* 145).

institute of Landscape Architects *see* 321:
Landscape Institute

Institution of Civil Engineers   311
Great George Street
London SW1P 3AA
tel 01–222 7722

Founded 1818

Aims:
Professional institute for the general
advancement of mechanical science. Seven
boards represent the main subdivisions of
airports, hydraulics and public health, maritime
and waterways, railways, roads, structures and
buildings, works construction.

Collections/Library:
Books and pamphlets (about 80,000) and
periodicals covering all branches of engineering.
Manuscripts and archives of the Institution.
      The Panel for Historical Engineering
Works was set up in 1971 to persuade members
of the Institution to take an interest in civil
engineering works which illustrate the history
and development of civil engineering and to
make both engineers and the public aware of our
engineering heritage and to maintain an index of
civil engineering works which merit recording or
preserving for the benefit of members of the
profession and of the public. In general,
buildings are only treated as civil engineering
works if the existence of external forces or the
limits of strength of the materials used is an
important factor in their design and needed
special knowledge. Some 650 historical civil
engineering works in GB have so far been
identified, and for over a third of these a detailed
description of the structure, with photographs,
references to published articles and so on, has
been compiled and deposited in the Institution's
library.

Enquiry services and conditions of use:
Available to members only. Rare material
available to research workers by arrangement.

Hours:
Mon–Fri 9.15–17.30

Publications:
Yearbook.
I.C.E. abstracts.
New civil engineer (journal).
*Early printed reports and maps (1665–1850) in the
Library of the Institution of Civil Engineers.*
Compiled by A. W. Skempton. London:
Thomas Telford, 1978.
M. F. Barbey. *Civil engineering heritage:
Northern England.* London: Thomas Telford,
1981, 178 pp. A guide to the civil engineering
works of historical importance in Northern
England. Based on the works of the Panel for
Historical Engineering Works.

Institution of Municipal Engineers   312
25 Eccleston Square
London SW1V 1NX
tel 01–834 5032/3

Founded 1873

Aims:
A professional institute for the science of
engineering and cognate subjects as applied to
the services undertaken by local authorities and
other public undertakings for the benefit of the
community.

Collections/Library:
Library.

Enquiry services and conditions of use:
For members only.

Institution of Structural Engineers   313
11 Upper Belgrave Street
London SW1X 8BH
tel 01–235 4535

Founded 1908

Aims:
To promote the science and art of structural
engineering. Founded in 1908 as the Concrete
Institute, became the Institution of Structural
Engineers in 1923.

Collections/Library:
Approximately 8,000 books, 15,000 pamphlets
and 200 periodical titles. Bibliographies covering
about 500 subject headings.

Enquiry services and conditions of use:
Library available to members of the Institution
only. Personal, postal and telephone enquiries
accepted.

5.2 Guide to societies, institutions and organisations

accepted./*continued*
Hours:
Mon–Fri 9.30–17.00 and until 18.00 on meeting
days (Thursdays, twice a month)

Publications:
The Structural engineer (journal).
Occasional publications.

Irish Architectural Archive *see* 339:
National Trust Archive

Irish Architectural Record Association   314
c/o National Library of Ireland
Kildare Street
Dublin 2
Ireland
tel Dublin 76 55 21

Founded 1939

Aims:
To collect records (mainly drawings and
photographs) of Irish buildings.

Collections/Library:
Hand list to the collection.

Enquiry services and conditions of use:
Personal, postal and telephone enquiries
accepted.

Hours:
10.00–22.00 (normally)

Publications:
Rosalind M. Elmes, *Catalogue of Irish
topographical prints and original drawings (in
Nat. Library).* Dublin. 1943.
*Irish architectural drawings: an exhibition to
commemorate the 25th anniversary of the Irish
Architectural Records Association.* 1965.

Activities:
Occasional exhibitions.

Irish Georgian Society   315
Castletown House
Celbridge
Co Kildare
Ireland
tel Dublin 288252

Founded 1958

Aims:
The preservation of 18th-century architecture in
Ireland.

Collections/Library:
None.

Enquiry services:
None.

Publications:
Newsletter.
Quarterly bulletin.
Appeal leaflets.
A list of publications for sale is available.

Activities:
Visits, tours, lectures, concerts.
Headquarters (Castletown House) run as a
museum.

Irish Institute of Pastoral Liturgy   316
College Street
Carlow
Ireland
tel Carlow (0503) 42942

Founded 1974

Aims:
To direct and co-ordinate work of various
advisory groups who assist bishops in liturgical
renewal, eg Art and Architecture Advisory
Panel, Music Panel, Advisory Service (on
matters relating to the liturgy: music, building
and adaptation of churches, planning).

Collections/Library:
Small specialised library mainly on matters
liturgical. A section is devoted to sacred art and
architecture. The Advisory Panel is presently
engaged in assembling a collection of slides and
photographs of recently renovated or newly built
churches in Ireland.

Enquiry services and conditions of use:
Personal, postal and telephone enquiries
accepted.

Hours:
Mon–Fri 9.00–17.30

Publications:
New liturgy (quarterly). Regularly carries article
on church art and architecture.
Episcopal Advisory Panel publications:
*Directory on the building and re-organisation of
churches.*
Disposal of liturgical objects.
A Document on confessionals.

Activities:
Compilation, in co-operation with An Foras
Forbartha, of a directory of all Roman Catholic
churches in Ireland.
Seminars for architects, artists and their clients
and for art and architecture students.

onbridge Gorge Museum Trust 317

The Wharfage
Ironbridge
Telford
Salop TF8 7AW
tel Ironbridge (095 245) 3522

Founded 1968

Aims:
To conserve for all time the outstanding remains
of industrialisation in the valley of the River
Severn between Coalbrookdale and Coalport, to
carry out research and educational activities, and
to collect data and documentary information
relating to the area.

Collections/Library:
The Museum's collections consist largely of
buildings preserved *in situ* but in addition there
is a major collection of decorative and
architectural ironwork manufactured by the
Coalbrookdale Company, a collection of
Coalport china, a collection of decorative wall
and floor tiles of Messrs Maw and Craven
Dunnill, together with the catalogues of
numerous local companies.

A research library on the history of
technology and industry, numbering some
10,000 volumes, may be consulted by
appointment. Of particular importance in the
collection are complete runs of many
nineteenth-century trade journals relating to the
iron, coal, clay and pottery industries. The
library is indexed.

Enquiry services and conditions of use:
Personal (library by appointment), postal and
telephone enquiries accepted.

Hours:
The Museum is open every day of the year
except Christmas day.
10.00–18.00 in the summer
10.00–17.00 in the winter

Publications:
*Transactions of the First International Congress on
the Conservation of Industrial Monuments, 1973*
(published 1975).
Guide books relating to the various museum
sites.

Activities:
The Museum Trust runs the Building
Conservation Training Course, under which
young craftsmen already established in the
building industry and architects and designers
involved in building conservation can gain
experience with established conservation
craftsmen.

Joint Committee 318

2 Chester Street
London SW1X 7BB
tel 01–235 3081

Founded 1968

Aims:
Brings together the Georgian Group, Society for
the Protection of Ancient Buildings, the
Victorian Society, the Civic Trust and the
Ancient Monuments Society. The object of the
Joint Committee was to discuss problems arising
from the official recognition of 'conservation
areas' in the Civic Amenities Act 1967. It has
widened the scope of its discussions to include all
matters of general concern to the built
environment, such as planning legislation and
taxation.

Publications:
Save the city. 1976 (reprint 1979).

Lambeth Palace Library 319

Lambeth Palace
Lambeth Palace Road
London SE1 7JU
tel 01–928 6222

Founded 1610

Aims:
Lambeth Palace Library is the historic library of
the Archbishops of Canterbury, and was
founded as a public library by Archbishop
Bancroft in 1610. The Church Commissioners
(*see* 258) are now responsible for its
administration.

Collections/Library:
The primary focus of the Library is on church
history. Records of the Commissioners for
Building Fifty New Churches in London and its
suburbs under the Act of 1711 are preserved in
Lambeth Palace Library. These documents
include contracts, deeds, accounts, surveyors'
reports, legal and parliamentary papers, and
plans. For an account of the Commission and its
work see H. M. Colvin, 'Fifty new churches' in
Architectural review, March 1950, revised and
incorporated in the catalogue by E. G. W. Bill
noted below.

The earlier records (1818–1850) of the
Incorporated Church Building Society (*see* 306),
founded in 1818 with the object of providing
financial assistance to those building or enlarging
churches, are available at the Lambeth Palace
Library. Nearly every church assisted is
represented by a file containing correspondence,
plans and elevations, estimates, and a certificate
of completion. Lewis's *Topographical dictionary*
(1831) mentions all grants made up to the date of
its publication.

publication./*continued*
Enquiry services and conditions of use:
Open to the public, with introduction, at the
Librarian's discretion.

Hours:
Mon–Fri 10.00–17.00

Publications:
Annual report.
A list of published catalogues of manuscripts and
archives is available on request.
World Microfilms publishes microfilm editions
of material from the collection, including '*The
Queen Anne Churches', papers of the Commission
for Building Fifty New Churches (1711–59),*
which includes the original Minute Books,
Accounts, Records, etc and a catalogue,
compiled by E. G. W. Bill, of the papers in
Lambeth Palace Library of the Commission for
Building Fifty New Churches in London and
Westminster, 1711–1759, was published as '*The
Queen Anne Churches*' (London: Mansell, 1979).

Landmark Trust   320
Shottesbrooke
Nr Maidenhead
Berkshire
tel Littlewick Green (0628 82) 3431

Founded 1965

Aims:
The Landmark Trust was established 'for
preserving small buildings, structures or sites of
historic interest, architectural merit, or amenity
value, and where possible finding suitable uses
for them; and for protecting and promoting the
enjoyment of places of historic interest or natural
beauty'. It is registered as a charity and is at
present responsible for about 70 different places,
many of them as a result of schemes undertaken
in co-operation with the National Trust, other
charities or local authorities. The current policy
of the Trust is to concern itself with: (a) minor
but handsome buildings of all kinds, into whose
construction went much thought and care,
which are part of our history, and which
contribute greatly to the scene; but whose
original use has disappeared and which cannot
be preserved from vandals, demolition or decay,
unless a new use, and a source of income, can be
found for them; (b) buildings or sites which,
while not necessarily outstanding in themselves,
occupy an important position in fine
surroundings that could easily be spoilt;
(c) places which the National Trust would like to
see preserved, but cannot see its way to
preserving itself. Within these categories the
Landmark Trust has a preference for buildings
or places, part at least of which can be let
furnished for short periods. This often enables a
new use to be found for a building without
spoiling it by the works needed for permanent

occupation; and it also helps to fulfil the second
object of the Trust – 'promoting the enjoyment
of places of historic interest or natural beauty'.

Publications:
Handbook of properties.

Landscape Institute (incorporating the   32
Institute of Landscape Architects)
12 Carlton House Terrace
London SW1Y 5AH
tel 01–839 4044

Founded 1929

Aims:
To promote a high standard of professional
service in relation to landscape design.

Collections/Library:
The Institute maintains a small reference library
of works in landscape architecture and a
collection of about 2,000 slides.

Enquiry services and conditions of use:
Available to non-members.
Personal callers by arrangement only. Postal and
telephone enquiries accepted.

Hours:
Tues, Thurs, 14.30–17.30 (Reading Room)

Liturgy Commission of the Roman Catholic   32
Bishops' Conference of England and Wales,
Department of Art and Architecture,
Conservation Sub-Committee
39 Eccleston Square
London SW1V 1PL
tel 01–821 0553

Founded 1977
(Department of Art and Architecture)

Aims:
The Conservation Sub-Committee of the
Department of Art and Architecture aims to
compile a register of information on all the
Roman Catholic churches of England and
Wales, together with their contents.

Collections/Library:
To date (March 1980) only the survey of the
Central Area of the Archdiocese of Westminster
is complete. This can be consulted at the
Secretariat, who will also be able to give
information on progress with other areas.

Enquiry services and conditions of use:
Personal enquiries, by appointment.

Hours:
Normal office hours

London Topographical Society   323

    c/o Stephen Marks, Hon Secretary
    Hamilton's
    Kilmersdon
    Nr Bath, Somerset.
    tel 01–567 9744 (Chairman, Peter Jackson)

    Founded 1880

    Aims:
    The London Topographical Society, founded as
    the Topographical Society of London, is a
    publishing society whose purpose is to assist the
    study and appreciation of London's history and
    topography by making available facsimiles of
    maps, plans and views, and by publishing
    research.

    Collections/Library:
    A portfolio of the Society's available maps, plans
    and views and copies of the books published by
    the Society can be inspected in the Bishopsgate
    Institute Reference Library. A register of
    research is being compiled by Frank Kelsall of
    the GLC Historic Buildings Division. It will
    include two sorts of unpublished research,
    research in progress and completed projects in a
    bibliography of unprinted material. Entries are
    arranged topographically (by London borough)
    or by subject for entries not confined to one
    place. The lists will be published by the Society.
    For further information contact Frank Kelsall,
    32 Beechhill Road, London SE9 1HH.

    Enquiry services:
    None.

    Publications:
    London topographical record.
    Books.
    Maps, plans and views.
    A list of publications is available from the
    Publications Secretary, Patrick Frazer, 36 Old
    Deer Park Gardens, Richmond, Surrey TW9
    2TL (tel 01–940 5419).

**London University. Courtauld Institute of
Art, Book Library** *see* 269: Courtauld Institute
of Art, Book Library

**London University. Courtauld Institute of
Art, Conway Library** *see* 446: Courtauld
Institute of Art, Conway Library

**London University. Institute of
Archaeology** *see* 310: Institute of Archaeology,
University of London

Mander and Mitchenson Theatre Collection
see 357: Raymond Mander and Joe Mitchenson
Theatre Collection

Mellon Centre for Studies in British Art *see*
347: Paul Mellon Centre for Studies in British
Art

Men of the Stones   324

    Alderman A. S. Ireson, MBE, FFS, FRSA,
    Secretary,
    The Rutland Studio
    Tinwell
    Stamford
    Lincolnshire PE9 3UD
    tel Stamford (0780) 3372

    Founded 1947

    Aims:
    A society advocating the use of stone and other
    natural and local building materials, for
    encouraging craftsmanship, and preserving the
    good architectural qualities of Stamford and
    other places in the limestone belt.

    Collection/Library:
    Extensive reference library on subjects relating
    to the aims and activities of the society.

    Enquiry services:
    Enquiries of a technical, aesthetic, craft or
    consultative nature related to the aims and
    objects of the society. Postal enquiries are
    preferred as this gives time for consideration of
    the problem, and for reference to specialist
    members when required.

    Publications:
    Annual report, includes a directory of member
    artists, firms and craftsmen.

    Activities:
    Meetings, talks, lectures, tours and visits.
    The society prepares reports on planning
    applications related to listed and similar
    buildings for planning authorities and the
    national learned societies, making
    recommendations when required.

Methodist Archives and Research Centre   325
Collection

    The John Rylands University Library of Manchester
    Deansgate Building
    Manchester M3 3EH
    tel Manchester (061) 834 5343
       or
    Connexional Archivist of the Methodist Church
    Southlands College
    Wimbledon Parkside
    London SW19 5NN
    tel 01–946 4375

5.2 Guide to societies, institutions and organisations

01–946 4375/*continued*
Founded 1962

Aims:
Central record repository for the Methodist
Church.

Collections/Library:
The collection of Methodist material comprises
over 26,000 books, a large number of pamphlets,
an extensive manuscript section, and much
association material. As the policy of the
Connexional Archivist has always been that local
material should as far as possible remain in the
locality, most of the manuscript material relating
to Methodist churches and their architects which
is extant, including architects' plans, will be
found in county record offices, circuit safes or
under the control of the Methodist District
archivists. Architectural information available in
the Collection is in general that to be obtained
from the large collection of centenary histories
and brochures in the Local History Section and
by searching through the collection of over 5,000
volumes of periodicals.

Enquiry services and conditions of use:
Personal, postal and telephone enquiries
accepted. Those wishing to use the Collection
should write to the library in advance stating
when they wish to visit the library and what type
of material they wish to see.

Hours:
Mon–Fri 9.30–17.30
Sat 9.30–13.00

Publications:
'The Methodist Archives and Research Centre',
reprint from the *Bulletin of the John Rylands
University Library of Manchester*, vol 60, no 2,
Spring 1978, pp 269–274.

Moated Site Research Group   326
  c/o F. A. Aberg, Hon Secretary
  29 Pine Walk
  Liss, Hampshire GU33 7AT
  tel Liss (073 082) 3881

Founded 1972

Aims:
The study of manorial earthworks, in particular
those bounded by a moat.

Collections/Library:
Index of moated manors.
Index of air photographs of moats.
Index of excavated moats.
Index of protected moats.
Collection of offprints and articles (c100).

Enquiry services and conditions of use:
Personal, postal and telephone enquiries
accepted.

Publications:
Annual report.

Activities:
Weekend seminars and courses are held annually
or bi-annually.

Museum of East Anglian Life   32
  Stowmarket
  Suffolk
  tel Stowmarket (044 92) 2229

Founded 1967

Aims:
To collect and preserve all kinds of materials
relating to the rural life of East Anglia.

Collections:
Abbot's Hall medieval tithe barn.
Edgar's Farmhouse (a 14th-century aisled hall
farmhouse re-erected on the museum site).
Abbot's Hall cottages (a pair of early
18th-century farmworkers' cottages).
Alton Watermill, mill house and cart lodge,
removed from Alton, nr Ipswich, and re-erected
on the museum site.

Enquiry services and conditions of use:
Enquiries by post or telephone.

Hours:
Museum open to the public from Easter to the
end of October.
Daily 11.00–17.30 Sun 14.00–17.30
Visitors at other times by arrangement.

Publications:
Guide to the Museum.
Leaflets describing the buildings.
Picture postcards.

Museum of London   328
  London Wall
  London EC2Y 5HN
  tel 01–600 3699

Founded 1911 (London Museum)

Aims:
Collection, display and interpretation of
materials relating to the archaeology and history
of London from prehistoric times to the present
day.

Collections/Library:
Combined collections of the former London
Museum and the Guildhall Museum.
Library and Department of Painting, Drawings
and Prints dealing specifically with the
topographical and social history of Greater
London. Indexes to illustrations are classified on

a topographical basis with subject
cross-references.
Examples of timber, stonework, etc from the
London area are housed in the period
departments (Roman, Medieval, Tudor and
Stuart and Modern).

Enquiry services and conditions of use:
Departments deal with public enquiries by post,
telephone and in person, but by appointment
only.

Hours:
Tues–Fri 10.00–17.00

Activities:
Notices of forthcoming exhibitions and general
information from the Communications
Department.
Notices of forthcoming lectures, workshops, etc
from the Education Department.

Mutual Households Association Ltd.   329
Cornhill House
41 Kingsway
London WC2B 6UB
tel 01–836 1624

Founded 1955

Aims:
To save, for the benefit of the nation, houses of
historic importance, architectural interest, or of
beauty, which may otherwise decay through the
inability of individual owners to keep them
going, and to create in them apartments for
retired and semi-retired people. It is a registered
charity and non-profit organisation for the
preservation of buildings.

Collections/Library:
None.

Enquiry services:
Personal, postal and telephone enquiries
accepted.

Hours:
Mon–Fri 8.30–16.30

Publications:
Annual report.
Illustrated brochure.

National Art Library *see* 415: Victoria and
Albert Museum Library

National Association of Almshouses   330
Billingbear Lodge
Wokingham
Berkshire RG11 5RU
tel Wokingham (0344) 52922

Founded 1949

Aims:
Seeks, among other things, to secure the
preservation and modernisation of almshouses.

Collections/Library:
A collection of black and white 35mm
photographic negatives of almshouses is held on
loan from the Royal Commission on Historical
Monuments, prints of which can be supplied in
accordance with the Royal Commission's price
list.

Enquiry services and conditions of use:
Postal and telephone enquiries accepted.

Hours:
Mon–Fri 9.30–17.30

Publications:
Year book.
Almshouses gazette (quarterly).

National Institute for Physical Planning and   331
Construction Research (An Foras
Forbartha)
St Martin's House
Waterloo Road
Dublin 4
Ireland
tel Dublin 764211

Founded 1964

Aims:
An environmental research institute providing
technical support services in relation to the
physical environment, both natural and
man-made. The Institute comprises four
divisions – planning, construction, roads and
water resources and an education–information
section. The conservation and amenity section of
the planning division is responsible for the
compilation of the National Heritage Inventory,
the terms of reference of which are to make an
inventory of all areas and items of environmental
importance in Ireland and to encourage an
awareness of Ireland's natural and man-made
heritage. The programme is to prepare and
up-date periodically a comprehensive inventory
on a county-by-county basis on (a) areas of
scientific importance (b) buildings and areas of
architectural or historic importance and (c) items
and areas of archaeological importance and
interest.

Collections/Library:
The National Heritage Inventory records are
unpublished, although parts are being published
(*see below*). A library is maintained.

5.2 Guide to societies, institutions and organisations

maintained./*continued*
Enquiry services and conditions of use:
Personal, postal and telephone enquiries
accepted. Information services (compilation of
bibliographies and inventories),
training–education programmes and advisory
services (including a Conservation and Amenity
Advisory Service) are available.

Hours:
Mon–Fri 9.15–13.00; 14.00–17.15

Publications:
The Institute has published some 150 research
publications and technical reports; a complete
list is available on request.
Publications from the National Heritage
Inventory:
Bray: architectural heritage. 1980.
Carlow: architectural heritage. 1980.
Cobh: architectural heritage. 1979.
Kinsale: architectural heritage. 1980.
Inventory of outstanding landscapes in Ireland.
1977.

National Library of Scotland 332
George IV Bridge
Edinburgh EH1 1EW
tel Edinburgh (031) 226 4531

Map Room
National Library of Scotland Annexe
Causewayside
Edinburgh EH9 1PH
tel Edinburgh (031) 667 7848

Founded 1682

Collections/Library:
The collections cover all fields of human
knowledge. As a copyright library (since 1710),
the library receives a copy of every work
published in the United Kingdom and the
Republic of Ireland.
   The Department of Printed Books includes,
besides periodicals and books, maps and official
publications. Manuscripts are looked after by the
Department of Manuscripts.

Special catalogues of interest include:
Bibliography of Scotland:
The nearest approach to a bibliography of
Scotland at its time of publication was probably
the work of Sir Arthur Mitchell and C. G. Cash
*A contribution to a bibliography of Scottish
topography* (2 vols, 1917). This consists of one
volume listing regional and local histories,
descriptions, and other relevant works arranged
in alphabetical order of regions and counties,
and by towns, parishes, etc, within the counties,
and a second volume arranged by subject. P. D.
Hancock's *A bibliography of works relating to
Scotland, 1916–1950* (2 vols, 1959–60), which is
similarly arranged continued the work of
Mitchell and Cash. A supplementary catalogue,

using the same arrangement and headings as
Mitchell and Cash, begun before the publication
of Hancock's work and consequently to some
extent overlapping it, is maintained by the
Library from its current accessions, that is,
mostly new books but including any appropriate
older books not found in Mitchell and Cash's
original work. The scope of the subject section
has now been greatly widened to cover almost
the whole range of Scottish bibliography. The
printed volumes of Mitchell and Cash and
Hancock are placed in the reading room. The
catalogue maintained by the Library is in
loose-leaf folders.

Art Books:
*The Union Catalogue of Art Books in Edinburgh
Libraries,* compiled in 1954 by Miss Ailsa
Robertson and recently revised and expanded
before its transfer to the National Library, is
kept up to date with entries submitted by the
participating libraries (Edinburgh University
Library, Napier College of Commerce and
Technology, the National Gallery of Scotland,
The National Library of Scotland, New College
Library, The Royal Scottish Academy, The
Royal Scottish Museum, The Scottish Arts
Council, The Scottish National Gallery of
Modern Art, The Scottish National Portrait
Gallery and The Society of Antiquaries of
Scotland/National Museum of Antiquities of
Scotland). Its scope is the bibliography of the
fine arts in the widest sense of that term, subject
covered include archaeology (selectively, works
about structures with marked or decorative
features), architectural plans (city planning,
cottage plans, etc) architecture (monographs,
etc) conservation, drawings (including
topographical drawings), guide books with
art–historical interest, interior decoration,
landscape gardening, pattern books and
restoration. Building materials and engineering
are not covered. Since 1973, 20th-century
publications have not been reported in the
assumption that copies received by statutory
deposit will be found in this library. The
catalogue is therefore intended to be as complete
as possible for all pre-1901 publications, all sale
and exhibition catalogues (which continue to be
fully reported), and all 20th-century as well as
earlier foreign books.

Manuscripts:
The Department of Manuscripts' main concern
is with Scottish manuscripts in the widest
possible sense, ie manuscripts written by
Scotsmen, manuscripts written in Scotland,
whatever the subject, and manuscripts written
about Scotland and Scottish affairs, whether by
Scotsmen or not. The index to manuscripts is
primarily of personal names; certain subjects are
included, but there is no complete subject index.
In its final form the catalogue of manuscripts
will be a series of printed volumes each

containing descriptions (arranged by manuscript and charter number) and index.

Enquiry services and conditions of use:
Admission to the reading rooms is by ticket; to the map room by signing the register of readers. Application forms for readers' tickets, including the special forms that must be completed by undergraduate students, the separately printed regulations governing admission to the main reading room and its use, the additional regulations for the use of the south reading room, and a leaflet describing the map room and its use, are obtainable on application.

Enquiries by telephone or letter of a general nature will be answered as fully and as expeditiously as possible within the scope of standard works of reference and the general knowledge and experience possessed by the staff of the reference services of the Library's printed or manuscript materials, but work that requires a great deal of research cannot be undertaken. Enquiries about books or manuscripts in the Library will be answered by the specialist staff concerned.

Hours:
Main reading room and south reading room Mon–Fri 9.30–20.30; Sat 9.30–13.00
Map room. Mon–Fri 9.30–17.00; Sat 9.30–13.00
The Library is closed on New Year's Day, the following week-day, Good Friday, Christmas Day and Boxing Day.

Publications:
A list may be obtained by writing to the publications officer.

Activities:
Exhibitions.

National Library of Wales   333
Aberystwyth
Dyfed SY23 3BU
tel Aberystwyth (0970) 3816/9

Founded 1907

Aims:
The collection, preservation and maintenance of manuscripts, printed books, periodical publications, newspapers, maps, photographs, paintings, pictures, engravings, drawings and prints, musical publications and works of all kinds especially works composed in Welsh or any other Celtic language which relate to the Welsh and other Celtic peoples as well as all works including audio-visual material which may help to attain the purpose for which the educational institutions existing in Wales were created and founded.

Collections/Library:
All subjects relating to Wales and the other Celtic countries and peoples. As a legal deposit library, however, with the right since 1911 to claim copies of nearly all British and Irish publications the Library has extensive collections in all subject fields. There is a card catalogue of authors and a partial catalogue of Celtic biographical and topographical material.

Manuscripts:
The Department of Manuscripts and Records contains over 30,000 volumes of manuscripts and about 3,500,000 deeds and other documents. The greater part of this material consists of collections of personal and estate papers, the records of the Church in Wales, the records of the Court of Great Sessions, and some of the records of the former counties of Brecon, Cardigan, Montgomery and Radnor (eg Quarter Sessions). There are items relating to architecture scattered throughout these collections but mainly in the collections of estate papers (relating to mansions and smaller buildings) and the records of the Church in Wales (relating to churches and parsonages). Brief descriptions of these collections are published in the *Annual report of the National Library of Wales* when they are received. The collections are later described in detail in typescript catalogues (c 600 volumes at present). There is a card index (in progress) to these catalogues in the reading room with a substantial number of cards filed under architecture. The most substantial group of material relating to architecture not included in the card index at present is the material described in the catalogues of the records of the Church in Wales. There are items in various sections of the Church in Wales catalogues, eg faculties, maps and plans, miscellaneous documents, correspondence, etc. There are also plans, etc relating to public undertakings among the records of the former counties of Brecon, Radnor and Montgomery deposited in the library. The papers of Sir Clough Williams-Ellis were deposited in the library in November 1978 but the plans and drawings relating to his architectural practice have been deposited with the British Architectural Library of the Royal Institute of British Architects. Most of the papers date from after 1951, the year in which his home, Plas Brondanw, was destroyed by fire. There is a substantial body of personal correspondence and also some files of correspondence, office accounts, and a few bills of quantities, etc, concerning commissions executed or intended to have been executed by Sir Clough (see the *Annual report of the National Library of Wales*, 1978–9).

Enquiry services and conditions of use:
Personal, postal and telephone enquiries accepted. Researchers and readers must be 18

■■■■ Societies, institutions and organisations

5.2 Guide to societies, institutions and organisations

be 18/*continued*
years of age and over and their applications for a
reader's ticket must be supported by a person of
recognised position.

Hours:
Mon–Fri 9.30–18.00
Sat 9.30–17.00

Activities:
Exhibitions.

Publications:
Annual report.
List of publications available on request.

National Monuments Advisory Council   334
Ely Place Upper
Dublin 2
Ireland
tel Dublin 764071 ext 28

Founded 1930

Aims:
To give advice and assistance to the
Commissioners of Public Works on any matter
arising on or relating to the carrying into
execution of the provisions of the National
Monuments Acts or any other matter affecting
national monuments and the protection and
preservation thereof. The Advisory Council is a
prescribed body under the Local Government
Planning and Development Acts. This means
that applications for planning permission which
might affect national monuments are referred to
Council by the various planning authorities. The
Council also examines development plans and
advises thereon.

Collections/Library:
None.

Enquiry services and conditions of use:
Personal, postal and telephone enquiries
accepted.

Hours:
Mon–Fri 9.30–17.30

National Monuments Record (England) *see*
365: Royal Commission on Historical
Monuments (England) including the National Monuments
Record

National Monuments Record of Scotland *see*
366: Royal Commission on the Ancient and
Historical Monuments of Scotland including the National
Monuments Record of Scotland

National Monuments Record for Wales *see*
367: Royal Commission on Ancient and
Historical Monuments in Wales including the National
Monuments Record for Wales

National Museum of Antiquities of Scotland   335
Queen Street
Edinburgh EH2 1JD
tel Edinburgh (031) 556 8921

Founded 1954

Collections/Library:
The collections of the Society of Antiquaries of
Scotland are now incorporated in the library of
the National Museum of Antiquities. The
Trustees attempt to acquire all publications
relevant to the museum collections within a
framework of representation of Scottish material
culture in general and the British background. In
addition, the sections on Scottish parish history,
local history and topography, genealogy and
family history, are being added to continually
with the acquisition of older material as well as
current publications.
   The Scottish Country Life Archive, started
in 1959, contains old photographs, drawings,
maps, records of objects, detailed information
and photographs from fieldwork, manuscript
sources, diaries, rentals, etc, and extracted
information from available documentary and
printed sources mainly concerned with
Scotland's agricultural development, but
including sections on the house, buildings,
towns, villages and townships. About fifteen per
cent of the Archive deals with vernacular
buildings in Scotland and their regional
variations.

Enquiry services and conditions of use:
Open to the public.

Hours:
Mon–Fri 10.00–17.00

Publications:
Annual report.
Short guide and information sheet on the
Country Life Archive.

National Piers Society *see* 348: Piers Information Bureau

National Railway Museum   336
Leeman Road
York YO2 4XJ
tel York (0904) 21261

Founded 1975

Aims:
To present the history and development of
British railway engineering, including the social
and economic aspects, over the past 150 years. A
branch of the Science Museum.

Collections/Library:
The library is the official repository for
'redundant' official railway negatives and
drawings under the terms of the Transport Act
1968. The collection does not currently include
architectural drawings.

Enquiry services and conditions of use:
The reference library can provide an enquiry
service on railway matters generally within the
limitations of its resources. Personal (by prior
arrangement only) and postal enquiries accepted.
Telephone use only in cases of extreme urgency.
A current reader's ticket must be held for
personal callers. These can be obtained on
application.

Hours:
Mon–Sat 10.00–18.00
Sun 14.00–18.00

Publications:
Guide to the museum, and other material
connected with the collection.

National Record of Industrial Monuments 337

Centre for the History of Technology, Science and
Society
School of Humanities and Social Sciences
University of Bath
Claverton Down, Bath BA2 7AY
tel Bath (0225) 61244

Founded 1965

Aims:
The National Record of Industrial Monuments
(NRIM) started work in 1965, but its origins go
back to 1959 when the Council for British
Archaeology set up a research Committee for
Industrial Archaeology, which planned and put
into operation the National Survey of Industrial
Monuments. The NRIM exists to compile a
non-intensive site record of industrial heritage
features in Great Britain classified according to
counties and industrial categories.

Collections/Library:
The records of the NRIM are prepared by
fieldworkers who enter the details of industrial
monuments onto standardised cards. The
records, which number about 10,000 entries at
present, are classified by county and by
industry, of which there are ten major categories.
The record is housed in index card boxes in the
above mentioned centre, and copies are held by
the National Monuments Record in London (*see*

365). County summaries have been issued from
time to time although none have been compiled
since 1973. Since then there have been very few
additions to the record.

Enquiry services and conditions of use:
Personal visits preferred, although some
applications can be dealt with by post and
telephone.

Hours:
Normal office hours.

Publications:
Noted in the *Annual report of the Centre for the
History of Technology, Science and Society.*

National Register of Archives *see* 364: Royal
Commission on Historical Manuscripts
(and National Register of Archives)

National Register of Archives (Scotland) 338

PO Box 36
HM General Register House
Edinburgh EH1 3YY
tel Edinburgh (031) 226 5101

Founded 1945

Aims:
The National Register of Archives (Scotland) is
a branch of the Scottish Record Office (*see* 387)
and exists to list and report on manuscript
material in private hands and to advise owners
on the care of their manuscripts.

Collections/Library:
The Surveys to which the Register's Source
Lists refer can be consulted in the Scottish
Record Office, at Register House and West
Register House, the National Register of
Archives at Quality Court, London and the
Libraries of the Scottish Universities. A *Source
list for architecture* is available.

Enquiry services and conditions of use:
In few cases can owners of manuscripts be
approached by researchers directly, therefore in
the first instance enquiries are channelled
through the Register.
Postal enquiries accepted.

Hours:
Mon–Fri 9.00–17.00

Publications:
Summaries of the most recent surveys appear in
the *Annual report of the Keeper of Records of
Scotland.*

5.2 Guide to societies, institutions and organisations

National Trust Archive   339
From Aug 1981,
Irish Architectural Archive
63 Merrion Square
Dublin 2
Ireland
tel Dublin 763430

Founded 1976

Aims:
To undertake the work of recording Ireland's
architectural wealth, and to promote public
appreciation of a frequently neglected heritage.
In establishing a national collection of
architectural records for Ireland, the Archive
hopes to become the recognised starting-point
for anyone seeking information on any Irish
building of note.

Collections/Library:
The collection, which is growing steadily,
presently consists of some 20,000 architectural
drawings and 18,000 photographs, as well as
books, manuscripts and engravings. The Irish
Georgian Society's collection of photographs has
been purchased by the Archive. The collection
covers architecture throughout Ireland, north
and south, and records buildings of all types and
periods.

Enquiry services and conditions of use:
Premises open to the public without
introduction or charge. The Archive can make
available, subject to normal copyright
restrictions, copies of any document in its
possession.

Hours:
Weekdays.

Activities:
Photographic surveys of notable buildings which
are about to be demolished.
Lectures.
Travelling exhibitions.

National Trust for Ireland (An Taisce)   340
41 Percy Place
Dublin 4
Ireland
tel Dublin 681944

Founded 1948

Aims:
Voluntary and independent conservation
organisation which aims to stimulate a greater
awareness and appreciation of our surroundings
through recommendations to the government on
legislation related to the environment, through
education, publications and the collection of
material.

Collections/Library:
An architectural photographic archive was
established in 1976 (*see* 339).

Publications:
An Taisce, Ireland's conservation journal.
Gardens of outstanding interest in Ireland (1980).
List of publications and educational slide sets
and filmstrips available on request. Slide sets are
available on Irish gardens, Irish archaeology,
Irish Victorian architecture, and architecture of
small Irish towns.

The National Trust for Places of Historic   341
Interest and Natural Beauty
42 Queen Anne's Gate
London SW1H 9AS
tel 01–222 9251

Founded 1895

Aims:
Preserves, for the benefit of the nation, buildings
and places of historic or architectural interest or
natural beauty.

Collections/Library:
Maintains a photographic library of slides, black
and white photographs and films. Fairly detailed
coverage of most of their properties.

Enquiry services:
Limited to the work and activities of the Trust.
While the Trust has regional offices throughout
England, Wales and Northern Ireland, enquiries
are dealt with from the London office.

Hours:
Mon–Fri 9.30–17.30

Publications
Annual report.
Annual opening arrangements:
Newsletter.
National Trust studies (annual).
Properties of the National Trust is a complete
register of the Trust's holdings.
Guide books to Trust properties.
Regional touring guides.
A list of the Trust's publications is available.
The National Trust guide (London: Jonathan
Cape, 1973), covers all the important properties
of the National Trust in England, Wales and
Northern Ireland.
Paul Johnson. *National Trust book of British
castles.* London: Granada, 1981.
J. M. Richards. *National Trust book of English
architecture.* London: Weidenfeld, 1981.

National Trust for Scotland for Places of   342
Historic Interest or Natural Beauty
5 Charlotte Square
Edinburgh EH2 4DU
tel Edinburgh (031) 226 5922

Founded 1931

Aims:
Preserves, for the benefit of the nation, buildings and places of historic or architectural interest or natural beauty.

Collections/Library:
None. A few films available for hire.

Enquiry services:
Limited to the work and activities of the Trust.

Publications:
Yearbook (includes a list of the Trust's publications).
Guide books to Trust properties.
The National Trust for Scotland guide (London: Jonathan Cape, 1981).

Newcomen Society for the History of Engineering and Technology   343
Science Museum
Exhibition Road
South Kensington
London SW7 2DD
tel 01–589 1793

Founded 1920

Aims:
National society promoting the study of the history of engineering and technology and seeking to secure the preservation of relevant records.

Collections/Library:
A small library of books pertaining to engineering history (including civil engineering). Not catalogued.

Enquiry services and conditions of use:
Postal and telephone enquiries accepted.

Hours:
Mon–Fri 9.15–18.15

Publications:
Transactions (annual).
Cumulative index to 'Transactions' vol 1–32.
Newcomen bulletin (three per year).
Extra publications (list available on request).

Activities:
Meetings, lectures, visits.

North Hertfordshire District Council, Planning Department   344
Council Offices
Gernon Road
Letchworth, Herts. SG6 9JF
tel Letchworth (046 26) 6500

Founded 1974

Collections/Library:
Bye-law archives for Letchworth Garden City 1904–47. This includes an almost complete sequence of development of the Garden City in its pre-1914 period which was notable for the excellence of individual houses together with innovation and experiment of the 1905 Cheap Cottage Competition. Work by M. H. Baillie Scott, Harrison Townsend, Halsey Ricardo, Curtis Green, Geoffrey Lucas, Randall Wells and a comprehensive coverage of Garden City buildings by Barry Parker and Raymond Unwin and other local practices – Bennett and Bidwell, Courteney Crickmer, and Cecil Hignett. A Letchworth Buildings Index has been compiled together with a summary working paper *Letchworth Garden City buildings index*, North Hertfordshire District Council, October 1976.

Enquiry services and conditions of use:
Enquiries to Mervyn Miller, ext 262. There is no full time archives staff and enquiries should be made by post or by appointment, or prior arrangement only if access to drawings is involved.

North Hertfordshire District Council Museums Services, First Garden City Museum   345
296 Norton Way South
Letchworth, Herts.
tel Letchworth (046 26) 3149

Founded 1976

Aims:
A permanent museum recording the development of and life in the First Garden City, Letchworth. The building was originally the Letchworth offices of Barry Parker and Raymond Unwin, built 1907 and extended 1937 as Barry Parker's home. In 1973 his widow sold the building to Letchworth Garden City Corporation and it has subsequently been extended and leased to North Hertfordshire District Council to form the First Garden City Museum.

Collections/Library:
The museum contains a comprehensive collection of documents, photographs, objects and artefacts relating to the Garden City Movement, the foundation of Letchworth Garden City (1903), its development and social history. The Barry Parker Collection includes practice records, drawings and photographs, covering the period 1895–1942, during which Parker was in practice; the partnership with Raymond Unwin (1896–1914) was responsible for three major model communities – Earswick (1902 onwards), Letchworth Garden City (1904 onwards), and Hampstead Garden Suburb (1905 onwards). The drawings, several thousand in

thousand in/*continued*
number, date from all periods, with a
comprehensive coverage of Garden City
buildings; individual houses by the practice;
housing and town planning schemes; furniture
and interior designs; and water colour sketches
by Barry Parker.

Note catalogue compiled by M. K. Miller
available for serious students. Catalogue,
Letchworth Garden City (1903–1978), annotated
by M. K. Miller gives an indication of the range
of material available relating to the development
of Letchworth.

The library contains an important
collection of books about the Garden City
Movement, the development of town planning
and Edwardian domestic architecture.

Enquiry services and conditions of use:
Personal (prior appointment necessary), postal
and telephone enquiries accepted. Enquiries to
the Curator, tel Letchworth (046 26) 5647, or to
the Local History Assistant (046 26) 3149.

Hours:
Museum: Mon–Fri 14.00–16.30
            Sat 10.00–1300 and 14.00–16.00
Collections: By appointment

Publications:
*Letchworth Garden City (1903–1978): a
commemorative exhibition, catalogue of exhibits.*
1978.

North of England Open Air Museum *see* 232:
Beamish North of England Open Air Museum

**Northern Ireland Historic Buildings
Council** *see* 301: Historic Buildings Council for
Northern Ireland

**Office of Population Censuses and Surveys,
incorporating the General Register** *see*
291–294: General Register Office

Ordnance Survey Department Library   346
Ordnance Survey Office
Romsey Road
Maybush
Southampton, Hants. SO9 4DH
tel Southampton (0703) 775555 ext 334/691

Founded 1791

Aims:
National survey and mapping authority.

Collections/Library:
35,000 books, reports and pamphlets. Specialises
in geodesy, surveying, cartography, printing,
archaeology.

Enquiry services and conditions of use:
Intended primarily as a technical reference
library for the use of the Department. Postal and
telephone enquiries accepted. Personal visits by
bona fide research students only by arrangement.

Hours:
Mon–Thurs 7.45–17.00
Fri 7.45–16.30

Publications:
Annual report.
Accessions lists.
Maps at various scales.
Leaflets describing Ordnance Survey services.
*The old series Ordnance Survey maps of England
and Wales: a reproduction of the 110 sheets of the
survey in early state in 10 volumes.* Lympne
Castle (Kent): Harry Margary. 1975– .
A history of the Ordnance Survey. Edited by W.
Seymour. Folkestone: Dawson, 1980.

Paul Mellon Centre for Studies in British Art   34?
20 Bloomsbury Square
London WC1A 2NP
tel 01–580 0311

Founded 1969

Aims:
To promote and encourage the study of
post-medieval British art prior to 1900.

Collections/Library:
The Centre is engaged in creating an extensive
photographic archive of British paintings,
sculpture, drawings and prints, now numbering
some 60,000. It does not include architecture.
However, as part of the Centre's initial
sponsorship of the *Buildings of Ireland* series,
they processed a large number of films for Prof
Alistair Rowan and hold the negatives though
they hold no information about content.

Enquiry services and conditions of use:
Personal callers accepted.

Hours:
Mon–Fri 9.30–17.00 (sometimes closed
13.00–14.00)

Activities:
Grants made to individual scholars to assist in
the completion of advanced research. Grants
made to institutions to assist in the cost of
producing scholarly catalogues.
The Centre underwrites the total cost of
publishing a number of books which fall within
the terms of the Centre's interest and is engaged
in publishing a series of books devoted to source
material connected with British art.

iers Information Bureau (of the National   348
iers Society)
 38 Holte Road
 Atherstone, Warwickshire CV9 1HN
 tel Atherstone (082 77) 2640

Founded 1973

Aims:
As the information department of the National
Piers Society since September 1979, it exists to
provide information on piers to all those who
wish it. In addition, it carries out its own
research.

Collections/Library:
Expanding collection of information, including
press cuttings and postcards, on all piers in
England and Wales, as well as some in Scotland
and abroad.

Enquiry services and conditions of use:
Postal enquiries (with SAE) accepted.

Publications:
National Piers Society newsletter (quarterly).

Activities:
The National Piers Society is drawing up a
directory of piers, owners and associated
societies. For further information contact Basil J.
Rushton, National Piers Society, 82 Speed
House, Barbican, London EC2.

lanning History Group   349
 c/o Professor Gordon E. Cherry
 Centre for Urban and Regional Studies
 J. G. Smith Building
 University of Birmingham
 PO Box 363
 Birmingham B15 2TT
 tel Birmingham (021) 472 1301 ext 2693

Founded 1974

Aims:
To provide a forum and a network of contacts
whereby academics and practising planners can
come together and learn of each others' work in
the field of history of planning studies. The
Group is international. While no particular
historical periods are to be excluded, nonetheless
the focus of current concern is from the 19th
century onwards.

Collections/Library:
None. A Research register is being compiled by
A. D. King, 58 Lidgett Lane, Roundhay, Leeds
LS8 1PL. It is published occasionally in the
Planning history bulletin (1979, no 2–).

Enquiry services and conditions of use:
No enquiry service.

Publications:
Planning history bulletin (1979–). (supersedes
Newsletter).
Membership list.
Dr A. R. Sutcliffe, *A history of modern town
planning: a bibliographic guide.* (Research
memorandum no 57). Centre for Urban and
Regional Studies, University of Birmingham,
Feb. 1977 (*see* 55).
A series *History of environmental planning* under
the editorship of Dr A. R. Sutcliffe and Prof
Gordon E. Cherry is being established.

Activities:
Occasional group meetings with pre-circulated
papers.
Conferences.

Property Services Agency (formerly Ministry   350
of Public Building and Works)
 Historical Library
 Room C103
 Whitgift Centre
 Wellesley Road
 Croydon CR9 3LY
 tel 01–686 8710 ext 4520 or 4589

Founded 1944 (Library Service)

Aims:
To provide a library and technical information
service to the staff of the Property Services
Agency.

Collections/Library:
Specialist collection on history of government
building and buildings. The PSA Library is
mainly concerned with providing information on
construction subjects to the staff of the Agency.
It also provides historical information about
government buildings it maintains in London
and elsewhere as well as on the history of
government works organisations.
    The Photographic Library has over 525,000
photographs: construction and maintenance of
government buildings at home and overseas;
some civil engineering, housing, roads and
motorways; royal parks and gardens; ancient
monuments and historic buildings.

Enquiry services and conditions of use:
Personal callers by prior appointment. The
collection may only be used if the information
required is not readily available elsewhere.
Photographic Library:
Photographs may be viewed in the Library.
Copies may be purchased.

Hours:
Mon–Fri 9.00–17.00.

Publications:
PSA in print: an annotated list (annual).
Bibliographies.

Bibliographies./*continued*
Current information in the construction industry
(fortnightly).
Construction references. Six-monthly list of
accessions and periodical articles with subject
and author indexes.
(All these publications deal with the
construction industry in general, but
occasionally contain material of historical
importance.)

Conservation Focal Unit
Room C415
Whitgift Centre
Wellesley Road
Croydon CR9 3LY
tel 01–686 8710 ext 4389

Aims:
To coordinate information and provide support
to PSA directorates and the UK territorial
organisation, in connection with the
maintenance, repair, alteration and extension of
buildings of special architectural and historical
interest, and the design of buildings in
conservation areas. The Unit also provides a
central source for conservation briefing and
publicity.

Collections/Library:
Regional registers of historic buildings in the
PSA estate are being compiled, with information
on the legal status of individual buildings, their
form and history, current and future use,
condition and problems. The records include
photographs and slides. It is intended to extend
recording to include all PSA buildings in
conservation areas.
The Unit also holds information on
materials, suppliers and specialists of particular
use in conservation to supplement the resources
of PSA technical libraries.

Enquiry services:
Advice can be given on materials and
techniques, design and detailing, planning and
other legal constraints.

Property Services Agency (Scottish Branch)   351
Room B110 (Library)
Argyle House
3 Lady Lawson Street
Edinburgh EH3 9SD
tel Edinburgh (031) 229 9191 ext 5188 (Library), ext
5184 (Photographs)

Collections/Library:
Books: c 5,000 books and pamphlets. General
reference texts. Book stock on construction
subjects (ie architecture, engineering, quantity
surveying, building legislation).
Periodicals: c 150 current titles, kept for two
years only.
Photographs: c 20,000 black and white and

colour, prints and transparencies, of current
departmental building projects in Scotland.
Indexes to the collection. All the photographs
are Crown copyright.

Enquiry services and conditions of use:
Personal, postal and telephone enquiries
accepted. Available to all employees of the PSA
and other government departments and to
private construction bodies, architects, building
and architectural students, and to members of
the public doing supervised research on
construction. Photographs can be loaned and
copy prints are available, (list of charges sent on
request).

Hours:
Mon–Thurs 8.30–17.00
Fri 8.30–16.30

Publications:
Library bulletin (monthly).

Public Record Office   35
Headquarters:
Ruskin Avenue
Kew
Richmond, Surrey TW9 4DU
tel 01–876 3444

Branch:
Chancery Lane
London WC2A 1LR
tel 01–405 0741

Founded 1838

Aims:
The preservation and making available of the
records of all the departments of central
government since the Norman Conquest of
1066.

Collections/Library:
Many classes of public records contain material
of interest to the architectural historian. Among
important groups of records are those of the
Ministry of Public Buildings and Works,
Exchequer, War Office, Admiralty, State
Papers, Domestic. Material is of many kinds,
ranging from medieval documents on the King's
works to plans of modern government buildings.
Owing to the obligation to pay a stamp duty on
apprenticeship indentures, there are, with the
records of the Inland Revenue, a series of
Apprenticeship Books covering a period from
1710 to 1811. These are of value as they contain
an entry of each apprenticeship, giving the name
of the apprentice, the name and trade of the
master and sometimes name of father and the
place of residence of each. Typescript indexes (t
1774) can be consulted at the Guildhall Library
(*see* 297) and the Society of Genealogists (*see*

400). The serious researcher should spend some time at the Public Record Office looking at their *Guide, Summary, Guide supplement,* printed, typed and manuscript lists, indexes, catalogues and calendars in order to learn the full extent of the sources available. Very many Public Record Office sources are also cited in volumes such as Colvin, *English architectural history: a guide to sources* (*see* 12), Emmison, *Archives and local history* (*see* 21), Mullins, *Texts and calendars* (*see* 39), etc.

Enquiry services and conditions of use:
Personal callers only. General advice can be given but detailed enquiries cannot be answered by the staff either by post or telephone except for certain topics (such as Census enquiries) when a paid search may be undertaken. Generally speaking, modern records are housed at Kew, while pre-Victorian ones are at Chancery Lane. Records are made available to readers only in the building in which they are stored.

Hours:
Mon–Fri 9.30–17.00

Publications:
Details of publications are given in Government publications: sectional list 24: *British national archives* (HMSO).
The following are of particular interest:
Guide to the contents of the Public Record Office. Vol 1, Legal records, etc. (HMSO, 1963). Vol 2, State papers and Departmental records (HMSO, 1963). Vol 3, Documents transferred to the Public Record Office 1960–1966 (HMSO, 1968).
Maps and plans in the Public Record Office. Vol 1, British Isles c 1410–1860 (HMSO, 1967). Vol 2, America and West Indies (HMSO, 1974).
List of documents relating to the household and wardrobe, John to Edward I (HMSO, 1964).
The British Transport Historical Records Collection: a provisional guide (*see* 10).
The following leaflets are available:
Information for readers.
Notes for new readers.
Records at Chancery Lane/Records at Kew (list).

Public Record Office of Northern Ireland 353
66 Balmoral Avenue
Belfast BT9 6NY
tel Belfast (0232) 661621

Founded 1924

Aims:
To preserve the records of Northern Ireland government departments and of the courts, as well as such private papers or records of public bodies as are deemed to be of historical interest.

Collections/Library:
The collection includes about 500 million documents. Lists, catalogues and detailed calendars are produced for each deposit as circumstances permit. Indexes of personal names, place names and subject may be consulted in the public search room. All index cards refer the user to the catalogues, etc.

Enquiry services and conditions of use:
Simple enquiries can be handled by telephone. As far as possible enquiries are handled free of charge, but where they involve the location of specific items in a large collection for which there is only a bundle list, a handling charge may be made. Those wishing to use the records are encouraged to visit the Office and to undertake their own research.

Hours:
Mon–Fri 9.30–16.45

Publications:
Details of publications are given in Government publications: sectional list 24: *British national archives* (HMSO).

Public Record Office (Scotland) *see* 387:
Scottish Record Office

Pugin Society 354
4 Boscombe Avenue
London E10 6HY
tel 01–539 3876

Founded 1974

Aims:
To foster Christian architecture and traditional crafts in a Christian social order.

Collections/Library:
A reference library and magazine/newspaper cuttings collection is maintained.

Enquiry services and conditions of use:
An information service is available to serious enquirers and the media. Photocopy service available. Personal use by appointment.

Publications:
The Keys of Peter (bi-monthly).
Contrasts (annual).

The Queen's University of Belfast, 355
Architecture and Planning Information
Service
The Science Library
The Queen's University of Belfast
Chlorine Gardens
Belfast BT9 5EQ
tel Belfast (0232) 661111 ext 4304

661111 ext 4304/*continued*
Founded 1966 (prior to that the School of
Architecture and the library were in the College
of Art)

Aims:
To help the staff and students in the
Departments of Architecture and Planning at
Queen's University find information from the
library's own collections and from the wider
network of library resources. A certain amount
of work is also carried out for practising
architects and planners and members of the
public.

Collections/Library:
In addition to the book collection, of about
10,000 volumes, the Queen's University
Architecture and Planning Library subscribes to
a wide range of journals and has a slide library, a
trade literature and an Irish collection.

Books and pamphlets. The stock includes both
recent material and a good collection of earlier
publications. Subjects covered include
architectural history, building and
environmental design, building construction and
materials, history and theory of planning,
landscape design and regional and urban
planning.

Reference books. The Library maintains a good
up-to-date collection of reference sources and
information retrieval tools.

Periodicals. The Library subscribes to about 200
journals including a number of foreign titles.

Slides. The Library has some 5,000 slides
available for loan to members of staff.

Trade literature. This fairly large collection
comprising manufacturers' catalogues, offprints
and a complete set of British Standards is
regularly updated.

Irish file. This collection consists of items,
mainly photocopies of articles, dealing with all
aspects of architecture and planning in Ireland.

Enquiry services and conditions of use:
The services are primarily for staff and students
of Queen's University, but, time permitting, are
available to others.

Hours:
Mon–Fri 9.00–17.30
Sat 9.00–12.30
Closed on public holidays.

Publications:
APIS bulletin. A weekly current awareness
publication listing books and journal contents of
interest to architects and planners. Not indexed.
Guides to sources of information in architecture
and planning.

Bibliographies covering a wide range of topics.
Guide to QUB Science Library (of which the
Architecture and Planning Information Services
is a part).
Instruction in library use.

Activities:
Courses are run at various levels and are linked
to the teaching programmes in the Departments
of Architecture and Planning.
    Small exhibitions are mounted in
conjunction with teaching programmes.
    Literature searches, using both manual and
computer bases, are carried out.

Railway and Canal Historial Society   35⬤
Hon Secretary (private address)
20 Neston Drive
Chester CH2 2HR
tel Chester (0244) 381472

Founded 1957

Aims:
To investigate and record historical details of
railways and canals.

Collections/Library:
Library housed at Birmingham City Library.
Index of research material held by research
officer is available (free to members).

Enquiry services and conditions of use:
Postal enquiries only.

Publications:
Journal (three per year).
Bulletin (six per year).
Local groups publish tour notes.

Activities:
Local groups organise lectures, tours and visits.

Raymond Mander and Joe Mitchenson   35⬤
Theatre Collection
5 Venner Road
London SE26
tel 01–778 6730

Founded c 1940

Aims:
Promoting the research and knowledge of the
history of the British theatre and drama.

Collections/Library:
The collection holds photographs of interiors
and exteriors of theatres, particularly London
theatres, as well as books, plans and other
material relating to their building and
subsequent use.

Enquiry services and conditions of use:
By appointment.

Redundant Churches Fund 358
St Andrew-by-the-Wardrobe
Queen Victoria Street
London EC4V 5DE
tel 01–248 3420

Founded 1969

Aims:
The preservation in the interests of the nation
and the Church of England, of churches and
parts of churches of historic or architectural
interest vested in the Fund together with their
contents so vested. It currently looks after about
125 churches.

Collections/Library:
None.

Enquiry services:
None.

Publications:
Annual report.
Guides to churches in the care of the Fund.

Registry of Business Names 359
England and Wales:
Companies House
55–71 City Road
London EC1Y 1BB
tel 01–253 9393

Northern Ireland:
Department of Commerce
43–47 Chichester Street
Belfast

Scotland:
102 George Street
Edinburgh EH2 3DJ
tel Edinburgh (031) 2255774/5

Founded 1916

Aims:
Registration of businesses carried on under
names other than those of the proprietor.
Registration is required whenever business is
being carried on in GB in names other than those
of the proprietors. It is required if: (a) an
individual uses a business name which differs in
any way from his true name; (b) a firm uses a
business name which differs in any way from the
true names or the full corporate names of all the
partners, or (c) a company wherever
incorporated uses a business name which differs
in any way from its full corporate name. A
person would be regarded as using his true name
if he uses his surname only or his surname with
the addition of all his forename(s) or all his
initial(s). A company's true name is the title
under which it is registered under the
Companies Acts.

Collections/Library:
Open access index of all business names
registered (approx 2.4m). The particulars of any
registered business name (eg changes of
partners) may be inspected for a fee of 5 pence.

Enquiry services and conditions of use:
Personal enquiries only.

Hours:
Mon–Fri 9.45–16.00

Religious Society of Friends 360
Friends House
Euston Road
London NW1 2BJ
tel 01–387 3601

Library Founded 1673

Collections/Library:
Large collection of books, periodicals, prints and
drawings, photographs, manuscripts and
archives on Quakerism and Quakers, including
material on the architecture of Friends meeting
houses.

Enquiry services and conditions of use:
Bona fide researchers may use the library at the
Librarian's discretion.

Hours:
Mon–Fri 9.30–17.30

**Roman Catholic Bishops' Conference of
England and Wales, Department of Art and
Architecture, Conservation Sub-Committee** *see* 322:
Liturgy Commission of the Roman Catholic Bishops'
Conference of England and Wales, Department of Art and
Architecture, Conservation Sub-Committee

Royal Academy of Arts Library 361
Burlington House
Piccadilly
London W1V 0DS
tel 01–734 9052

Founded 1768

Aims:
To help practising artists and art historians with
their research queries.

Collections/Library:
The Royal Academy is the oldest institution in
Great Britain that is solely devoted to the fine
arts. It can provide information about the Royal
Academy and its history, members, exhibitors
and exhibitions. The library contains about
15,000 books dealing mainly with the fine arts,
and including many 17th, 18th and 19th-century

19th-century/*continued*
books on architecture as well as complete sets of
Royal Academy exhibition catalogues and works
dealing with members of the Royal Academy
and manuscript material connected with the
Academy. The Academy's collection includes
architectural drawings.

Enquiry services and conditions of use:
Personal, postal and telephone enquiries
accepted.
Friends of the Royal Academy is available to all.

Hours:
Mon–Fri 14.00–17.00

Publications:
The manuscript *Register of students of the Royal
Academy of Arts, 1769–1922* is available on
microfilm from EP Microfilm Ltd.
For publications described elsewhere in this
guide *see* 92, 119.

Royal Archaeological Institute 362
c/o 304 Addison House
Grove End Road
St John's Wood
London NW8 9EL
No telephone

Founded 1844

Aims:
To promote and popularise the study of
antiquities of every period in the history of the
British Isles. It constantly exerts its influence for
the preservation of national antiquities, and the
maintenance of high standards of excavation,
research and publication. Membership is
conditional on election by Council after
sponsorship.

Collections/Library:
No library of its own, but members (excluding
associate members) have access to the library of
the Society of Antiquaries of London (*see* 396).

Enquiry services:
None.

Publications:
Archaeological journal (annual). Indexes to
volumes 1 to 75 are available. The remainder is
being completed.

Activities:
The Session: Monthly meetings between
October and May, on Wednesdays in the rooms
of the Society of Antiquaries, Burlington House,
Piccadilly, London. Papers read (usually
illustrated) deal with recent excavations and
field-work, various aspects of the history of
architecture and art, etc. Guests may be
admitted.

Annual one week meeting during the summer.
Members only.
Afternoon or day excursions during the spring
and autumn to ancient sites and buildings in or
near London. Members only.

Royal College of Music 36
Prince Consort Road
London SW7
tel 01–589 3643

Founded 1882

Aims:
The advancement of the art of music; the
promotion and supervision of musical
instruction; and the encouragement and
promotion of the cultivation of music as an art.

Collections/Library:
Although the library has no specific section
relating to buildings for music and their
architects, they do have a section relating to the
history of musical institutions which may
contain references to their building, and there is
a section relating to acoustics. The Department
of Portraits holds about 200 black and white
prints of concert halls, theatres and the Royal
College of Music.

Enquiry services and conditions of use:
Personal, postal and telephone enquiries
accepted. Open to students and the general
public for enquiries, but not for loans.

Hours:
Library:
Mon–Fri 10.00–17.30 in term time.
Opening hours during the vacation may be
limited.
Department of Portraits:
Mon–Fri 10.00–17.00

Royal Commission on Historical 36
Manuscripts (and National Register of
Archives)
Quality House
Quality Court
Chancery Lane
London WC2A 1HP
tel 01–242 1198

Founded 1869

Aims:
Appointed by Royal Warrant dated 2 April 186
reconstituted in 1959. To make enquiry in Grea
Britain and Northern Ireland as to the existence
and location of manuscripts, including records
and archives of all kinds of value for the study o
history, other than records which are for the
time being public records by virtue of the Publi

Records Act; with the consent of the owners or custodians to inspect and report upon them; with the consent of the owners to reproduce and publish or assist the publication of such reports; to record particulars of such manuscripts and records in a National Register of Archives; to promote and assist the proper preservation and storage of such manuscripts and records; to assist those wishing to use such manuscripts or records for study or research; to consider and advise upon general questions relating to the location and use of such manuscripts and records; to promote the co-ordinated action of all professional and other bodies concerned with the preservation and use of such manuscripts and records; to carry out in place of the Public Record Office the statutory duties of the Master of the Rolls in respect of manorial and tithe documents.

Collections/Library:
The Commission maintains the National Register of Archives as a central collecting point for unpublished information on manuscript sources. This contains 22,000 reports on manuscript collections dealing principally with the records and papers of individuals of note, families and estates, local authorities, religious institutions and bodies, business and industrial undertakings. Aids and indexes to the information contained in the Register include short-title, personal and subject indexes.

Enquiry service and conditions of use:
The Search Room, containing reports, indexes etc of the National Register of Archives is open to the public for reference. No written introduction or reader's ticket required. Postal enquiries accepted only for limited and specific enquiries. No telephone enquiries.

Hours:
Mon–Fri 9.30–17.00

Publications:
A complete list of the Commission's reports and other publications is contained in Government publications: sectional list 17: *Publications of the Royal Commission on Historical Manuscripts* (HMSO).
Report of the Secretary to the Commissioners (annual, HMSO).
Accessions to repositories and reports added to the National Register of Archives (annual).
Architectural history and the fine and applied arts: sources in the National Register of Archives. 1969–74. 5 vols. (*see* 101).
Record repositories in Great Britain (*see* 207).

see also National Register of Archives (Scotland) (338) and Scottish Record Office (387).

Royal Commission on Historical Monuments (England) including the National Monuments Record

365

Fortress House
23 Savile Row
London W1X 1AB
tel 01–734 6010

Founded 1908

Aims:
To make a record of all ancient and historical monuments in England up to 1714 (now up to 1855). To make surveys of buildings of special architectural or historic interest which are threatened with destruction, and which are not yet published in the Commission's *Inventories*. To maintain a central archive of material relating to English ancient monuments and historical buildings.

Collections/Library:
A comprehensive collection of photographs, with some prints, engravings and architectural drawings of historic buildings in England, covering all periods, styles and dates. The collection is well indexed under county and name of town or village. Architectural details, stained glass, murals, tombs, aerial views, etc are included among the 1,000,000 photographs and 20,000 measured drawings. Copies of many photographs can be supplied.

The library houses extensive indexes of measured drawings and photographs to be found in other collections.

Inventories of every surviving building up to 1850 and selected monuments after that date are being collected, county by county. Their archives consist of detailed records of the monuments in all the counties so far surveyed.

The NMR is the official central repository for the lists of English buildings of architectural and historic interest compiled by the Department of the Environment.

The NMR possesses files of sales catalogues of houses, which may include plans of estates.

The NMR holds one of the two sets of the 'Goodhart-Rendel index of nineteenth-century churches and their architects' (*see* 168).

Copies of all National Record of Industrial Monuments cards (*see* 337) are held by the NMR.

The library maintains an index of buildings threatened with demolition.

A small collection of books and periodicals is also maintained.

Enquiry serves and conditions of use:
Available to the public.
Personal, postal and telephone enquiries accepted.

accepted./*continued*
Hours:
Mon–Fri 10.00–17.30

Publications:
Inventories (*see* 120).
Occasional publications.
Reports.
A complete list of the Commission's publications is given in Government publications: sectional list 27 (*see* 1).

Royal Commission on the Ancient and   366
Historical Monuments of Scotland
including the National Monuments Records
of Scotland
54 Melville Street
Edinburgh EH3 7HF
tel Edinburgh (031) 225 5994/5

Founded 1908

Aims:
To make a record of all ancient and historical monuments in Scotland. To make surveys of buildings of special architectural or historic interest which are threatened with destruction, and which are not yet published in the Commission's *Inventories*. To maintain a central archive of material relating to Scottish ancient monuments and historical buildings.

Collections/Library:
A comprehensive collection of about 140,000 photographs and 50,000 drawings, together with a library of some 7,000 books and periodicals relating to Scottish architecture and topography. The bulk of the material relates to Scottish architecture of all periods up to about 1930, some of the principal constituents being the plans and elevations prepared from original field surveys by the Commission's staff from 1909 onwards; a series of surveys of historic houses and vernacular buildings; a collection of drawings from the London office of William Burn (1789–1870), transferred from the RIBA; an important corpus of National Art Survey Drawings; and a large collection of drawings from the office of Sir Robert Lorimer, extending from 1891 to his death in 1929.
Indexes:
1. Principal card index. Open access. Drawings and photographs in NMRS collection. Topographical by location.
   a. Photographs. Open access. Boxed and shelved. Alphabetical within counties.
   b. Drawings. On application.
2. Summary guide index. Open access. 90 vols. Looseleaf. Alphabetical within a county system. References to source material in NMRS, public and private collections, printed books, pamphlets, etc. Cross-reference to Architects' File.
3. Library index. Open access. 27 vols. Books,

pamphlets and manuscripts. Part 1: Alphabetical by names. Part 2: Alphabetical by titles. Manuscripts: 1 vol. Alphabetical by collections.
4. Architects' file. Open access. 9 vols. Alphabetical by architects' names. Sculptors and masons included. Cross-reference to Summary guide. Entries divided into ecclesiastical, public, domestic, unexecuted, outside Scotland. Dates and references given.
A photographic copying service is available and a public loans service of photographs.

Enquiry services and conditions of use:
Available to the public.
Personal (preferably), postal and telephone enquiries accepted.

Hours:
Mon–Fri 9.30–17.00

Publications:
Inventories (*see* 122).
Occasional publications.
Reports.
Catalogue of aerial photographs (1979).
Recording Scotland's heritage: the work of the Royal Commission on the Ancient and Historical Monuments of Scotland (1975).
C. Cruft, 'Drawings in the collection of the National Monuments Record of Scotland', in *Scottish Georgian Society Bulletin*, vol 1, 1972, pp 35–9.
A complete list of the Commission's publications is given in Government publications: sectional list 27 (*see* 1).

Royal Commission on Ancient and   367
Historical Monuments in Wales including
the National Monuments Record for Wales
Edleston House
Queen's Road
Aberystwyth
Dyfed SY23 2HP
tel Aberystwyth (0970) 4381/2

Founded 1908

Aims:
To make a record of all ancient and historical monuments in Wales. To make surveys of buildings of special architectural or historic interest which are threatened with destruction, and which are not yet published in the Commission's *Inventories*. To maintain a central archive of material relating to Welsh ancient monuments and historical buildings.

Collections/Library:
A collection of photographs, available for loan, but not yet indexed. A collection of drawings, available for loan, which are indexed. Original material collected by investigators, including plans and other drawings, written descriptions,

and photographs, together with an integrated card index to all records held by the Commission.
Copies of all published *Inventories*, and the original material upon which they were based.
A general archaeological, architectural and historical reference library.

Enquiry services and conditions of use:
Available to the public.
Personal (for specific or general enquiries, but consultation of records by appointment), postal (for specific requests) and telephone enquiries (for specific requests if absolutely unavoidable) accepted.

Hours:
Mon–Fri 9.00–17.00

Publications:
Inventories (see 121).
Occasional publications.
Reports.
A complete list of the Commission's publications is given in Government publications: sectional list 27 (*see* 1).

Royal Fine Art Commission   368
2 Carlton Gardens
London SW1Y 5AA
tel 01–930 3935

Founded 1924

Aims:
The Commission is required to advise Departments of State on, and to call their attention to, any prospect or development which may appear to affect amenities of a national or public character.

Collections/Library:
None.

Enquiry services:
Postal enquiries only.

Hours
Mon–Fri 9.30–17.00

Publications:
Periodic report (published by HMSO).

Royal Fine Art Commission for Scotland   369
22 Melville Street
Edinburgh EH3 7NS
tel Edinburgh (031) 225 5434

Founded 1927

Aims:
To enquire into and report on questions of

public amenity or of artistic importance relating to Scotland which might be referred to them by the Department of State and to advise on similar questions referred to them by public or quasi-public bodies. The Commission advises on the quality of the built environment insofar as this affects the public interest (including considerations of urban environmental planning, design, architecture and conservation) and also on works of art in relation to building exteriors and interiors.

Publications:
Periodic report (published by HMSO).

Royal Horticultural Society   370
Lindley Library
Royal Horticultural Society Hall
Vincent Square
London SW1P 2PE
tel 01–834 4333

Founded 1804

Aims:
To collect information respecting the cultivating of all plants and trees and to encourage every branch of horticulture.

Collections/Library:
Over 36,000 books. Includes material on glasshouses and other horticultural buildings.

Enquiry services and conditions of use:
Open to the public by prior application to the Secretary.

Hours:
Mon–Fri 9.30–17.30

Publications:
The Lindley Library. Catalogue of books, pamphlets, manuscripts and drawings. (London, 1927).

The Royal Incorporation of Architects in   371
Scotland
15 Rutland Square
Edinburgh EH1 2BE
tel Edinburgh (031) 229 7205

Founded 1916

Aims:
To organise and unite in fellowship the architects of Scotland and to combine their efforts for the general advancement of Scottish architecture and for the promotion of the efficiency of the profession of architecture.

Collections/Library:
Books and material on Scottish architecture.

architecture./*continued*
Enquiry services and conditions of use:
Personal, postal and telephone enquiries
accepted.

Hours:
Mon–Fri 9.15–13.00; 14.30–17.00

Publications:
Annual report.
Newsletter/Journal: *Prospect* (quarterly).
Monographs (eg *69 recent industrial projects.*
1979).
Guides.
Kalendar.

Royal Institute of British Architects 372
66 Portland Place
London W1N 4AD
tel 01–580 5533

Founded 1834

Aims:
Professional institute for the general
advancement of architecture and the knowledge
of the various arts and sciences connected
therewith.
Founded in 1834 as the Institute of British
Architects; became the Royal Institute of British
Architects in 1866.

Collections/Library:
British Architectural Library (*see* 236, 237).
In addition to the Library, various departments
maintain collections or provide information
which may be of interest to the researcher.

Press office:
Maintains a clipping file from the major national
newspapers, which can be personally inspected.
Maintains biographical files of living British
architects.
Maintains photographic portrait files for living
British architects.

Clients Advisory Service:
Maintains practice files (including photographs
of work) and brochures for current RIBA
member practices. Fully indexed by building
type.

Membership records:
Records of RIBA members, but for 19th century
and early 20th century records see the British
Architectural Library.

Archives:
Many valuable series of archives of the RIBA
from the 1830s to the present day, and of some
associated societies, or societies which have
merged with it, such as the Architects'
Benevolent Society and the Society of
Architects, are preserved in the Institute.

The archives include minutes of meetings
of Council and of ordinary general meetings;
minutes of the various standing committees;
ledgers, journals, cash books; manuscripts of
prize essays and of sessional papers;
correspondence with members and others;
biographical files on architects;
recommendations and declarations of Fellows,
Associates and Licentiates; nomination papers of
Fellows, Associates and Honorary Associates;
and other administrative series. *Bona fide*
researchers may consult these archives under
appropriate safeguards.
Some of the early archives are held by the
Library. For the Institute's archives not held by
the Library, contact the Administration
Department.

Enquiry services and conditions of use:
Contact the appropriate department.

Hours:
Mon–Fri 9.30–17.00

Publications:
'Yellow pages, a classified directory to RIBA
services, activities and resources', in *RIBA
Journal*, vol 85, no 12, Dec 1978.
For publications described elsewhere in this
guide *see:* 45, 46, 47, 48, 49, 123, 124, 125, 127,
128, 155, 196, 213, 585.

Activities:
Lectures, exhibitions etc.
Bookshop.

The Royal Institute of the Architects of 373
Ireland
8 Merrion Square
Dublin 2
Ireland
tel Dublin 761703

Founded 1839

Aims:
The governing body of the architectural
profession in Ireland. Its objects are the
advancement of architecture and the associated
arts and sciences, the promotion of high
standards of professional conduct and practice,
the protection of the interests of architectural
training and education.

Collections/Library:
The collection of architectural books has been
dispersed to other libraries.

Enquiry services:
No active information unit.

Publications:
Annual report.
Yearbook.

Royal Institution of Chartered Surveyors 374
12 Great George Street
Parliament Square
London SW1P 3AD
tel 01–222 7000

Founded 1868

Aims:
A professional institution concerned with land,
property and buildings, and the training and
professional standards of chartered surveyors.

Collections/Library:
32,000 volumes on statistics, law,
photogrammetry, land surveying, agriculture,
land agency and estate management, building
and construction, housing and property
management, landlord and tenant, planning and
development, rating and valuation, architecture,
fine arts and chattels, estate agency. Special
collections: historical collections on land
surveying, building, economics, fine arts, Board
of Agriculture Reports (19th century); Royal
Commission Reports on land use (19th century);
topographical collections; *Victoria county
histories.*

Enquiry services and conditions of use:
Open to the public for reference.

Hours:
Mon–Fri 9.30–17.30

Royal Scottish Academy 375
The Mound
Edinburgh EH2 2EL
tel Edinburgh (031) 225 6671

Founded 1826

Aims:
The Royal Scottish Academy of Painting,
Sculpture and Architecture was founded to
encourage the practice of the fine arts in
Scotland, by showing to the public
representative collections of works, mainly by
Scottish artists of the time.

Collections/Library:
The Library can provide information about the
Royal Scottish Academy and its history,
members, exhibitors and exhibitions. The
Library contains books dealing with the fine arts
as well as complete sets of Royal Scottish
Academy exhibition catalogues and works
dealing with members of the Academy and
manuscript material connected with the
Academy.

Enquiry services and conditions of use:
The Library exists primarily for the use of

members and associates of the Academy and its
honorary academicians. Apart from these the
Library is purely for reference. However,
requests for information received from outside
bodies and private individuals are dealt with and
information supplied by letter, telephone and
personally to those who call at the Academy.

Hours:
Mon–Fri 10.00–13.00 or by appointment

Publications:
Annual report.
Exhibition catalogues.
For publications described elsewhere in this
guide *see: 89, 129.*

Royal Society for the Encouragement of 376
Arts, Manufactures and Commerce
8 John Adam Street
Adelphi
London WC2N 6EZ
tel 01–839 2366

Founded 1754

Aims:
The aims of the Royal Society of Arts (styled
Royal in 1908) are the advancement,
development, and application of every
department of science in connection with arts,
manufactures, and commerce. It serves as a
liaison between the various practical arts and
sciences, and provides a medium for the
announcement by leading authorities of recent
developments of more than specialised interest.

Collections/Library:
The Society's library is divided into three
sections:
1. The lending section, which contains over
   5,000 books devoted mainly to the industrial
   and fine arts and the background of the
   Society's history (including technological,
   economic, art and architectural history).
2. The reference section, which contains about
   3,000 books, covers the same subject range as
   the lending section and includes two special
   collections: one devoted to the major
   international exhibitions, and the other
   consisting of the early library of the Society,
   with other works published before 1830.
3. The Society's early archives, consisting of
   approximately 10,000 manuscript items of the
   18th and early 19th centuries.
All books and periodicals are listed in the card
catalogue by author and subject.

Enquiry services and conditions of use:
Personal, postal and telephone enquiries
accepted.

Hours:
Mon–Fri 9.30–12.30; 13.30–17.30

5.2 Guide to societies, institutions and organisations

13.30–17.30/*continued*
Publications:
Journal (monthly).
The Royal Society of Arts, 1794–1954, by Derek
Hudson and Kenneth William Luckhurst
(London: John Murray, 1954). Supplemented
by a *Bibliography of the Society's history*
(London: The Society, 1980) containing a list of
the Society's publications since 1954.

Activities:
Ordinary meetings for the reading of papers are
held regularly on Wednesdays from November
to May.
        Courses of lectures of an expository and
semi-technical character are delivered on
Mondays. Normally, three courses of three
lectures each are given during the Session.

Royal Society of Ulster Architects   377
    51 Malone Road
    Belfast BT9 6RY
    tel Belfast (0232) 668846

Founded 1901

Aims:
The general advancement of architecture.

Collections/Library:
The library was handed over to Queen's
University, Belfast (*see* 355). A photographic
library of members' work is at present under way
and it is hoped this will develop into a useful
up-dated record of architecture in the province.

Enquiry services and conditions of use:
Personal, postal and telephone enquiries
accepted.

Hours:
Mon–Fri 9.30–13.00; 14.30–17.30

Publications:
Annual yearbook and directory.

Activities:
Lectures, exhibitions, visits, conferences,
competitions, mid-career education.

Royal Town Planning Institute   378
    26 Portland Place
    London W1N 4BE
    tel 01–636 9107

Founded 1914

Aims:
To further the theory and practice of town and
country planning. The chartered professional
institution for town planners.

Collections/Library:
Library of some 10,000 volumes and 100 current
periodicals. Classified by UDC with an author
and classified catalogue with alphabetical subject
index. Includes a collection of regional surveys
and plans prepared in the 1930s.

Enquiry services and conditions of use:
Personal, postal and telephone enquiries
accepted.

Hours:
Mon–Thurs 9.00–17.00
Fri 9.00–16.30

Publications:
Planner (journal).
Newsletter.
Books.
Conference proceedings.
Seminar proceedings.
Consultation documents.

Activities:
Conferences and seminars.

Ryedale Folk Museum   379
    Hutton-le-Hole
    Yorkshire
    tel Lastingham (075 15) 367

Founded 1966

Aims:
To collect and display bygones reflecting the life
and times of the district and the reconstruction
of buildings, especially those of cruck
construction.

Enquiry services and conditions of use:
Postal enquiries should be addressed to the
curator.

Publications:
Newsletter (bi-annual).
Guide book.

The Saltire Society   380
    Saltire House
    13 Atholl Crescent
    Edinburgh EH3 8HA
    tel Edinburgh (031) 228 6621

Founded 1936

Aims:
To perpetuate, strengthen and develop the
cultural heritage of Scotland.

Collections/Library:
Library of about 2,000 books on Scottish
literature, history and culture and biography.

Archives (in preparation) of the Society's annual Awards for Good Design in Housing, Restoration and Reconstruction of Housing and Housing Area Improvement.

Enquiry services and conditions of use:
Personal, postal and telephone enquiries accepted.

Hours:
Mon–Fri 9.15–13.00; 2.30–17.00

Publications:
Newsletters.
A list of publications is available.

Activities:
Meetings in branches.
Conferences.
Awards in crafts, art, school projects, housing, historical research.
Musical activities.
Art exhibitions.
Conservation and amenity.

AVE Britain's Heritage   381
3 Park Square West
London NW1 4LJ
tel 01–486 4953

Founded 1975

Aims:
A conservation pressure group formed to arouse concern about the continuing destruction of historic buildings. A group of journalists, architects and planners who welcome correspondents able to send details of threats to historic buildings, SAVE campaigns through press releases and reports for the retention and rehabilitation of old buildings for social and economic as well as architectural reasons.

Collections/Library:
None.

Enquiry services and conditions of use:
Personal (preferably by appointment), postal and telephone enquiries accepted.

Publications:
Annual report usually appears in periodicals.
Occasional reports often appear in periodicals.
Books and booklets, eg:
The best buildings in Britain (1981). A catalogue of Grade I listed buildings in England and Wales and of Category A buildings in Scotland. A basic reference book to structures designated as of special architectural or historic interest.
The Fall of Zion: northern chapel architecture and its future, by Ken Powell (1980). A survey of non-conformist architecture in the north of England.

Lost houses of Scotland (1980). Documents nearly 400 country houses.
Off the rails: saving railway architecture (1977).
Offprints of SAVE reports and copies of books and booklets are available from the SAVE office.
A list of publications in print is available.

Save London's Theatres Campaign   382
8 Harley Street
London W1N 2AB
tel 01–636 6367

Founded 1972

Aims:
The saving of theatre buildings in the Greater London area, and ensuring their continued use for live entertainment. The Campaign is a pressure group sponsored by British Actors Equity Association.

Collections/Library:
Collection consists solely of reports and leaflets of the Campaign.

Enquiry services and conditions of use:
Postal enquiries only.

Hours:
Normal office hours.

Publications:
Annual report.
Propaganda leaflets.

Activities:
General approaches to national and local government; more specific approaches around certain theatre buildings which have been under threat. Also petitions, meetings and demonstrations about threatened theatres.
Efforts to obtain legislation to protect theatre buildings, resulting so far in the Theatres Trust Act and the consequent setting up of the Theatres Trust (*see* 406).

Science Museum Library   383
South Kensington
London SW7 5NH
tel 01–581 4734 (library enquiry desk) or 589 3456 (museum switchboard)

Founded 1883

Aims:
Museum of science and technology.

Collections/Library:
Pictorial collections, including all kinds of pictorial media, illustrating the history of science and technology; some will include architectural subjects, eg railway prints may illustrate railway

railway/*continued*
stations or other buildings. The Simmons
Collection of records relating to British
windmills and watermills consists of some 240
folders of typed information collected from
many sources, and approximately 300 maps of
various dates on which the locations of mills have
been marked. The records, which are arranged
by county, are supplemented by photographic
prints of many mills, from over 2,000 negatives.

Enquiry services and conditions of use:
Personal, postal and telephone enquiries
accepted. Reader's ticket required to consult rare
printed books, archival material and
manuscripts, prints and drawings.

Hours:
Daily except Sundays and Bank Holiday
weekends. 10.00–17.30

Publications:
A brief guide to the Science Museum Library.
Catalogue of pre-1641 printed books.
Photocopying service prices.
Photograph and lantern slide service.

Scottish Churches Architectural Heritage Trust

384

15 North Bank Street
The Mound
Edinburgh EH1 2LP
tel Edinburgh (031) 225 8644

Founded 1978

Aims:
To raise funds for the repair and maintenance of
church buildings in Scotland which are in public
use for worship. To encourage the highest
standard of care and workmanship, by attaching
appropriate conditions to grant aid, by
stimulating knowledgeable interest in those
responsible for their upkeep and helping to
increase expertise in the professions and craft
trades concerned.

Collections/Library:
A very small collection of conservation source
books and reference material for maintenance.
Not for public use.

Enquiry services and conditions of use:
Telephone/written assistance will be given for
problems involved with fund raising,
restoration, repairs, locating a suitable architect,
location of craftsmen etc. Source of assistance
with history research for Scottish churches.

Hours
Mon–Fri 9.00–17.00

Publications:
Annual report.
Newsletter.

Guide to grants available for church buildings.
Factsheet on the Trust.
Brochures.
Poster.

Activities:
Exhibitions, conferences, tours, heritage
churches walks.

Scottish Civic Trust *see* 260: Civic Trust

Scottish Development Department

38

New St Andrews House
Edinburgh EH1 3SX
tel Edinburgh (031) 556 8400

Branches:
Ancient Monuments Branch
17 Atholl Crescent
Edinburgh EH3 8JN
tel Edinburgh (031) 229 9321
(note: a move is planned)

Historic Buildings Branch
25 Drumsheugh Gardens
Edinburgh EH3 7RN
tel Edinburgh (031) 226 3611

Scottish Office Library
New St Andrews House
Edinburgh EH1 3TG
tel Edinburgh (031) 556 8400 ext 5633

Aims:
The Scottish Development Department
discharges in Scotland many of the functions
undertaken in England by the Departments of
the Environment and Transport. It is
responsible for most matters affecting the
physical environment in Wales, including
housing, planning, comprehensive development
and ancient monuments and historic buildings.

The Ancient Monuments Branch is responsible
for the preservation and display of ancient
monuments in the care of the Secretary of State,
statutory protection of ancient monuments and
rescue archaeology.

The Historic Buildings Branch deals with the
listing of buildings of special architectural or
historic interest, grants towards the repair or
maintenance of buildings of outstanding
architectural or historic interest and towards the
preservation or enhancement of the character or
appearance of conservation areas.

The Scottish Office Library's object is the
collection, organisation and dissemination of all
the information needed to further the work of
the department.

Collections/Library:
Ancient Monuments Branch:
Maintains a schedule of monuments classed as of
national importance, whether or not in state
care.
Holds information and descriptions for each
monument.

Historic Buildings Branch:
Maintains a complete list for Scotland of
buildings of special architectural or historic
interest, and maps showing where they are.
Holds photographs of all buildings on lists
revised since 1978. The negatives are in the
collection of the National Monuments Record of
Scotland (*see* 366).
Holds complete lists of conservation areas in
Scotland, with maps showing boundaries of the
areas.
Holds files of Historic Buildings Council cases
(confidential).

Scottish Office Library:
The Library has four main libraries and several
sub-libraries, and architecture features in several
of them. The Library's stock of books,
pamphlets, government publications and
periodicals covers: local government; housing;
social and environmental planning; roads, traffic
and transport; countryside and recreation, etc.

Enquiry services and conditions of use:
Personal, postal and telephone enquiries
accepted. Reference facilities for the public. For
enquiries concerning listed buildings, listed
buildings consent and grants, contact the
Historic Buildings Branch.

Hours:
Mon–Thurs 8.30–17.00
Fri 8.30–16.30

Publications:
Scottish Office publications list (annual).

Ancient Monuments Branch:
Guide books to monuments in the care of the
state.
Lists of ancient monuments.
Postcards, slides.

Historic Buildings Branch:
Scotland's listed buildings (1981).

Library:
Library bulletin (monthly accessions list).

cottish Georgian Society   386
39 Castle Street
Edinburgh EH1 3BH
tel Edinburgh (031) 225 8391

Founded 1956

Aims:
To encourage the protection, preservation,
study and appreciation of buildings of merit and
historic interest of all periods in Scotland.

Collections/Library:
None.

Enquiry services and conditions of use:
Personal, postal and telephone enquiries
accepted.

Hours:
Wed 14.00–17.00
Thurs and Fri 9.30–17.00

Publications:
Annual report.
Bulletin (approximately every two years).

Activities:
Lectures, architectural walks and tours open to
members. With the three subsidiary groups
(North-East Group, Strathclyde Group and
Highland Group) examine and comment to the
planning authority on all applications for listed
building consent whether for alteration or
demolition. Representations are made at public
enquiries and advice is given to applicants and
their architects.

Scottish Record Office   387
PO Box 36
HM General Register House
Edinburgh EH1 3YY
tel
HM General Register House:
Edinburgh (031) 556 6585
West Register House:
Edinburgh (031) 226 5101

Founded 1774

Aims:
Preservation of public, local and private archives
in Scotland. The National Register of Archives
(Scotland) (*see* 338), which forms part of the
Scottish Record Office, is responsible for the
listing of private archives in private custody, the
dissemination of information regarding such
archives, and advice to owners on archive
problems.

Collections/Library:
HM General Register House, Princes Street,
Edinburgh is the headquarters of the Scottish
Record Office and the repository for the
principal legal registers and the older historical
records. The main holdings include: state papers
and administrative records of pre-Union (1707)
Scotland, including records of the Scottish
Parliament, Privy Council and Exchequer;
records of the post-Union Scottish Exchequer;

5.2 Guide to societies, institutions and organisations

Exchequer;/*continued*
registers of the Scottish seals—Chancery (Great Seal), Privy Seal and Signet; registers of the Court of Session, High Court of Judiciary, Sheriff, Commissary and other courts; registers of Sasines and Deeds and notarial and diligence records; local records, including local authority records, heritors' records, and valuation rolls; Church records; gifts and deposits (private archives); and miscellaneous series. Lists and other guides to the records are available for consultation in the Historical Search Room.

The Register House Plans (RHP) collection, over 40,000 in number, consists largely of manuscript plans with engraved, lithographed and marked Ordnance Survey plans and some printed maps. The nucleus of the RHP series came from the records of the Court of Session, mostly plans produced as evidence in such cases as the division of commodities. On to this nucleus has been added a vast number of plans from diverse sources, especially from private owners, from the Scottish-based modern government departments, from the sherriff courts and from the Scottish region of the British Railways Board. There are more than 10,000 British Rail plans. As a by-product of the work of the National Register of Archives (Scotland), the RHP also includes photocopies of valuable plans in private custody. Estate plans, for all parts of Scotland, bulk largely in the collection. Though there are a few earlier ones, the vast majority of the plans are post-1740. Many of these plans are illustrated with 'vignettes', pictorial designs which often portray visually the buildings which the plan portrays cartographically. The 19th-century urbanisation of Scotland is illustrated by many feuing plans, proposals for building elegant suburbs. Architectural plans in the RHP series cover a complete range of buildings. The Department of the Environment has deposited a series of plans of well-known public buildings, such as Edinburgh Castle and the Royal Scottish Academy. The records of the heritors, who in each parish were responsible for the maintenance of kirk and manse, have produced plans of ecclesiastical buildings throughout Scotland. Mainly from private depositors have come plans of domestic architecture—plans, elevations and sections of the homes of all social classes. There are also plans of work buildings, such as mills, byres, stables, steadings and hothouses. A large number of plans relate to communications and transport, especially railways. These include detailed architectural plans of station buildings. Not all the plans in the RHP series are Scottish. There are plans of military fortifications abroad, plans of settlements in the colonies, notably Australia and Canada, and also some English plans.

Because they come into the Scottish Record Office in no logical order, the Register House Plans are listed in a running reference system.

Each plan is given the next chronological RHP number and a description which locates it topographically. If it is a Scottish plan, the location is by the civil parish and county existing immediately before the local government reorganisation of 1975. Technical drawings are listed by name of the source company in contrary order. The lists describing the plans are bound into volumes covering about twelve hundred plans each. These volumes are available in the Scottish Record Office's Historical and West Search Rooms and also in the National Library of Scotland. A quicker access to particular plans is by means of the card indexes, which are kept in both search rooms. The main card index is a topographical one, covering the whole plan collection, but there are also subsidiary card indexes for various categories of research, such as architecture and communications. The architectural card index is arranged by subject (commercial, domestic, ecclesiastical, farm buildings and steadings, garden ornaments and furniture, interiors, public buildings, railway buildings). Within each type the arrangement is by parish. There is also a card index to the names of architects, surveyors and firms, which refers to a plan number, but does not give detail of what the building is, where it is, or when it was built. For such details one must consult the lists in the bound volumes. A more detailed guide, though as yet covering only a small proportion of the collection, is the *Descriptive list of plans in the Scottish Record Office* which is being published by HMSO. These volumes describe the plans in considerable detail, including size, scale and National Grid reference.

The West Register House, Charlotte Square, Edinburgh, serves as a branch repository for modern records and series requiring specialised storage. The main holdings include: records of government departments and nationalised industries in Scotland (including the Scottish railway archives); court processes and warrants of legal registers; maps and plans; and the Scottish Record Office's microfilm library. Lists and other guides are available in the West Search Room.

Standard reference books are available for consultation on open shelves in the search rooms. In addition the Scottish Record Office maintains a small reference library dealing mainly with Scottish history, law and topography.

A new *Guide to the Scottish Record Office* is in preparation. M. Livingstone, *Guide to the public records of Scotland* (1905), although greatly out-of-date, is still useful for the older historical records. Details of accessions each year are given in the *Annual report of the Keeper of the Records of Scotland*. A Summary Catalogue of all the Scottish Record Office's holdings may be consulted in the Historical and West Search Rooms. Many Scottish Record Office sources a also cited in other publications, such as Dunbar 'Source materials for Scottish architectural history' (see 20).

Enquiry services and conditions of use:
Records which are open to public examination may be inspected without charge for historical purposes by personal callers. For those who are unable to make a personal search the Scottish Record Office is normally prepared to answer, without charge, specific postal enquiries, eg for the will of a particular person, or requests for photocopies which provide sufficient information for the documents to be readily identifiable, or enquiries for information regarding sources for particular subjects of historical research. In some cases the Office may, for a fee, undertake searches over such periods and subject to such conditions as the Keeper of the Records of Scotland may prescribe for particular classes of records. The Keeper has discretion to reduce or waive the fee in appropriate cases and reserves the right to decline searches. The Scottish Record Office cannot undertake general genealogical searches which should be referred to the Scots Ancestry Research Society, 20 York Place, Edinburgh EH1 3EP or from private record agents (list available on request). Postal enquiries should be addressed to: The Keeper of the Records of Scotland, Scottish Record Office, PO Box 36, HM General Register House, Edinburgh EH1 3YY.

Hours:
Historical Search Room (HM General Register House):
Mon–Fri 9.00–16.45
Sat 9.00–12.00
West Search Room (West Register House):
Mon–Fri 9.00–16.45

Publications:
Details of publications are given in Government publications: sectional list 24: *British national archives* (HMSO).
 The following are of particular interest:
Source lists on various subjects, eg *Source list of material on art and architecture in Scottish Record Office. Part 1. Private muniments.* This has been compiled and circulated (copy in BAL) but is undergoing extensive revision and amplification with a view to publication.
Guide to the Scottish Record Office (in course of preparation).
Letterpress and photo-litho publications including *Accounts of the Masters of Works 1529–1650* (2 vols) and *Descrptive lists of plans in the Scottish Record Office.*
SRO Leaflet no 1: *History of the national archives.*
SRO Leaflet no 2: *HM General Register House.*
SRO Leaflet no 3: *The West Register House.*
SRO Leaflet no 5: *Scottish Record Office: facilities for historical research.*

SRO Leaflet no 6: *Scottish Record Office: facilities for local history groups.*
SRO Leaflet no 8: *Scottish Record Office: Register House Plans Collection.*
SRO Leaflet no 9: *Scottish Record Office: sources for family history.*

Scottish Society for Industrial Archaeology 388
Honorary Secretary
c/o Museum of Transport
23 Albert Drive
Glasgow G41
tel Glasgow (041) 423 8000

Founded 1967

Aims:
To further the study of industrial archaeology in Scotland.

Collections/Library:
None.

Sir John Soane's Museum 389
13 Lincoln's Inn Fields
London WC2A 3BP
tel 01–405 2107

Founded 1833

Aims:
Founded for the benefit of students and amateurs of the arts.

Collections/Library:
The general collection consists of Egyptian, Greek, Roman and other antiquities, casts and models, permanently exhibited as arranged by Sir John Soane. Also exhibited are paintings, drawings and engravings, notably Hogarth, Canaletto and Turner.
 The library, containing 3,500 titles of which 1,940 are concerning art and architecture, is that of Sir John Soane, and represents his collection at the time of his death in 1837.
 There is a collection of 30,000 architectural drawings, especially Adam, Dance and Soane.
 Catalogues and indexes of all sections are available at the Museum. There are no published catalogues (other than the Adam catalogue listed below), but copies from microfilm can be obtained.

Enquiry services and conditions of use:
The library is available for study by the public on prior application.

Hours:
Tues–Sat 10.00–17.00

5.2 Guide to societies, institutions and organisations

10.00–17.00/*continued*
Publications:
A new description of Sir John Soane's Museum,
4th ed, 1977.
*The drawings of Robert and James Adam in Sir
John Soane's Museum, with the Catalogue of the
drawings and designs of Robert and James Adam
in Sir John Soane's Museum.* Compiled by Walter
L. Spiers. Microfilm of drawings and printed
catalogue. Cambridge: Chadwyck-Healey;
Teaneck (NJ): Somerset House, 1979.
Sir John Summerson at Sir John Soane's Museum.
A tape cassette accompanied by 24 slides.
Produced by Pidgeon Audio Visual (*see* 474).

Society for Medieval Archaeology   390
University College
London WC1E 6BT
tel 01–387 7050 ext 232

Founded 1957

Aims:
To further the study of post-Roman archaeology
(c 400 to 1500 AD), and to co-ordinate the work
of archaeologists and historians in this field.

Collections/Library:
None.

Enquiry services:
None.

Publications:
Medieval archaology (annual).
Monographs.

Activities:
Annual conference.

Society for Promoting Christian Knowledge   391
Holy Trinity Church
Marylebone Road
London NW1 4DU
tel 01–387 5282

Founded 1699

Aims:
Missionary society and publishing body. At
home, Christian publishing and bookselling;
overseas, support of indigenous Christian
literature operations.

Collections/Library:
Over 25,000 file copies of SPCK publications,
including many on church and cathedral
architecture and decorative arts.
    Some information can be derived also from
the Society's archives, eg on various
church-building activities during the 18th, 19th
and 20th centuries.
    Titles of SPCK publications under subject

headings can be found in classified catalogues
available through Archivist and Librarian. Title
have been entered in a File Copy index under
their first letter, in approximately the order in
which they went out of print. Each has its own
shelf number.
    The rich archives of the earlier decades of
the 18th century have been card-indexed. For
subsequent periods recourse must be had to the
volume indexes.

Enquiry services and conditions of use:
Personal (by appointment), postal and telephon
enquiries accepted.

Hours:
Irregular, but receptionist (9.00–17.00) is able t
expedite telephone enquiries.

**Society for the Interpretation of Britain's
Heritage**   39
Ian Parkin, Hon Secretary
47 Grange Park Avenue
Wilmslow, Cheshire SK9 4AJ
tel Wilmslow (0625) 525271

Founded 1975

Aims:
To act as a forum for the exchange of views and
news on the interpretation of the urban and rur
heritage of Britain. Membership of the Society i
drawn from those individuals who are concerne
with studying, planning and managing
interpretive facilities in all parts of the country.

Publications:
Interpretation (thrice yearly newsletter).

Activities:
Meetings.

**Society for the Promotion of the
Preservation of Early English Parish
Churches**   39
1 Headley Lane
Thornton
Bradford, West Yorkshire BD13 3LX
No telephone

Founded 1977

Aims:
To promote and foster an interest in the
preservation of English churches, that is earlier
parish churches up to the years 1650–1700.

Collections/Library:
1. Collection of photographic slides (35mm full
frame) covering the subjects of church art and
architecture.
All counties—exteriors; interiors; details.

Indexed A–Z by individual church.
2. Collection/library of church
literature—church guides, parish magazines,
histories, prints and postcards from 1850
onwards.
All counties of England only.
Indexed A–Z by individual church.

Enquiry services and conditions of use:
General enquiry service on all aspects of church
art, architecture and history. Postal enquiries
only. Loan of photographic slides to accredited
study groups (applications by post).

Publications:
Ashlar (quarterly). Publication on the subject of
church art, architecture and history, with topical
news and events. Illustrated.
Church guides.
Monographs.

Activities:
Advice on the design and layout of parish
magazines with artwork service for Church of
England churches.
Lectures/courses on the appreciation of church
art and architecture; aspects of church
preservation and restoration.
Conferences.
The promoting of exhibitions on aspects of
church art etc.
Photographic recording for societies etc (eg
cathedral treasures for the Worshipful Company
of Goldsmiths, London, 1979; restoration of All
Saints, Harewood, for Redundant Churches
Fund, 1979).
Recording projects for societies, etc (eg
grave-stone inscriptions, St Thomas's, Bradley,
Hudds. for the Council for Places of Worship,
1979–80).

Society for the Protection of Ancient Buildings   394
55 Great Ormond Street
London WC1N 3JA
tel 01–405 2646 or 4541

Founded 1877

Aims:
Founded by William Morris, the Society advises
on all problems affecting old buildings, giving
technical advice on their treatment and repair.
Buildings, ecclesiastical and secular, large and
small, including mills, barns, dovecotes and
bridges are within the scope of the Society.
The Wind and Watermill Section of the Society
was set up in 1929 (originally as the Windmill
Section, coverage was extended to watermills
later).

Collections/Library:
The Society maintains a modest library of
books, pamphlets and slides.

The Society has the country's most extensive
archive on the conservation of historic buildings.
The archive, dating from 1877, contains case
studies and photographic records. It is largely
organised by individual buildings.

An inventory of pre-Victorian barns in England
and Wales is being established.

Enquiry services and conditions of use:
Facilities are limited and access to the archives is
restricted to *bona fide* researchers, strictly by
appointment.

Hours:
Mon–Fri 9.30–17.30

Publications:
SPAB News (1980– , quarterly).
Literature on the history and care of old
buildings, their features and fittings. A list of
publications may be obtained on application.

Activities:
The Society investigates cases of buildings
(mainly pre-1714) suffering from neglect or
threatened by damaging treatment or with
destruction; prepares surveys and reports on the
historical areas of cities, towns and villages;
arranges conferences, lectures, walks and
exhibitions; maintains an index of houses
threatened with demolition and provides
possible purchasers with information. A one
week historical buildings repair course is held
annually in October. The Society is one of the
bodies to whom all applications to demolish
listed buildings are submitted statutorily.

Society for Theatre Research   395
77 Kinnerton Street
London SW1X 8ED
No telephone

Founded 1948

Aims:
The Society for Theatre Research provides a
meeting point for all those – scholars, research
workers, actors, producers and lovers of the
theatre – who are interested in its history and
technique. It encourages further research into
these subjects and is especially anxious to link it
to modern theatre practice. Through its
world-wide membership the Society is able to
act as a clearing house for historical and technical
information.

Collections/Library:
The library and collections have been handed
over to the Theatre Museum (at present c/o the
Victoria and Albert Museum, South
Kensington, London SW7 2RL, pending the
completion and opening of the Theatre Museum
in Covent Garden)(*see* 404).

(see 4.04)/*continued*
Enquiry services and conditions of use:
Facilities available for answering queries
regarding the history of the British theatre and
stage.

Publications:
Annual report.
Theatre notebook (three times per year).
Index to 'Theatre notebook', vols 1–25.
Bulletin (occasional newsletter).
Occasional publications.

Activities:
Monthly lecture meetings, Oct–March.
Annual public lecture in May.
Occasional special events.

Society of Antiquaries of London   396
Burlington House
Piccadilly
London W1V 0HS
tel 01–734 0193 or 437 9954

Founded 1707

Aims:
The study of antiquity and the history of former
times. Its interests include archaeological
investigation and the preservation of historic
buildings.

Collections/Library:
The library contains c 130,000 books and
periodicals. Currently some 300 foreign and 250
English periodicals are taken. The aim is to
provide Fellows with a good range of books and
periodicals covering their multifarious interests
(archaeological research, genealogy, heraldry,
documents, records, prehistory, topography,
classical, European and British architecture of all
periods, vernacular, religious, and industrial
architecture, preservation of monuments, etc),
and in some fields, eg British archaeology, it is
unrivalled in the completeness and extent of its
collection. Besides the author catalogue, there is
a very large subject catalogue which, though
variable in quality, can be a very useful research
tool. The subject and topographical card index
started in 1924. Printed catalogues exist for the
19th century.
    Collection of 800 manuscripts and 557 early
printed books (1500–1641), of which 212 are
English and 345 foreign.
    Collection of 30,000 prints and drawings
which relate for the most part to the study of
architecture, antiquities and topography. This
collection is topographically indexed.
    The Society possesses a complete set of
rubbings of all the monumental brasses at
present known in the British Isles. The
rubbings, with the detailed catalogue and related
books and illustrations, forms the best collection
of materials on brass rubbings.

There are numerous other collections of a
specialised character. They include rubbings of
inscriptions and marks on bells, plans of castles,
photographs of roof bosses, etc.
    The Society holds more than 20,000 slides
forming a rather haphazard collection, mainly o
the older 3¼in size. A large proportion are of
architectural subjects and may be borrowed by
Fellows of the Society.

Enquiry service and conditions of use:
Postal enquiries preferred.
Use of the collections by arrangement.

Hours:
Mon–Fri 10.00–17.00
Sat 10.00–13.00 usually closed August.

Publications:
Antiquaries journal (1921– ; annually in 2 parts)
        Supersedes the Society's *Proceedings.*
—— *Index to vols 1–10.*
—— *Index to vols 21–30.*
—— *Index to vols 31–40.*
Proceedings (1861–1920).
—— *Index to 2nd series, vols 1–20* (1861–1905).
—— *Index to 2nd series, vols 21–32* (1907–1920).
Archaeologia (1770– ; now every two years).
—— *Index to vols 1–50* (1770–1887).
—— *Select index to vols 51–100* (1888–1966).
Research reports.
A list of publications and off-prints is available
from the Society.
The *Early minute books, 1717–1900* is available
on microfilm from Oxford Microform
Publications.
The most complete source of information about
the history and activities of the Society is *A
history of the Society of Antiquaries*, by Dr Joan
Evans (The Society, 1956).
Details of the Society's collections and
possessions are given in *The Society of
Antiquaries of London: notes on its history and
possessions,* prepared by Dr R. L. S.
Bruce-Mitford (1951) and in *The Society of
Antiquaries of London: a short guide to its history,
activities and possessions* (The Society, 1968).

Activities:
Meetings at which papers are read.

Society of Antiquaries of Scotland   39
National Museum of Antiquities of Scotland
Queen Street
Edinburgh EH2 1JD
tel Edinburgh (031) 556 8921 ext 68

Founded 1780

Aims:
The study of the antiquities and history of
Scotland (including architecture).

Collections/Library:
The Society's collections were handed over to the Crown in 1851, now incorporated in the National Museum of Antiquities (*see* 335).

Enquiry services:
From the librarian of the National Museum of Antiquities.

Publications:
Proceedings of the Society of Antiquaries of Scotland (annual from 1855), previously *Archaeologia Scotica*.

Activities:
Meetings to hear papers read (open to members).
Annual one-day conference (open to members).

Society of Architectural Historians of Great Britain

398

c/o Miss Anne Riches, Hon Secretary
25 Drumsheugh Gardens
Edinburgh EH3 7RN
tel Edinburgh (031) 226 3611
(private: office)

Founded 1956

Aims:
Encouragement of the study of the history of architecture and through its journal to publish the results of original research.

Collections/Library:
None, however a Research Register is kept of work completed but not published and research in progress. Extracts are published from time to time and updated. Further information on work recorded in the Register may be had from Dr F. Taylor, FSA, Register of Research, Society of Architectural Historians of Great Britain, The John Rylands University Library of Manchester, Oxford Road, Manchester, M13 9PP.

Enquiry Services:
None.

Publications:
Architectural history: Journal of the Society of Architectural Historians of Great Britain (annual).
Newsletter (twice a year, available to members only).
Occasional monographs, eg *Modern houses in Britain 1919–39* (1977) (*see* 712); *Architectural drawings from Lowther Castle, Westmorland*, edited by Howard Colvin, J. Mordaunt Crook and Terry Friedman (1980).
Research register (*see* 156).
List of members.

Activities:
Annual weekend residential conference.
Annual lecture and symposium.
Continental study tour (annual).
Annual book award.

Society of Decorative Crafts

399

Cymbeline
West Hanningfield
Chelmsford
Essex
tel Chelmsford (0245) 400640

Founded 1975

Aims:
The objects for which the Society of Decorative Crafts is established are:
(a) to re-establish and maintain a high standard of craftsmanship in all branches of the decorative arts and associated crafts.
(b) to improve the status, training and qualifications of members.
(c) to promote and encourage craftsmanship by means of meetings, educational courses, conferences, seminars, publications and like means.
(d) to provide courses of education, to provide educational material, to hold examinations and to award recognition of success to examinees achieving such standards as may from time to time be decided by the society.
(e) to organise competitions and similar events and to make awards for activities associated with the crafts.
(f) to act in association with any other company, associations, institute, society, body or person in pursuit of the objects of the society.
Membership is open to all decorative craftsmen or women in various forms providing they satisfy certain criteria set by the Council. This criteria will be based largely on proven craft ability with less emphasis on educational attainments.

Many of the Society's members have done preservation work and thus there is amongst its membership a great deal of technical information available, especially in the fields of gilding, graining and marbling on or within the fabric of buildings.

Society of Friends *see* 360: Religious Society of Friends

Society of Genealogists

400

37 Harrington Gardens
London SW7 4JX
tel 01–373 7054

Founded 1911

Founded 1911/continued
Aims:
To promote, encourage and foster the study,
science and knowledge of genealogy.

Collections/Library:
The Society possesses a large library of
genealogical material, including a considerable
amount of topographical material and the
publications of record and archaeological
societies.

Enquiry services and conditions of use:
The library is available to non-members on
payment of a fee. A small research department
undertakes paid research work into family
history. The Society can also give the names of
searchers, either for general research or to search
in a particular area.

Hours:
Tues 10.00–18.00
Wed 10.00–20.00
Thurs 10.00–20.00
Fri 10.00–18.00
Sat 10.00–17.00

Publications:
A list of parishes in Boyd's marriage index. 4th ed,
1980.
National index of parish registers. To be
published in twelve volumes. Vols 1–3 cover
general sources of births, marriages and deaths
before 1837, sources for non-conformist
genealogy and sources for Roman Catholic and
Jewish genealogy. The remaining volumes are
on specific regions. Published by Phillimore for
the Society.
Parish register copies. Part 1: Society of
Genealogists Collection. 5th ed, 1980.

South East Wales Industrial Archaeology   401
Society
c/o Mrs A. E. Thompson, Secretary
19 Cefn Coed Gardens
Cyn Coed
Cardiff CF2 6AX
tel Cardiff (0222) 761547

Founded 1965/66 (disbanded 1981)

Aims:
Investigating, recording and publishing
industrial sites in SE Wales.

Collections/Library:
None.

Enquiry services:
Postal enquiries should be addressed to the
Secretary.

Publications:
Journal.

Activities:
Winter lecture programme (fortnightly).
Summer evening visits to industrial sites.
Field projects.

Standing Conference for Local History   40
26 Bedford Square
London WC1B 3HU
tel 01–636 4066

Founded 1948

Aims:
To bring together representatives of its forty-tw
member County Local History Committees and
sixty-four national bodies and universities so tha
co-ordinated action may be taken to aid the
development of the study of local history and the
provision of services necessary for such study.

Collections/Library:
None.

Enquiry services and conditions of use:
Membership is open by invitation to national
and local bodies. Postal enquiries accepted. An
information and advisory service is provided.

Hours:
Mon–Fri 9.15–17.30

Publications:
The Local historian (quarterly journal).
Armorial bearings of the sovereigns of England.
Building stones of England and Wales.
Hedges and local history.
Directory of national organisations (see 215).
How to read a coat of arms.
Landscapes and documents.
Local history exhibitions.
Local history and folklore.
Local history societies in England and Wales: a list
(*see* 216).
Logic of open field systems.
Maps for the local historian: a guide to British
sources (*see* 27).
Recognisable qualifications in local history.
Tithes and the Tithe Commutation Act, 1836.
Writing a church guide.

Activities:
Meetings, conferences.
Initiates special projects.

Surrey County Council, Antiquities of the
County of Surrey *see* 485: Surrey County
Council, Antiquities of the County of Surrey

Terra Cotta Association 1937   403
Drayton House
30 Gordon Street
London WC1H 0AN
tel 01–388 0025

Aims:
To offer information and advice through the
experience and knowledge of members to those
concerned with the repair and restoration of
terracotta and faience clad buildings.

Collections/Library:
None.

Enquiry services and conditions of use:
Enquirers are referred to member companies.

_____

Theatre Museum   404
Victoria and Albert Museum
South Kensington
London SW7 2RL
tel 01–589 6371

Founded 1974

Aims:
The Theatre Museum is devoted to the
performing arts. It is administered by the
Victoria and Albert Museum under the
Department of Education and Science. It will
reopen in the mid 1980s in the Flower Market,
Covent Garden.

Collections/Library:
The Gabrielle Enthoven Theatre Collection,
which was first established in the Victoria and
Albert Museum in 1925, includes architectural
plans of theatres and views of the interiors and
exteriors of buildings. The collection includes
photographs and other representations of
theatres, including opera houses, circuses and
concert halls. There is a card index to this
material. Copy prints are available, though
restricted. The museum does not hold the
copyright on all their material and cannot assist
in tracing the copyright owner.

The collections and libraries formed by the
Theatre Museum Association, the Friends of the
Museum of Performing Arts and the Society for
Theatre Research are now part of the Museum's
collections.

Enquiry services and conditions of use:
The service is restricted to specific enquiries and
is only available to personal users by
appointment.

Hours:
Tues–Thurs 10.00–13.00; 14.00–14.30
The Museum is closed until it reopens in its new
premises.

Publications:
Postcards.
Theatre Museum cards.
Catalogues of exhibitions.
Reading lists.

Theatres' Advisory Council   405
4–7 Great Pulteney Street
London W1R 3DF
tel 01–434 3901

Aims:
Provides guidance or other assistance on the
safe-guarding or restoration of existing theatre
buildings.

_____

Theatres Trust   406
10 St Martin's Court
St Martin's Lane
London WC2N 4AJ

Founded 1977

Aims:
Established under an Act of Parliament for the
better protection of theatres for the benefit of the
nation.
    The Trust was designed as a channel to
raise private funds towards theatres threatened
with extinction by building regulations or
general financial pressures, and is also entitled to
comment upon any planning proposal under
consideration by a local authority which involves
a theatre.

_____

The Thirties Society   407
Clive Aslet, Hon Secretary
c/o Country Life
King's Reach Tower
Stamford Street
London SE1 9LS
tel 01–261 6969

Founded 1979

Aims:
To stimulate the study and appreciation of the
architecture of the 1920s and '30s, and to
safeguard the best examples from destruction or
mutilation.

Collections/Library:
The Society intends to build up a library of
relevant books, documents, cuttings, albums
and photographs for members to consult.

Publications:
Thirties Society Journal (1981– ; annual).

Activities:
Submission to the Department of the
Environment of lists of notable buildings worthy
of statutory protection.
Campaigns to save notable buildings.
Visits, walks, lectures, seminars, conferences,
film showings, etc.

5.2 Guide to societies, institutions and organisations

Town and Country Planning Association   408
17 Carlton House Terrace
London SW1Y 5AS
tel 01–930 8903/4/5

Founded 1899

Aims:
Founded as the Garden Cities Association it is
an educational charity which promotes public
understanding of planning and environmental
problems and promotes national, regional and
local planning policies based on a contemporary
interpretation of the principles first enunciated by
Sir Ebenezer Howard – harmonisation of the
built and natural environments, dispersal of
population and employment to new towns so as
to relieve urban overcrowding, the reversion of
land values to the community and the
encouragement of public participation in
decision making.

Collections/Library:
A small collection of books covering all aspects of
town and country planning, including
conservation and urban design. The collection
includes a number of earlier books relating
especially to the garden cities movement and
related subjects. Press cuttings are kept for one
year and journals for two years. Card index by
subject and author.

Enquiry services and conditions of use:
The staff can give advice and information on
aspects of planning, especially the New Towns,
but cannot undertake research, looking up
references, etc. Postal and telephone enquiries
are accepted. The library is for the use of
members, but others may use it by arrangement
with the Information Officer.

Hours:
Mon–Fri 9.30–17.30

Publications:
Annual report.
Town and country planning (monthly).
Bulletin of environmental education (monthly).
Planning bulletin (weekly).
Various leaflets on planning aid, discussion
papers on current topics and policy statements
on a wide range of planning and environmental
subjects.

Activities:
Annual international study tour of British New
Towns.
Conferences, seminars and short study tours.
Environmental education service for schools.
Promotes the establishment of urban study
centres, through the Council for Urban Study
Centres (CUSC).
Promotes town trails.

Transport Trust   40
Michael Lindsey-Smith, Director
Terminal House
Shepperton
Middlesex TW17 8AS
tel Walton (98) 28950 ext 250
or
Bryan Woodriff
Centre for Industrial Archaeology
School of Liberal Studies
Kingston Polytechnic
Penrhyn Road
Kingston upon Thames
Surrey KT1 2EE
tel 01–549 1366 ext 523

Founded 1965

Aims:
To promote and encourage the permanent
perservation for the benefit of the nation of
transport items of historical and/or technical
interest including books, drawings, films and
photographs of all forms of transport by rail,
road, air and water. Additionally, to arrange
displays and rallies of historical transport for the
benefit of the public.

Collections/Library:
Transport Trust Library and Archive:
The Trust is frequently offered rare books,
drawings and photographs on transport subjects
which might otherwise be dispersed. Its present
holdings, still being set up, are housed in the
library of the University of Surrey, Guildford.

Transport Trust Historical Structures Research
Unit:
The Trust, with the help of Kingston
Polytechnic Centre for Industrial Archaeology,
has compiled a catalogue of over 1,000 important
transport-related structures (bridges, canals,
stations, viaducts, etc). The work is continuing
but *bona fide* researchers may view the material
upon application to the Centre for Industrial
Archaeology, where it is presently housed.

Publications:
The Transport Trust Journal (1965–1975).
Travelback, Journal of the Transport Trust
(1976–1978).
Yesteryear transport (1979– ; quarterly).
Historic transport guide (1974– ; annual).

Ulster Architectural Heritage Society   41
181A Stranmillis Road
Belfast BT9 5DU
tel Belfast (0232) 660809

Founded 1967

Aims:
To promote the appreciation and enjoyment of good architecture of all periods; to encourage the preservation of buildings and groups of buildings of artistic merit or historic interest; and to encourage public awareness and appreciation of the beauty, history and character of local neighbourhoods in Northern Ireland and their surroundings.

Collections/Library:
None.

Hours:
Mon–Fri 9.00–13.00; 14.00–17.00

Publications:
Annual report.
Newsletters.
Monographs, eg:
Classical churches in Ulster, by James Stevens Curl (1980).
Lists and surveys (*see* 136).
List of publications available on request.

Activities:
Outings to places of interest, lectures, talks for members and their guests.

Ulster Folk and Transport Museum   411
Cultra Manor
Holywood
Co Down BT18 0EU
tel Holywood (023 17) 5411

Founded 1958

Aims:
A national institution established by Act of Parliament to collect, preserve and exhibit material illustrative of traditional life in Ulster and Irish transport history.

Collections/Library:
Library and archives, covering both the material and non-material aspects of Ulster folklife.

Open air museum of re-erected buildings representing the variety of Ulster urban and rural vernacular building, mainly in the period 1880–1910. Buildings include a byre dwelling, two cotters' houses, three farmhouses, a spade mill, a flax mill, a weaver's house, a rectory, a national school and a church.

Hours:
Museum:
Oct–April, Mon–Sat 11.00–17.00
                Sun 14.00–17.00
May–June, Mon, Thurs, Fri, Sat 11.00–19.00
                Tues, Wed 11.00–21.00
                Sun 14.00–19.00
July–Sept, Mon–Sat 11.00–19.00
                Sun 14.00–19.00

Publications:
Ulster folklife (annual).

Unitarian Historical Society   412
6 Ventnor Terrace
Edinburgh EH9 2BL
tel Edinburgh (031) 667 4360

Aims:
The study of Unitarian history.

Collections/Library:
The Society's library is absorbed into Dr Williams's Library, Gordon Square, London (*see* 282).

Enquiry services and conditions of use:
Personal, postal and telephone enquiries accepted.

Publications:
Transactions of the Unitarian Historical Society (annual).

United Reformed Church History Society   413
86 Tavistock Place
London WC1H 9RT
tel 01–837 7661

Founded 1972

Aims:
Incorporates the Congregational Historical Society (founded 1899) and the Presbyterian Historical Society of England (founded 1913). To facilitate study of the history of Congregational, Presbyterian and United Reformed Church denominations and to collect archives, books, records and pictures.

Collections/Library:
The collection includes architectural details and some pictures and plans of many Congregational and Presbyterian churches.

Enquiry services and conditions of use:
Personal, postal and telephone enquiries accepted.

Hours:
Tues and Fri 10.15–12.15; 13.00–15.30

Publications:
Journal (twice yearly).

University of London. Courtauld Institute of Art, Book Library *see* 269: Courtauld Institute of Art, Book Library

5.2 Guide to societies, institutions and organisations

**University of London. Courtauld Institute
of Art, Conway Library** *see* 446: Courtauld
Institute of Art, Conway Library

**University of London. Institute of
Archaeology** *see* 310: Institute of Archaeology,
University of London

Vernacular Architecture Group 414
c/o Chy an Whyloryan
Wigmore
Leominster
Herefordshire HR6 9UD
tel Wigmore (056 886) 356

Founded 1952

Aims:
To promote the study of lesser traditional
buildings, particularly in the UK and Eire.

Collections/Library:
Library is held at the Royal Commission on
Ancient and Historical Monuments in Wales (*see*
367). A bibliography of books and articles on
vernacular architecture (including social and
economic aspects) is maintained. A card index of
dated buildings is also kept.

Enquiry services:
Enquiries should be addressed to the Secretary.

Publications:
A Bibliography on vernacular architecture
(London: David and Charles, 1972).
Supplemented by *Current bibliography of
vernacular architecture, 1970–1976* (Vernacular
Architecture Group, 1979) (*see* 96 and 113).
Vernacular architecture (annual).

Activities:
Annual conference.

Victoria and Albert Museum Library 415
South Kensington
London SW7 2RL
tel 01–589 6371 ext 331

Founded 1837

Aims:
Founded in 1837 as the library of the
Government School of Design, its aims at first
were to provide design information and
precedents for artisans and manufacturers. In
1857 the library became part of the South
Kensington Museum and its scope was widened
to cover art history in general. The publication
of a catalogue-cum-desiderata list, *The universal
catalogue of books on art* (1866–70) confirmed its

comprehensive scope, and it was named the
National Art Library. Its prints and drawings
were formed into a separate museum department
in 1909, and it remains an academic book library
comprehensively covering the history of fine and
applied art of all periods and countries.

Collections/Library:
The library contains about 750,000 volumes.
The holdings of the library relating to
architecture include:
A large, representative collection of architectural
source books, 16th–18th century, together with
books in related fields such as topography,
perspective, etc.
A rich collection of 19th-century source books.
A comprehensive collection of books, from the
19th century to the present, dealing with the
history and aesthetics of architecture, but not
including technical works.
Runs of the major architectural periodicals from
the 19th century to the present.
Archival material: architects' letters, etc,
including a collection of A. W. N. Pugin's
notebooks and diaries.

The library's catalogues and indexes include:
Book author catalogue: pre-1890 acquisitions (in
printed volume).
Book author catalogue: post-1890 acquisitions
(on cards).
Manuscripts catalogue (on cards).
General subject index (two series, 1905–1930,
1930 to date, in guard books), which is arranged
alphabetically. The section devoted to
architecture is sub-divided by period, region and
type.
There are separate sheaf catalogues of guides to
country houses and churches.

Enquiry services and conditions of use:
Open to the public for occasional use of the
general stock. Regular readers should apply for
readers' tickets. For use of restricted material
(rare, precious, fragile), written application
should be made in advance, or regular readers
should obtain tickets endorsed for special
collections. There is no access to the stacks.
Reading room staff will advise readers on the use
of the library and will assist with enquiries or
refer them to senior staff. Extensive searches for
information are not undertaken. Complex
enquiries should be sent in writing (address
letters to Keeper of the Library) and will be dealt
with by senior staff. Only enquiries answerable
from the library catalogues or standard reference
books can be dealt with by telephone.

Hours:
Mon–Thurs 10.00–17.30
Sat 10.00–13.00; 14.00–17.30

Publications:
The Museum's publications are listed in

Government publications: sectional list 55 (HMSO).
List of accessions (irregular).

Some publications relating to architecture include:
Michael E. Keen, *A bibliography of the trade directories of the British Isles, in the National Art Library* (*see* 38).
Marble halls: drawings and models for Victorian secular buildings (exhibition catalogue, 1973) (*see* 606).
Victorian architectural source books displayed in the exhibition 'Marble halls' (catalogue, 1973).
Victorian church art (exhibition catalogue, 1971–2).
M. I. Wilson, *Early British topography* (catalogue of library holdings, 1977).

The author catalogue of the library was published by G. K. Hall (Boston, Mass) in 1972 (10 vols).

Activities:
The Museum occasionally organises exhibitions of architectural interest, and the regular lecture programme includes lectures on architecture.

Victoria and Albert Museum, Department of Prints and Drawings and Paintings   416
South Kensington
London SW7 2RL
tel 01–589 6371 ext 348

Founded 1852

Collections/Library:
The collection includes approximately 5,000 designs by architects, primarily British, plus approximately 1,000 measured drawings. Artist catalogue and subject index available in the Print Room.

Enquiry services and conditions of use:
The Print Room is open to personal callers.

Hours:
Mon–Thurs and Sat 10.00–16.30

Publications:
The Museum's publications are listed in Government publications: sectional list 55 (HMSO).
Handbook to the Dept. of Prints and Drawings and Paintings (1964).
A series of published catalogues is in course of preparation.
A microfilm edition of the collection of the architectural drawings in the Victoria and Albert Museum has been published by EP Microform Ltd. (23 reels). It contains some 14,000 drawings and provides a definitive coverage of the

drawings in the Museum by English architects, and of buildings in England designed by overseas architects. On the whole, the microfilm does not include other designs, for furniture, metalwork, wallpaper, ceilings, fabrics and so on, by the architects and artists whose work appears on the film. The microfilm is fully indexed.

Victoria and Albert Museum. Theatre Museum *see* 404: Theatre Museum

---

Victorian Society   417
1 Priory Gardens
London W4 1TT
tel 01–994 1019

Founded 1958

Aims:
To preserve the best of Victorian and Edwardian architecture, and also to study the art and history of the period. It is particularly concerned to protect important nineteenth and early twentieth-century buildings, both public and private, industrial monuments, and historical areas.
   The Society co-operates with the Department of the Environment in compiling lists of important buildings of the period. The Society is represented at public inquiries all over Britain. It commissions reports and initiates campaigns to save major buildings. It also advises local authorities on the designation and enhancement of conservation areas, and is represented on many Conservation Area Advisory Committees. The Society consults on all listed building applications involving demolition.

Collections/Library:
A collection of literature on Victorian subjects is in the course of cataloguing.
Notes on visits and walking tours.

Enquiry services and conditions of use:
Specialist advice to householders on preservation, repairs, interior design and decoration is available from the Society, as well as architectural itineraries and information on buildings in danger.

Publications:
Annual report.
Newsletter.

Activities:
Lectures, conferences, visits, tours and other activities to promote understanding and appreciation of all aspects of the Victorian and Edwardian periods.
Regional Groups in Avon, Birmingham,

5.2 Guide to societies, institutions and organisations

Birmingham,/*continued*
Hampshire, Leicester, Liverpool, Manchester,
South Yorkshire, West Yorkshire and South
Wales have their own programmes of events and
campaigns.

Weald and Downland Open Air Museum   418
Singleton, near Chichester
West Sussex
tel Singleton (0243 63) 348

Aims:
A private, non-profit-making organisation that
has brought together a collection of historic
buildings, saved from destruction and re-erected
on the 40 acres of the museum site. The main
focus is on traditional small scale vernacular
building, with special reference to the South-east
(Sussex, Kent, Surrey, Hampshire).

Collections/Library:
The museum includes examples of buildings
from the South-east of England. It also provides
a Library and Research Centre for information,
education and research into vernacular
architecture. The collection includes J. R.
Armstrong's photographic collection and mss
plans, etc consisting mainly of some 60,000
2×2in black and white transparencies – mostly
photographs of buildings and details of these,
but also on microfile, plans, drawings and texts
(such as inventories, etc). In addition to these,
there are smaller, more specialised collections,
left by members of the Wealden Buildings Study
Group. At present these collections are only
tentatively arranged and catalogued. The task of
more detailed cross-indexing etc, will begin as
soon as facilities are available at the museum. All
the material will be available for reference by
students and others interested in the subjects.
Future cataloguing will also include the location
and scope of other material of cognate interest at
present available in other institutions such as
record offices, local libraries, or in the possession
of individuals.

The reference collection can be divided (and is at
present arranged) as follows:
A. Vernacular building within the catchment
area of the museum (approximately Sussex,
Kent, South Surrey and East Hampshire).
(About 45% of the collection).
  1. Buildings rebuilt or in store at the museum,
  mostly recorded in considerable detail.
  2. Buildings with which the museum has been
  closely associated, eg offered to the museum,
  or involving efforts to preserve or advice
  concerning restoration given.
  3. Buildings recorded, often in considerable
  detail, by members of the Wealden Buildings
  Study Group and other individuals.
  4. Surveys of particular villages or parishes.
  5. General records of buildings demolished
  within the last thirty years (since the collection
  was started).

Note: 4 and 5 are arranged geographically, bu
a few categories, such as farm buildings,
barns, granaries, etc, and specific forms of
houses, such as the Wealden (or recessed hall
type of medieval house, have been grouped
separately within their own categories. In
addition there are fringe collections of
buildings having varying connection with
vernacular building, such as parish churches,
which are covered in some detail for West
Sussex, and some of the greater houses and
mansions.
B. Vernacular building in the British Isles but
outside the museum's catchment area, including
records from most of the Spring conferences
organised by the Vernacular Architecture Grou
– arranged on a county or regional basis. (About
20% of the collection).
C. 1. Other museums of the open air type
  concerned with vernacular building. Most of
  the museums in this country and in western
  Europe are covered – some in considerable
  detail.
  2. Vernacular building typical of various
  regions in Europe. (About 20% of the
  collection).
D. Fringe subjects:
  1. Relevant social and economic history,
  including brick and tile making, stone
  working, woodcraft, use of timber, etc.
  2. Archaeological evidence of early buildings,
  reconstructions, etc.
  3. Maps of various kinds, geological,
  distribution maps, landscape forms, etc.

Enquiry services and conditions of use:
Personal, postal and telephone enquiries
accepted. Student or other credentials required.

Hours:
Museum:
April–Oct, Tues–Sun
(also Mon, July–Aug) 11.00–18.00
Nov, Wed, Sat, Sun 11.00–17.00
Dec–March, Sun 11.00–16.00

Publications:
List of publications available.

Welsh Folk Museum   41
Sain Ffagin
Cardiff CF5 2NP
tel Cardiff (0222) 569441

Founded 1947

Aims:
To teach the world about Wales, and the Welsh
people about their own background; to re-create
and study the daily life of the Welsh people in
the past.

Collections/Library:
The collections include 14 re-erected buildings
from all parts of Wales, eg a 15th-century
timber-framed house from Clwyd, a
16th-century timber-framed house from Powys,
a 17th-century stone and timber barn from
Clwyd, an 18th-century longhouse from Powys,
a 17th–18th-century stone farmhouse from
Glamorgan, an 18th-century quarryman's
cottage from Gwynedd, as well as several craft
buildings, eg a tannery, working flour-mill,
woollen mill, and smithy.
The library includes an architectural section
which is particularly strong on Welsh vernacular
architecture.
    There is a small collection of building
materials, eg panels, trusses, etc.
    There is a collection of approximately
10,000 black and white photographs and slides,
and some 500 colour, of Welsh vernacular
architecture. Indexes are available at the
museum. The material is not available for loan,
but copy prints can be provided. Most of the
material is their copyright. The photographic
collection is open, by appointment, from
9.00–13.00; 14.00–16.00, weekdays.

Enquiry services and conditions of use:
Personal (by appointment), postal and telephone
enquiries accepted. Library enquiries should be
addressed to the archivist. Informal advice about
dating and restoring buildings is available.

Hours:
8.30–14.30 (office closed 13.00–13.40).
Museum grounds open daily 10.00–17.00 (18.00
in summer), Sun 14.30–17.00

Publications:
Annual report.
Guidebook.
Handbooks to several of the re-erected buildings.
Publications list available.

Activities:
Easter courses, often on architectural subjects.

Welsh Office 420
    Crown Buildings
    Cardiff CF1 3NQ
    tel Cardiff (0222) 38066

Includes:
Ancient Monuments Branch
Historic Buildings Branch
Welsh Office Library

Founded 1969

Aims:
The Welsh Office is responsible for most matters
affecting the physical environment in Wales,
including housing, planning, comprehensive

development and ancient monuments and
historic buildings.

The Ancient Monuments Branch is responsible
for the preservation and display of ancient
monuments in the care of the Secretary of State,
statutory protection of ancient monuments and
rescue archaeology.

The Historic Buildings Branch deals with the
listing of buildings of special architectural or
historic interest, grants towards the repair or
maintenance of buildings of outstanding
architectural or historic interest and towards the
preservation or enhancement of the character or
appearance of conservation areas.

The Library's object is the collection,
organisation and dissemination of all the
information needed to further the work of the
department.

Collections/Library:
Ancient Monuments Branch:
Maintains a schedule of monuments classed as of
national importance, whether or not in state
care. Holds folders for each monument,
containing descriptions.

Historic Buildings Branch:
Maintains a complete list for Wales of buildings
of special architectural or historic interest. (37
vols, one for each district authority).
Holds a modest collection of photographs,
chiefly of buildings which have been
grant-aided.
Holds complete lists of conservation areas in
Wales, with maps showing boundaries of the
areas.

Library:
The Library has a stock of about 22,500 books,
pamphlets and government publications and
receives about 400 periodicals. Subjects covered
by the library include: local government;
housing; social and environmental planning;
roads, traffic and transport; countryside and
recreation, etc.

Enquiry services and conditions of use:
Personal, postal and telephone enquiries
accepted. Reference facilities for the public. For
enquiries concerning listed buildings, listed
buildings consent and grants, contact the
Historic Buildings Branch.

Hours:
Mon–Fri 8.30–17.00

Publications:
Ancient Monuments Branch:
Guide books to monuments in the care of the
state.
List of ancient monuments.
Postcards, slides.

5.2 Guide to societies, institutions and organisations

slides./*continued*
Library:
Accessions list (monthly).
Select bibliographies.

Wesley Historical Society 421
39 Fair Street
St Columb Major
Cornwall
tel St Columb Major (063 72) 287

Founded 1896

Aims:
The study of all aspects of Methodist history.

Collections/Library:
Lending library for members at Southlands
College, Wimbledon Parkside, London SW19
5NN.

Publications:
Proceedings (thrice yearly).

Whitehouse, Museum of Building and 422
Country Life
Aston Munslow
Salop
tel Munslow (058 476) 661

Founded 1966

Aims:
The preservation and restoration of the
Homestead, a house dating from pre-Norman
times, undercroft, cruck hall, 1580 cross-wing
and Georgian addition, dovecote of 1250 AD
and other surrounding buildings including a
17th-century cider house, 1680 stable,
16th-century open bay house (now converted to
barn), cart shed, granary etc.

Collections/Library:
Educational facilities for students and adult
courses are in preparation.

Publications:
The White House, by G. W. Tonkin.
A house, its country and its people, by Constance
Purser.

William Morris Gallery 423
Lloyd Park
Forest Road
London E17 4PP
tel 01–527 5544 ext 390

Founded 1950

Aims:
Life and work of William Morris and associates,
including Pre-Raphaelite painters, the Arts and
Crafts movement and the work of Frank
Brangwyn.

Collections/Library:
The Morris Collection contains material relating
to all aspects of the work of William Morris and
the firm of Morris & Co. This includes designs
by Morris, Burne-Jones, Rossetti and other
members of the firm, as well as furniture, woven
textiles, chintzes, tapestries, embroideries,
stained glass and wallpapers, letters and
manuscripts by Morris and a set of books printed
at his Kelmscott Press. The Brangwyn gift
consists mainly of 19th and 20th-century
paintings. A. H. Mackmurdo, architect, designer
and founder of The Century Guild, bequeathed
a collection of furniture, textiles and metalwork
designed by The Century Guild. There are also
small collections of ceramics by William De
Morgan and the Martin Brothers, and works by
Walter Crane, C. F. A. Voysey and others.
The Gallery's reference library contains
books and periodicals relating to the period,
which may be consulted by appointment. The
photograph collection includes approximately 50
black and white negatives, prints of which can be
made to order, of photographic views of houses
associated with Morris, and buildings designed
by A. H. Mackmurdo, as well as plans and
elevations of Mackmurdo buildings. A catalogue
of the A. H. Mackmurdo and Century Guild
collections (including architectural plans by
Mackmurdo) is available for sale.

Enquiry services and conditions of use:
Personal, postal and telephone enquiries
accepted. It is essential to make an appointment
to use the Library/Reference facilities.

Hours:
Gallery:
Mon–Sat 10.00–17.00
First Sunday in each month, 10.00–12.00;
14.00–17.00
Library/Reference Collection:
By appointment.

Publications:
35mm colour slides (sets and single slides). List
available on request.
Postcards, greeting cards.
Catalogues of the collection, eg. *A. H.
Mackmurdo and The Century Guild.*
A list of publications is available on request.

This section begins with some useful publications for picture researchers, historians and lecturers, and is followed by a list of organisations and individuals with collections of architectural photographs and slides.

In some cases photographic records may be the only resource for a particular building, especially if the building has been demolished or altered. But a search for visual documentation might require looking further than the photographic and slide collections listed here. Books and journals often contain photographs, prints, drawings, etc and the sources listed elsewhere in this guide should assist in locating such illustrations (eg in section 2.1, Victoria and Albert Museum, *Topographical index to measured drawings*). Architectural drawings and topographical drawings are often invaluable sources of visual information - some of the major collections are indicated under the name of the organisation in section 5.2 (eg British Architectural Library Drawings Collection, Sir John Soane's Museum, Victoria and Albert Museum, etc) while some guides, indexes and catalogues of this type of illustration will be found in sections 1 (eg Barley's *Guide to British topographical collections*) and 2.1 (eg Royal Institute of British Architects, Drawings Collection, *Catalogue of the Drawings Collection of the RIBA*).

British catalogue of audiovisual materials. 424
First experimental ed. London: British Library, Bibliographic Services Division, 1979. 487pp. Supplement, 1980. London: British Library, Bibliographic Services Division, 1980. 200pp.
One of the largest lists to be published of audiovisual materials currently available for purchase or hire in the UK. It contains records of some 5,300 items covering all subject areas. Types of material covered include slides, filmstrips, spoken word sound recordings, tape/slide presentations, 8mm film loops, OHPs, educational kits and a small number of 16mm films. Arranged in classified subject order. There is an author-title-series index and a subject index as well as a list of publishers and distributors.

British Industrial and Scientific Film Association. 425
Film guide for the construction industry, including information on slide packages and slide/tape programmes. Lancaster; London etc: Construction Press, 1979. 123pp.
Arranged in five parts. The contents list gives the main subject headings under which the film titles and descriptions are listed. It is arranged on the basis of UDC classification and basically takes the form of four main groups (civil engineering, building, planning and architecture). The main part of the book consists of the titles and descriptions of some 800 films, given in the order shown by the subject list. For each film the following details are generally provided: title, distributor, production company and sponsor, date of production, length of film, whether black and white or colour and brief description of film including intended audience. An alphabetical title index and a list of distributors is provided. The final section is devoted to the other audio-visual media. Despite its title, includes many films about architectural history, including films on individual architects (Adam, Mackintosh, Lutyens), building types (cinemas, castles, factories) etc.

British Universities Film Council 426
Audio-visual materials for higher education, 1979–80. Part 1: History and the arts.
Edited by James Ballantyne. 4th ed. London: The Council, 1979. 103pp.
Lists nearly 3,000 items from 250 distributors which have been viewed and recommended for inclusion by over 500 subject specialists. Materials are included only if considered to be suitable for degree-level teaching or research purposes. The media covered are: films, videotapes, sound-recordings, tape-slide programmes or slide-sets with substantial accompanying booklets, and film loops. Slides (except as above, but Appendix II lists some of the major suppliers in the UK) and filmstrips are not included.

The main body of the catalogue lists all materials in accordance with the Universal Decimal Classification scheme of which an outline of the main divisions is given. The subjects covered include archaeology and industrial archaeology, architecture and town planning. Under each title full technical details are given together with credits, date of production and synopsis of contents. There are two indexes: a title index and a subject index, as well as a list of distributors and their addresses and a section listing other useful catalogues. The previous edition was published in 1977. The next edition is planned for 1981–82.

■ Photographs, slides and films

6.1 Published directories to sources of architectural photographs, slides and films

Evans, Hilary   427
The art of picture research: a guide to current practice, procedure, techniques and resources. 2nd ed. Newton Abbot: David and Charles, 1979. 208pp.

> An important work of reference for all picture researchers, concentrating on the sources, procedures and pitfalls of picture research. All the various fees, copyrights and other rights are covered. Index.

Evans, Hilary and Mary, *compilers*   428
Picture researcher's handbook: an international guide to picture sources and how to use them. 2nd ed. London: Saturday Ventures, 1979. 328pp.

> Entries are arranged in three groups: general, regional and specialist (eg art, which includes architecture). Individual entries give the name of the collection, general description of material, address and telephone, approximate number of items, research procedures and procedures for loan and copying. Subject index and alphabetical index.

Wall, John, *compiler*   429
Directory of British photographic collections. Compiled at the National Photographic Record, a department of the Royal Photographic Society. London: Heinemann, 1977. 226pp. Bibl pp 225–226.

> Particularly useful for the sections on arts and crafts, which includes architecture, buildings, church architecture, commercial architecture, vernacular architecture and street furniture, and the section on geography, which lists local history collections of public libraries, museums, record offices, etc. Each entry provides the name of the owner of the collection, address and telephone number, dates when collections were begun or terminated, names of photographers, subjects covered, size of collection and forms of material held, retrieval aids, conditions of access, copying facilities, charges, and notes on the collection. Useful information is provided on: copyright; photographic agencies; fees; 'library' and 'archive'; loan services; on making the best use of photographic collections; picture researchers; and photographic galleries.

For other items relating to this section see:

5.1 **Published directories to societies, institutions and organisations**
198 *ARLIS directory of members.*
199 *ASLIB directory.*
205 *The Environment: sources of information for teachers.*
207 Historical Manuscripts Commission. *Record repositories in Great Britain.*

209 Howard. *Directory of theatre research resources in Great Britain.*
210 Howard. *Directory of theatre research resources in Greater London.*
211 *The Libraries, museums and art galleries yearbook.*
212 Library Association. Reference, Special and Information Section. *Library resources.*

5.2 **Guide to societies, institutions and organisations**
239 British Film Institute.

■ **6.2**

Guide to sources of architectural photographs and slides

> There is a general introduction at the beginning of section 6.1 which also covers this section.

Aerofilms Ltd   43
Gate Studios
Station Road
Boreham Wood, Herts. WD6 1EJ
tel 01–207 0666

> This, the first commercial aerial photographic company in the world, holds many thousands of black and white prints and colour transparencies showing British architecture from the air. While the collection began in 1919, it also includes the Mills Collection (1890–1910) of ground-level views of London. Prints must be bought, although they do supply xerox copies. Colour transparencies are available on loan. Various leaflets on the collection are available, as is a book: *The Aerofilms book of aerial photographs: a guide to Aerofilms Library.* They hold the copyright for nearly all their material. Open Mon–Thurs 9.00–17.30, Fri 9.00–16.30.

Malcolm Aird Associates Ltd   43
Stanfield Studio
87 Hampstead High Street
London NW3 1RE
tel 01–435 7440

> A general collection which includes about 1,000 35mm colour transparencies of places in Britain (landscapes, buildings, places of historical interest). Material can be loaned and copy prints are available. They own the copyright on all their material. Open normal office hours.

Ancient Art and Architecture Photo-Library   43
6 Kenton Road
Harrow-on-the-Hill
Middlesex HA1 2BL
tel 01–422 1214

This collection, begun in 1960, contains over 7,000 black and white film negatives and colour transparencies of architecture from prehistoric times to the 19th century, with the emphasis on the historical aspect rather than the technical. Lists and indexes are available at their premises. Material can be loaned and copy prints are available. They hold the copyright on all their material. Personal (by appointment), postal and telephone enquiries are accepted, although the material is only available to accredited picture researchers, authors of books or articles and users of pictures for publication where fees can be paid for reproduction. The collection is open from 9.00 to 17.30.

Architectural Association Slide Library 433
36 Bedford Square
London WC1B 3ES
tel 01–636 0974

A collection of over 60,000 35mm slides (colour and black and white) covering architecture of all periods and countries, as well as certain allied subjects. It also holds archival collections of negatives including the F. R. Yerbury collection and the E. R. Jarrett bequest. There is no catalogue of the whole collection, but there is selective subject indexing. The slides are filed in drawers which give open access to the borrower. The basic divisions of the slide collection are: historical building (arranged chronologically); twentieth century building (arranged by building type); town planning; and fine and applied art and other subjects. Within each subject heading, the sequence normally is: British; European; USA; other countries. Within each of these sub-sections, slides are ordered alphabetically by place. A general information leaflet and occasional selective catalogues are available. A history and description of the Slide Library appears in *The Architectural Association annual review, 1980* (pp 7–62) and has been reprinted as a separate publication. The library loans slides for lecturing and other educational purposes, supplies prints for publication, duplicate transparencies, etc, and mounts slide presentations and exhibitions. They do not hold the copyright on all their material, but will help in tracing the copyright owner. The collection is available to members of the Architectural Association and the public. There is a hire charge for material borrowed. Personal, postal and telephone enquiries are accepted. Notice is required for access to the negative collection, and queries about its contents. The Slide Library is to take on the responsibility for the storage and development of an AA Drawings collection. The library is open Mon–Fri from 10.00–17.30.

Architectural Press Ltd 434
9 Queen Anne's Gate
London SW1H 9BY
tel 01–222 4333

The collection contains black and white and some colour photographs that have been used in *Architectural review*, *Architects' journal* and other Architectural Press publications. Photographs are not available for loan. Prints can be purchased of those photographs which are Architectural Press copyright, but photos are not necessarily their copyright. Reproduction fees are charged. Access is by appointment only.

James Austin 435
22 Godesdone Road
Cambridge CB5 8HR
tel Cambridge (0223) 59763

Collection, begun in 1965, of very good quality black and white photographs of European architecture. British architecture numbers about 1,000 photographs, but will be extended over the next years. Duplicated catalogues and lists are available as are copy prints. Nearly all the material is the owner's copyright. The collection is open Mon–Fri from 9.00–12.30 and 14.30–18.00. Personal use by appointment only. Postal and telephone enquiries accepted.

B. T. Batsford Ltd 436
4 Fitzhardinge Street
London W1H 0AH
tel 01–486 8484

Collection of black and white photographs taken for books that they published in the past. Particularly interesting collection of Victorian and Edwardian photographs. Copyright to be cleared in some cases. They are not open to the public, and do not normally lend photographs.

John Beecham Library 437
26 Ormonde Street
Sunderland SR4 7PH
tel Sunderland (0783) 76668

A collection, begun in 1957, of about 8,000 colour transparencies (and some monochrome) in 35mm or 6 × 7cm or 4 × 5in, by John Beecham, Senior Lecturer in Environmental Studies in the Polytechnic, Sunderland. About half the collection is devoted to architectural subjects, with the emphasis on northern England. Specific sets are available on Hadrian's Wall and Roman northern Britain, stone monuments of England, abbeys of northern England and the Border, castles of northern England (especially Saxon) and southern

6.2 Guide to sources of architectural photographs and slides

southern/*continued*
England, and industrial archaeology (bridges, buildings). Material can be loaned and copy prints are available. All the material is the owner's copyright. Personal, postal and telephone (after 18.00) use accepted.

Berkshire Architectural Records Committee Collection   438

Berkshire Record Office
Shire Hall
Reading RG1 3EE
tel Reading (0734) 55981 ext 230

The Berkshire Architectural Records Committee Collection was originally compiled (c 1941) to provide a photographic record of buildings in danger during the war. It was extended to include all buildings of architectural or historic interest, though it is by no means complete in this respect yet. The collection contains several hundred prints (negatives are held by the Reading Museum) of secular and ecclesiastical buildings in Berkshire (including the Vale of White Horse). Most photographs date from 1941–1950. Catalogues and lists are available and copy prints can possibly be made by arrangement. The collection is open Mon–Wed 9.00–17.00; Thurs 9.00–19.30 (after 17.00 by appointment); Fri 9.00–16.30. Personal callers are welcome. Preliminary enquiries may, however, be made by post or telephone.

Bodleian Library. Department of Western Manuscripts   439

Oxford OX1 3BG
tel Oxford (0865) 44675

The Dept of Western Manuscripts produce filmstrips collated from their manuscript collection, eg *Medieval buildings and architecture, from 9 English and Continental mss of the 15th and 16th centuries.* Catalogue of the filmstrips supplied. All colour 35mm.

Ted Bottle   440

114 Meadow Lane
Agar Nook
Coalville, Leicestershire
tel Coalville (0530) 34133

A collection of about 500 colour transparencies (interior views) and about 80 colour prints (exterior views) of theatre buildings by an amateur photographer. All types of theatres, from 1845 to the early 20th century, in all parts of the UK are included in this expanding collection. Special attention is focussed on auditoriums, plaster work and decoration, and backstage and mechanical features. Copy prints are available for reproduction and publication. At present there are no fees, except the cost of

reproduction and postage. The owner holds the copyright on all the material. Access to the collection is by arrangement.

Brecht-Einzig Ltd   44

65 Vineyard Hill Road
Wimbledon Park
London SW19 7JL
tel 01–946 8561 or 947 7053

This substantial collection, begun in the early 1960s, includes prints, film negatives, slides and transparencies, both black and white and colour of modern British architecture. All building types are represented. Duplicated lists of buildings photographed are available on request Copy prints are available for sale, display, reproduction and publication. A handling/search fee is charged. Copyright must be cleared in some cases, but they assist in tracing the copyright owner. The collection is open Mon–Fri from 9.15–17.15, by appointment.

British Museum. Department of Prints and Drawings *see* 242.

British Tourist Authority Photographic Library   44

239 Old Marylebone Road
London NW1 5QT
tel 01–262 0141

Over 140,000 colour transparencies and black and white photographs, of historic houses, churches, cathedrals, etc. Prints must be bought Colour transparencies are loaned. Naturally the photographs tend to be filled with happy tourists, rather than building detail. The library is organised by counties and by subject (sports, travel, theatres, restaurants, inns, hotels, etc). They own the copyright on all their material. A research fee is charged for postal and telephone use, but not for personal use. Open Mon–Fri 11.00–16.00.

J. Allan Cash Ltd, Worldwide Photographic Library   44

74 South Ealing Road
London W5 4QB
tel 01–840 4141

A worldwide general collection, begun about 1936, which includes approximately a quarter million black and white negatives and 150,000 colour transparencies, including subjects of an architectural type. They will probably only have well-known buildings. A catalogue is available on request. Material is available for loan and copy prints can be supplied. The library is open Mon–Fri 9.30–17.30. Personal, postal and telephone requests accepted.

J. H. Cordingly 444

83 Sandy Lane
Romily
Stockport SK6 4NH

A private collection, begun in 1968, which has
been compiled by the owner for his own use as a
lecturer, though it is available for copies and
reproduction. The collection, all 35mm colour
transparencies, includes about 2,000
representations of Stuart and Georgian
churches, 4,500 of English architecture and
decoration (mainly large houses), 1,000 Scots
towers and houses, and 300 of Irish subjects.
About half the transparencies are of interiors,
including details of stucco, murals, etc. The
collection mostly covers the period between 1500
and 1830. None of the material is available for
loan. The owner holds the copyright on all the
material. Use of the collection is by post only.

Country Life Magazine 445

King's Reach Tower
Stamford Street
London SE1 9LS
tel 01–261 7058

A collection of about 250,000 black and white
film and glass negatives of country houses and
related subjects in Britain and Ireland which
were taken for *Country life* magazine (founded in
1897). Copy prints are available, subject to the
owner's consent in appropriate cases. The issue
number and page number of *Country life* must
be quoted or their index consulted. They own
the copyright on all their material. Access to the
collection is by appointment.

Courtauld Institute of Art, Conway Library 446

University of London
20 Portman Square
London W1H 0BE
tel 01–935 9292

The Conway Library is a photographic study
collection of western architecture, architectural
drawings, sculpture, etc. Black and white
photographs are filed under main headings,
topographically. Architects' names are supplied
if known. Regular photographic campaigns in
England and abroad are undertaken to record
buildings and sculpture and manuscripts. Prints
can be bought if the library owns the negative.
There are no catalogues or indexes. Photographs
from the collection appear in *Courtauld Institute
of Art illustration archives*, a quarterly periodical
(London: Harvey Miller, 1977–   ). Use of the
collection is at the discretion of the Director of
the Institute. Personal, postal and telephone
enquiries accepted. During term the library is
open Mon–Fri from 10.00–19.00, during
vacations Mon–Fri from 10.00–18.00.

Denness Collection of Colour Prints 447

7 Hudshaw Gardens
Hexham, Northumberland NE46 1HY
tel Hexham (0434) 3677

A private collection, begun in 1962, of about
11,000 3 × 5 in colour prints of British
architectural subjects. The photographer, Mrs
Barbara Denness, specialises in architectural
subjects of historical interest. Included in the
collection are Wren and Hawksmoor London
churches, medieval churches in Suffolk, fortified
manors, Border towers and castles, Georgian
towns, Saxon churches in Northumbria and the
South and many pictures of street furniture
(fountains, horse troughs, lamp-posts, signposts,
bootscrapers, bollards, etc). Copy prints are
available. There are no standard fees for
publication etc as this is not a commercial
concern. Personal (by appointment), postal and
telephone use is accepted.

Department of the Environment 448

Room 401
Hannibal House
Elephant and Castle
London SE1 6TD
tel 01–703 6380

They will supply black and white prints and lend
colour transparencies of buildings under their
jurisdiction, ie ancient monuments and historical
buildings, public statutes and memorials,
government buildings (palaces, embassies,
army, navy and air force buildings) and royal
parks.

Department of the Environment Slide Library 449

Room 601
Prince Consort House
Albert Embankment
London SE1 7TF
tel 01–211 6926 or 5406

Formed in 1954 to meet the needs of planners
and architects in the former Ministry of Housing
and Local Government, the collection has grown
steadily over the years, the content being
expanded to illustrate many of the
responsibilities and interests of both the DOE
(including PSA) and Dept of Town Planning.
Out of a total collection of 40,000 35mm colour
slides, approximately 14,000 relate to British
architectural history. Slides are mainly of
modern buildings in Britain, but also include
ancient monuments, buildings of architectural
and historic interest, new towns, Good Design
in Housing Awards and housing
development/improvement. There is a
published catalogue, arranged in two sections: a

sections: a/*continued*
classified section which lists all slides held by
subject, and a geographical section, which lists
slides by location. A list of all the subjects held
on a card index in the library is included in the
catalogue. The library operates a loan service
only; slides are not available for sale. The loan
service (normally a two week period) is available
to *bona fide* organisations only, not students.
There are a number of slides in the collection
that are not available for loan outside the
department, ie where restriction of use has been
made or in the case of sale sets, either
department or those obtained commercially (but
source information can be made available). The
library is open Mon–Fri from 9.00–13.00 and
14.00–17.00. Personal use (with prior
arrangement) is preferred, though postal use is
possible. Telephone enquiries are limited to
general information only.

Design Council Slide Library 450
The Design Centre
28 Haymarket
London SW1Y 4SU
tel 01–839 8000

A collection, begun in the 1950s, of about 35,000
black and white prints and 16,000 slides, mainly
colour, covering all forms of industrial design,
including furniture, architecture and building as
well as design theory (eg movements such as art
nouveau), exhibitions (eg the Festival of Britain)
and town planning and environmental subjects.
A catalogue of the slide collection is available.
Material can be loaned (in UK only) and copies
are available for sale, reproduction and
publication. The collection is open from
Mon–Fri 10.00 to 17.00. Personal and postal
requests are accepted.

C. M. Dixon 451
13 Danescourt
Dover, Kent CT16 2QE
tel Dover (0304) 208056

Mostly an archaeology collection, but also quite
a large collection of vernacular architecture and
early periods. All the material is colour, but can
be converted to black and white prints if they are
wanted. Fees (publication, search and holding),
by negotiation. Access by appointment.

Keith Ellis Collection 452
75 Bellclose Road
West Drayton, Middlesex UB7 9DF
tel West Drayton (81) 48997

This collection, begun in 1964, is an illustrative
and picture library featuring churches and other
historical buildings, mainly in greater London
and specifically on City of London churches. It

holds 100 black and white and 50 colour prints
and about 2,500 black and white and 1,000
colour film negatives on architectural subjects.
While the collection is mainly black and white,
the emphasis is now on colour. A simple subject
guide to the collection is available on application
and additional catalogues and subject indexes are
housed in the collection. Copy prints are
available. They own the copyright on all their
material. Hours by appointment.

Mary Evans Picture Library 45
1 Tranquil Vale
Blackheath, London SE3 0BU
tel 01–318 0034

The aim of this commercial picture library is to
provide visual documentation of the past, from
pre-history to the present, although after about
1910, the coverage is only selective. The
emphasis of the collection is on social life, and
pictures are filed under more than 1,000 subject
headings, including architecture. They have
hardly any photographs, but many thousands of
prints, mainly 18th–19th century which can be
borrowed. There is no charge for borrowing
pictures on approval for up to one month, but a
service fee may be charged to cover the cost of
research, postage, handling, etc. A service fee is
generally charged if no pictures, or only a small
proportion, are ultimately used. They also offer
copies for sale. The material is mostly black and
white, though there is some colour. They hold
the copyright on virtually all their material.
Researchers are free to do their own research in
their archives, by appointment. Pictures may be
requested by telephone, letter or personal visit.
The library is open Mon–Fri from 9.30–17.30.

Great Dixter (Quentin Lloyd) 45
Little Dixter
Northiam, East Sussex
tel Northiam (07974) 3160

A collection of between 2,500 and 3,000 black
and white prints, glass negatives, glass positives
and lantern slides, taken by the photographer
Nathaniel Lloyd between 1913 and 1935. Most
of the photographs are of domestic architecture
in Britain. The material is not available for loan
or for publication. Copy prints are not available.
There is no access to the collection.

Dr Ivan Hall 45
7 Hengate
Beverley, N Humberside
tel Beverley (0482) 864378

A private collection for teaching and research
begun in 1956. It comprises thousands of black
and white prints, film negatives and lantern

slides. Architecture is the dominant subject of the collection, with the emphasis on the neo-classical period, though covering the whole range from Roman, through medieval and renaissance and some Victorian. Particular features of the collection are building materials used in the late 18th century, especially for ornament (pewter, ironwork, plaster, etc) and pattern book derivations. Material cannot be loaned, except under special circumstances. Copy prints are available. The owner does not hold the copyright on all the material. Personal, postal and telephone enquiries accepted. Open normal office hours.

obert Harding Picture Library   456
5 Botts Mews
Chepstow Road
London W2 5AG
tel 01–229 2234/5

A general collection of black and white prints and colour slides, begun in 1972, of which about 1,000 relate to British and Irish architecture, both historical and modern. Original slides are supplied for copying, and copy prints can be supplied for black and white. Virtually all the material is their copyright. The collection is open from 9.30–17.30 (closed 13.00–14.00), and personal, postal and telephone enquiries are accepted.

he Iris Hardwick Library of Photographs   457
13 Duck Street
Cerne Abbas
Dorset DT2 7LA
tel Cerne Abbas (030 03) 502

A collection of black and white prints and colour transparencies begun in the late 1960s and including illustrations of village churches and cottages, mostly in the West Country, as well as gardens and garden design, garden features and planning. Copy prints are available for publication and the library owns the copyright on all their material. Personal (by appointment only), postal and telephone use acceptable.

live Hicks   458
72 Brentham Way
London W5 1BE
tel 01–997 7974 or 636 6255

A personal collection built up specifically during very extensive travel in Britain over many years. It contains over 20,000 35mm colour lantern slides and over 5,000 monochrome film negatives of British and Irish architecture and landscape, including historic and vernacular architecture, prehistoric structures, Roman buildings, cathedrals, abbeys, parish churches,

castles, fortifications, houses, cottages, bridges, windmills, public buildings, garden buildings, early development of housing and modern architecture. The collection is particularly strong on the medieval period, and especially full for most major medieval churches, including glass and sculpture. It is representative up to c 1830. The last 150 years are less fully covered. Original material is not available on loan except under most exceptional circumstances, and except on approval with a view to publication. Copy prints or transparencies can be prepared for sale, display, reproduction or publication. Fees are negotiable. The owner holds the copyright on all the material, but some photographs require permission from and payment to the building owner for publication. The collection is not open to visitors in the ordinary way, but facilities may be made available to people undertaking serious and significant research under some circumstances.

Michael Holford   459
119 Queens Road
Loughton, Essex
tel 01–508 4358

A general art history collection, begun about 1968, with about 2,000 images of British architecture (Saxon to 19th century, castles, churches, cathedrals and houses). Good quality, large format colour transparencies, which may be hired for reproduction. Copy prints are not available for sale. The owner holds the copyright on all the material. The collection is open Mon–Fri from 9.30–17.00, and personal, postal and telephone use is accepted, although restricted to editorial use only.

Angelo Hornak   460
10 Exeter Mansions
106 Shaftesbury Avenue
London W1V 7DH
tel 01–437 2920

A good, fast-growing collection of mainly colour transparencies. Transparencies are available for loan against standard reproduction fees. Access by appointment.

Dr Quentin Hughes's Collection   461
Liverpool School of Architecture
University of Liverpool
PO Box 147
Liverpool L69 3BX
tel Liverpool (051) 709 6022 ext 2920;
evenings Liverpool (051) 728 7905

A collection, begun in 1950, of approximately 1,000 black and white film negatives and 1,000 colour transparencies of military architecture in

6.2 Guide to sources of architectural photographs and slides

architecture in/*continued*
Britain, which is part of a much larger collection of negatives, photographs and colour transparencies of military architecture in Europe and the British Empire with particular reference to such places as Malta and Gibraltar. It also contains many photographs of secular and ecclesiastical buildings. There are no indexes to the collection and material cannot be loaned, although copy prints are available. For selections of pictures borrowed on approval and not used, or where very few are used from a large number, a fee is charged on the work involved. These fees are for borrowing the material. In the case of transparencies only copies are sold but originals may be borrowed for reproduction upon payment of a deposit. All the material is the copyright of the owner. Open normal office hours. Personal use (by appointment) and postal use accepted. Telephone use (if essential) must be confirmed in writing.

John R. Hume   462
Department of History
University of Strathclyde
Glasgow G1 1XQ
tel Glasgow (041) 552 4400 ext 2363 or 2225

A collection, begun in 1964, which includes approximately 35,000 prints and film negatives and 5,000 colour transparencies of industrial buildings and related machinery, civil engineering structures and some domestic and ecclesiastical buildings, mainly 1750 – date. Aids to the collection comprise a single copy chronological list, a partial card index and a partial geographical index. Material cannot be loaned and while copy prints can be supplied, there are no facilities for 'official' print-making, so that it is difficult to guarantee delivery dates of copy prints. Not all the photographs are the owner's copyright, but assistance is provided in tracing the copyright holder. There are no facilities for personal consultation. Postal and telephone enquiries are welcome, but not 'blanket' enquiries.

Irish Tourist Board   463
Baggot Street Bridge
Dublin 2
Ireland
tel Dublin 765871

The primary aim of the library is to promote tourism and, therefore, the majority of their slides and photographs are related to items of scenic interest and to particular tourist attractions. In black and white they have a certain amount of material dating back to the late 1930s which was purchased by the tourism association which preceded the present day Irish Tourist Board. Typed lists of some of the older black and white negatives are available. There

are lists of ancient monuments and county lists. Castles, country houses and cathedrals are well represented. The colour transparency library is of much more recent origin. Cross reference list to the colour library are available. There are list for: pre-Christian monuments and ruins; Georgian architecture; modern buildings; buildings of interest; castles; manors, mansions country houses etc; cottages; abbeys, monastic ruins, round towers; cathedrals and churches; museums, galleries and libraries; and pubs, restaurants and shops. Black and white photographs may be ordered. All colour materia is available for loan in the form of 35mm slides or 2¼in transparencies. All material is copyright of the Irish Tourist Board. Reproduction fees are charged for commercial use, but they do not charge reproduction fees to magazines. The library is open Mon to Fri from 10.00–12.30; 14.00–16.00.

Peter Jennings   46
26 Rowan Close
St Albans, Herts AL4 0ST
tel St Albans (0727) 61835

This collection, begun in 1970, is being built into a complete record of surviving British windmills, supplemented by interior views and historic pictures. It comprises 400 historic black and white prints and 50 colour prints, 600 black and white film negatives and 800 (6 × 7cm) colour slides (although 35mm is also available). Loan is by arrangement. Copy prints are available. The owner holds the copyright on all the material. Personal use is by appointment only. Postal and telephone enquiries accepted.

A. F. Kersting   46
37 Frewin Road
London SW18
tel 01–874 1475

Almost certainly the most extensive collection o architectural photographs taken by one person. The collection contains about 60,000 black and white prints and 15,000 colour transparencies, though not all are specific to Great Britain. Very good quality interiors and exteriors. Material ca be loaned or copied. Open Mon–Fri 9.00–18.00 appointments preferred.

Lucinda Lambton Library   46
14 Rawlinson Road
Oxford
tel Oxford (0865) 56909 or 55869

A collection of about 20,000 colour transparencies, mainly architectural, covering subjects such as architectural curiosities, industrial archaeology, the history of the lavatory, railway stations, Victorian restaurants and hotels, vernacular and curious buildings, street furniture, shops and pubs, cemeteries and churchyards. The collection covers the period from Roman times to the present. Special attention is given to artistic composition and the unusual. There is a subject index. Copy prints are available and material can be loaned. All the material is the copyright of the collection. Fees are negotiable. Personal, postal and telephone use is accepted. The Library is open from 8.30 to 24.00.

Peter Laws 467

2 Donnington Road
Penzance, Cornwall TR18 4PH
tel Penzance (0736) 3544

A private collection, begun in 1937. Originally of buildings in Maidstone and vicinity, represented by 55mm ($2\frac{1}{4}$in sq) negatives and prints. From 1944 to 1961 the photographs (55mm negatives) are mainly of buildings in Cambridgeshire and East Anglia. From 1961 the collection is mainly of 35mm colour slides including a great many transparencies from old photographs, including 19th and early 20th-century postcards, particularly of Cornish subjects, such as churches. The categories of the slide collection and approximate numbers are: National Trust buildings (300), buildings in Penzance (250), 20th-century architecture in the UK (120), railway buildings (100), south-west Ireland (100), lighthouses in the UK and Ireland (100), buildings in the Isles of Scilly (130), 19th-century architecture (100), buildings designed by Silvarus Trevail FRIBA (75), buildings designed by Edmund Sedding, senior (1836–68), Edmund Sedding, junior (1863–1921) and John D. Sedding (1838–1891) (60), Cornish churches (100), Bedfordshire buildings (50), buildings in the UK (250), industrial archaeology – bridges, watermills, windmills, canal buildings, warehouses, foundries, engine houses etc in Britain and Ireland (250). Many of the slides reflect the photographers' interest in the vernacular styles of building and the use of different building materials. Photographs can be loaned by arrangement and copy prints can be provided. The owner holds the copyright on most of the material. Open normal office hours. Personal, postal and telephone enquiries accepted.

W. Leary 468

52 St Peter's Way
Plemstall Park
Mickle Trafford, Chester CH2 4EJ
tel Mickle Trafford (0244) 300031

A personal collection, begun in 1965 and terminated in 1977, which includes

approximately 500–600 black and white prints and film negatives of Lincolnshire Methodist chapels, used and unused and demolished. Copy prints are available and all the material is the owner's copyright. Access to the collection is by letter to the owner.

Mansell Collection 469

42 Linden Gardens
London W2 4ER
tel 01–229 5475

A general historical picture library, predominantly pre-1930s. They supply prints on loan for publication and other reproduction purposes, and all prints issued must be returned after use. A fee is charged for the use of Mansell Collection material, the amount being dependent upon the way it is used. A loan and research fee is charged if nothing from a selection is finally used. Fees can be advised on application. Most of the material in the Mansell Collection is Mansell copyright, or out of copyright. In a few cases copyright must be cleared and whenever possible they assist in advising where to apply for permission.

While not principally an architectural collection, their architecture section is fairly comprehensive in scope, including folders on various techniques of architectural construction, architectural details, various kinds of mainly domestic buildings, reconstructions of buildings from earlier cultures, and separate folders for most architectural styles and/or periods. The topographical section includes a large number of prints of buildings classified not by what they are but by where they are. They also have plates from many early architectural publications, such as Pyne's *Royal residences*, Nash's *Mansions of England in the olden times*, *Architecture of the Renaissance in England*, *Vitruvius Britannicus*, various volumes of Kip engravings, etc. There is no catalogue.

They are normally open to visitors from 10.00–17.00, but appointments are absolutely necessary to visit the collection, and, as they tend to get quite booked up in advance, they require between one and two weeks' notice. They also deal with postal requests, and telephone requests of not more than six subjects where the description of what is required is quite straightforward.

National Art Slide Library *see* 493: Victoria and Albert Museum, National Art Slide Library

National Monuments Record: England, Scotland, Wales *see* 365–367

National Trust for Places of Historic Interest and Natural Beauty *see* 341

Norfolk and Norwich Archaeological 470
Society's Collection
Garsett House
St Andrew's Hall Plain
Norwich NR3 1AT

> The photographic collection, begun in the early
> 1900s is devoted to architecture and furnishings
> (especially church furniture) chiefly in Norfolk.
> It contains 1,274 prints, 50 postcard views, 831
> film negatives, 432 glass negatives, 2 glass
> positives and 12 lantern slides. All material is
> black and white. A manuscript list of subjects
> and a card index of parishes represented is held
> in the library. No material is available for loan
> and although copy prints are not normally
> available, any request would be considered. The
> Society owns the copyright on all negatives and
> some prints. The library is open Mon–Fri from
> 9.00–17.30, and while free to members of the
> Society, a charge of £1.00/day is made to
> non-members.

Photo Precision 471
Caxton Road
St Ives
Huntingdon, Cambridgeshire PE17 4LS
tel Huntingdon (0480) 64364

> A collection of about 20,000 colour photographs
> of stately homes, museums, cathedrals, parks,
> zoos and other places of interest, mostly in the
> British Isles. Material can be loaned or copied.
> The collection is open Mon–Fri from
> 9.00–17.00, preferably by appointment.

Photolog Library (Dr W. H. Findlay) 472
9 Rosemount Place
Perth PH2 7EH
tel Perth (0738) 24157

> An architectural collection, containing
> approximately 1,000 black and white prints (10
> × 8in), 1,200 film negatives and 500 colour
> transparencies of all types of buildings, from all
> periods, in Perth. Copy prints are available and
> all material is the copyright of the collection.
> The collection is open by appointment.

Picturepoint Ltd 473
770 Fulham Road
London SW6 5SJ
tel 01–736 5865

> A general collection of about ½ million colour
> transparencies, which, while including
> illustrations from archaeological remains to
> contemporary architecture, does not hold

anything very detailed. There are no catalogues
or guides to the collection. Material is loaned on
approval. They hold the copyright on all
material either as agents or as principals. The
collection is open Mon–Fri from 9.30–17.30,
but is not available to single individuals without
backup from a company of proven financial
standing.

Pidgeon Audio Visual 47
Orders and enquiries to:
World Microfilms Publications
62 Queen's Grove
London NW8 6ER

> Pidgeon Audio Visual was set up in 1978 to
> publish this continuing library of cassette/slides
> by architects and other eminent commentators
> on architecture and design. The cassettes presen
> half-hour talks accompanied by 24 colour slides.
> Sets, produced and in preparation, include Sir
> John Summerson at Sir John Soane's Museum,
> Jack Pritchard (Lawn Road and the Thirties),
> Alison and Peter Smithson, Philip Dowson,
> Nicholas Grimshaw, Peter Cook, Richard
> Rogers, Cedric Price, Theo Crosby, Denys
> Lasdun, Norman Foster, Edward Cullinan and
> James Stirling. The cassette/slide sets are
> available for sale only.

Pitkin Pictorials 47
11 Wyfold Road
London SW6 6SG
tel 01–385 4351

> A collection of photographs used in the
> guidebooks to notable buildings, cathedrals,
> stately homes, city views, museums, castles,
> gardens and monuments which are published by
> the company. Material can be loaned or copied.
> Open Mon–Fri from 9.15–17.15. Visits by
> appointment.

A. F. Plunkett Collection 47
29 Margetson Avenue
Thorpe St Andrew
Norwich NA7 0DG
tel Norwich (0603) 35164

> This collection, begun in 1931, concentrates
> chiefly on Norfolk architecture (ecclesiastical,
> military, domestic, etc, from medieval to
> modern), but includes small representations of
> some other English and Welsh counties. The
> collection includes 5,566 black and white prints,
> 5,579 film negatives, and 623 black and white
> lantern slides.

. Poole 477
7 Fernhill Avenue
Weymouth, Dorset
tel Weymouth (0305) 2768

This private collection, begun in 1950, contains
about 1,500 35mm colour transparencies of
domestic architecture (in traditional materials; of
the industrial revolution; of 20th-century
suburban growth; and of recent 'self-conscious'
planners' response), country houses and
churches of Dorset, and town and village streets,
especially, but not exclusively, Dorset. The
emphasis of the collection is on traditional
architecture and provenance and use of local
materials such as stone, brick, cob etc and on
regional styles, particularly Dorset.
Transparencies cannot generally be loaned, but
copy prints are available to order. The owner
holds the copyright on all the material. As this is
a private collection, it is not regularly accessible.

ostal Publicity Photographic Library 478
Room 435
Postal Headquarters
St Martin's-le-Grand
London EC1A 1HQ
tel 01–432 3513

The library illustrates all aspects of the postal
service with prints and transparencies, both
monochrome and colour. All photographs are
filed alphabetically under subject (eg Buildings:
historic with postal association, Letterboxes:
Victorian, Edward VII, etc, and Post offices:
historic, in London, modern exteriors, etc). The
library includes several thousand photographs of
buildings and street furniture, mainly of the 19th
and 20th centuries. Standard prints, both
monochrome and colour, are on glossy paper
and are $8\frac{1}{2} \times 6\frac{1}{2}$in (216 × 165mm) in size. Other
sizes and surface textures are available only to
order. Colour transparencies vary within the
following size ranges: 35mm, $2\frac{1}{4} \times 2\frac{1}{4}$in (58 ×
58mm), 5 × 4in (127 × 101mm) and 10 × 8in
(254 × 203mm). Copies of the photographs can
be supplied for reference, reproduction or
display and a scale of fees is available on request.
Appointments to inspect and select material may
be made during normal office hours.

adio Times Hulton Picture Library 479
35 Marylebone High Street
London W1M 4AA
tel 01–580 5577

A commercial library providing pictures for
publication or exhibition purposes. It covers
historical subjects from pre-history to 1957. The
collection as a whole numbers over six million
illustrations, including prints (both engravings
and photographs), glass negatives and even some
original art works. Colour material forms a
comparatively small part of the collection. They
hold the copyright on most of their material.
Prints, usually 8 × 6in, are lent for commercial
reproduction or sold for exhibition purposes.
Supply normally takes about two weeks. There
is no handling fee. Illustrations are not provided
for individual research.

One of the topics they isolate in the
collection is architecture, which is divided into
historical (before 1921) and modern (after 1921).
Within each section there are sub-sections by
type of building, part of building, etc. The
strictly architectural material is supplemented by
a large amount of material classified as
topographical. Here the architecture will be
incidental rather than central but may,
nevertheless, be quite important. The collection
is particularly useful for finding pictures of
buildings no longer standing. The catalogues
and indexes are for staff use only.

The library is open Mon–Fri from
9.30–17.30. Personal and telephone requests are
accepted, but postal requests are preferred.

**Science Museum Library. H. E. S. Simmons
Collection** *see* 383.

Slide Centre Ltd 480
143 Chatham Road
London SW11 6SR
tel 01–223 3457

Principally involved in supplying colour slides
and filmstrips for educational purposes from a
large stock or originals. A catalogue is available
giving details of the architecture series (eg
outlines of architecture, 1,000 years of English
architecture, the English parish church, the
British castle, the development of the domestic
house, stained glass in England, etc) and the
building series (eg stone age burial chambers,
bronze age stone circles, iron age dwellings and
hill fortresses, cathedrals and major churches,
castles, major houses, etc). Other relevant
material is listed in the sections on geography,
environmental studies and history. In all, they
hold about 1,500 colour slides of British
architecture, covering most building types and
periods, from prehistory to modern. They do
not hold the copyright on all their material, but
will assist in tracing the copyright owner.
Personal (by arrangement), postal and telephone
use is accepted. Open Mon–Fri from
9.30–16.30.

6.2 Guide to sources of architectural photographs and slides

Edwin Smith Collection 481
The Coach House
Windmill Hill
Saffron Walden, Essex CB10 1RR
tel Saffron Walden (0799) 23373

Approximately 60,000 photographs taken by
Edwin Smith between 1945 and 1971, organised
by his widow, Olive Smith. Particularly fine
quality black and white photographs and some
1,000 colour transparencies. Card indexes to the
collection. No loan facilities. The collection
holds the copyright on all the material. Personal
access to the collection is granted only in
exceptional circumstances. Postal enquiries are
preferred.

J. C. D. Smith 482
Old Arch
Four Forks
Spaxton Bridgwater, Somerset TA5 1AA
tel Spaxton Bridgwater (027 867) 404

The largest specialist private collection of
photographs of English medieval woodcarvings
(misericords, bench-ends, church details).
Approximately 8,000 black and white prints and
8,000 negatives, 500 black and white and 200
colour lantern slides and 100 colour film
negatives. There are indexes to the collection.
Prints can be loaned by arrangement and copy
prints are available. All the material is Mr
Smith's copyright.

Jessica Strang 483
86 Cambridge Gardens
London W10 6HS
tel 01–969 7292

A collection, begun in 1975 and still growing, of
about 9,000 35mm colour slides of existing
buildings of all periods. The emphasis of the
collection is on graphics, architectural detail and
domestic interiors (1960–1980). London
architectural, sculptural and design details are
particularly well-represented, with about 3,000
slides. A subject list of London details is
available and a guide and card indexes are in
preparation. Subject indexes are available at the
library only. Material is loaned free for seven
days and fees are charged for longer loan and for
reproduction. Copy prints are not available.
Search and service fees are charged, although
individuals may make their own search free of
charge. All the material is Jessica Strang's
copyright. Personal (by appointment), postal
and telephone use is accepted.

Suffolk Record Office 48
Bury St Edmunds Branch
School Hall Street
Bury St Edmunds IP33 1RX
tel Bury St Edmunds (0284) 63141

Ipswich Branch
County Hall
Ipswich IP4 2JS
tel Ipswich (0473) 55801

The Suffolk Record Office and its predecessors
have sought over the past twenty-five years to
build up a photographic archive which will
effectively facilitate the study of that particular
aspect of the county's history – its physical
appearance at differing points in time – which
photographs alone can illuminate with accuracy
and succinctness. Grouped together in the
strongrooms of the two branch offices are a
number of collections which represent, in some
cases the work of a single photographer, and, in
others, the zeal of an individual collector.
Together they provide a broad and often highly
detailed coverage of specific places and subjects
at dates spread across the spectrum of
photographic history from the mid-nineteenth
century to the present.
The photographic collections are available
for study to all *bona fide* users, that is, to those
who have a specific and legitimate object to
pursue in examining them. Because of the
difficulties involved in handling fragile glass
negatives, and of storing large quantities of
individual prints, full acccess to the material can
only be arranged where advance notification of a
visit, either by letter or telephone, has been
received. The Photographic Section of the
Record Office can, in most cases, make copies of
photographs though technicalities of copyright
and ownership and difficulties of reproduction
may, in some cases, preclude this. Price lists for
copying are available on request.
The guide which follows attempts to give
some brief account of the origins, style and
content of the principal collections in the Record
Office and to indicate the nature and scope of the
finding aids at present available to searchers.

The Suffolk Photographic Survey (Ipswich)
In 1954 Mr R. B. Pratt of Capel St Mary
conceived the idea of bringing together in a
single place a collection of photographs which
would illustrate as fully as possible the life of the
county in former times. The Survey, as it came
to be called, today comprises more than 9,000
negatives and prints which, in their range – of
time, place and subject – go far towards
achieving his initial goal of comprehensiveness.
Buildings of all types, people, activities – both
work and play, vehicles and vessels, industry and
agriculture, crafts and customs are reflected here
across the broadest span of time, with a heavy

emphasis on the last years of the nineteenth century and the early years of this. A number of smaller collections have been absorbed into the overall structure, principal among these being a large number of negatives of photographs printed in the *East Anglian Daily Times* up until the 1950s. Card indexes of subjects and places provide access to the main part of the collection which is arranged partly in topographical, and partly in subject sequence.

The Alexander Collection (Ipswich K420)
Views of Ipswich and a few other parishes, dating from the 1850s and 1860s, taken by Richard Dykes Alexander (1788–1865).

The Burrows Collection (Ipswich S9)
An album of some 200 photographs including views of Ipswich and neighbouring parishes, dated c 1858, taken by Robert Burrows (1810–1883).

The Cowell Collection (Ipswich K400)
The years preceding and following the First World War saw the publication of numerous series of postcards, produced all over the country by local printers. Prominent among those in the Ipswich area was the Christchurch Series, printed by Messrs Cowell of the Buttermarket. It is the glass negatives from which these were produced that are preserved in this collection. Dating principally from the years 1905 to 1908, with a few from the 1920s, the 1,500 half-plate negatives cover villages and towns from Lowestoft to Clare and into north Essex, though there is a concentration on the area within twenty miles of Ipswich, which, together with Felixstowe, forms the focal point of the collection. The coverage is of typical postcard type – street scenes, principal buildings, churches and beauty spots, but the photographer is often at pains to include people in his shots, and, as a result, they frequently provide fascinating and lively glimpses into the life of the period. A full catalogue and index is in preparation.

The East Suffolk Building Record (Ipswich)
This collection represents the fruits of an attempt made by the Ipswich and East Suffolk Record Office in 1967, in conjunction with the County Planning Department, to make a photographic survey of all buildings listed by the then Ministry of Housing and Local Government as being of outstanding architectural or historical interest. The work was carried out by amateurs within their own areas and the coverage, as a result, varies considerably, in terms both of completeness and technical quality, from parish to parish. In all some 160 out of a possible total of 317 parishes made some sort of return. Some give a complete coverage of all listed buildings within the parish,

others only partially so. Photographs are usually of frontages, and few architectural details, few shots of the rear or sides of buildings, and no interiors, are included. The photographs exist in the form of some 2,500 35mm negatives and strip prints, of which the most satisfactory have been enlarged to half-plate size. These enlargements are arranged in envelopes in alphabetical sequence of parish and individual parish envelopes may be requested. The photographs should be used in conjunction with the Schedules of Listed Buildings, also available in the Record Office. It is important, finally, to remember that the Building Record covers only the eastern half of the county.

The Felixstowe Collection (Ipswich JI14)
An unusual collection which appears to represent the output of an unidentified professional photographer working in Felixstowe between 1924 and 1949. Like most other collections of this type, it contains numbers of local views in and around the town, but it is uncommon in its heavy emphasis upon recording local events and society activities. Work commissioned by businesses and authorities is also reflected in shots of, for example, shop fronts, estate show houses and hospital interiors. The photographs survive as 300 half-plate negatives, some on glass, others on film, and are stored in labelled envelopes for ease of identification. A number of them were damaged by storage in damp conditions before their transfer to the Record Office and are unsuitable for copying.

The Frith Collection (Ipswich and Bury)
Francis Frith was Britain's earliest publisher of postcards and for a long period the best known and most successful. He and his assistants set themselves the task of recording in photographs the whole of the country, and systematically set about making their survey by railway and by hired horse and trap. From his large 10×8in glass negatives were run off initial sets of sepia toned prints and, at a later stage, the masters from which the postcards were printed. In 1971, when the firm went into liquidation, Frith's negatives and prints were sold off and some 500 of the sepia prints were purchased for the then East and West Suffolk Record Offices. They cover the period from the 1890s to the 1920s, and are spread broadly (and somewhat thinly) across the face of the county, with a predictable emphasis on beauty spots and larger towns, in particular the seaside resorts. The Frith prints covering the eastern half of the county are filed at the Ipswich branch office in alphabetical sequence of place, and those for the western half (7 towns only) at the Bury branch office, under the reference 2630.

The Gillson Collection (Ipswich JI6)
F. W. Gillson's photographic business operated

operated/*continued*

in Ipswich for a period of more than thirty years from 1923, first in Brooks Hall Road and later in Norwich Road, and it is therefore regrettable that his surviving negatives cover only the short period from 1926 to 1930. The thousand or so glass and film negatives of half-plate size which have survived are of what might be described as postcard content: street scenes, village views, attractive buildings, beaches and so on. The collection is heavily weighted towards Ipswich scenes but also covers towns and villages within about a twenty mile radius of the town. There is, in addition, a small amount of material relating to the area around Burwell in east Cambridgeshire, this no doubt deriving from some personal connection with the area. The quality of the material is very variable. In general, photographs taken using film negative are of poor technical quality and would not lend themselves readily to enlargement. A manuscript catalogue of the collection, made probably by Gillson himself, is in the Record Office. This unfortunately is arranged alphabetically by title rather than by place so that the Ancient House, Ipswich is indexed under 'A' rather than 'I' and the beach at Felixstowe under 'B'.

The Girling Collection (Ipswich HA203)
An architect by profession, Frank Girling was a keen photographer and a man of catholic interests. For nearly forty years until his death in 1966, he applied himself to the making of a photographic record of those fields in which his manifold interests lay, and the results, bequeathed to the Record Office, amount to many thousands of negatives and prints, in two series. The first is a set of 144 albums, of which 30 deal with Suffolk buildings and views arranged by parish, 16 cover other counties, 28 are concerned with ecclesiastical architecture and fittings, 34 with domestic buildings and architectural detail and the remainder with mills, prehistoric remains and sites, farm activities, market houses, merchants' marks (Girling's *English merchants' marks* was published in 1962) and so on. These subjects are repeated and supplemented by others ranging from sundials to fungi and gypsies, in a series of 75 box files containing notes, cuttings and photographs. A summary catalogue of both albums and boxes is available in the Record Office, though the contents of each are not individually detailed.

The Lovell Collection (Ipswich JI11)
For 15 years between 1914 and 1929, a motor cycle combination travelled the roads of Suffolk bearing R. T. Cooper, author of a series of articles on *Suffolk parishes, their history and romance*, published in the *East Anglian Daily Times* under the name 'Yeoman', and Edmund Lovell, photographer and friend. The result of these weekend excursions, apart from the articles, was a series of eight photograph albums compiled by Lovell and containing some 3,500

photographs of churches, their exteriors and details, houses, from the large mansion to the picturesque cottage, village streets, and river scenes. Some 300 parishes, including some over the border in north Essex and south Norfolk, are covered. There is no index to the items, but each of the albums bears on its fly-leaf a list of the parishes dealt with. The photographs survive only as prints of quarter-plate and smaller sizes, so that reproduction may be difficult, though the technical quality is excellent.

The Munro-Cautley Collection (Ipswich JI5)
H. Munro-Cautley, FSA, ARIBA, the author of *Suffolk churches and their treasures* (1937) and *Royal arms and commandments in our churches* (1934) was a keen amateur photographer, and the preparatory work for his two volumes included the taking of almost a thousand glass plate negatives of ecclesiastical architecture and fittings. His photographic work was precise, patient and careful. In the preface to *Suffolk churches* he records that much of his photographic work was done from specially erected scaffolding, and many of the shots of individual details are unequalled elsewhere. Furnishings, fittings, architectural features and exteriors are all included in the collection though there is little coverage of details and buildings of later than 17th century date. Over 200 churches are dealt with to a greater or lesser degree. The photographs of Royal arms and commandments are national rather than local in coverage. A manuscript catalogue of the photographs made by Munro-Cautley is available in the Record Office. Arranged alphabetically by parish, it directs the searcher to the relevant negative box, but does not indicate which features of the church are covered.

The Newham Collection (Bury 890)
As relaxation from his work as a GP in the Market Weston of the 1940s and 1950s, Dr H. B Newham turned to photography, which he combined with a keen interest in ecclesiology, to make a series of 400 quarter plate glass negatives. Concentrating largely on the areas of Norfolk and Suffolk readily accessible to him, he took as his principal subject church fittings and furnishings, and in particular woodcarving, but his camera accompanied him on journeys to other parts of the country where his other architectural interests such as dovecotes and mills were allowed full rein. At home in Market Weston, he was a keen recorder of local people, buildings and events.

In addition to the negatives, a series of some 400 three inch square glass transparencies of similar subjects survive. In the early 1950s, Dr Newham also adopted the practice of mounting prints, as he developed them, in simple chronological sequence within albums. Devoid of any subject arrangement, these volumes form a fascinating amalgam of his interests, family and villagers placed side by side with church chests and dovecotes, architectural curiosities and copies of early photographs of the Market Weston area.

A manuscript list of the negatives, with a place index to those plates taken before 1955 was kept by Dr Newham in a notebook, which is now stored with the collection.

The Spanton–Jarman Collection (Bury K 505)
The 1864 Post Office Directory of Bury St Edmunds includes mention of one Willam Spanton who, at his 'repository of arts and West Suffolk photographic establishment' at 16 Abbeygate Street carried on the business of 'house decorator, carver and gilder and paper hanger, plumber, glazier and painter', not to mention photographer. From these beginnings grew the business which later came to absorb that of another Bury photographer, J. W. Clarke, and to involve members of the Jarman family, who maintain the firm to this day. Some 4,000 glass plates of differing sizes, covering the period from the 1860s to the Second World War are now lodged at the Bury branch office. 200 or more parishes in Suffolk, Essex and Norfolk feature, by far the largest number of photographs being of Bury St Edmunds. Subjects covered include churches, large houses, inns, village views, family groups, paintings and engravings, but there are many types of material which are unparalleled in other collections; election hustings at Angel Hill, the operating theatre at the West Suffolk General Hospital, the construction of a canal and the opening of a light railway are typical of a number of plates of unusual value for the nineteenth century social historian.

Available to searchers are a typescript place index, detailing the subjects photographed in each parish, a manuscript index of personal names covering both photographic sitters and portrait paintings, and a manuscript catalogue of the collection, arranged in groups according to the size of the negative, and indicating, for each item, title, original plate number, size and type of negative.

Copies of photographs in this collection are available on special request only.

The Vick Collection (Ipswich J 14)
When, at the end of the last century, William Vick, 'family and commercial photographic artist' retired after thirty years in his Ipswich studio in London Road, the 10,000 or more glass negatives that represented his work were purchased by public subscription and placed in the Ipswich Museum, whence they were eventually transferred to the Record Office. The incredible richness and variety of this collection reflects both the diversity of the work of a professional photographer in the nineteenth century and the many interests of a man who was a leading figure in the Ipswich Scientific Society

and in other local scholarly organisations. In addition to many thousands of family portraits and groups, the collection includes local street scenes and some rural buildings, shop premises (many later printed and used as billheads or advertisements) and photographs of objects of antiquarian and artistic interest. The geographical coverage is largely limited to Ipswich, though occasional forays to surrounding towns and villages are recorded. The collection consists entirely of glass plates of sizes varying from 10×8in to small quarter-plate size. An index by Vick himself to the 10×8 in plates survives, but is patchy in its coverage, idosyncratic in its organisation and handicapped by later disturbances to the arrangement of the plates. A new alphabetical arrangement is at present under way. One series of half-plate negatives is contained in labelled boxes which facilitate identification. The family photographs and many thousands of half and quarter plates are in many cases as yet unidentified.

Other Collections
Apart from the major collections listed above, the two branch offices contain many thousands of photographs scattered amongst the archives in their custody. There are a number of small groups of negatives and prints discovered in attics and sheds, last remnants of a grandparent's hobby, many of them of considerable aesthetic or historical interest.

While the amateur photographer flourished at home, his professional counterpart derived an increasing amount of his income from work for commercial enterprises, and often quite extensive collections of photographs have become an integral part of series of business archives. Amongst the records of the Cobbold family, for instance, are a series of prints of public houses owned by their Ipswich brewery.

Surrey County Council, Antiquities of the County of Surrey
485

County Planning Department
County Hall
Kingston upon Thames KT1 2DT
tel 01–546 1050 ext 3664 or 3667

The photographic collection is maintained by the Conservation and Historic Buildings Section, which provides a specialist advisory service to the eleven district councils in Surrey. The collection is supported by a filing system incorporating architects' reports and general correspondence. The photographic record, begun in 1950, has grown in response to the demands of development control questions and committee work in relation to grants, plaques and possible cases for statutory listing. The collection, all black and white, comprises approximately 18,500 prints, 12,500 film negatives and 4,000 glass negatives of all types

6.2 Guide to sources of architectural photographs and slides

all types/*continued*
and periods of buildings of architectural or
historic interest in Surrey. There is a card index
to the collection. Material cannot be loaned, but
copy prints are available. The Council holds the
copyright on all the material. Photographs of
buildings in that area of the county which
became part of Greater London in 1965 are
deposited in the Surrey Record Office, in
County Hall. The collection is open normal
office hours and personal, postal and telephone
use is accepted.

Dr Jennifer Tann 486
University of Aston Management Centre
158 Corporation Street
Birmingham B4 6TE
tel Birmingham (021) 359 3611 ext 488

This collection, begun in 1960, is exclusively of
industrial and working-class housing of the 18th
and 19th centuries. It comprises about 800 black
and white prints and film negatives and 1,000
colour transparencies. Subject indexes are
available. Copy prints can be provided. The
owner holds the copyright on all the material.
Hours are by appointment. Postal use preferred.

Theatre Museum *see* 404.

Douglas Thompson 487
1 Petticoat Lane
Bury St Edmunds, Suffolk IP33 3NS
tel Bury St Edmunds (0284) 3126

This collection, begun in the 1930s, comprises
7,500 black and white prints and 10,000 film
negatives of railway stations. The views are
mainly from the platform. The material is
catalogued by location. There are no loan
facilities, but copy prints are available. The
owner holds the copyright on the majority of
items. Personal access is by arrangement.

Trans-Globe Film Distributors Ltd 488
23 Crisp Road
London W6 9RL
tel 01–748 0017

A collection of 35mm colour transparencies of
interiors and exteriors of historic houses,
monuments, castles, etc in England, Scotland,
Wales and Northern Ireland. Includes National
Trust and privately owned properties. A
catalogue is available for sale. Material is not
available for loan. Copies are available for
reproduction. Access to the collection is only by
appointment. Postal and telephone requests are
accepted.

**University of Aberdeen, G. W. Wilson
Collection** 48
University Library
King's College
Aberdeen AB9 2UB
tel Aberdeen (0224) 40241

A collection of 40,000 black and white glass
negatives of British architectural subjects, datin
c 1860–c 1910. Copy prints are available for
reproduction and publication. All the material i
their copyright. Use of the collection is in perso
or by post. Open from 9.15–16.30.

**University of Cambridge, Committee for
Aerial Photography** 49
Mond Building
Free School Lane
Cambridge CB2 3RF
tel Cambridge (0223) 358381

The main purpose of this small department of
the University is to obtain and make available
aerial photographs needed by other faculties at
Cambridge for teaching or research. They are
prepared to help with similar needs arising
elsewhere, in so far as they can with their limite
resources. The Committee sponsors a series of
flights for reconnaissance and photography
deliberately planned for research. The
photographs taken in the course of these flights
form the University Collection of Aerial
Photographs, now approaching a third of a
million negatives, with prints to match and
supporting maps and lantern slides. The
collection relates mainly to the United Kingdom
but there is extensive cover of Ireland. There is
little or no cover for much of London and of th
country extending up the Thames as far as
Windsor, and for areas around Liverpool,
Manchester, Prestwick and Renfrew airports.

The principal subjects served by the
collection are agriculture, archaeology,
architecture, ecology, geology, geography,
history, land use, planning and soil science, an
the photographs also illustrate many different
aspects of the social and economic past and
present of the country. There are many
photographs of great country houses, castles,
religious houses, cathedrals, industrial
buildings, in addition to views of towns and
villages. The earliest photographs were taken in
1945, but the photography was comparatively
restricted in the first five years and the main
mass of the collection dates from between 1949
and the present.

A detailed catalogue is kept at the
collection, in the form of a typed list, in which
the photographs are recorded in the sequence i
which they were taken. The main system for
retrieving information from the collection is a
detailed card index arranged by locality and by
subject, with abundant cross-referencing.

The greater part of the collection consists of low level oblique photographs, but there is also an appreciable and growing quantity of precision vertical survey photographs. Most of the reproductions are in black and white though they have some thousands of colour photographs, mostly in the form of transparencies. The negatives are on aerial survey film: for the oblique photographs these are either 5½in or 70mm square; the frame size of the vertical survey photographs is 9in square.

The collection is regarded as an archive and copies are not available on loan. Prints of the photographs may be consulted by serious enquirers by appointment at any reasonable time, Mon–Fri, and copies can be supplied at a standard scale of charges. If an order involves any appreciable search of the collection, an appropriate search fee is charged. The copyright of the greater part of the material is held by the University (the remainder being Crown Copyright). Reproduction fees are ordinarily charged when photographs are required for publication, although fees may be waived if the publication is in a work of scholarship, such as a learned journal, from which neither author or publisher derive any direct financial gain.

University of East Anglia, Photographic Library   491

School of Fine Arts
University of East Anglia
Norwich NR4 7TJ
tel Norwich (0603) 56161

A large collection, begun in 1966, covering all the arts, including architecture, which contains approximately 70,000 black and white prints and film negatives, 40,000 black and white lantern slides and 40,000 35mm colour slides. About one third of the collection is devoted to architecture. It is particularly strong on medieval architecture. Copies are available for sale and reproduction, but not for loan. Not all the material is their copyright, though they will assist in tracing the copyright owner. The collection is open to personal users Mon–Fri from 9.00–17.00.

University of St Andrews   492

University Library
St Andrews
Fife, Scotland KY16 9TR
tel St Andrews (0334) 76161 ext 514

The photographic collection, begun in 1839, is predominantly black and white and includes about 100,000 prints, 30,000 film negatives, 5,000 glass negatives, a few glass positives, 500 lantern slides as well as a few colour prints and 500 colour lantern slides representing all building types for periods and locations throughout Britain and Ireland. Most of the

architectural subjects are to be found in the reference print collection of Valentine & Sons Ltd, Dundee, photographic publishers until 1967. Aids to the collection include single copy catalogues and lists and sheaf indexes, but subject indexes do not exist for architecture. Copy prints are available. Not all the material is their copyright and only limited assistance can be offered in tracing the copyright owner. The collection is open during term time Mon–Fri from 9.00–1300 and 14.00–17.00, and during vacations Mon–Fri from 9.00–13.00 and 14.00–16.00. Personal and postal use is accepted, but access is at the discretion of the librarian. Telephone requests are not accepted.

Victoria and Albert Museum, National Art Slide Library   493

South Kensington
London SW7 2RL
tel 01–589 6371 ext 262

A slide collection, begun in 1898, which in the past concentrated on the history of painting, rather than architecture. British and Irish architecture, at present, accounts for less than 10% of the holdings and is represented by over 6,000 black and white and 4,000 colour 35mm slides, covering the period from medieval onwards, catalogued under 'country houses', 'secular' and 'ecclesiastic'. A descriptive leaflet is available and master catalogues can be inspected in the visitors' room. Slides are not available for sale, display, reproduction or publication, but are available for loan for lectures. One week's notice in advance is required for any given lecture and 40 slides per lecture may be borrowed. £1.00 is payable in advance if slides are to be sent by the library by post, otherwise the library facilities are free, but available to UK residents for use within the UK only. Lost or damaged slides are charged at £0.50 each. The library is open Mon–Thurs from 10.00–17.00. Slides may be borrowed in person or by post. Only basic information is given over the telephone.

Weidenfeld and Nicolson Ltd   494

91 Clapham High Street
London SW4 7TA
tel 01–622 9933

An archive, begun in the early 1960s, of photographs which have appeared in their publications. The collection numbers about 40,000 photographs, most of them black and white prints. The photographs are filed under the name of the book they were collected for. There are no subject indexes or cross-references, so there is no point in enquiring, for example, if they have a photograph of a particular cathedral. They have only done a couple of general books on architecture, so this subject does not feature large in the collection. Users are, however,

however,/*continued*
welcome to look through the photographs and
books, and material can be loaned. They do not
hold the copyright on most of the photographs,
but try to help trace the copyright owner. Open
Mon–Fri from 9.30–17.00. Personal (by prior
appointment), postal and telephone use
accepted.

Andy Williams Photographic Library   495
3 Levylsdene
Merrow
Guildford, Surrey
tel Guildford (0483) 72778

A collection, begun in 1960, of about 5,000 5 ×
4in colour transparencies. Landscape is the main
subject of the collection, but there is a good
selection of material on cathedrals, cottages,
great houses and castles in Britain, and buildings
and scenes in London. There is an A–Z index to
the collection with special reference to castles,
London etc. Copy prints are available for
reproduction and publication. All the material is
the collection's copyright. Visits to the collection
are preferably by appointment, but they are
willing to send selections by post.

Woodmansterne Ltd   496
Greenhill Crescent
Holywell Industrial Estate
Watford, Herts WD1 8RD
tel Watford (0923) 28236/45788

The Woodmansterne Picture Library, begun in
1952, contains about 5,000 British architectural
subjects, from prehistoric times to the 20th
century. Subjects include cathedrals, churches,
country houses, landscape design, parks and
gardens and townscapes as well as special
collections of National Trust properties,
National Trust for Scotland properties, the
William Morris Gallery, etc. Most of the subjects
are of well-known buildings. Material is available
as 35mm colour transparencies, which can be
purchased, and most subjects can also be
supplied on loan (against a fee) in 6 × 9cm, and
sometimes 9 × 12cm, positive format. Slide sets,
colourslide cassettes, colourslide recordings,
slidebooks, visual guides and lectures for hire are
also available. Subject and geographical
catalogues can be supplied. They own the
copyright on most of their material and will
assist in tracing the copyright owner in cases
where they don't. Publication and reproduction
fees are based on the recommendations of
BAPLA and the IIP. Personal, postal and
telephone use is accepted. The library is open
Mon–Fri from 9.00–16.00.

John and Patricia Woolverton Colour   49`
Library
Cobblers Cottage
Eardisland
Leominster, Herefordshire HR6 9BD
tel Leominster (05447) 584

A collection of over 3,000 5 × 4in colour
transparencies of landscape and architectural
subjects in the UK. Abbeys, cathedrals, castles,
stately homes, manor houses, period cottages,
etc are generally shown in a landscape scene.
Transparencies are available for loan. They hold
the copyright on all their material. Personal (by
appointment), postal and telephone use
accepted.

Yorkshire Architectural and York   49`
Archaeological Society
c/o The Castle Museum
York
tel York (0904) 53611

The Evelyn Collection of Slides is an
architectural collection begun in 1900 and
terminated in 1930 which contains
approximately 2,500 black and white lantern
slides, mainly of local buildings. Processing of
the collection (ie copying each slide to produce a
master negative, a 2 × 2in transparency and a
contact print mounted in a card index system for
reference purposes) is being done voluntarily by
members of the Society, and it may be some
considerable time before this is completed.
Catalogues and lists are in preparation.
Meanwhile, access is available on a limited basis
to architects, archaeologists, historians, etc and
those with a particular interest in local history.
Potential users should write to Mr S. Heppell,
Keeper of the Evelyn Collection.

For other items relating to this section *see:*

0 Civic Trust.
2 Commonwealth War Graves Commission.
5 Council for Places of Worship.
7 Council for the Protection of Rual England.
8 Council for the Protection of Rural Wales.
3 Department of Finance, Works Division Library.
4 Department of Health and Social Security.
9 Department of the Environment for Northern Ireland, Historic Monuments and Buildings Branch.
4 Ecclesiological Society.
5 Edinburgh City Libraries.
8 Friends of Friendless Churches.
0 The Garden History Society.
5 The Georgian Group.
6 Greater London Council.
7 Guildhall Library.
9 Institute of Advanced Architectural Studies, University of York.
1 Institution of Civil Engineers.
4 Irish Architectural Record Association.
6 Irish Institute of Pastoral Liturgy.
1 Landscape Institute (incorporating the Institute of Landscape Architects).
6 Moated Site Research Group.
0 National Association of Almshouses.
5 National Museum of Antiquities of Scotland.
6 National Railway Museum.
9 National Trust Archive (Ireland).
0 National Trust for Ireland (An Taisce).
1 National Trust for Places of Historic Interest and Natural Beauty.
2 National Trust for Scotland for Places of Historic Interest or Natural Beauty.

345 North Hertfordshire District Council Museums Services, First Garden City Museum.
347 Paul Mellon Centre for Studies in British Art.
350 Property Services Agency.
351 Property Services Agency (Scottish Branch).
359 Raymond Mander and Joe Mitchenson Theatre Collection.
360 Religious Society of Friends.
363 Royal College of Music.
365 Royal Commission on Historical Monuments (England) including the National Monuments Record.
366 Royal Commission on the Ancient and Historical Monuments of Scotland including the National Monuments Record of Scotland.
367 Royal Commission on Ancient and Historical Monuments in Wales including the National Monuments Record for Wales.
372 Royal Institute of British Architects.
377 Royal Society of Ulster Architects.
383 Science Museum Library.
385 Scottish Development Department, Ancient Monuments Branch and Historic Buildings Branch.
393 Society for the Promotion of the Preservation of Early English Parish Churches.
404 Theatre Museum.
407 The Thirties Society.
409 Transport Trust.
413 United Reformed Church History Society.
418 Weald and Downland Open Air Museum.
419 Welsh Folk Museum.
420 Welsh Office, Ancient Monuments Branch and Historic Buildings Branch.
423 William Morris Gallery.

This section begins with general books on architectural history, including dictionaries of terms, then lists books on the various periods and styles, the history of building construction, details and decoration and concludes with sections devoted to various building types.

At the end of each section references are provided to items elsewhere in the book which relate to that section, whether monographs, bibliographies, catalogues, periodicals, organisations or photograph collections. For example, if trying to locate information on theatres, besides the books on theatres listed in section 7.11: Building types: recreational, the reader will be referred to items described elsewhere, such as directories of theatre research resources, periodical indexes in which it is possible to trace articles on theatres, library catalogues which will list additional books on the subject, collections of photographs of theatre buildings and organisations with an interest in or information about theatre buildings. Thus the sections on periods and styles, building construction, details and decoration and building types are designed to be more than a list of some of the more useful publications on the subject, but to serve as a mini-guide to sources of information on the subject.

.1
General

(General histories of architecture, dictionaries and glossaries, histories of the architectural profession, patronage, vernacular architecture, etc)

The Architect: chapters in the history of the profession. Edited by Spiro Kostof. New York: Oxford University Press, 1977. 371pp. Bibl refs.   **499**
Partial contents: 'The rise of the professional architect in England', by John Wilton-Ely.
> The chapter by J. Wilton-Ely portrays the role of the architect in England from medieval to modern times in the course of the transition from an agrarian to a capitalist society. The author contrasts the models of Smith, the first Englishman calling himself an architect, Pratt the gentleman architect and Jones the scholar-architect, with the professionalism of Wren, Hawksmoor and Vanbrugh. The influence of treatises, pattern books and folios on architectural practice is also noted.

Atkinson, Thomas Dinham   **500**
A glossary of terms used in English architecture. London: Methuen, 1906. 335pp.
> Limited to the historical aspect of architecture.

Atkinson, Thomas Dinham   **501**
Local style in English architecture: an enquiry into its origin and development. London: Batsford, 1947. 183pp. Microfiche, London: Architectural Press.
> In three parts. Part 1: Factors determining local variation; eg geology and geography, race, religion, the foreigner, wealth, transport, fashion. Part 2: Variations in particular features; eg the parish church plan, the steeple, timber construction, buildings and roofs, church furniture. Part 3: General view of local variations. The first outline of characteristic types of buildings from different English districts. Mainly devoted to ecclesiastical buildings.

Briggs, Martin S.   **502**
Architect in history. New York: Da Capo Press, 1927 (1974 reprint). 400pp. Includes bibliographies. (Da Capo Press series in architecture and decorative art)
> Up to the end of the middle ages the book deals with the evolution of the architect in Europe generally, for the renaissance period it concentrates on Italy, France and England and for the nineteenth century it confines itself to England. Index includes references to competitions, drawing, town planning, assistants, use of models, education, remuneration of architects, etc.

Brunskill, R. W.   **503**
Illustrated handbook of vernacular architecture. New ed. London: Faber and Faber, 1978. 249pp. Bibl pp 228–242.
> Concerns itself with the architecture of the lesser houses – manor houses, farm houses and cottages – and of barns, stables and mills, inns and shops, and early industrial buildings close to the domestic scale. Materials and methods of

7.1 General

methods of/*continued*
construction used for walls, roofs, staircases,
windows, doorways and other features are dealt
with. The appendices show how to study the
subject, make extensive detailed records and
carry out surveys. Index.

Craig, Maurice and **Fitz-Gerald**,   504
Desmond John Villiers
**Ireland observed: a handbook to the buildings and
antiquities.** With a section on Dublin by D. Newman
Johnson. Cork: Mercier Press, 1970. 119pp. Bibl
pp 109–111.
> A gazetteer providing brief entries for buildings.
> Glossary.

Curl, James Stevens   505
**English architecture: an illustrated
glossary.** Newton Abbot: David and Charles, 1977.
192pp. Bibl pp 189–191.
> Includes Scottish terms.

Dunbar, John G.   506
The architecture of Scotland. 2nd rev ed.
London: Batsford, 1978. 209pp. Bibl pp 198–199.
> An introduction, intended for the general
> reader, to the historic buildings of Scotland as
> they exist today, including lairds' houses of
> post-medieval date, the greater and lesser
> country mansions of the later Stuart and
> Georgian eras, urban and rural buildings of
> traditional character, the architecture of the
> industrial revolution, as well as the ancient
> monuments. Covers, mainly in a chronological
> approach, the period from the middle ages to the
> beginning of the Victorian era. Each chapter
> includes a list of buildings or sites worth visiting.
> Index.

Fletcher, *Sir* Banister   507
**Sir Banister Fletcher's 'A history of
architecture'.** 18th ed. Revised by J. C. Palmes.
London: Athlone Press, 1975. 1390pp.
> Comprehensive world wide coverage, with brief
> mentions of architects. Good bibliographies at
> the end of each chapter. Index.

Harbison, Peter, **Potterton**, Homan   508
and **Sheehy**, Jeanne
**Irish are and architecture from prehistory to the
present.** London: Thames and Hudson, 1978. 272pp.
Bibl pp 265–272.
> Separate chapters on the architecture of the early
> Christian period, 432–1170, Norman and later
> medieval Gaelic Ireland, 1170–1600, the 17th
> century, 18th century, 19th century and the 20th
> century. Index includes names of architects and
> places.

Harris, John and **Lever**, Jill   50
**Illustrated glossary of architecture,
850–1830.** London: Faber and Faber, 1966. 78pp,
224 plates. Bibl pp 77–78.
> The terms of architecture in general use for the
> study of British architecture. Largely of
> ecclesiastical and larger domestic buildings. The
> definitions are brief, but most of them are
> followed by references to a photograph
> illustrating them, with the pertinent features
> indicated by pointers.

Hay, George   51
Architecture of Scotland. 2nd ed, rev and enl.
Stocksfield (Northumberland): Oriel Press, 1977.
96pp.
> A reliable little guide intended for the general
> reader. The main text is preceded by a glossary
> and outline, and followed by four suggested
> architectural tours and a general index.

Hilling, John B.   51
**The historic architecture of Wales: an
introduction.** Cardiff: University of Wales, 1976.
234pp. Bibl pp 218–222.
> Surveys architecture in Wales from prehistoric
> times to the early years of the 20th century.
> Includes early Celtic settlements, vernacular
> architecture, chapels, country mansions,
> industrial buildings, as well as medieval castles
> and churches. Index of architects, engineers and
> designers working in Wales and their buildings,
> pp 224–227. Gives the architects' dates and
> names and dates of buildings mentioned in the
> text. Index.

House and Garden   51
Dictionary of design and decoration.
London: Collins, 1973. 541pp.
> A comprehensive, fully illustrated work of
> reference to the applied arts and architecture.
> Deals with decorators and their designs,
> architects and their buildings, industrial
> designers and their products. Includes
> biographical entries. Sections on English
> architecture, Irish architecture, Anglo-Saxon
> architecture, Georgian architecture, etc.

Jenkins, Frank   51
**Architect and patron: a survey of
professional relations and practice in England
from the sixteenth century to the present day.**
London: Oxford University Press, 1961. 254pp. Bibl
notes.
> Index of names and subjects. Buildings are
> indexed under place names.

aye, Barrington   514
**he development of the architectural
  profession in Britain.** London: Allen and Unwin,
  1960. 223pp. Bibl pp 178–200.
     A sociological analysis of the origin and
     development of professionalism among
     architects in Britain. Beginning with the
     medieval master-masons, the professional
     activities of architects in Britain are traced
     through intervening centuries up to 1945.
     Architectural education, professional conduct,
     the growth of professional associations, public
     competitions, are among the topics dealt with.
     Index.

idson, Peter, **Murray**, Peter and   515
hompson, Paul
history of English architecture. 2nd rev ed.
  Harmondsworth: Penguin Books, 1979. 394pp.
  Bibl pp 370–372. (Pelican Books).
     A short guide to the successive stages of building
     in England from Anglo-Saxon times to the
     present.

ittle, Bryan   516
nglish historic architecture. London:
  Batsford, 1964. 256pp. Bibl pp 241–242.
     A brief survey concentrating on buildings of the
     more important and monumental type from
     prehistory to 1914. Index.

lurray's architectural guides. Edited by John   517
etjeman and John Piper
  Murray's Berkshire architectural guide. Edited by John
  Betjeman and John Piper. London: J. Murray, 1949.
  163pp.
  Murray's Buckinghamshire architectural guide. Edited
  by John Betjeman and John Piper. London:
  J. Murray, 1948. 132pp.
  Murray's Lancashire architectural guide. By Peter
  Fleetwood-Hesketh. London: J. Murray, 1955.
  194pp.

lellist, John B.   518
ritish architecture and its background.
  London: Macmillan, 1967. 361pp. Bibl pp 331–334.
     A concise, introductory text. Part 1 covers the
     classical and European background; part 2,
     architecture in Britain 1066–1800, part 3, the
     nineteenth and twentieth centuries. Index
     includes names of architects and buildings (listed
     under cities and towns).

sborne, Arthur Leslie   519
**he Country Life pocket guide to English
  domestic architecture.** London: Country Life,
  1967. 303pp.
     A revised edition of the author's *Dictionary of
     English domestic architecture* (1954). A
     descriptive and illustrated glossary.

Penoyre, John and Jane   520
**Houses in the landscape: a regional study of
  vernacular building styles in England and
  Wales.** London, Boston: Faber and Faber, 1978.
  175pp. Bibl pp 165–166.
     Divides the country into ten regions, with a
     chapter devoted to each. Within each chapter
     there is a map showing the pattern of use of
     building materials in the region and its general
     geology, colour plates of a range of characteristic
     buildings, concentrating on their external
     appearance, and line drawings illustrating local
     traits. Index.

Petzsch, Helmut   521
Architecture in Scotland. London: Longman,
  1971. 146pp. Bibl pp 141–142.
     An introductory guide to the building and
     architecture of Scotland from prehistory to the
     present day. Each chapter includes a list of
     buildings and sites to see as well as
     recommended further reading.

Pevsner, *Sir* Nikolaus   522
**Englishness of English art: an expanded
  and annotated version of the Reith Lectures
  broadcast in October and November, 1955.**
  London: Architectural Press, 1956. 208pp.
     Concerned primarily with the art of painting,
     though chapter 4 deals with the perpendicular
     style of architecture, while chapter 7 is devoted
     to the picturesque. Index.

Pride, Glen L   523
Glossary of Scottish building. [n.p.]:
  G. Pride, 1975. 96pp. Bibl pp 95–96.
     Includes some 4,000 terms, of which about 20%
     are in current use. Where terms of identical
     meaning have been and are being used both in
     England and Scotland they have been omitted.
     Only a very few terms are illustrated with line
     drawings.

    524
Spirit of the age. London: British Broadcasting
  Corp, 1975, 1976 reprint. 240pp.
     Contents: 'The medieval world', by Alec
     Clifton-Taylor; 'A new heaven, a new earth', by
     Roy Strong; 'The cult of grandeur', by Robert
     Furneaux Jordan; 'A sense of proportion', by
     John Julius Norwich; 'Landscape with
     buildings', by John Summerson; 'All that
     money could buy', by Mark Girouard; 'A full
     life and an honest place', by Patrick Nuttgens;
     'Dreams and awakenings', by Hugh Casson.
     Based on eight films first shown on BBC-2 in the
     Autumn of 1975.

7.1 General

Watkin, David   525
English architecture: a concise history.
London: Thames and Hudson, 1979. 216pp. Bibl
pp 203–206. (The world of art library).
> A brief outline from Saxon times to the present,
> which concentrates on the major masterpieces.
> Glossary. Index.

Watkin, David   526
The rise of architectural history. London:
Architectural Press, 1980. 204pp. Bibl pp 191–196.
> An outline study of architectural history,
> primarily in England, from the seventeenth
> century to the present day. The approach is
> mainly chronological. Chapters are devoted to
> the continental and American background,
> English antiquarians and the gothic revival (the
> 17th and 18th centuries, 1800–1840, Pugin to
> Comper, Ferguson to Banister Fletcher,
> Lethaby), the history of the 'English tradition'
> 1900–1945 (Blomfield and the Edwardians,
> classicism and the country house, the second
> World War), the establishment of art history (the
> impact of Germany, the impact of Colvin),
> Victorian and neoclassical studies and some
> recent tendencies. While describing the
> development of the study of architectural
> history, the book also, in its textual references to
> the publications of the writers of architectural
> history, serves as a bibliography of the most
> important and influential writings on
> architectural history and provides biographical
> information about the authors. Index.

Yarwood, Doreen   527
The architecture of Britain. London:
Batsford, 1976. 276pp. Bibl pp 263–266.
> Covers the period 450 AD to the present.
> Concentrates on the most significant of the
> buildings. A condensed version of *The
> Architecture of England*. Also includes Scotland
> and Wales. Index.

Yarwood, Doreen   528
**The architecture of England from
pre-historic times to the present day.** London:
Batsford, 1963. 672pp. Bibl pp 640–646.
> Includes the majority of famous and masterly
> works, in their own right and in order to
> illustrate the designs of their individual
> architects whose careers are summarised. A
> number of lesser-known buildings considered
> typical of their age are also included. Index.

For other items relating to this section see items
in:

1. **How to find out: guides to the literature**
   1 *Ancient monuments and historic buildings.*
     Government publications sectional list no 27.
   2 *Architectural periodicals index.*
   4 Avery Architectural Library. *Catalog.*
   5 Avery Architectural Library. *An index to
     architectural periodicals.*
   9 British Tourist Authority. *Town trails and urban
     walks.*
   12 Colvin. *English architectural history: a guide to
      sources.*
   15 Courtauld Institute of Art, University of
      London. *Annual bibliography of the history of
      British art.*
   20 Dunbar. *Source materials for Scottish
      architectural history.*
   23 Goodey. *Urban walks and town trails.*
   24 *Guide to the literature of art history.*
   25 Guildhall Library. *London buildings and sites: a
      guide for researchers in Guildhall Library.*
   26 Harley. *Historian's guide to ordnance survey maps.*
   27 Harley. *Maps for the local historian.*
   28 Harris. *Sources for architectural history in
      England.*
   29 Harvard University, Graduate School of Design.
      Catalog of the library.
   30 Harvey. *Architectural archives.*
   31 Harvey. *Sources for the history of houses.*
   33 Humphreys. *A handbook to county bibliography.*
   35 Iredale. *Discovering local history.*
   36 Iredale. *Discovering your old house.*
   37 Iredale. *Local history research and writing.*
   39 Mullins. *Texts and calendars.*
   44 *RILA.*
   45 Royal Institute of British Architects, Library.
      Catalogue.
   46 Royal Institute of British Architects, Library.
      *Comprehensive index to architectural periodicals,
      1956–70.*
   47 Royal Institute of British Architects, Library.
      RIBA Annual review of periodical articles.
   48 Royal Institute of British Architects, Library.
      RIBA Booklist.
   49 Royal Institute of British Architects, Library.
      RIBA Library bulletin.
   50 Sheehy. *Guide to reference books.*
   56 Upcott. *A bibliographic account of the principal
      works relating to English topography.*
   57 *Urban history yearbook.*
   58 Walford. *Guide to reference material.*

2.1 **Biographical dictionaries, encyclopaedias,
   directories, surveys and indexes**
   59 *Allgemeines Lexikon der bildende Künstler von der
      Antike bis zur Gegenwart . . .*
   63 Architectural Publication Society. *The dictionary
      of architecture.*
   70 Brett. *Buildings in the town and parish of Saint
      Helier.*
   71 Briggs. *Everyman's concise encyclopaedia of
      architecture.*

7.1 General

for other items relating to this section/*continued*
318 Joint Committee.
320 Landmark Trust.
323 London Topographical Society.
327 Museum of East Anglian Life.
328 Museum of London.
331 National Institute for Physical Planning and Construction Research (An Foras Forbartha).
332 National Library of Scotland.
333 National Library of Wales.
334 National Monuments Advisory Council.
335 National Museum of Antiquities of Scotland.
338 National Register of Archives (Scotland).
339 National Trust Archive.
340 National Trust for Ireland (An Taisce).
341 National Trust for Places of Historic Interest and Natural Beauty.
342 National Trust for Scotland for Places of Historic Interest or Natural Beauty.
347 Paul Mellon Centre for Studies in British Art.
350 Property Services Agency.
352 Public Record Office.
353 Public Record Office of Northern Ireland.
355 The Queen's University of Belfast, Architecture and Planning Information Service.
364 Royal Commission on Historical Manuscripts (and National Register of Archives).
365 Royal Commission on Historical Monuments (England) including the National Monuments Record.
366 Royal Commission on the Ancient and Historical Monuments of Scotland including the National Monuments Record of Scotland.
367 Royal Commission on Ancient and Historical Monuments in Wales including the National Monuments Record for Wales.
368 Royal Fine Art Commission.
369 Royal Fine Art Commission for Scotland.
379 Ryedale Folk Museum.
380 The Saltire Society.
381 SAVE Britain's Heritage.
385 Scottish Development Department, Ancient Monuments Branch and Historic Buildings Branch.
387 Scottish Record Office.
392 Society for the Interpretation of Britain's Heritage.
394 Society for the Protection of Ancient Buildings.
398 Society of Architectural Historians of Great Britain.
402 Standing Conference for Local History.
410 Ulster Architectural Heritage Society.
414 Vernacular Architecture Group.
415 Victoria and Albert Museum Library.
416 Victoria and Albert Museum, Department of Prints and Drawings and Paintings.
418 Weald and Downland Open Air Museum.
419 Welsh Folk Museum.
420 Welsh Office Ancient Monuments Branch and Historic Buildings Branch.
422 Whitehouse, Museum of Building and Country Life.

6.2 Guide to sources of architectural photographs and slides
430 Aerofilms Ltd.
431 Malcolm Aird Associates Ltd.
452 Ancient Art and Architecture Photo-Library.
433 Architectural Association Slide Library.
438 Berkshire Architectural Records Committee Collection.
442 British Tourist Authority Photographic Library.
443 J. Allan Cash Ltd, Worldwide Photographic Library.
446 Courtauld Institute of Art, Conway Library.
447 Denness Collection of Colour Prints.
448 Department of the Environment.
453 Mary Evans Picture Library.
456 Robert Harding Picture Library.
459 Michael Holford.
460 Angelo Hornak.
463 Irish Tourist Board.
465 A. F. Kersting.
469 Mansell Collection.
471 Photo Precision.
472 Photolog Library (Dr W. H. Findlay).
473 Picturepoint Ltd.
475 Pitkin Pictorials.
476 A. F. Plunkett Collection.
478 Postal Publicity Photographic Library.
479 Radio Times Hulton Picture Library.
480 Slide Centre Ltd.
481 Edwin Smith Collection.
483 Jessica Strang.
484 Suffolk Record Office.
489 University of Aberdeen, G. W. Wilson Collection.
490 University of Cambridge, Committee for Aerial Photography.
491 University of East Anglia, Photographic Library.
492 University of St Andrews.
493 Victoria and Albert Museum, National Art Slide Library.
494 Weidenfeld and Nicolson Ltd.
496 Woodmansterne Ltd.
497 John and Patricia Woolverton Colour Library.
498 Yorkshire Architectural and York Archaeological Society.

7.6 Details, decoration and ornament
660 Fleming. *The Penguin dictionary of decorative arts.*
675 *Oxford companion to the decorative arts.*
678 Stafford. *An illustrated dictionary of ornament.*

7.7 Building types: general
685 Pevsner. *A history of building types.*

7.9 Building types: ecclesiastical
761 Child. *Discovering church architecture.*

7.2

Prehistory to medieval

(Ancient monuments, Anglo-Saxon, Carolingian,
Decorated, Early Christian, Gothic, Perpendicular,
Romanesque, etc)

Bony, Jean   529
**The English decorated style: gothic
architecture transformed, 1250–1350.** Oxford:
Phaidon, 1979. 315pp. Bibl pp 297–307. (The
Wrightsman lectures).
> Based on the author's Wrightsman Lectures at
> the Institute of Fine Arts, New York, in 1969.
> Chapters deal with the impact of the French
> rayonnant style in gothic England, court style
> and the decorated vocabulary, space, linear
> patterns and networks, and the decorated style in
> the history of gothic architecture. Index.

Childs, V. Gordon and **Simpson**, W. Douglas   530
Scotland. 5th ed. Edinburgh: HMSO, 1967.
139pp. Bibl p 133. (Illustrated regional guides to
ancient monuments in the ownership or guardianship
of the Ministry of Public Buildings and Works, 6).
> Prehistoric remains as well as early Christian or
> Celtic monastic sites and sculptured stones;
> Viking settlements, Norse chapels, medieval
> abbeys, castles and sculptured stones; and later
> domestic buildings.

Clapham, *Sir* A. W.   531
English romanesque architecture. Oxford:
Clarendon Press, 1930–34. 2 vols.
> Concerned with ecclesiastical architecture from
> the 7th–12th centuries. Indexes in each volume.

Conant, Kenneth John   532
**Carolingian and romanesque architecture,
800 to 1200.** 3rd rev ed. Harmondsworth: Penguin
Books, 1973. 345pp. Bibl pp 321–328. (The Pelican
history of art).
> Not devoted exclusively to Britain, but like the
> rest of the Pelican series, one of the best books
> on its subject. Index.

Feachem, Richard   533
Guide to prehistoric Scotland. 2nd ed.
London: Batsford, 1977. 223pp. Bibl pp 215–223.
> Gives in succinct form full information about
> most of the important ancient sites in Scotland.
> The gazetteer is arranged by type of site with the
> Ordnance Survey map reference and route
> details in each case. Index.

Harbison, Peter   534
**Guide to the national monuments in the
Republic of Ireland,** including a selection of other
monuments not in state care. 2nd ed. Dublin: Gill
and Macmillan; London: Macmillan, 1975. 284pp.
Bibl pp 269–270.
> Mainly monuments erected before 1700. Brief
> histories and descriptions. Includes
> bibliographical references for each monument.
> Glossary. Index.

Harvey, John H.   535
The mediaeval architect. London: Wayland,
1972. 296pp. Bibl pp 262–278.
> Treats the medieval architect in Europe with
> emphasis on Britain. Includes chapters on the
> education of the architect; methods (drawing,
> models and moulds); and organisation and
> professionalism. Appendix of sources. General
> index and index of architects, including artists
> and craftsmen.

Harvey, John   536
The perpendicular style, 1330–1485.
London: Batsford, 1978. 308pp. Bibl pp 271–275.
> An important survey of the English style of late
> medieval architecture known as perpendicular
> which, in the course of six chapters, traces the
> origins of the style during the second quarter of
> the fourteenth century, describes the
> development of the court or official form over a
> period of 150 years, and considers the principal
> regional variations during that period. An
> introduction, two preliminary chapters and an
> epilogue are devoted to various aspects of the
> style including its precursors, its principal
> characteristics, the master masons who helped to
> develop the form, and its relation to the political
> scene of late medieval England. The buildings
> discussed are essentially ecclesiastical structures
> – cathedral, abbey and parish churches – rather
> than military and domestic works. Includes a
> table of dated buildings and a glossary. Index of
> subjects; index of medieval architects and artists;
> and topographical index of places in Great
> Britain.

Henry, Françoise   537
**Irish art in the early Christian period to AD
800.** Ithaca (New York): Cornell University Press,
1965. 256pp. Bibl pp 206–213.
> Concise history of art and architecture.
> Bibliographical references in the footnotes to the
> text. A standard history.

Henry, Françoise   538
**Irish art during the Viking invasions,
800–1020.** Ithaca (New York): Cornell University
Press, 1967. 236pp. Bibl pp 206–213.
> Concise history of art and architecture in
> Ireland. Bibliographical references in the
> footnotes to the text. Sequel to Henry, *Irish art
> in the early Christian period.*

Henry, Françoise   539
Irish art in the romanesque period,
    1020–1170. Ithaca (New York): Cornell University
    Press, 1970. 240pp.
        Concise history of art and architecture in
        Ireland. Good selection of plates and maps.
        Bibliographical references in the footnotes to the
        text. Sequel to Henry, *Irish art during the Viking
        invasions.*

Hubert, Jean, **Porcher**, Jean and **Volbach**, W. F.   540
The Carolingian renaissance. New York:
    Braziller, 1970. 380pp. Bibl pp 323–338. (The Arts of
    mankind).
        Illustrated handbook of Carolingian art and
        architecture. Provides chronological table,
        glossary-index, and good comprehensive
        bibliography with its own index by subject.
        Collections of plans, elevations, reconstructions
        and maps. For the beginning student.

Kendrick, *Sir* Thomas D.   541
Anglo-Saxon art to AD 900. London:
    Methuen, 1938. 228pp.
        Concise history of art and architecture in
        England from the Roman period to 900AD.
        Bibliographical references in the footnotes.
        Index.

Kendrick, *Sir* Thomas D.   542
Late Saxon and Viking art. London:
    Methuen, 1949. 152pp.
        Concise history of the art and architecture of
        England in the 10th century and Scandinavian
        art of the 9th and 10th centuries. Bibliographical
        references in the footnotes. Index. Sequel to
        Kendrick, *Anglo-Saxon art*; together they form a
        standard history of the arts of the middle ages in
        England.

Simpson, W. Douglas   543
The ancient stones of Scotland. London:
    Robert Hale, 1965. 254pp.
        A general survey of the ancient monuments of
        Scotland from prehistory up to the 18th century,
        omitting inhabited castles, churches still in use,
        and burghal architecture. Index to places.

Stalley, Roger Andrew   544
Architecture and sculpture in Ireland,
    1150–1350. Dublin: Gill and Macmillan; London:
    Macmillan, 1971. 149 pp.

Thomas, Nicholas   545
Guide to prehistoric England. 2nd ed.
    London: Batsford, 1976. 270pp. Bibl pp 258–264.
        Gives, in succinct form, full information about
        most of the important ancient sites in England.
        The arrangement of the gazetteer is by county
        and the relevant Ordnance Survey map
        references and route details are added in each
        case. Index.

Webb, Geoffrey   546
Architecture in Britain: the middle ages.
    2nd ed. Harmondsworth: Penguin Books, 1965.
    234pp. Bibl pp 222–224. (Pelican history of art).
        A history of architecture in Britain from the 7th
        century to 1548, with the emphasis on
        ecclesiastical architecture. Excludes military
        architecture. A standard work. Glossary. Index.

For other items relating to this section see items in:

.2 Indexes to research and theses

3. How to find out about architects and buildings: unpublished sources, indexes and catalogues

5.2 Guide to societies, institutions and organisations

for other items relating to this section/*continued*

385 Scottish Development Department, Ancient Monuments Branch and Historic Buildings Branch.
387 Scottish Record Office.
391 Society for Medieval Archaeology.
393 Society for the Promotion of the Preservation of Early English Parish Churches.
394 Society for the Protection of Ancient Buildings.
396 Society of Antiquaries of London.
397 Society of Antiquaries of Scotland.
398 Society of Architectural Historians of Great Britain.
402 Standing Conference for Local History.
410 Ulster Architectural Heritage Society.
411 Ulster Folk and Transport Museum.
414 Vernacular Architecture Group.
415 Victoria and Albert Museum Library.
418 Weald and Downland Open Air Museum.
419 Welsh Folk Museum.
420 Welsh Office, Ancient Monuments Branch and Historic Buildings Branch.
422 Whitehouse, Museum of Building and Country Life.

6.2 Guide to sources of architectural photographs and slides
437 John Beecham Library.
439 Bodleian Library. Department of Western Manuscripts.
451 C. M. Dixon.
458 Clive Hicks.
482 J. C. D. Smith.
491 University of East Anglia, Photographic Library.
496 Woodmansterne Ltd.

7.5 Building construction: materials and methods
618 Andrews. *The mediaeval builder and his methods.*
621 Charles. *Medieval cruck building and its derivatives.*
623 Crossley. *Timber building in England from early times to the end of the seventeenth century.*
626 Fitchen. *The construction of gothic cathedrals: a study of medieval vault construction.*
633 Innocent. *The development of English building construction.*
634 Knoop. *The mediaeval mason: an economic history of English stone building in the later middle ages and early modern times.*
637 Lloyd. *A history of English brickwork.*
639 Mason. *Framed buildings of England.*
641 Salzman. *Building in England down to 1540.*
644 West. *The timber-frame house in England.*
645 Wight. *Brick building in England from the middle ages to 1550.*

7.8 Building types: domestic
704 Fedden. *The country house guide.*
725 MacGibbon. *Castellated and domestic architecture of Scotland from the 12th to the 18th century.*
726 MacKenzie. *The mediaeval castle in Scotland.*
733 Renn. *Norman castles in Britain.*
743 Thompson. *Military architecture in England during the middle ages.*
744 Tipping. *English homes.*
745 Toy. *The castles of Great Britain.*
748 Wood. *The English mediaeval house.*

7.9 Building types: ecclesiastical
752 Allen. *The great church towers of England, chiefly of the perpendicular period.*
754 Bond. *Gothic architecture in England.*
755 Bond. *An introduction to English church architecture.*
757 Butler. *Mediaeval monasteries of Great Britain.*
759 Champneys. *Irish ecclesiastical architecture.*
763 Clifton-Taylor. *The cathedrals of England.*
765 Cook. *The English cathedral through the centuries.*
766 Cook. *English collegiate churches of the middle ages.*
767 Cook. *The English mediaeval parish church.*
768 Cook. *English monasteries in the middle ages.*
769 Cook. *English abbeys and priories.*
770 Cowan. *Mediaeval religious houses: Scotland.*
771 Cruden. *Scottish abbeys.*
776 Gilyard-Beer. *Abbeys: an illustrated guide to the abbeys of England and Wales.*
777 Gwynn. *Medieval religious houses: Ireland.*
778 Harvey. *Cathedrals of England and Wales.*
782 King. *Handbook to the Welsh cathedrals.*
783 Knowles. *Medieval religious houses, England and Wales.*
784 Leask. *Irish churches and monastic buildings.*
788 Little. *Abbeys and priories in England and Wales.*
792 Petrie. *The ecclesiastical architecture of Ireland anterior to the Anglo-Norman invasion.*
794 Taylor. *Anglo-Saxon architecture.*
797 Williams. *The Welsh church from conquest to reformation.*

7.12 Building types: education and welfare
829 Clay. *The mediaeval hospitals of England.*
830 Godfrey. *The English almshouse.*

7.15 Landscape and planning
848 Barley. *The plans and topography of medieval towns in England and Wales.*
864 Platt. *The English medieval town.*

7.3

Renaissance to neoclassic

(Baroque, Elizabethan, Georgian, Gothick, Greek Revival, Palladian, Regency, Rococo, Romanticism, etc)

Belcher, John and **Macartney**, Mervyn E., *editors*   547
Later renaissance architecture in England:
   a series of examples of the domestic buildings erected subsequent to the Elizabethan period.
   With introductory and descriptive text. London: Batsford, 1897–1901. 2 vols.

Briggs, Martin S.   548
Goths and vandals: a study of the
   destruction, neglect and preservation of historical buildings in England. London: Constable, 1952. 251pp. Bibl pp 243–244.
   Mainly concerned with the facts of destruction,

decay, and efforts at preservation since the reformation and the renaissance in England, about 1520–1950. Index of persons and buildings.

Burke, Joseph   549
English art, 1714–1800. Oxford: Clarendon
Press, 1976. 425pp. Bibl pp 401–409. (Oxford history of English art, 9).
A critical history of the trends and developments in painting, sculpture, architecture, landscape gardening and the decorative arts, covering the period from the publication of the first volume of Colen Campbell's *Vitruvius Britannicus* (1715) and the Georgian rule of taste through the rococo, neoclassicism and the transition to romanticism. The bibliography is neither comprehensive, exhaustive nor current. Index.

Chalklin, C. W.   550
The provincial towns of Georgian England, a study of the building processes, 1740–1820.
London: Edward Arnold, 1974. 367pp.
Bibl pp 342–352. (Studies in urban history, 3).
Examines the urban growth phenomenon of the 18th and early 19th centuries and its relation to the demands of industry and trade. Assesses the role of the land promoter and house builder, the costs and returns of building enterprise, the logistics and business mechanisms of such building operations, and the control on land speculation. Index.

Crook, J. Mordaunt   551
The Greek revival: neo-classical attitudes in British architecture, 1760–1870. London:
J. Murray, 1972. 204pp. Bibl pp 165–187.
The first part of the book deals with the rediscovery of Greece in the 17th, 18th and early 19th centuries, the second part is concerned with architectural theory, and the third is a photographic survey of the buildings themselves. Index.

Cruickshank, Dan and **Wyld**, Peter   552
London: the art of Georgian building.
London: Architectural Press, 1975, 232pp.
Bibl pp 226–230.
Deals with the speculative terrace house between 1680 and 1830. In four parts: facades; details; materials; and axonometric summary. Useful section containing references to contemporary pattern books. Street index.

Davis, Terence   553
The gothick taste. Newton Abbot: David and Charles, 1974. 168pp. Bibl pp 165–166.
Essay on and illustrations of the work of the 18th century gothicists, including the great and lesser houses, landscapes and garden buildings, church architecture and furniture. Index.

Downes, Kerry   554
English baroque architecture. London:
Zwemmer, 1966. 135pp. Bibl pp xv–xvi.
Includes royal palaces, the great country houses, town houses and inns, churches, minor public buildings, universities and gardens and garden buildings. Index of persons. Index of places. Index of other names, titles and topics.

Knoop, Douglas and **Jones**, G. P.   555
The London mason in the seventeenth century. Manchester: Manchester University Press, 1935. 92pp. Bibl pp 65–67.
Includes (p 2) a 60 name list of principal biographical notices with page references to the text.

Pilcher, Donald   556
The Regency style, 1800 to 1830. London:
Batsford, 1947. 120pp.
Deals with architecture, design, planning and landscape gardens. Index.

Richardson, *Sir* Albert E.   557
Monumental classic architecture in Great Britain and Ireland during the eighteenth and nineteenth centuries. London: Batsford, 1914.
123pp. Bibl pp 113–115.
The development of neo-classic architecture from the Roman Palladian (1730–1790) through the Graeco-Roman (1780–1820), Greek (1820–1840) to the neo-Greek and Italian. Index.

Sitwell, Sacheverell   558
British architects and craftsmen: a survey of taste, design and style 1600–1830. New ed revised by Mark Girouard. London: Pan Books, 1960.
320pp.
Relates the work of British architects and craftsmen to the general European background and tradition. Index.

Steegman, John   559
The rule of taste from George I to George IV. London: Macmillan, 1936. 203pp.
Bibl pp 193–195.
Traces the various changes in the arts of architecture, gardening and painting as reflected in the outlook of those classes of society which, from the early 18th to the early 19th centuries, recognised themselves as the arbiters of taste. Explains the circumstances in which the fashion for antique styles arose. Ends at 1832. Index.

Summerson, *Sir* John   560
Architecture in Britain, 1530–1830. 6th rev
  ed. Harmondsworth: Penguin Books, 1977. 611pp.
  Bibl pp 569–576. (Pelican history of art).
      A standard text on British architecture from the
      early renaissance to the Greek and gothic
      revivals. In addition to the main text, two long
      appendices deal with Scottish architecture and
      English architecture in the American colonies.
      The index generally lists buildings in towns
      under the name of the town in which they are
      situated but buildings and streets in London,
      Paris and Rome are indexed directly under their
      names.

Summerson, *Sir* John   561
Georgian London. 3rd rev ed. London: Barrie
  and Jenkins, 1978. 350pp. Bibl pp 329–331.
      While dealing specifically with London, it makes
      a valuable contribution to the study of Georgian
      architecture and the whole problem of the
      growth of a city. Index.

Vitruvius Britannicus   562
  1. Campbell, Colen
  Vitruvius Britannicus or the British architect (vols 1, 2
  and 3). Introduction by John Harris. First published
  in three volumes, London, 1715–1725; reissued in
  one volume. (Vol 1 of the three-volume facsimile ed.)
  New York: Benjamin Blom, 1967.

  2. Badeslade, J. and others
  Vitruvius Britannicus or the British architect (the
  hitherto unpublished vol 4) by J. Badeslade and J.
  Rocque (first announced 1739) and (vols 4 and 5) by
  John Woolfe and James Gandon (first published in
  two volumes, 1767–71) reissued in one volume. (Vol
  2 of the three-volume facsimile ed.) New York:
  Benjamin Blom, 1967.

  3. Richardson, George
  The new Vitruvius Britannicus . . . (first published in
  two volumes, 1802–1808) reissued in one volume.
  (Vol 3 of the three-volume facsimile ed.) New York:
  Benjamin Blom, 1970.

  4. Breman, Paul and Addis, Denise
  *Guide to Vitruvius Britannicus: annotated and
  analytical index to the plates.* Foreword by John
  Harris. (Vol 4 to the *Vitruvius Britannicus).* New
  York: B. Blom, 1972. 132pp.
      A main source of the English country house and
      secular architecture of the late 17th and 18th
      centuries. The index volume includes an
      alphabetical register containing proper names of
      architects, decorators, gardeners, patrons, or
      buildings to be found in the index volume.

Wiebenson, Dora   56
Sources of Greek revival architecture.
  London: Zwemmer, 1969. 136pp. Bibl notes.
  (Studies in architecture, 8).
      Describes the patrons, the travellers and the
      special characteristics of the individual voyages,
      and their source in traditional architectural
      theory. The various ways in which the material
      from the archaeological publications of the
      travellers entered the vocabulary of early 19th
      century architecture is also suggested. Index.

Wittkower, Rudolf   56
Palladio and English Palladianism. London:
  Thames and Hudson, 1974. 224pp.
  Bibl notes pp 207–220.
      Contains 13 essays written between 1945 and
      1969 on the theme of Palladio and his influence
      in England, especially on Inigo Jones,
      Burlington and Kent. Index.

Wren Society   56
Publications. Vols I–XX, 1924–43. Oxford:
  Oxford University Press, 1924–43. 20 vols.
      Original drawings and documents relating to
      Wren and his contempoaries. There is an index
      in vol 20 to vols 1–19.

For other items relating to this section see items in:
1.   **How to find out: guides to the literature**
    1 *Ancient monuments and historic buildings.*
      Government publications sectional list no. 27.
    2 *Architectural periodicals index.*
    4 Avery Architectural Library. *Catalog.*
    5 Avery Architectural Library. *An index to
      architectural periodicals.*
    6 Baggs. *Copy books.*
    7 Baggs. *Pattern books and vernacular architecture
      before 1790.*
    8 Barley. *A guide to British topographical
      collections.*
   12 Colvin. *English architectural history: a guide to
      sources.*
   15 Courtauld Institute of Art, University of
      London. *Annual bibliography of the history of
      British art.*
   19 Dobai. *Die Kunstliteratur des Klassizismus und
      der Romantik in England.*
   20 Dunbar. *Source materials for Scottish
      architectural history.*
   22 Georgian Group. *Recommended books on
      Georgian architecture and decoration.*
   24 *Guide to the literature of art history.*
   25 Guildhall Library. *London buildings and sites: a
      guide for researchers in Guildhall Library.*
   28 Harris. *Sources for architectural history in
      England.*
   29 Harvard University, Graduate School of Design.
      Catalog of the library.
   30 Harvey. *Architectural archives.*

31 Harvey. *Sources for the history of houses.*
35 Iredale. *Discovering local history.*
36 Iredale. *Discovering your old house.*
37 Iredale. *Local history research and writing.*
39 Mullins. *Texts and calendars.*
40 Norton. *Guide to the national and provincial directories of England and Wales, excluding London, published before 1856.*
44 *RILA.*
45 Royal Institute of British Architects, Library. *Catalogue.*
46 Royal Institute of British Architects, Library. *Comprehensive index to architectural periodicals.*
47 Royal Institute of British Architects, Library. *RIBA Annual review of periodical articles.*
48 Royal Institute of British Architects, Library. *RIBA Booklist.*
49 Royal Institute of British Architects, Library. *RIBA Library bulletin.*
50 Sheehy. *Guide to reference books.*
56 Upcott. *A bibliographic account of the principal works relating to English topography.*
57 *Urban history yearbook.*
58 Walford. *Guide to reference material.*

2.1 Biographical dictionaries, encyclopaedias, directories, surveys and indexes

59 *Allgemeines Lexikon der bildende Künstler von der Antike bis zur Gegenwart . . .*
63 Architectural Publication Society. *The dictionary of architecture.*
65 Beard. *Georgian craftsmen and their work.*
67 Bennett. *Leicestershire architects. 1700–1850.*
68 *A Bibliography of Leicestershire churches.*
69 *Biographical dictionary of British gardeners.*
70 Brett. *Buildings in the town and parish of Saint Helier.*
71 Briggs. *Everyman's concise encyclopaedia of architecture.*
72 *Buildings of England*, series.
73 *Buildings of Ireland*, series.
74 *Buildings of Scotland*, series.
75 *Buildings of Wales*, series.
76 *Burke's guide to country houses*, series.
78 Colvin. *A biographical dictionary of British architects, 1600–1840.*
79 Colvin. *The history of the King's works.*
80 Committee for the Survey of the Memorials of Greater London. *Survey of London.*
83 Department of the Environment. Directorate of Ancient Monuments and Historic Buildings. *Lists of buildings of archaeological or historic interest.*
84 *The Dictionary of national biography.*
87 Eden. *Dictionary of land surveyors and local cartographers of Great Britain and Ireland, 1550–1850.*
88 *Gazetteer of pre-1914 theatres.*
91 Graves. *A dictionary of artists who have exhibited works in the principal London exhibitions from 1760 to 1893.*
92 Graves. *The Royal Academy of Arts: a complete dictionary of contributions and their work, from its foundation in 1769 to 1904.*
93 Graves. *The Society of Artists of Great Britain 1760–1791. The Free Society of Artists 1761–1793. A complete dictionary of contributors and their work from the foundation of the societies to 1791.*
95 Gunnis. *Dictionary of British sculptors, 1660–1851.*
96 Hall. *A bibliography on vernacular architecture.*
97 Harris. *Catalogue of British drawings for architecture, decoration, sculpture and landscape gardening 1550–1900 in American collections.*
98 Harris. *A country house index.*
101 Historical Manuscripts Commission. *Architectural history and the fine and applied arts: sources in the National Register of Archives.*
105 Jamilly. *Anglo-Jewish architects, and architecture in the 18th and 19th centuries.*
109 Linstrum. *West Yorkshire architects and architecture.*
111 Loeber. *A biographical dictionary of engineers in Ireland, 1600–1730.*
112 Loeber. *A biographical dictionary of Irish architects, 1600–1730.*
113 Michelmore. *Current bibliography of vernacular architecture (1970–1976).*
114 Musgrave. *Obituary prior to 1800.*
116 Pevsner. *A dictionary of architecture.*
118 Richards. *Who's who in architecture from 1400 to the present day.*
120 Royal Commission on Historical Monuments (England). *Inventories.*
121 Royal Commission on the Ancient and Historical Monuments in Wales. *Inventories.*
122 Royal Commission on the Ancient and Historical Monuments of Scotland. *Inventories.*
127 Royal Institute of British Architects, Drawings Collection. *Catalogue of the Drawings Collection of the RIBA.*
128 Royal Institute of British Architects, Library. *Index of architects of several countries and many periods (except English mediaeval).*
130 Scottish Development Department. *Lists of buildings of architectural or historic interest.*
132 *Shell guides*, series.
133 *The Shell guide to Wales.*
135 Spain. *Theatre architects in the British Isles.*
136 Ulster Architectural Heritage Society. *Historic buildings, groups of buildings, areas of architectural importance.*
137 Victoria and Albert Museum. *Topographical index to measured drawings of architecture which have appeared in the principal architectural publications.*
138 *The Victoria history of the counties of England.*
140 Ware. *A short dictionary of British architects.*

2.2 Indexes to research and theses

146 ASLIB. *Index to theses.*
147 *British and German-language theses.*
148 *Comprehensive dissertation index.*
149 *Dissertation abstracts international.*
150 Institute of Historical Research. *History theses, 1901–70.*
151 Institute of Historical Research. *Historical research for university degrees in the United Kingdom.*

402 Standing Conference for Local History.
410 Ulster Architectural Heritage Society.
411 Ulster Folk and Transport Museum.
414 Vernacular Architecture Group.
415 Victoria and Albert Museum Library.
416 Victoria and Albert Museum, Department of Prints and Drawings and Paintings.
418 Weald and Downland Open Air Museum.
419 Welsh Folk Museum.
420 Welsh Office, Ancient Monuments Branch and Historic Buildings Branch.
422 Whitehouse, Museum of Building and Country Life.

5.2 Guide to sources of architectural photographs and slides

444 J. H. Cordingly.
455 Dr Ivan Hall.
496 Woodmansterne Ltd.

7.1 General

513 Jenkins. *Architect and patron.*
514 Kaye. *The development of the architectural profession in Britain.*
526 Watkin. *The rise of architectural history.*

7.4 Nineteenth and twentieth centuries

571 Clark. *The gothic revival.*
581 Germann. *Gothic revival in Europe and Britain.*
593 Macaulay. *The gothic revival, 1745–1845.*

7.5 Building construction: materials and methods

623 Crossley. *Timber building in England from early times to the end of the seventeenth century.*
627 Harris. *Discovering timber-framed buildings.*
633 Innocent. *The development of English building construction.*
637 Lloyd. *A history of English brickwork.*
639 Mason. *Framed buildings of England.*
641 Salzman. *Building in England down to 1540.*
644 West. *The timber-frame house in England.*
645 Wight. *Brick building in England from the middle ages to 1550.*

7.6 Details, decoration and ornament

647 Amery. *Period houses and their details.*
648 Amery. *Three centuries of architectural craftsmanship.*
649 Bankart. *The art of the plasterer.*
650 Beard. *Decorative plasterwork in Great Britain.*
651 Beveridge. *English renaissance woodwork, 1660–1730.*
653 Cornforth. *The quest for comfort: English interiors 1790–1848.*
654 Croft-Murray. *Decorative painting in England, 1537–1837.*
655 Curran. *Dublin decorative plasterwork of the seventeenth and eighteenth centuries.*
656 Davie. *Old English doorways.*
657 Dutton. *The English interior, 1500–1900.*
658 Edinburgh New Town Conservation Committee. *The care and conservation of Georgian houses: a maintenance manual.*
659 Entwisle. *The book of wallpaper.*
660 Fleming. *The Penguin dictionary of decorative arts.*
661 Fletcher. *Chimney pots and stacks.*
662 Fowler. *English decoration in the 18th century.*
663 Gardner. *English ironwork of the XVIIth and XVIIIth centuries.*
664 Gloag. *Early English decorative detail.*
665 Gloag. *A history of cast iron in architecture.*
666 Godfrey. *The English staircase.*
667 Harris. *English decorative ironwork, 1610–1836.*
668 Jourdain. *English decoration and furniture of the early renaissance, (1500–1650).*
669 Jourdain. *English decorative plasterwork of the renaissance.*
670 Jourdain. *English interior decoration, 1500–1830.*
671 Jourdain. *English interiors in smaller houses from the restoration to the Regency, 1660–1830.*
672 Kelly. *The book of English fireplaces.*
673 Lister. *Decorative cast ironwork in Great Britain.*
674 Lister. *Decorative wrought ironwork in Great Britain.*
675 *Oxford companion to the decorative arts.*
676 Ramsey. *Small Georgian houses and their details, 1750–1820.*
677 Shuffrey. *The English fireplace.*
678 Stafford. *An illustrated dictionary of ornament.*
679 Stratton. *The English interior: a review of the decoration of English homes from Tudor times to the XIXth century.*
680 Sugden. *A history of English wallpaper, 1509–1914.*
681 Thornton. *Seventeenth-century interior decoration in England, France and Holland.*
682 Turner. *Decorative plasterwork in Great Britain.*
683 West. *The fireplace in the home.*
684 Wilson. *The English country house and its furnishings.*

7.8 Building types: domestic

687 Airs. *The making of the English country house, 1500–1640.*
689 Barley. *The English farmhouse and cottage.*
698 Craig. *Classic Irish houses of the middle size.*
706 Garner. *The domestic architecture of England during the Tudor period.*
707 Georgian Society. *Records of 18th-century domestic architecture and decoration in Dublin.*
710 Gotch. *The English home from Charles I to George IV.*
713 Guinness. *The Palladian style in England, Ireland and America.*
714 Harris. *The artist and the country house: a history of country house and garden view painting in Britain, 1540–1870.*
716 Hill. *Scottish castles of the 16th and 17th centuries.*
721 Latham. *In English homes.*
724 Macartney. *English houses and gardens in the 17th and 18th centuries.*
725 MacGibbon. *Castellated and domestic architecture of Scotland from the 12th to the 18th century.*
734 Richardson. *The smaller English house of the later renaissance.*
735 Sadleir. *Georgian mansions in Ireland.*
736 Savidge. *The parsonage in England.*
740 Stevens. *Old Jersey houses and those who lived in them.*
744 Tipping. *English homes.*
749 Woodforde. *Georgian houses for all.*

Selective bibliography

7.4 Nineteenth and twentieth centuries

for other items relating to this section/*continued*
7.9 Building types: ecclesiastical

7.10 Building types: industrial and commercial

7.11 Building types: recreational

7.12 Building types: education and welfare

7.13 Building types: transport

7.15 Landscape and planning

7.4

Nineteenth and twentieth centuries

(Arts and Crafts, New Brutalism, Contemporary, Edwardian, Gothic Revival, Modern Movement, Queen Anne Style, Victorian, etc)

Arts Council [of Great Britain]   566
Ten years of British architecture, '45–55.
Introductory text by Sir John Summerson. London, 1956. 60pp. Bibliographies.
Catalogue of an exhibition which selectively illustrates the progress of architecture in Britain during the decade after the war. Includes sections on schools, housing, industrial, commercial, health and transport buildings and private houses. No index. For an expanded version *see* 574.

Banham, Reyner   567
The new brutalism: ethic or aesthetic?
London: Architectural Press, 1966. 196pp. (Documents of modern architecture).
A study of the development of a movement in British architecture, primarily associated with the work of Alison and Peter Smithson, which emerged in the 1950s. Index of names in the text.

Boase, T. S. R.   568
English art 1800–1870. Oxford: Clarendon Press, 1959, 352pp. Bibl pp 321–330. (Oxford history of English art, 10).
Treats painting, sculpture and architecture, surveying the major movements of the period. Index includes names of architects and buildings by place.

Burton, Lawrence   569
A choice over our heads: a guide to architecture and design since 1830. London: Talisman Books, 1978. 192pp. Bibl pp 172–191.
An introductory guide to architecture and design in Britain, Europe and the United States. Part 1: An outline of architecture since 1830; An outline of design since 1830; Town planning since 1830. Part 2: A guide to movements and ideas (in dictionary form). Part 3: A guide to individual architects and designers (in dictionary form). Part 4: A guide to places and museums. No index.

Casson, *Sir* Hugh   570
New sights of London: the handy guide to contemporary architecture. London: London Passenger Transport Board, 1938. 54pp. (London-in-your-pocket).
Includes various building types: domestic, commercial and industrial, public, civic and ecclesiastical, power and communications, recreational, hospitals and welfare, education and the arts. Index of architects. Useful for the modern movement.

Clark, Kenneth (*Baron* Clark)   571
The gothic revival: an essay in the history of taste. 3rd ed. London: J. Murray, 1962. 236pp.
A study in the history of gothic taste and its evolution from 1720 to 1870. Index.

Crook, J. Mordaunt   572
Victorian architecture: a visual anthology.
London, New York: Johnson Reprint, 1971.
300 plates from the *Builder*, the *Building news*, the *Architect*, and the *British architect*, in chronological order, selected and annotated, with an index of architects, patrons and places.

Curl, James Stevens   573
Victorian architecture: its practical aspects.
Newton Abbot: David and Charles, 1973. 128pp.
Bibl pp 120–124.
> Not a history of Victorian architecture, but a
> consideration of Victorian railway and factory
> architecture, housing, hospitals, prisons, pubs,
> churches and public buildings in the light of new
> materials and technology. The emphasis is on
> the Victorian's functional approach to design
> and construction problems. Index.

Dannatt, Trevor   574
**Modern architecture in Britain: selected
examples of recent building.** With an introduction
by John Summerson. London: Batsford, 1959.
216pp. Bibl pp 214–215.
> Provides a representative survey of work done in
> Britain from 1945 to 1958. The material is
> grouped into four sections: industrial and service
> buildings, office buildings, shops and
> showrooms, schools, housing and individual
> houses and churches and other public buildings.
> An expanded version of the Arts Council
> exhibition catalogue (*see* 566). No index.

Davey, Peter   575
**Arts and crafts architecture: the search for
earthly paradise.** London: Architectural Press,
1980. 176pp. Bibl pp 214–218.
> Discusses the development of arts and crafts
> ideals in building from about 1840 to 1920.
> Concentrates mainly on Britain. Includes brief
> biographies of many arts and crafts architects.
> Index of names and buildings.

Dixon, Roger and **Muthesius**, Stefan   576
Victorian architecture. London: Thames and
Hudson, 1978. 288pp. Bibl pp 250–251. (The World
of art library).
> Concise study organised by building type:
> domestic architecture (country houses, smaller
> houses, terraced and semi-detached houses,
> flats); buildings for entertainment (clubs, hotels,
> public houses, theatres and music halls); new
> building types (glasshouses, railway stations,
> workhouses, hospitals, barracks, prisons,
> cemeteries, pumping stations, baths and market
> halls), buildings for industry and commerce
> (factories, warehouses, office buildings, shops),
> civic architecture; churches; and architecture for
> education (schools, colleges and universities).
> Includes a dictionary of about 400 architects
> (pp 252–270) providing birth and death dates
> and short list of selected works with their dates.
> Index.

Dyos, H. J. and **Wolff**, Michael, *editors*   577
The Victorian city, images and reality.
London: Routledge and Kegan Paul, 1973. 2 vols.
> Deals with the city's growth, fabric, institutions,
> health, poverty, politics, religion, diversions,
> and the way in which writers, artists,
> photographers, and ordinary people responded
> to it. Index.

Eastlake, Charles L.   578
A history of the gothic revival. Edited with an
introduction by J. Mordaunt Crook. 2nd rev ed of
original 1872 ed. Leicester: Leicester University
Press; New York: Humanities Press, 1970. 652pp.
Bibl pp 145–163. (Victorian library).
> Introduction, appendix of selected examples of
> gothic buildings erected between 1820 and 1870,
> bibliography and index by J. Mordaunt Crook.
> The standard textbook on Victorian gothic.
> Index of persons and places.

Fawcett, Jane, *editor*   579
Seven Victorian architects. London: Thames
and Hudson, 1976. University Park: Pennsylvania
State University Press, 1977. 160pp. Bibl refs.
(Victorian Society. Papers).
> Contents: Introduction, by Nikolaus Pevsner;
> 'William Burn: the country house in transition',
> by David Walker; 'Philip and Philip Charles
> Hardwick: an architectural dynasty', by
> Hermione Hobhouse; 'Sydney Smirke: the
> architecture of compromise', by J. Mordaunt
> Crook; 'John Loughborough Pearson: noble
> seriousness', by David Lloyd; 'George Frederick
> Bodley: climax of the gothic revival', by David
> Verey; 'Alfred Waterhouse: civic grandeur', by
> Stuart Allen Smith; and 'Edwin Lutyens: the
> last high Victorian', by Roderick Gradidge.
> Check-lists of chief works of each of the
> architects discussed and photographs of their
> buildings. Index.

Ferriday, Peter, *editor*   580
Victorian architecture. London: Cape, 1973.
306pp.
> Twelve articles on individual architects: 'Charles
> Robert Cockerell', by E. M. Dodd; 'Sir Charles
> Barry', by Peter Fleetwood-Hesketh; 'A. W. N.
> Pugin', by Alexandra Gordon Clark; 'Sir Joseph
> Paxton', by Robert Furneaux Jordan; 'William
> Butterfield', by Paul Thompson; 'Sir Gilbert
> Scott', by David Cole; 'William Burges', by
> Charles Handley-Read; 'G. E. Street', by Joseph
> Kinnard; 'Richard Norman Shaw', by Nikolaus
> Pevsner, 'Philip Webb', by John
> Brandon-Jones; 'C. F. A. Voysey', by John
> Brandon-Jones; and 'John Francis Bentley', by
> Halsey Ricardo. Also general articles: 'Victorian
> prolegomena', by Nikolaus Pevsner; 'The
> Victorian architectural profession', by Frank

by Frank/*continued*
Jenkins; 'The country house of the 19th
century'; 'The Victorian home'; and 'Victorian
public buildings', all by H. S. Goodhart-Rendel.
Index lists names of buildings under place.

Germann, Georg   581
Gothic revival in Europe and Britain:
    sources, influences and ideas. Translated from
the German by Gerald Onn. London: Lund
Humphries with the Architectural Association, 1972.
263pp.
    Considers the gothic revival in European
architecture as a whole. No bibliography, but
extensive marginal notes. Index.

Girouard, Mark   582
Sweetness and light: the 'Queen Anne'
    movement, 1860–1900. Oxford: Clarendon Press,
1977. 250pp. Bibl notes pp 230–242.
    The 'Queen Anne' style of architecture
flourished in the last 40 years of the 19th
century. The author shows how it developed as
the increasingly self-confident and liberal upper
middle class of the 1870s shook off the
constrictions and soberly religious overtones of
rigid gothicism. The main protagonists, all
originally dedicated gothicists, were met with
'professional fury and public delight' but
succeeded because the style suited exactly the
demands of the market. The move towards
'sweetness and light' and the wide variety of
influences, from Japan to Amsterdam, are
explored in depth. Illustrates the development of
the style from domestic origins to terrace houses,
commercial buildings, the London Board
schools, artists' houses, blocks of flats, seaside
resorts and the 'Queen Anne' shopfront. Index
includes names of architects and buildings, by
location.

Goodhart-Rendel, H. S.   583
English architecture since the Regency: an
    interpretation. London: Constable, 1953. 296pp.
    Covers the period from 1820 to the 1930s. A
pioneering work in the re-evaluation of Victorian
architecture. List of architects whose work is
mentioned. Index.

Goodhart-Rendel, H. S.   584
'Rogue architects of the Victorian era', in
    RIBA Journal, vol 56, April 1949, pp 251–259.
    A paper read at the RIBA dealing with more
than a dozen lesser-known architects of the late
Victorian and Edwardian period, including
E. B. Lamb, John Shaw, James Wild, Thomas
Harris, Alexander Thomson, William
Butterfield, R. L. Roumieu, Joseph Peacock, E.
Bassett Keeling, Frederick Pilkington, Edward
Prior and James Maclaren.

Gotch, J. A., *editor*   58⌐
The growth and work of the Royal Institute
    of British Architects, 1834–1934. London: Royal
Institute of British Architects, 1934. 188pp.
    A history of the RIBA which reflects the history
of the development of the architectural
profession in Britain. No index.

Hersey, George L.   58⌐
High Victorian gothic: a study in
    associationism. Baltimore, London: Johns Hopkins
University Press, 1972. 234pp. Bibl pp 212–224.
(Johns Hopkins studies in nineteenth century
architecture).
    Not a survey of high Victorian gothic but a study
of emotional and analytical reactions to the
movement. The first two chapters survey
associational writings from the mid-18th to the
mid-19th centuries. The third chapter illustrates
how the Ecclesiological Society converted this
associational theory into high Victorian gothic
practice. The fourth chapter is a series of
associational interpretations of major high
Victorian gothic monuments. Index.

Hitchcock, Henry-Russell   58⌐
Architecture: nineteenth and twentieth
    centuries. 4th ed. Harmondsworth: Penguin Books,
1968. 520pp. Bibl pp 631–648. (Pelican history of
art).
    A standard text which is international in scope
but which devotes a considerable proportion of
the book to Britain. The bibliography includes a
section listing monographs and periodical
articles on individual architects. The index lists
buildings under towns and cities. Country
houses are entered under their own names.

Hitchcock, Henry-Russell   58⌐
Early Victorian architecture in Britain.
    London: Trewin Coppleston, 1972. Orig publ,
London: Architectural Press; New Haven: Yale
University Press, 1954. 2 vols.
    Vol 1 contains the text and vol 2 the illustrations.
Extends beyond the range of better-known
architects to include lesser-known names. Covers
the period from the 1830s to 1851. Index with
buildings listed under cities and towns, except
country houses whose names are considered to
represent their location. An important work.

Jackson, Anthony   58⌐
The politics of architecture: a history of
    modern architecture in Britain. London:
Architectural Press, 1970. 219pp. Bibl pp 207–213.
    An account of the buildings of the international
modern movement in Britain since the 1920s.
Index.

Jencks, Charles   590
Modern movements in architecture.
    Harmondsworth: Penguin Books, 1973. 432pp.
    Bibl pp 397–398.
        Includes a chapter (pp 239–99) on British
        architecture covering the post-war period to
        c 1970. Index.

Jordan, Robert Furneaux   591
Victorian architecture. Harmondsworth:
    Penguin Books, 1966. 278pp. Bibl pp 263–267.
    (Pelican books).
        Concentrates on Britain. Index includes names
        of buildings and persons.

Kornwolf, James D.   592
**M. H. Baillie Scott and the arts and crafts
    movement: pioneers of modern design.**
    Baltimore, London: Johns Hopkins Press, 1972.
    588pp. Bibl pp 561–568. (The Johns Hopkins studies
    in nineteenth century architecture).
        While concerned primarily with the life and
        work of Baillie Scott, the book discusses his work
        in terms of that which preceded, accompanied
        and followed it; in particular with the design of
        the smaller country house and its furnishings.
        There is a general index to movements,
        architects, etc and an index of works by Baillie
        Scott and other architects. Text footnotes
        throughout the book give additional sources of
        information.

Macaulay, James   593
The gothic revival, 1745–1845. Glasgow, etc:
    Blackie, 1975. 451pp. Bibl pp 403–415.
        Primarily considers Scotland and northern
        England. Appendices provide chronological
        indexes of ecclesiastical buildings in Scotland
        and in northern England, and of secular
        buildings in Scotland and in northern England.
        Index.

McKean, Charles and **Jestico**, Tom, *editors*   594
Modern buildings in London: a guide.
    London: Warehouse, 1976. 113pp.
        Covers the period 1965–75. The 101 buildings
        include developments, offices, social services
        buildings, examples of rehabilitation and repair,
        infill and extensions. Each project is illustrated
        and accompanied by the name of the
        architectural office or practice responsible, with,
        wherever possible, the name of the actual
        designer or job architect involved, the title of the
        building, address, date of completion and closest
        public transport. The various sections include
        the main guide, which arranges the buildings in
        six geographical areas, roughly based on the
        London borough boundaries, a supplementary
        list of buildings, travel notes and maps. A
        glossary of terms is included. Index to the
        buildings.

Macleod, Robert   595
**Style and society: architectural ideology in
    Britain, 1835–1914.** London: RIBA Publications,
    1971. 144pp.
        Deals with the ideals and intentions of the
        architects of the Victorian and Edwardian
        period, with key statements grouped in each area
        of study: the gothic revival; the 'Queen Anne'
        style; arts and crafts; the 'grand manner'; the
        rise of professionalism; and the start of
        architectural education. Index.

Marriott, Charles   596
Modern English architecture. London:
    Chapman and Hall, 1924. 268pp. Bibl pp 255–256.
    (Universal art series).
        Includes ecclesiastical, civic, commercial,
        industrial and domestic architecture, housing
        schemes and monuments and memorials.
        Alphabetical list of 87 architects, pp 227–52.

Mills, Edward D.   597
**The new architecture in Great Britain,
    1946–53.** London: Standard Catalogue, 1953. 209pp.
    Bibl p 209.
        Fifteen examples of important buildings
        covering a range of types: civic, religious,
        educational and domestic. Comments on the
        technical, economic and aesthetic considerations
        appear alongside the photographs and plans.
        Includes a section on the period 1935–46, with a
        chronological list of important modern buildings
        in this period.

Museum of Modern Art   598
Modern architecture in England. New York:
    Museum of Modern Art, 1937. 102pp. Reprinted,
    New York: Arno Press, 1969. 103pp. Bibl refs.
        Contains short essays by Henry
        Russell-Hitchcock on British 19th-century and
        modern architecture, and modern architecture in
        England, and by Catherine K. Bauer on
        elements of English housing practice.
        Predominantly photographs and plans
        illustrating the modern movement in England.
        Biographical section on the architects
        represented in this exhibition catalogue.

Muthesius, Hermann   599
**Die englische Baukunst der Gegenwart:
    Beispiele neuer englischer Profanbauten.**
    Leipzig: Cosmos, 1900. 4 portfolios.
        Examples of late-19th-century architecture,
        mainly in London, illustrated with plans and
        photos.

7.4 Nineteenth and twentieth centuries

Muthesius, Stefan 600
**The high Victorian movement in
architecture, 1850–1870.** London: Routledge and
Kegan Paul, 1972. 252pp. Bibl pp 243–246.
> The emphasis is on the work of the master
> architects of the period, especially in the light of
> contemporary architectural theory. Index.

Naylor, Gillian 601
**The arts and crafts movement: a study of its
sources, ideals and influences on design theory.**
London: Studio Vista, 1971. 203pp. Bibl pp 195–198.
> Examines the nature of the handicraft aesthetic
> as it developed in England in the 19th century,
> and outlines its impact on design theory in
> Europe and the US. Index.

Olsen, Donald J. 602
The growth of Victorian London. London:
Batsford, 1976. 384pp. Bibl refs pp 358–373.
> Contents: 1. A topography of values. 2. London
> in 1837: the Georgian legacy. 3. The rejection
> and destruction of Georgian London. 4. The
> preservation and extension of Georgian London.
> 5. The villa and the new suburb. 6. Salubrious
> dwellings for the industrious classes. 7. Grand
> lines of communication. 8. London in 1901: the
> Victorian legacy. Index.

Pevsner, *Sir* Nikolaus 603
**Pioneers of modern design, from William
Morris to Walter Gropius.** rev ed.
Harmondsworth: Penguin Books, 1960, 1975
printing (with revisions). 264pp. Bibl notes pp
219–253. (Pelican books).
> A revised and largely rewritten edition of
> *Pioneers of the modern movement* (London: Faber
> and Faber, 1936, reprinted by the Museum of
> Modern Art, NY, in 1950 under the title,
> *Pioneers of modern design*). From the arts and
> crafts movement to the Bauhaus, dealing in a
> largely biographical form, with the parts played
> by the most important architects in the
> development of the modern movement. Not
> confined to Britain. The classical statement of
> the 'progressive' interpretation of the 19th
> century.

Pevsner, *Sir* Nikolaus 604
**Some architectural writers of the nineteenth
century.** Oxford: Clarendon Press, 1972. 338pp.
> A book about architects writing about
> architecture which includes the English
> archaeologists of the early 19th century, the
> great gothicists, the Italianate revivalists and
> ends with Morris. Index.

Pevsner, *Sir* Nikolaus 605
Studies in art, architecture and design. Vol
2: Victorian and after. London: Thames and Hudson,
1968. 288pp. Bibl notes pp 269–276.
> A collection of essays of which most originally
> appeared in journals, on working class housing,
> high Victorian design, the Design and Industries
> Association, the return to historicism, as well as
> on individual figures, including Matthew Digby
> Wyatt, William Morris, Mackmurdo, Voysey,
> Mackintosh and George Walton. Index.

Physick, John and **Darby**, Michael 606
**Marble halls: drawings and models for
Victorian secular buildings: (catalogue of an)
exhibition, August-October 1973, (held at the)
Victoria and Albert Museum.** London: Victoria
and Albert Museum, 1973. 220pp.
> The drawings and models are arranged in
> chronological order within each of the following
> sections: national buildings, country houses,
> town houses, commercial buildings, schools and
> colleges; asylums, prisons and hospitals; civic
> buildings; town planning; theatres, music halls
> and clubs; railways; exhibition buildings;
> bridges and lighthouses; hotels, inns and
> boarding houses; museums, libraries and
> galleries; and memorials. Catalogue entries
> include bibliographical references. There is a
> biographical dictionary of Victorian architects
> (pp 21–30). Index of lenders, people and places.

Reilly, *Sir* Charles H. 607
**Representative British architects of the
present day.** London: Batsford, 1931. 172pp.
> Contents: Professor S. D. Adshead; Robert
> Atkinson; Sir Herbert Baker; Sir Reginald
> Blomfield; Arthur J. Davie; E. Guy Dawber;
> Clough Williams-Ellis; W. Curtis Green;
> H. V. Lanchester; Sir Edwin Lutyens; Sir Giles
> Gilbert Scott; Walter Tapper.

Richards, *Sir* J. M. 608
An introduction to modern architecture.
New and rev ed. London: Cassell, 1961. 176pp.
Bibl pp 164–172. Originally published by Penguin
Books, 1940.
> The development of modern architecture in the
> 20th century, its background, growth and
> thought behind it. Index.

Royal Institute of British Architects 609
**One hundred years of British architecture,
1851–1951.** London: Royal Institute of British
Architects, 1951. 48pp.
> Catalogue of an exhibition held at the RIBA in
> connection with the Festival of Britain.

ervice, Alastair   610
**dwardian architecture: a handbook to
building design in Britain, 1890–1914.** London:
Thames and Hudson, 1977. 216pp. Bibl pp 193–197.
> Concise study of this period with its many styles
> and developments: late gothic and Byzantine
> church architecture, the arts and crafts
> revolution of house design, the attempts to
> create a new free style from historical
> precedents, the English baroque of town halls,
> and the revival of purer classicism combined
> with the use of new structural techniques. These
> are seen through the work of Norman Shaw,
> Arthur Mackmurdo, Beresford Pite,
> J. F. Bentley, Voysey, Edward Prior, William
> Lethaby, Reginald Blomfield, Edwin Lutyens,
> Charles Rennie Mackintosh and many others.
> Includes a list of the most important architects of
> the period (pp 197–216) providing birth and
> death dates, and short list of their principal
> works with their dates. Index.

ervice, Alastair, *editor*   611
dwardian architecture and its origins.
London: Architectural Press, 1975. 504pp.
Bibl pp 489–490.
> Deals with the period from 1870–1914, mainly
> by essays on specific architects. Includes a list of
> principal British architects of the late Victorian
> and Edwardian period, giving birth and death
> dates. Index.

harp, Dennis   612
**visual history of twentieth-century
architecture.** [London]: Heinemann, 1972. 304pp.
Bibl p 10.
> A pictorial record in chronological sequence
> within decades of major buildings from 1900 to
> 1970. The book provides a chronology of
> buildings erected in this period and an index.
> Not confined to Britain.

teegman, John   613
**ictorian taste: a study of the arts and
architecture from 1830 to 1870.** With a foreword by
Sir Nikolaus Pevsner. Reissue of 1950 issue published
by Sidgwick and Jackson entitled *Consort of taste,
1830–1870*. London: Nelson's University
Paperbacks, 1970. 338pp. Bibl notes.
> The battle of styles. Index.

ummerson, *Sir* John   614
he architecture of Victorian London.
Charlottesville: University Press of Virginia, 1976.
109pp.
> Divided into three sections, each covering about
> 20 years. Deals with the period 1873–1901 and
> discusses the public buildings, railways,
> churches, new estate developments and the
> drainage system. No index.

Summerson, *Sir* John   615
**The turn of the century: architecture in
Britain around 1900.** [Glasgow]: University of
Glasgow Press, 1976. 25pp.
> The text of the W. A. Cargill Memorial Lecture
> delivered in 1975, which surveys the architects
> practising at the turn of the century generation
> by generation. No index.

Victoria and Albert Museum   616
**Exhibition of Victorian and Edwardian
decorative arts. Catalogue.** London: HMSO,
1952. 150pp.
> Useful for architects and craftsmen of the arts
> and crafts period. Gives biographical details and
> bibliographies. Index of artists, designers and
> manufacturers.

Willis, Peter   617
New architecture in Scotland. London: Lund
Humphries, 1977. 96pp.
> A selection of 28 buildings since the early 1960s,
> including domestic, religious, educational,
> commercial and medical buildings. Index of
> architects.

For other items relating to this section see items in:

1.   **How to find out: guides to the literature**
> 2 *Architectural periodicals index.*
> 4 Avery Architectural Library. *Catalog.*
> 5 Avery Architectural Library. *An index to
> architectural periodicals.*
> 10 *The British Transport Historical Records
> collection.*
> 13 Cossons. *The BP book of industrial archaeology.*
> 14 Coulson. *A bibliography of design in Britain,
> 1851–1970.*
> 15 Courtauld Institute of Art, University of
> London. *Annual bibliography of the history of
> British art.*
> 18 Department of the Environment Library.
> *Catalogues.*
> 24 *Guide to the literature of art history.*
> 25 Guildhall Library. *London buildings and sites: a
> guide for researchers in Guildhall Library.*
> 26 Harley. *Historian's guide to ordnance survey maps.*
> 28 Harris. *Sources for architectural history in
> England.*
> 29 Harvard University, Graduate School of Design.
> *Catalog of the library.*
> 30 Harvey. *Architectural archives.*
> 32 Hudson. *Industrial archaeology: a new
> introduction.*
> 34 *Industrial archaeologists' guide.*
> 35 Iredale. *Discovering local history.*
> 37 Iredale. *Local history research and writing.*
> 41 Open University. *Arts: . . . history of architecture
> and design 1890–1939: project guide.*
> 43 Parris. *British Transport historical records.*

for other items relating to this section/*continued*
44 *RILA.*
45 Royal Institute of British Architects, Library. *Catalogue.*
46 Royal Institute of British Architects, Library. *Comprehensive index to architectural periodicals, 1956–70.*
47 Royal Institute of British Architects, Library. *RIBA Annual review of periodical articles.*
48 Royal Institute of British Architects, Library. *RIBA Booklist.*
49 Royal Institute of British Architects, Library. *RIBA Library bulletin.*
50 Sheehy. *Guide to reference books.*
51 Smith. *How to find out in architecture and building.*
52 Smith. *A critical bibliography of building conservation.*
54 Storey. *Primary sources for Victorian studies.*
55 Sutcliffe. *The history of modern town planning: a bibliographic guide.*
57 *Urban history yearbook.*
58 Walford. *Guide to reference material.*

2.1 Biographical dictionaries, encyclopaedias, directories, surveys and indexes
59 *Allgemeines Lexikon der bildende Künstler von der Antike bis zur Gegenwart . . .*
60 *Architects', engineers' and building-trades directory, 1868.*
61 *The Architect's valuator and directory of architects, etc 1890.*
62 Architectural Association. *Brown book series, sessions 1859 to 1918.*
63 Architectural Publication Society. *The dictionary of architecture.*
64 Avery Architectural Library. *Avery obituary index.*
66 Bell. *A biographical index of British engineers in the 19th century.*
67 Bennett. *Leicestershire architects, 1700–1850.*
68 *A bibliography of Leicestershire churches.*
69 *Biographical dictionary of British gardeners.*
70 Brett. *Buildings in the town and parish of Saint Helier.*
71 Briggs. *Everyman's concise encyclopaedia of architecture.*
72 *Buildings of England*, series.
73 *Buildings of Ireland*, series.
74 *Buildings of Scotland*, series.
75 *Buildings of Wales*, series.
77 Clarke. *Church builders of the nineteenth century.*
78 Colvin. *A biographical dictionary of British architects, 1600–1840.*
79 Colvin. *The history of the King's works.*
80 Committee for the Survey of the Memorials of Greater London. *Survey of London.*
81 *Contemporary architects.*
82 *The Contractors', merchants' and estate manager's compendium and catalogue. 1900.*
83 Department of the Environment, Directorate of Ancient Monuments and Historic Buildings. *Lists.*
84 *The Dictionary of national biography.*
85 *Directory of official architects and planners. 1967–1973/4.*

86 *Directory of official architecture and planning, 1974/75– .*
87 Eden. *Dictionary of land surveyors and local cartographers of Great Britain and Ireland, 1550–1850.*
88 *Gazetteer of pre-1914 theatres.*
89 Gordon. *The Royal Scottish Academy of Painting, Sculpture and Architecture, 1826–1976.*
90 Gradidge. *Check list of architects, 1820–1939.*
91 Graves. *A dictionary of artists who have exhibited works in the principal London exhibitions from 1760 to 1893.*
92 Graves. *The Royal Academy of Arts: a complete dictionary of contributors and their work, from its foundation in 1769 to 1904.*
94 Gray. *Edwardian architecture.*
95 Gunnis. *Dictionary of British sculptors, 1660–1851.*
97 Harris. *Catalogue of British drawings for architecture, decoration, sculpture and landscape gardening 1550–1900 in American collections.*
98 Harris. *A country house index.*
100 Hatje. *Encyclopaedia of modern architecture.*
101 Historical Manuscripts Commission. *Architectural history and the fine and applied arts: sources in the National Register of Archives.*
102 *The Industrial archaeology of the British Isles,* series.
103 *Industrial archaeology of the British Isles,* series.
104 Institute of Registered Architects. *Official year book and list of members. 1972– .*
105 Jamilly. *Anglo-Jewish architects, and architecture in the 18th and 19th centuries.*
106 Johnson. *Works exhibited at the Royal Society of British Artists, 1824–1893 and at the New English Art Club, 1888–1917.*
107 *Kelly's local London, provincial and other directories.*
109 Linstrum. *West Yorkshire architects and architecture.*
110 *List of the fellows and members of the Royal Institute of British Architects, etc. 1854.*
115 *Obituaries from 'The Times'.*
116 Pevsner. *A dictionary of architecture.*
117 *The Register of architects. 1933– .*
118 Richards. *Who's who in architecture from 1400 to the present day.*
119 Royal Academy. *Royal Academy exhibitors, 1905–1970.*
123 Royal Institute of British Architects. *The RIBA directory. 1966/67–1972.*
124 Royal Institute of British Architects. *RIBA directory of members. 1974– .*
125 Royal Institute of British Architects. *RIBA directory of practices. 1972– .*
126 Royal Institute of British Architects. *The kalendar. 1886/87–1965/66.*
127 Royal Institute of British Architects, Drawings Collection. *Catalogue of the Drawings Collection of the RIBA.*
128 Royal Institute of British Architects, Library. *Index of architects of several countries and many periods (except English mediaeval).*
129 *The Royal Scottish Academy, 1826–1916, a complete list of the exhibited works.*

for other items relating to this section/*continued*

250 Buildings of England Office.
251 Business Archives Council.
252 Business Archives Council of Scotland.
256 Charles Rennie Mackintosh Society.
257 Chiltern Open Air Museum.
260 Civic Trust.
262 Commonwealth War Graves Commission.
269 Courtauld Institute of Art, Book Library.
270 Crown Estates Commissioners.
271 Decorative Arts Society 1890–1914.
272 Department of Education and Science.
273 Department of Finance, Works Division Library.
274 Department of Health and Social Security.
275 Departments of the Environment and Transport, Library.
276 Department of the Environment, Directorate of Ancient Monuments and Historic Buildings (England).
277 Department of the Environment, Regional offices concerned with listed buildings casework.
278 Department of the Environment for Northern Ireland.
279 Department of the Environment for Northern Ireland, Historic Monuments and Buildings Branch.
280 Design and Industries Association.
281 Design History Society.
285 Edinburgh City Libraries.
291 General Register Office.
292 General Register Office (Ireland).
293 General Register Office (Northern Ireland).
294 General Register Office for Scotland.
296 Greater London Council.
297 Guildhall Library.
298 Hampstead Garden Suburb Archives.
300 Historic Buildings Council for England.
301 Historic Buildings Council for Northern Ireland.
302 Historic Buildings Council for Scotland.
303 Historic Buildings Council for Wales.
310 Institute of Advanced Architectural Studies, University of York.
311 Institution of Civil Engineers.
312 Institution of Municipal Engineers.
313 Institution of Structural Engineers.
314 Irish Architectural Record Association.
317 Ironbridge Gorge Museum Trust.
323 London Topographical Society.
327 Museum of East Anglian Life.
328 Museum of London.
331 National Institute for Physical Planning and Construction Research (An Foras Forbartha).
332 National Library of Scotland.
333 National Library of Wales.
337 National Record of Industrial Monuments.
338 National Register of Archives (Scotland).
339 National Trust Archive.
340 National Trust for Ireland (An Taisce).
341 National Trust for Places of Historic Interest and Natural Beauty.
342 National Trust for Scotland for Places of Historic Interest or Natural Beauty.
343 Newcomen Society for the History of Engineering and Technology.
344 North Hertfordshire District Council, Planning Department.
345 North Hertfordshire District Council Museums Services, First Garden City Museum.
346 Ordnance Survey Department Library.
347 Paul Mellon Centre for Studies in British Art.
350 Property Services Agency.
352 Public Record Office.
353 Public Record Office of Northern Ireland.
355 The Queen's University of Belfast, Architecture and Planning Information Service.
359 Registry of Business Names.
361 Royal Academy of Arts Library.
364 Royal Commission on Historical Manuscripts (and National Register of Archives).
365 Royal Commission on Historical Monuments (England) including the National Monuments Record.
366 Royal Commission on the Ancient and Historical Monuments of Scotland including the National Monuments Record of Scotland.
367 Royal Commission on Ancient and Historical Monuments in Wales including the National Monuments Record for Wales.
368 Royal Fine Art Commission.
369 Royal Fine Art Commission for Scotland.
371 The Royal Incorporation of Architects in Scotland.
372 Royal Institute of British Architects.
373 The Royal Institute of the Architects of Ireland.
374 Royal Institution of Chartered Surveyors.
375 Royal Scottish Academy.
376 Royal Society for the Encouragement of Arts, Manufactures and Commerce.
377 Royal Society of Ulster Architects.
378 Royal Town Planning Institute.
379 Ryedale Folk Museum.
380 The Saltire Society.
381 SAVE Britain's Heritage.
383 Science Museum Library.
385 Scottish Development Department.
387 Scottish Record Office.
388 Scottish Society for Industrial Archaeology.
392 Society for the Interpretation of Britain's Heritage.
394 Society for the Protection of Ancient Buildings.
398 Society of Architectural Historians of Great Britain.
399 Society of Decorative Crafts.
400 Society of Genealogists.
401 South East Wales Industrial Archaeology Society.
402 Standing Conference for Local History.
407 The Thirties Society.
408 Town and Country Planning Association.
410 Ulster Architectural Heritage Society.
411 Ulster Folk and Transport Museum.
415 Victoria and Albert Museum Library.
416 Victoria and Albert Museum, Department of Prints and Drawings and Paintings.
417 Victorian Society.
418 Weald and Downland Open Air Museum.
419 Welsh Folk Museum.
420 Welsh Office.

422 Whitehouse, Museum of Building and Country Life.
423 William Morris Gallery.

.2 Guide to sources of architectural photographs and slides
433 Architectural Association Slide Library.
434 Architectural Press Ltd.
436 B. T. Batsford.
441 Brecht-Einzig Ltd.
449 Department of the Environment Slide Library.
450 Design Council Slide Library.
466 Lucinda Lambton.
467 Peter Laws.
474 Pidgeon Audio Visual.
483 Jessica Strang.
496 Woodmansterne Ltd.

.1 General
502 Briggs. *Architect in history.*
513 Jenkins. *Architect and patron.*
514 Kaye. *The development of the architectural profession in Britain.*
526 Watkin. *The rise of architectural history.*

.3 Renaissance to neoclassic
548 Briggs. *Goths and vandals.*
551 Crook. *The Greek revival: neo-classical attitudes in British architecture, 1760–1870.*
557 Richardson. *Monumental classic architecture in Great Britain and Ireland during the eighteenth and nineteenth centuries.*

.5 Building construction: materials and methods
628 Herbert. *Pioneers of prefabrication: the British contribution in the nineteenth century.*
631 Hix. *The glass house.*

.6 Details, decoration and ornament
652 Cooper. *The opulent eye: late Victorian and Edwardian taste in interior design.*
653 Cornforth. *The quest for comfort: English interiors 1790–1848.*
654 Croft-Murray. *Decorative painting in England, 1537–1837.*
657 Dutton. *The English interior, 1500–1900.*
659 Entwisle. *The book of wallpaper.*
665 Gloag. *A history of cast iron in architecture.*
680 Sugden. *A history of English wallpaper, 1509–1914.*

.7 Building types: general
685 Pevsner. *A history of building types.*

.8 Building types: domestic
695 Burnett. *A social history of housing, 1815–1970.*
696 Calder. *The Victorian home.*
709 Girouard. *The Victorian country house.*
712 Gould. *Modern houses in Britain, 1919–39.*
718 Jackson. *Semi-detached London: suburban development, life and transport, 1900–39.*
728 Muthesius. *Das englische Haus/The English house.*
736 Savidge. *The parsonage in England.*

740 Stevens. *Old Jersey houses and those who lived in them.*
741 Sutcliffe. *Multi-storey living: the British working-class experience.*
742 Tarn. *Five per cent philanthropy: an account of housing in urban areas between 1840 and 1914.*
750 Yorke. *The modern house in England.*

7.9 Building types: ecclesiastical
758 Carr. *The Commissioners' churches of London, 1818–1837.*
780 Howell. *Victorian churches.*
785 Lidbetter. *The Friends meeting house.*
786 Lindley. *Chapels and meeting houses.*
789 Little. *Catholic churches since 1623.*
791 Muthesius. *Die neuere kirchliche Baukunst in England.*
793 Port. *Six hundred new churches: a study of the Church Building Commission, 1818–56, and its church building activities.*
796 White. *The Cambridge movement: the ecclesiologists and the gothic revival.*

7.10 Building types: industrial and commercial
798 Artley. *The golden age of shop design: European shop interiors, 1880–1930.*
799 Brockman. *The British architect in industry, 1841–1940.*
801 Buchanan. *Industrial archaeology in Britain.*
802 Dan. *English shop fronts old and new.*
803 Dean. *English shop fronts from contemporary source books, 1792–1840.*
806 Geist. *Passagen: ein Bautyp des 19. Jahrhunderts.*

7.11 Building types: recreational
814 Adamson. *Seaside piers.*
816 Girouard. *Victorian pubs.*
817 Glasstone. *Victorian and Edwardian theatres.*
818 Howard. *London theatres and music halls, 1850–1950.*
820 Lindley. *Seaside architecture.*
821 Mickleburgh. *Guide to British piers.*
824 Sharp. *The picture palace and other buildings for the movies.*
825 Southern. *The Victorian theatre, a pictorial survey.*
826 Taylor. *The golden age of British hotels.*

7.12 Building types: education and welfare
831 Robson. *School architecture.*
832 Seaborne. *The English school.*
833 Thompson. *Library buildings of Britain and Europe.*

7.13 Building types: transport
835 Biddle. *Victorian stations.*
836 Binney. *Railway architecture.*
839 Harris. *Canals and their architecture.*
841 Meeks. *The railway station.*
843 Ruddock. *Arch bridges and their builders, 1735–1835.*

7.5 Building construction: materials and methods

7.5

Building construction: materials and methods

(Brick, building regulations, carpentry, cob, glass,
lead, pisé, prefabrication, stabilised earth, stone,
structure, thatch, tile, timber and timber-frame, turf,
vaulting, wattle, etc)

Andrews, Francis B.   618
The mediaeval builder and his methods.
     Wakefield: EP Publishing, 1974. 117pp.
     Bibl pp 97–99.
          From mid-13th to the 15th century. *The
          mediaeval builder and his methods* was originally
          published in *Transactions of the Birmingham
          Archaeological Society*, 48, 1925 and *Further
          notes on the mediaeval builder*, which is included
          in this publication, originally appeared in
          *Transactions of the Birmingham Archaeological
          Society*, 55, 1931. Discusses the work of the
          masons, bricklayers, carpenters, plumbers,
          glaziers and painters, and the materials that were
          used. No index.

Billett, Michael   619
Thatching and thatched buildings. London:
     R. Hale, 1979. 208pp.
          Describes the historical development of thatch
          and thatched buildings, outlines the craft of
          thatching and describes over five hundred
          thatched villages in England, categorised on a
          county basis throughout the different regions of
          England. Thatched buildings, such as inns,
          restaurants, churches, barns and walls are
          included as well as cottages. Index.

Brunskill, Ronald and **Clifton-Taylor**, Alec   620
English brickwork. London: Ward Lock,
     1977. 160pp. Bibl p 154. (A Hyperion book).
          Shows, by word, diagram and illustrations, how
          bricks have been used in architecture in the
          various parts of the country from medieval times
          up to the present. Part 1 surveys the history of

English brickwork, the clays and methods of
firing, the bonding, the mortar, the virtuosity of
the craftsmen of the later 17th and early 18th
centuries, and the evolution of substitute
materials. This section is followed by a glossary
with illustrations explaining the terms used. Part
3 consists of photographs arranged
chronologically, but with special attention to
periods and types of building in which brick was
particularly popular. An appendix describes a
method of systematic recording of brickwork.
The book covers the past two centuries of
brickwork largely disregarded in Nathaniel
Lloyd's *History of English brickwork* (*see* 637).
Index.

Charles, F. W. B.   62
**Medieval cruck-building and its
     derivatives: a study of timber-framed
     construction based on buildings in
     Worcestershire.** London: Society for Medieval
     Archaeology, 1967. 70pp. Bibl. (Society for Medieval
     Archaeology. Monograph series no 2).
          Primarily concerned with Worcestershire but
          still of general significance. Assesses the
          technical problems faced by the medieval
          carpenters in design, assembly and erection of
          timber-frame structures. Index.

Clifton-Taylor, Alec   62
The pattern of English building. 3rd ed.
     London: Faber and Faber, 1972. 466pp.
     Bibl pp 410–414.
          Gives a comprehensive picture of the pattern of
          building over the whole of England, with the
          emphasis on domestic buildings rather than
          ecclesiastical. Deals with the materials used,
          relating them to the geology and geography of
          the country and the historical background.
          Includes a glossary (pp 403–409) and a place
          index arranged alphabetically by English
          counties, Ireland, Isle of Man, Scotland and
          Wales.

Crossley, Fred H.   62.
**Timber building in England from early
     times to the end of the seventeenth century.**
     London: Batsford, 1951. 168pp. Bibl pp 160–162.
     (The British art and building series).
          The first section deals with religious buildings
          and the second with secular. Index.

Davey, Norman   62-
Building stones of England and Wales.
     London: Bedford Square Press for the Standing
     Conference for Local History, 1976. 47pp. Bibl p 44.
          Describes the various rock types, the quarries,
          the mason's art, surface stones and geological
          erratics. Maps show the distribution of quarry
          workings and tables list those still active. No
          index.

Elsden, J. Vincent and **Howe**, J. A.　　625
The stones of London. London: Colliery
　　Guardian Co, 1923. 205pp.
　　　　A brief, descriptive guide to the principal stones
　　　　used in London, with selected examples of
　　　　buildings in which they may be seen. Index.

Fitchen, John　　626
**The construction of Gothic cathedrals: a
　　study of medieval vault erection.** Oxford:
　　Clarendon Press, 1961. 344pp. Bibl pp 317–336.
　　　　Deals with the various types of vaulting.
　　　　Glossary. Indexes of authors, subjects, places
　　　　and buildings.

Harris, Richard　　627
Discovering timber-framed buildings. 2nd
　　ed. Aylesbury: Shire Publications, 1979. 96pp.
　　Bibl p 93. ('Discovering' series, no 242).
　　　　A brief introduction to the subject, which shows
　　　　how timber buildings were built and how they
　　　　vary from region to region. Concentrates on
　　　　houses, cottages and barns built in the sixteenth,
　　　　seventeenth and eighteenth centuries. Index.

Herbert, Gilbert　　628
**Pioneers of prefabrication: the British
　　contribution in the nineteenth century.**
　　Baltimore, London: Johns Hopkins University Press,
　　1978. 228pp. Bibl pp 213–219. (The Johns Hopkins
　　studies in nineteenth-century architecture).
　　　　Describes the designing, financing and
　　　　large-scale production of prefabricated
　　　　structures such as houses, barracks, theatres and
　　　　storehouses. Index.

Hewett, Cecil A.　　629
English cathedral carpentry. London:
　　Wayland, 1974. 176pp.
　　　　Describes the carpenters' work that still survives
　　　　in English cathedrals. Chapters are devoted to
　　　　ridged main-span roofs, lean-to roofs, apse roofs,
　　　　polygonal chapter house roofs, doors and the few
　　　　surviving windlasses and capstans that hoisted
　　　　materials during building. The appendix lists the
　　　　carpentered contents of each cathedral. Glossary.
　　　　Index of people. Index of places.

A History of technology.　　630
　　Vol 1: From early times to fall of ancient empires;
　　edited by Charles Singer . . . [and others]. 1954.
　　827pp.
　　Vol 2: The Mediterranean civilizations and the
　　middle ages, c700 BC to cAD 1500; edited by Charles
　　Singer . . . [and others]. 1956, 1957 printing (with
　　corrections). 803pp.
　　Vol 3: From the renaissance to the industrial
　　revolution, c1500 –c1750; edited by Charles Singer
　　. . . [and others]. 1957. 766pp.

　　Vol 4: The industrial revolution, c1750 to c1850;
　　edited by Charles Singer . . . [and others]. 1958.
　　728pp.
　　Vol 5: The late nineteenth century, c1850 to c1900;
　　edited by Charles Singer . . . [and others]. 1958.
　　888pp.
　　Vol 6: The twentieth century, c1900 to c1950; edited
　　by Trevor I. Williams. Part 1. 1978. 690pp.
　　Vol 7: The twentieth century, c1900 to c1950; edited
　　by Trevor I. Williams. Part 2. 1978. pp 691–1530.
　　Oxford: Clarendon Press, 1954–78.
　　　　An essential work of reference. The following
　　　　chapters are particularly relevant:
　　　　Vol 1. Ch 12: Building in wattle, wood and turf.
　　　　　　　　Ch 17: Building in brick and stone.
　　　　Vol 2. Ch 12: Building construction.
　　　　Vol 3. Ch　4: Windmills.
　　　　　　　　Ch 10: Building construction.
　　　　　　　　Ch 16: Bridges.
　　　　Vol 4. Ch　7: Watermills.
　　　　　　　　Ch 15: Building and civil engineering
　　　　　　　　construction.
　　　　Vol 5. Ch 20: Building materials and techniques.
　　　　Vol 7. Ch 36: Civil engineering.
　　　　　　　　Ch 37: Building and architecture.
　　　　Bibliographies and indexes in each volume.

Hix, John　　631
The glass house. London: Phaidon, 1974.
　　Cambridge (Mass): MIT Press, 1974 (paperback
　　1981). 208pp. Bibl pp 197–198.
　　　　Traces the development of the glasshouse from
　　　　the 17th century to the present. Not limited just
　　　　to horticultural buildings, as it also discusses the
　　　　Crystal Palace and other buildings for the
　　　　International Exhibition as well as glass as a
　　　　material for houses. International in scope, there
　　　　is nonetheless, a great deal of information on
　　　　British conservatories, palm houses and
　　　　exhibition buildings. Index.

Hudson, Kenneth　　632
The fashionable stone. Bath: Adams and
　　Dart, 1971. 120pp. Bibl pp 114–116.
　　　　Examines both the economics and techniques of
　　　　limestone quarrying and mining since the 17th
　　　　century, and analyses the reputation of Bath and
　　　　Portland stone. Index.

Innocent, Charles Frederick　　633
**The development of English building
　　construction.** New impression with new
　　introduction and bibliography by Sir Robert
　　de Z. Hall. Reprint of 1916 ed. Newton Abbot: David
　　and Charles Reprints, 1971. [26] 294pp.
　　Bibl pp [XII–XVIII].
　　　　From primitive times to the 19th century, with
　　　　sections on timber buildings, walls, floors, slated
　　　　roofs, thatching, doors, windows and chimneys.
　　　　Based mainly on evidence from northern and
　　　　western England. Index. Despite its age, still an
　　　　important work.

7.5 Building construction: materials and methods

Knoop, Douglas   634
**The mediaeval mason: an economic history
of English stone building in the later middle
ages and early modern times.** Manchester:
Manchester University Press, 1933. 294pp. Bibl pp
279–283.
> Deals with the administration and organisation
> of the medieval building industry and provides
> detailed information about masons and their
> organisation. A standard work. Index.

Knowles, C. C. and **Pitt**, P. H.   635
**A history of building regulation in London,
1189–1972, with an account of the District
Surveyors' Association.** London: Architectural
Press, 1972. 164pp.
> By-laws regulating the construction of buildings
> were originally concerned with matters of safety
> and fire precautions, but they came to set
> standards of building practice and of town
> planning and to regulate many aspects of urban
> settlement. London's building regulations were
> widely taken as a model elsewhere and the
> standards they laid down inevitably had a
> powerful effect on construction and hence on
> architectural style. This book traces these
> developments. Index.

Lloyd, Nathaniel   636
**Building craftsmanship in brick and tile
and in stone slates.** Cambridge: Cambridge
University Press, 1929. 99pp.
> Deals with tiled roofs, weather-tiling, leadwork
> to chimneys, dormers, brick chimney caps, uses
> of brick, plain tiles used with brick, brick and
> tile fireplaces, bonds and their products and
> stone slate roofs through text, photographs and
> drawings. Index.

Lloyd, Nathaniel   637
**A history of English brickwork, with
examples and notes of the architectural use and
manipulation of brick from mediaeval times to
the end of the Georgian period.** London: H. G.
Montgomery, 1925. 449pp.
> The standard work. Index.

Mainstone, Rowland   638
Developments in structural form. London:
Allen Lane, 1975. 350pp. Bibl pp 327–328. Published
in association with RIBA Publications.
> An important book for understanding the
> pattern of development, from prehistoric times
> to the present, of structures (wide-span
> buildings, bridges, multi-storey buildings and
> towers), structural elements (arches and
> catenaries; vaults, domes and curved
> membranes; beams and slabs; trusses, portal
> frames and space frames; supports, walls and

foundations), and structural materials (stone,
brick, concrete, timber, iron and steel,
reinforced concrete, prestressed concrete and
new composite materials). International in
scope. Glossary of structural terms. Index of
subjects and index of places, buildings and
bridges (indexed under place name).

Mason, R. T.   639
Framed buildings of England. Horsham:
Coach Publishing House, 1973. 136pp. Bibl notes.
> Detailed descriptive handbook of timber-framed
> building from medieval times to the early 18th
> century. Glossary and index.

Rural Industries Bureau   640
The thatcher's craft. London: The Bureau,
1960. 228pp. (Publication no 69).
> The standard work on the subject giving full
> practical information on thatching in Britain and
> including a brief history of thatching and a
> glossary of thatching terms.

Salzman, L. F.   641
**Building in England down to 1540: a
documentary history.** Oxford: Clarendon Press,
1952. Reprinted, Kraus Reprint. 629pp. Bibl notes
p xvi.
> Deals with contemporary documentary evidence
> on the actual processes of building. Index of
> persons and places; index of subjects. The index
> provides an excellent glossary of medieval
> building terms. A standard work.

Shore, B. C. G.   642
**Stones of Britain, a pictorial guide to those
in charge of valuable buildings.** London: Leonard
Hill, 1957. 303pp.
> A technical study of British building stones for
> the preservationist. Index.

Weaver, Lawrence   643
English leadwork: its art and history.
London: Batsford, 1909. 268pp. Bibl pp 251–257.
> Covers all aspects of leadwork. Includes fonts,
> rain-water pipe-heads, cisterns, medieval leaded
> spires, renaissance steeples, domes, lanterns and
> walls, statuary, etc. Index.

West, Trudy   644
The timber-frame house in England.
Photographs and drawings by Paul Dong. Newton
Abbot: David and Charles, 1971. 222pp.
> A general introduction. Chapters on the manor
> house, the town house, medieval and early
> Tudor, the plan, fireplaces and chimneys,
> roofing, cladding and decoration, restoration
> and preservation. Index.

Wight, Jane A.   645
**Brick building in England from the middle
    ages to 1550.** London: John Baker, 1972. 439pp.
Bibl pp 400–406.
        Contents: The development of building in brick;
        the manor-house complex; defence and the
        major castles; brick buildings erected by
        bishops; ecclesiastical building and the
        reformation conversions; terracotta; Hampton
        Court. Select gazetteer of buildings with
        brickwork before 1450. Index.

Williams-Ellis, *Sir* Clough, **Eastwick-Field**,   646
John and Elizabeth
Building in cob, pisé and stablized earth.
        Rev and enl ed. London: Country Life, 1947. 164pp
        plus 30 plates.
        A revised and enlarged edition of Clough
        Williams-Ellis' *Cottage building in cob, pisé, chalk
        and clay*. A technical rather than historical
        treatment. Index.

For other items relating to this section see items in:

7.6 Details, decoration and ornament

■■■■ **7.6**

Details, decoration and ornament

(Ceilings, chimneys, doorways, fireplaces, furnishings, gateways, interior design, ironwork, painting, plasterwork, stained glass, staircases, wallpaper, woodwork, etc)

Amery, Colin, *editor* 64
Period houses and their details. London: Architectural Press; New York: Whitney Library of Design, 1974. 17pp plus 212 plates.
> Measured drawings and photographs illustrating mainly 18th-century facades and interior and exterior details such as woodwork, stonework, ironwork, doorways, chimney-pieces, staircases, etc which were originally published as 'The practical exemplar of architecture', in the *Architectural review*, 1906–1927. No index.

Amery, Colin, *editor* 64
Three centuries of architectural craftsmanship. London: Architectural Press; New York: Nichols, 1977. 221pp. Bibl pp 1–3 (3rd sequence).
> Brief introduction to illustrations of three centuries (17th, 18th and early 19th) of commercial, domestic and religious building with focus on doorways, gateways, ironwork, archways and panelling. The measured drawing and photographs were previously published during the 1920s, either as part of 'The practical exemplar of architecture' or in *Houses of the Wren and early Georgian periods* by Tunstall Smith and Christopher Woodbridge. No index.

Bankart, George P. 64
The art of the plasterer, an account of the decorative development of the craft chiefly in England from the XVIth to the XVIIIth century, with chapters on the stucco of the classic period and of the Italian renaissance, also on sgraffito, pargetting, Scottish, Irish and modern plasterwork. London: Batsford, 1908. 350pp.
> Includes an index.

Beard, Geoffrey 650
Decorative plasterwork in Great Britain.
London: Phaidon, 1975. 262pp. Bibl p 253.
Records chronologically the history of
plasterwork in churches, public buildings and
country houses from Tudor to Regency times,
with a special chapter on Scotland. Includes a
dictionary of over 300 plasterers with a
chronological list of documented works. A
revised and expanded dictionary of craftsmen
appears in Geoffrey Beard's *Craftsmen and
interior decoration in England, 1660–1820*
(Edinburgh): J. Bartholomew and Son, 1981, pp
241–296). Index of places. Index of persons.

Beveridge, Thomas J. 651
English renaissance woodwork, 1660–1730.
London: Technical Journals, 1921. 27pp. Microfiche,
London: Architectural Press.
A selection of the finest examples, monumental
and domestic, chiefly of the period of
Christopher Wren. Includes 80 plates from
measured drawings.

Cooper, Nicholas 652
**The opulent eye: late Victorian and
Edwardian taste in interior design.** With
photographic plates by H. Bedford Lemere. London:
Architectural Press, 1976. 258pp.
Annotated photographs of the period
1890–1914. Index.

Cornforth, John 653
**The quest for comfort: English interiors
1790–1848.** London: Barrie and Jenkins, 1978.
144pp.
A follow-up to Fowler and Cornforth, *English
decoration in the 18th century* (*see* 662). The
illustrations, from contemporary sources,
provide views of great houses, town houses,
collectors' houses, the Old English style, houses
of writers and artists. Index of houses.

Croft-Murray, Edward 654
Decorative painting in England, 1537–1837.
Vol 1: Early Tudor to Sir James Thornhill. London:
Country Life, 1962. 326pp. Bibl pp 277–291.
Vol 2: The eighteenth and early nineteenth centuries.
Feltham: Country Life, 1970. Bibl pp 327–45.
The standard work, lavishly illustrated, dealing
with painting as the decorative complement to
architecture in the adornment of ceilings, walls
and woodwork. Detailed catalogue with
biographies of the artists and lists of their known
work, and bibliographies. Index.

Curran, C. P. 655
**Dublin decorative plasterwork of the
seventeenth and eighteenth centuries.** London:
Tiranti, 1967. 124pp plus plates. Bibl pp 113–115.
Includes a list of Dublin plasterers, providing
known dates of their activities. Index to people
and places.

Davie, W. Galsworthy 656
**Old English doorways: a series of historical
examples from Tudor times to the end of the
XVIII century**; illustrated . . . from photographs
specially taken by W. Galsworthy Davie; with
historical and descriptive notes on the subjects
including . . . drawings and sketches by H. Tanner,
Junr. London: Batsford, 1903. 44pp. Microfiche,
London: Architectural Press.

Dutton, R. 657
The English interior, 1500–1900. London:
Batsford, 1948. 192pp. Microfiche, London:
Architectural Press. (British art and building).
From the first waves of the renaissance from
Italy to the end of the 19th century.

**Edinburgh New Town Conservation
Committee** 658
**The care and conservation of Georgian houses:
a maintenance manual.** 2nd ed. London:
Architectural Press with Edinburgh New Town
Conservation Committee, 1980. 224pp. Bibl. pp
211–214.
A maintenance manual for the New Town of
Edinburgh. It is aimed at the architect and
consists mainly of a series of information sheets
covering almost every conceivable aspect of the
construction and conservation of New Town
Georgian, including substructure, external
walls, roofs, internal details and external works.
While specific to Edinburgh, the information it
contains is of wider interest. Index.

Entwisle, E. A. 659
**The book of wallpaper: a history and an
appreciation.** Rev ed. Bath: Kingsmead Reprints,
1970. 151pp plus plates. Bibl p 151.
From the 16th century to the present. Index.

Fleming, John and **Honour**, Hugh 660
The Penguin dictionary of decorative arts.
London: Allen Lane, 1977. 896pp.
A guide to the decorative arts of the West from
the middle ages to the present. There are
approximately 4,000 entries which provide
definitions of stylistic and technical terms,
accounts of materials and processes of working,
biographies of leading craftsmen and designers,
and brief histories of most notable factories.
Some entries include brief bibliographies.

7.6 Details, decoration and ornament

Fletcher, Valentine   661
**Chimney pots and stacks: an introduction to
    their history, variety and identification.** Fontwell
(Sussex): Centaur Press, 1968. 114pp.
Bibl pp 109–110.
    A general history of European chimneys, but
    concentrating mainly on Britain. Index.

Fowler, John and **Cornforth**, John   662
English decoration in the 18th century.
Rev ed. London: Barrie and Jenkins, 1978. 288pp.
Bibl pp 267–69.
    Its approach is fundamentally one of social
    history: explaining how new forms of decoration
    were introduced and came to be used in the
    context of life in a great house. Concentrates on
    the decoration of the country house, including
    upholstery, painting, lighting, heating, picture
    hanging and morning decorations. Indexes of
    names, houses and subjects.

Gardner, J. Starkie   663
**English ironwork of the XVIIth and XVIIIth
    centuries, an historical and analytical account
    of the development of exterior smithcraft.**
London: Batsford, 1911. 336pp. Bibl pp 245–256.
Microfiche, London: Architectural Press. Reprinted,
New York: B. Blom, 1972; Boston (Mass): Milford
House, 1973; London: Victoria and Albert Museum,
1978. 3 vols.
    Includes gates, railings, balustrades,
    stair-ramps, grilles, fanlights, lampholders,
    brackets, signs and vanes. List of smiths and
    designers. Index.

Gloag, John   664
**Early English decorative detail: from
    contemporary source books and some early
    drawings.** With an introduction by John Gloag.
London: Tiranti, 1965. 19pp plus 203 plates.
    From early Tudor to the mid-18th century.
    Index to buildings.

Gloag, John and **Bridgwater**, Derek   665
A history of cast iron in architecture.
London: Allen and Unwin, 1948. 395pp. Bibl notes.
    The emphasis is placed on the particular
    significance the history of cast iron has had on
    the rise of British industry and the character of
    British architecture since the first industrial
    revolution. Covers the period 1650–1945. Index.

Godfrey, Walter H.   666
**The English staircase: an historical
    approach.** London: Batsford, 1911. 74pp plus 63
plates.
    An historical account of its characteristic types in
    England and Scotland from medieval times to
    the end of the 18th century. Index.

Harris, John   667
**English decorative ironworks from
    contemporary source books, 1610–1836: a
    collection of drawings and pattern books,
    including A new booke of drawings by John
    Tijou 1693; A new book of iron work by J. Jores
    1756; The smith's right hand by W. and J.
    Welldon 1765; A book of designs by J. Bottomley
    1793; Ornamental iron work by I. and J. Taylor,
    c 1795;** etc. London: Alec Tiranti, 1960. 18pp plus
154 plates.
    A comprehensive source book to the subject
    which assembles all the pattern books similar to
    Tijou and which includes engravings from
    various other works and some original drawings.
    Index.

Jourdain, Margaret   668
**English decoration and furniture of the
    early renaissance, (1500–1650) . . . .** London:
Batsford, 1924. 305pp. Microfiche, London:
Architectural Press. (The Library of decorative art,
vol 1).
    An account of the development and
    characteristic forms during the Tudor,
    Elizabethan and Jacobean periods. Indexes to
    illustrations and text.

Jourdain, Margaret   669
**English decorative plasterwork of the
    renaissance, a review of its design during the
    period from 1500–1800.** London: Batsford, 1926.
258pp. Microfiche, London: Architectural Press.
    Shows Elizabethan, Stuart, Georgian and Adam
    friezes, overmantles, panels, ornament and
    detail. Index of plasterers (pp ix–xiii). Index to
    text and illustrations.

Jourdain, Margaret   670
**English interior decoration, 1500–1830: a
    study in the development of design.** London:
Batsford, 1950. 84pp, plates.
    The influences, decorative painting, woodwork,
    plaster, staircases, chimney-pieces and doors are
    treated in chapters devoted to specific periods.
    Index.

Jourdain, Margaret   671
**English interiors in smaller houses from the
    restoration to the Regency, 1660–1830.** London:
Batsford, 1923. 202pp. Microfiche, London:
Architectural Press.
    Stuart, Georgian and Regency design.
    Illustrations of interiors, chimney pieces,
    staircases, doors, ceilings, metalwork and
    carving.

Kelly, Alison   672
The book of English fireplaces. Feltham:
Country Life Books, 1968. 96pp.
     A general history of fireplaces from earliest times
to the present. Index.

Lister, Raymond   673
Decorative cast ironwork in Great Britain.
London: G. Bell, 1960. 258pp. Bibl pp 239–247.
     Discusses the technique, and includes a chapter
on architectural cast ironwork. Glossary. Index.

Lister, Raymond   674
**Decorative wrought ironwork in Great
Britain.** London: G. Bell, 1957. 265 pp.
Bibl pp 245–256.
     Discusses the technique and includes a chapter
on architectural wrought ironwork. Glossary.
Index.

Oxford companion to the decorative arts.   675
Edited by Harold Osborne. Oxford: Clarendon
Press, 1975. 865pp. Bibl pp 851–865.
     Concentrates on fine craftsmanship. It extends
to all the main fields of craftsmanship as well as
to a number of minor and specialist crafts.
Entries are also provided for important
craftsmen, schools, etc throughout the world,
and for particular cultures or periods.

Ramsey, Stanley C. and **Harvey**, J. M. D.   676
**Small Georgian houses and their details,
1750–1820.** New ed. London: Architectural Press,
1972. 230pp.
     Measured drawings and photographs of
Georgian exteriors, interiors and details which
were originally published in two volumes as
*Small houses of the late Georgian period,
1750–1820.* Vol 1: Exteriors (1919), vol 2:
Details and interiors (1923).

Shuffrey, L. A.   677
**The English fireplace: a history of the
development of the chimney, chimney-piece,
and firegrate, with their accessories, from the
earliest times to the beginning of the 19th
century.** London: Batsford, 1912. 234pp.
Microfiche, London: Architectural Press.
     Illustrated . . . from photographs chiefly by W.
Galsworthy Davie with many other illustrations.
Covers in great detail the Elizabethan and
Jacobean periods. Index.

Stafford, Maureen and **Ware**, Dora   678
An illustrated dictionary of ornament. With
an introduction by John Gloag. London: Allen and
Unwin, 1974. 246pp. Bibl pp 243–244.
     Includes some 1,000 definitions and 2,500 line
drawings. Covers basic ornamental motifs,
devices and terms used in architecture, furniture
design, sculpture etc and defines styles of
ornament and decoration. Definitions include
reference to historical origin, but are more
concerned with character, use, appearance and
application; the relationship between
architectural and ornamental styles is referred to.
Index of persons and places.

Stratton, Arthur   679
**The English interior: a review of the
decoration of English homes from Tudor times
to the XIXth century.** London: Batsford, 1920.
87pp. Microfiche, London: Architectural Press.
     Traces the development of the English interior
as a whole from medieval times to the 19th
century. Index.

Sugden, Alan Victor and **Edmondson**,   680
John Ludlam
A history of English wallpaper, 1509–1914. London:
Batsford, 1925. 281pp. Bibl pp 280–81.
     Beginning with the first attempts to use paper
bearing a design or picture as a form of
decoration in substitution for the costly gilt
embossed leathers and figured textiles of the
period, the development in technical and artistic
achievement is traced down to World War I.
Includes a section on mill records, historical
notes on well-known wallpaper firms. Index.

Thornton, Peter   681
**Seventeenth-century interior decoration in
England, France and Holland.** New Haven,
London: Yale University Press for the Paul Mellon
Centre for Studies in British Art, 1978, 1979 printing
(with corrections). 427pp. Bibl refs.
     Developed in response to a need for
reconstructions of historical interiors at
important buildings under the Victoria and
Albert Museum's direction, the book tells how
household furnishings were made, what they
were made of, and how they were used. The
emphasis is on the use of textiles (curtains, floor
and furniture coverings). Shorter discussions of
panelling, chimney furniture, porcelain, and the
decoration appropriate to rooms of specific
purpose. Index.

Turner, Laurence   682
Decorative plasterwork in Great Britain.
London: Country Life, 1927. 271pp.
     Each chapter is devoted to a specific period,
from 1504–1789, in a chronological
arrangement. Index.

7.6 Details, decoration and ornament

West, Trudy   683
The fireplace in the home. Line illustrations
    by P. C. Young. Newton Abbot: David and Charles,
    1976. 160pp.
        A general history of English fireplaces from early
        times to the present. Index.

Wilson, Michael I.   684
The English country house and its
    furnishings. London: Batsford, 1977. 216pp.
    Bibl pp 210–211.
        An account of the architectural development and
        the furnishings of the country house from
        medieval times to the Victorians. Includes a
        chapter on the gardens and a list of some houses
        for visiting in England (arranged by counties).
        Index.

For other items relating to this section see items in:

1.   **How to find out: guides to the literature**
    2 *Architectural periodicals index.*
    4 Avery Architectural Library. *Catalog.*
    5 Avery Architectural Library. *An index to*
       architectural periodicals.
    6 Baggs. *Copy books.*
    7 Baggs. *Pattern books and vernacular architecture*
       before 1790.
    14 Coulson. *A bibliography of design in Britain,*
       1851–1970.
    15 Courtauld Institute of Art, University of
       London. *Annual bibliography of the history of*
       British art.
    19 Dobai. *Die Kunstliteratur des Klassizismus und*
       der Romantik in England.
    22 Georgian Group. *Recommended books on*
       Georgian architecture and decoration.
    24 *Guide to the literature of art history.*
    29 Harvard University, Graduate School of Design.
       Catalog of the library.
    41 Open University. *Arts: . . . history of architecture*
       and design 1890–1939: project guide.
    44 *RILA.*
    45 Royal Institute of British Architects, Library.
       Catalogue.
    46 Royal Institute of British Architects, Library.
       Comprehensive index to architectural periodicals,
       1956–70.
    47 Royal Institute of British Architects, Library.
       RIBA Annual review of periodical articles.
    49 Royal Institute of British Architects, Library.
       RIBA Library bulletin.
    50 Sheehy. *Guide to reference books.*
    52 Smith. *A critical bibliography of building*
       conservation.
    58 Walford. *Guide to reference material.*

2.1 **Biographical dictionaries, encylopaedias,**
    directories, surveys and indexes
    63 Architectural Publication Society. *The dictionary*
       of architecture.

    65 Beard. *Georgian craftsmen and their work.*
    95 Gunnis. *Dictionary of British sculptors,*
       1660–1851.
    97 Harris. *Catalogue of British drawings for*
       architecture, decoration, sculpture and landscape
       gardening 1550–1900 in American collections.
    127 Royal Institute of British Architects, Drawings
       Collection. *Catalogue of the Drawings Collection*
       of the RIBA.

3.   **How to find out about architects and buildings:**
    unpublished sources, indexes and catalogues
    161 British Architectural Library. Classified
       catalogues.
    164 British Architectural Library. Periodicals subjec
       index.
    167 British Architectural Library, Drawings
       Collection. Indexes.
    169 Kendrick. Nineteenth century stained glass.

4.3 **Some of the most important periodicals**
    182 *The Architect.*
    183 *The Architects' journal.*
    185 *Architectural review.*
    186 *The British architect.*
    188 *The Builder.*
    189 *Building news.*
    192 *Country life.*
    197 *The Studio.*

5.1 **Published directories to societies, institutions**
    and organisations
    200 *The Building Centre and CIRIA guide to sources*
       of information.
    202 *Conservation sourcebook.*
    208 *House's guide to the construction industry.*

5.2 **Guide to societies, institutions and organisations**
    225 Art Workers' Guild.
    227 Association for Studies in the Conservation of
       Historic Buildings.
    236 British Architectural Library.
    237 British Architectural Library. Drawings
       Collection.
    240 British Institute of Interior Design.
    244 British Society of Master Glass Painters.
    249 Building Conservation Trust.
    265 Council for Places of Worship.
    269 Courtauld Institute of Art, Book Library.
    271 Decorative Arts Society 1890–1914.
    280 Design and Industries Association.
    281 Design History Society.
    289 Furniture History Society.
    295 The Georgian Group.
    297 Guildhall Library.
    309 Institute of Advanced Architectural Studies,
       University of York.
    315 Irish Georgian Society.
    317 Ironbridge Gorge Museum Trust.
    365 Royal Commission on Historical Monuments
       (England) including the National Monuments
       Record.
    366 Royal Commission on the Ancient and Historica
       Monuments of Scotland including the National
       Monuments Record of Scotland.

7.7

Building types: general

Pevsner, *Sir* Nikolaus   685
A history of building types. London: Thames and Hudson, 1976. 352pp. Bibl pp 295–328.
The building types covered are national monuments, government buildings (parliaments, ministries, town halls and law courts), theatres, libraries, museums, hospitals, prisons, hotels, exchanges and banks, warehouses and offices, railway stations, market halls and exhibition buildings, shops and department stores, and factories. Particularly useful for the 19th century. The emphasis is on the stylistic rather than the functionalist aspects. Excellent bibliographies. Index.

7.8

Building types: domestic

(Castles, cottages, country houses, farmhouses, flats, parsonages, suburban housing, vernacular houses, working-class and middle-class housing, etc)

Addy, Sidney Oldall   686
The evolution of the English house. Revised and enlarged from the author's notes by John Summerson. London: Allen and Unwin, 1933. 252pp. Bibl pp 240–242. First published 1898.
The development of vernacular domestic building in England. Index of subjects and places.

Airs, Malcolm   687
The making of the English country house, 1500–1640. London: Architectural Press, 1975. 208pp. Bibl pp 195–205.
The builders, the building process, materials, and the workmen are discussed. Index.

7.8 Building types: domestic

Automobile Association 688
**AA guide to stately homes, castles and
gardens.** 1977– . Basingstoke: AA; London:
Distributed by Hutchinson. Annual.
A comprehensive guide to over 2,000 places of
interest in Great Britain. Arranged into 20
geographical areas. Entries give map locations,
brief descriptions and opening hours. Index to
towns and places of interest. Includes a greater
range of places than does *Historic houses, castles
and gardens* (*see* 717), but does not include Eire.
From 1980 entitled *AA stately homes, museums,
castles and gardens in Britain.*

Barley, M. W. 689
The English farmhouse and cottage.
London: Routledge and Kegan Paul, 1961. 297pp.
Deals primarily with the vernacular architecture
of the 16th and 17th centuries, using fieldwork
and documents in local record offices as a major
source of information. Index.

Barley, M. W. 690
**The house and home: a review of 900 years
of house planning and furnishing in Britain.**
London: Studio Vista, 1971. 208pp. Bibl pp 75–76.
First published 1963.
The vernacular house from the middle ages to
the 20th century seen as the expression of social
needs. Mainly photographs, with a brief text.

Braun, Hugh Stanley 691
Elements of English architecture. Newton
Abbot: David and Charles, 1973. 194pp.
A study of the growth and development of
architectural construction, planning and design
of the vernacular tradition in house-building.

Briggs, Martin S. 692
The English farmhouse. London: Batsford,
1953. 242pp. Microfiche, London: Architectural
Press. (The new heritage series).
An historical survey describing both the
chronological development of the farmhouse and
its distinctive regional features in the different
areas of England. Includes some houses which
are not strictly farmhouses as well as a section on
19th-century farmstead layouts.

Brown, R. Allen 693
English castles. 3rd ed. London: Batsford,
1976. 240pp. Bibl notes pp 225–235.
An account of the origins, development,
construction and purpose of the English castle as
both residence and fortress. Index.

Brown, R. J. 69
The English country cottage. London: Robert
Hale, 1979. 272pp. Bibl p 262.
Traces the development of the cottage from the
single-roomed peasant's cot of the middle ages,
through the 16th and 17th centuries, to the
model and picturesque cottages of the 18th and
19th centuries, and up to the brick cottages of
the 20th century. The construction and
distribution of each type of cottage
(timber-framed, mud, stone and brick) is
discussed together with the methods employed
to weatherproof them and the types of roof
coverings used in various parts of the country.
There are chapters on chimneys and fireplaces,
floors, ceilings and stairs, and doors and
windows. Place index and general index.

Burnett, John 69
A social history of housing, 1815–1970.
Newton Abbot: David and Charles, 1978. 344pp.
Bibl notes pp 315–338.
Concentrates on the ordinary house, its location,
size, rooms and amenities and its occupants. The
book describes the kinds of accommodation,
existing and new, available during this period,
analyses the factors that determined the 'built
form', and measures and accounts for the
changes that occurred in housing quality and
standards. Chapters cover rural housing,
middle-class suburban housing, council housing
and inter-war speculative housing. Index.

Calder, Jenni 69
The Victorian home. London: Batsford, 1977.
238pp. Bibl pp 233–234.
Not an architectural study, but a study of life in
the Victorian home which has useful chapters on
working-class homes and the interior. Index.

Camesasca, Ettore, *editor* 69
History of the house. With a foreword by Sir
Robert Matthew. London and Glasgow: Collins,
1971. 432pp.
Chronicles the history from prehistoric shelters
to the 20th century in almost every continent.
Describes not only the physical structure of
houses, but also the life and society of the
inhabitants, their taste in furnishing and
decoration, the evolution of the equipment they
employed and the effect of changes in society on
dwellings which already existed. While Great
Britain forms only a small part of this
international survey, it is a good introduction
and useful for comparisons with what was
happening elsewhere. Index.

Craig, Maurice   698
Classic Irish houses of the middle size.
London: Architectural Press; New York:
Architectural Book Publishing, 1976. 170pp.
Bibl p 167.
Deals with the 17th-, 18th- and early
19th-century houses which were occupied by
minor gentry, prosperous farmers,
manufacturers and traders. Index.

Cruden, Stewart   699
The Scottish castle. Edinburgh: Nelson, 1960.
272pp. Bibl pp 247–257.
A survey of the development of the Scottish
castle from the earliest broch to the Hanoverian
fortifications. Index of names, places, buildings.
Reference has been made to a revised edition,
1963, but no copy was seen.

De Breffny, Brian   700
Castles of Ireland. London: Thames and
Hudson, 1977. 208pp.
96 castles from the 12th-20th centuries arranged
in alphabetical order. Index of castles by
counties. An historical introduction describes
their architectural evolution.

De Breffny, Brian and **ffolliott**, Rosemary   701
**The houses of Ireland: domestic
architecture from the medieval castle to the
Edwardian villa.** London: Thames and Hudson,
1975. 240pp. Bibl p 233.
A scholarly study. Index includes architects and
buildings.

The Destruction of the country house,   702
1875–1975. By Roy Strong, Marcus Binney,
John Harris and others. London: Thames and
Hudson, 1974. 192pp.
Its lists and photographic records of country
houses destroyed in England, Scotland and
Wales make it a valuable tool for the
architectural historian.

Dutton, Ralph   703
The English country house. 2nd ed. London:
Batsford, 1943–44. 120pp. Microfiche, London:
Architectural Press.
Covers the period c 1066–1850, from the
English vernacular, through the rise of the
architect to the cult of the antique, with a
chapter on the garden. Index.

Fedden, Robin and **Kenworthy-Brown**, John   704
**The country house guide: historic houses in
private ownership in England, Wales and
Scotland.** London: Jonathan Cape, 1979. 431pp.

An illustrated guide to some 215 privately owned
country houses that are open to the public for at
least twenty days a year. Includes chapters on
private houses and their visitors (by John
Kenworthy-Brown), the building materials (by
Alec Clifton-Taylor), the middle ages (by John
Harvey), private ownership and the future (by
John Cornforth) and castles and mansions of
Scotland (by Colin McWilliam). Glossary. Index
(includes names of architects).

Fleming, John   705
**Scottish country houses and gardens open to
the public.** London: Country Life, 1957. 128pp (in
1954 ed.)
Illustrations of the principal country houses of
Scotland open to the public, arranged
chronologically, with accompanying text. Index.

Garner, Thomas and **Stratton**, Arthur   706
**The domestic architecture of England
during the Tudor period.** London: Batsford, 1929.
2 vols.
Photographs and measured drawings of country
houses with historical and descriptive text. A
topograpical list of subjects illustrated in both
volumes appears in each volume, as does an
index to the descriptive text and illustrations.
Vol 1 covers stone houses and brick houses, vol 2
covers timber houses, exterior details, interiors
of early Tudor halls and rooms and interior
details.

Georgian Society [of Dublin]   707
**Records of 18th-century domestic
architecture and decoration in Dublin.** Dublin:
Dublin University Press for the Society, 1909–13.
Reprinted 1969. 5 vols.
Predominantly illustrations with explanatory
text. Index in each volume and complete index
(in three parts: persons, places and subjects) to
the series in vol 5. Vol 5 includes a catalogue of
Georgian houses in Ireland (pp 81–107),
arranged by county, and supplying name and
parish, architect and date, original and present
owner, authorities consulted, and descriptive
notes.

Girouard, Mark   708
**Life in the English country house: a social
and architectural history.** New Haven, London:
Yale University Press, 1978. 344pp. Bibl notes
pp 319–331.
Traces the evolution of the country house from
the middle ages to 1940. The emphasis is on how
the houses functioned. Index.

7.8 Building types: domestic

Girouard, Mark   709
The Victorian country house. Rev and enl ed.
New Haven, London: Yale University Press, 1979.
467pp. Bibl notes pp 444–454.
> Covers country houses, ie a house built as a
> centre of a sizeable estate, not simply a house
> built in the country, constructed between 1840
> and 1890. Chapter 3 is a catalogue of country
> houses (not including those given separate
> chapters in the main body of the book). Irish and
> Scottish sections cover only houses partly or
> wholly designed by English architects. At the
> end of each entry brief details are given of where,
> if anywhere, illustrations, plans and further
> information can be found. There is a section
> (pp 436–444) providing biographical notes on
> architects, giving birth and death dates, a brief
> biography and a list of country houses with
> dates. General index. An in-depth exploration of
> the social, political and technological
> background of the country house.

Gotch, J. Alfred   710
**The English home from Charles I to
George IV: its architecture, decoration and
garden design.** London: Batsford, 1918. 410pp.
Microfiche, London: Architectural Press.
> A review of the development of house building,
> decoration and garden design from early Stuart
> times to the beginning of the 19th century.

Gotch, J. Alfred   711
**The growth of the English house: from
early feudal times to the close of the eighteenth
century.** 2nd ed. London: Batsford, 1928. 214pp.
Microfiche of 1st ed, 1909, London: Architectural
Press.
> A short history of its architectural development.

Gould, Jeremy   712
Modern houses in Britain, 1919–39. London:
Society of Architectural Historians of Great Britain,
1977. 64pp. Bibl refs. (Architectural history
monographs, 1).
> The modern movement house, with special
> emphasis on construction and aesthetic effect.
> The work of Connell, Ward & Lucas, Tecton,
> Gropius & Fry and Mendelsohn & Chermayeff
> is criticised in detail. Gazetteer of more than
> 300 houses gives, as far as possible, the address
> of each house, name of architect and client,
> dates of construction and a reference to the
> principal contemporary publication. Index of
> architects.

Guinness, Desmond and **Sadler**, Julius
Trousdale, *Jr.*   713
**The Palladian style in England, Ireland and
America.** London: Thames and Hudson, 1976.
184pp. Bibl pp 179–180.

> One section is devoted to England and another
> to Ireland. Valuable for the study of the
> country house. Index.

Harris, John   714
**The artist and the country house: a history
of country house and garden view painting in
Britain, 1540–1870.** London: Philip Wilson for
Sotheby Parke Bernet, 1979. 376pp. Bibl p 366.
> Besides distinguishing the house painters and
> studying their works in relation to landscape
> and topographical painting in general, it brings
> together a corpus of illustrations that serve as a
> visual quarry for historians of architecture and
> gardening and provides a brief history of each
> house, which focuses on any unusual
> architectural features that are brought out in the
> painting. Illustrates over 400 house views.
> Index.

Harvey, Nigel   715
**A history of farm buildings in England and
Wales.** Newton Abbot: David and Charles, 1970.
227pp. Bibl.

Hill, Oliver   716
**Scottish castles of the 16th and 17th
centuries.** With an introduction by Christopher
Hussey. London: Country Life, 1953. 280pp. Bibl
pp 275–276.
> The introduction covers the historical
> background, followed by sections on the origins
> and characteristics, the castles of the 16th and
> 17th centuries, decoration and equipment, and
> contemporary life. Includes an historical chart,
> 1500–1700, and a glossary. Index.

**Historic houses, castles and gardens
in Great Britain and Ireland.** 1972– .   717
Dunstable: ABC Travel Guides. Annual.
> Includes most of the habitable properties which
> are open to the public, including privately
> owned and 'lived-in' mansions regularly opened
> to the public, together with the majority of
> houses and gardens under the control of the
> National Trust and the National Trust for
> Scotland. Castles and estates administered by
> the Department of the Environment and
> Secretary of State for Scotland are included
> where applicable as are the houses under the
> care of local civic authorities. There is a
> supplementary list of properties open by
> appointment only, printed at the end.
> Information provided includes name,
> address and location of property (and map
> reference), brief description, opening times and
> admission charges, catering facilities and coach
> and rail tours and bus services. Many properties
> have their own illustrated advertisements. Index
> to all houses, castles and gardens.

Jackson, Alan A. 718
**Semi-detached London: suburban
development, life and transport, 1900–39.**
London: Allen and Unwin, 1973. 381pp. Bibl pp
361–369.
> The roles of the speculative builder, the estate
> developer and the local authorities in London's
> suburban development. Appendix 6:
> specifications and plans of London's surburban
> houses. Index.

Jones, Sydney R. 719
**English village homes and country
buildings.** London: Batsford, 1936. 120pp. (British
heritage series).
> A survey of English villages – the historical
> background, the village in the landscape, village
> architecture and local styles in rural
> architecture. Index.

Jordan, R. Furneaux 720
A picture history of the English house.
London: Edward Hulton, 1959. 160pp.
> A general outline of developments in larger
> houses.

Latham, Charles 721
**In English homes; the internal character,
furniture and adornments of some of the most
notable houses of England historically.** London:
Country Life, 1907–09. 3 vols.
> Stately homes from the 16th–18th centuries.
> Continued by H. Avray Tipping, *English homes*
> (*see* 744).

Leask, Harold G. 722
Irish castles and castellated houses.
Dundalk: Tempest Dundalgen Press, 1941.
Reprinted 1973. 170pp.
> A general survey from the 11th–17th centuries
> of the military architecture of Ireland. Index.

Lloyd, Nathaniel 723
**A history of the English house, from
primitive times to the Victorian period.** London:
Architectural Press, 1931 (1975 reprint). 487pp.
> Following the general text, which is arranged by
> centuries, are over 900 photographic illustrations
> with descriptive text arranged chronologically
> within sections, eg plans and exteriors, external
> wall treatment, windows, chimneys, interiors,
> ceilings, fireplaces, staircases, metalwork. Index
> includes buildings by place and architects listed
> alphabetically under 'architects'.

Macartney, Mervyn 724
**English houses and gardens in the 17th and
18th centuries: a series of bird's eye views
reproduced from contemporary engravings by
Kip, Badeslade, Harris and others.** With
descriptive notes by Mervyn Macartney. London:
Batsford, 1908. 34pp. Microfiche, London:
Architectural Press.

MacGibbon, David and **Ross**, T. 725
**Castellated and domestic architecture of
Scotland from the twelfth to the eighteenth
century.** Edinburgh: David Douglas, 1887–92. 5
vols.
> Traces the historical sequence of the various
> phases of architecture in the old castles and
> houses of Scotland. Vol 5 includes some
> churches, post-reformation. 'Scottish sundials',
> vol 5, pp 357–514. Early Scottish masters of
> works, master masons and architects, vol 5, pp
> 515–569. Indexes in each volume. General index
> to the whole work in vol 5 (pp 571–595).
> Topographical list (arranged by county) of
> buildings described in the whole work, vol 5, pp
> 597–603. The standard work.

MacKenzie, W. Mackay 726
The mediaeval castle in Scotland. London:
Methuen, 1927. Reprinted, New York: Arno, 1976.
249pp plus 31 plates.
> Contents include the mote and bailey castle,
> 12th–13th centuries, the earlier stone castles,
> 13th–14th centuries, the parts of the castle,
> palatial castles and towers. Index.

Mercer, Eric 727
**English vernacular houses: a study of
traditional farmhouses and cottages.** London:
HMSO, 1975. 246pp. Bibl refs. At head of title:
Royal Commission on Historical Monuments,
England.
> A study of small rural houses, tracing their
> history from the middle ages to the 19th century.
> Covers all the major aspects of vernacular
> architecture from house-plans and construction
> methods to the influence of the homes of the
> great upon smaller dwellings. Glossary of
> technical terms. Indexes of names and places (by
> county) and of subjects.

Muthesius, Hermann 728
**Das englische Haus: Entwicklung,
Bedingungen, Anlage, Aufbau, Einrichtung und
Innenraum.** 2. durchgesehene Aufl. Berlin:
Wasmuth, 1908–11. 3 vols.
The English house. By Hermann Muthesius.
Edited with an introduction by Dennis Sharp and a
preface by Julius Posener; translated [from the
German] by Janet Seligman. London: Crosby
Lockwood Staples; New York: Rizzoli, 1979. 246pp.

7.8 Building types: domestic

246pp./continued
While beginning around 450, the emphasis is on
the smaller house of the late 19th century. The
English edition is a slightly abridged version of
the German second edition, consolidated into
one volume. The first part deals with the
changes in the period and the great architects.
The second part deals with the 'geography' of
the house, its planning, layout and social
structure. The last part describes house interiors
and design. It has an index to the names of
artists, craftsmen, architects and an index to
buildings (under their names for country houses
and under places for other houses).

O'Neil, B. H. St. J.   729
**Castles: an introduction to the castles of
    England and Wales.** 2nd ed. London: HMSO,
1973. 76pp.
    An introduction to the subject which deals
    mainly with castles in the care of the
    Department of the Environment.

Peate, Iorwerth C.   730
The Welsh house, a study in folk culture.
    2nd ed. Liverpool: H. Evans and Sons, Brython
    Press, 1944. Bibl pp 188–195.
        A pioneering work. Houses as an aspect of folk
        culture.

Prizeman, John   731
Your house: the outside view. London:
    Hutchinson, 1975. 128pp.
        An illustrated review of the history of the
        ordinary house from moated castle to suburban
        semi. Particular emphasis on the use of colour
        for different types of architecture.

Reid, Richard   732
The Shell book of cottages. London: Michael
    Joseph, 1977. 256pp. Bibl pp 248–249.
        The earlier chapters briefly discuss the elements
        of cottages, eg plans, walling, roofs, interiors
        and the cult of the picturesque. The remainder
        of the book sketches the regional differences.
        Includes a glossary and a directory of places to
        visit. Index of names and places.

Renn, D. F.   733
Norman castles in Britain. 2nd ed. London:
    J. Baker; New York: Humanities Press, 1973. 369pp.
    Bibl references.
        Comprehensive history of and guide to over 800
        castles. Glossary. No index.

Richardson, *Sir* A. E. and **Eberlein**,   734
H. Donaldson
**The smaller English house of the later renaissance,
    1660–1830, an account of its design, plan and
    details.** London: Batsford, 1925. 286pp.

Classifies the smaller types of houses, and
considers the evolution of plan, materials and
craftsmanship, and varieties in composition.
Index.

Sadleir, Thomas U. and **Dickinson**, Page L.   735
**Georgian mansions in Ireland: with some
    account of the evolution of Georgian
    architecture and details.** Dublin: Printed for the
    authors at the Dublin University Press, 1915. 103pp
    plus 80 plates.

Savidge, Alan   736
**The parsonage in England: its history and
    architecture.** With a foreword by Sir Nikolaus
    Pevsner. London: SPCK, 1969. 239pp.
    Bibl pp 225–228.
        Covers the period from before the reformation to
        1963. Indexes to parsonages and places and to
        architects and artists.

Simpson, W. Douglas   737
Scottish castles. Edinburgh: HMSO, 1964 (4th
    impression). 49pp. Bibl.
        Aims to give a general conspectus of the origin
        and development of the Scottish castle. While
        dealing primarily with castles in the Ministry's
        custody, also contains a number of others.

Sinclair, Colin   738
The thatched houses of the old Highlands.
    Edinburgh, London: Oliver and Boyd, 1953. 82pp.
        Gives technical particulars of the construction of
        these houses and their variations in different
        localities (the Hebridean type, the Skye type and
        the Dailriadic type) as well as something of the
        way of life of the people who built and lived in
        them.

Smith, Peter   739
**Houses of the Welsh countryside: a study in
    historical geography.** London: HMSO, 1975.
    604pp. Bibl refs. At head of title: Royal Commission
    on Ancient and Historical Monuments in Wales.
        The definitive work on its subject. Describes the
        development of Welsh domestic architecture
        from the late middle ages to the industrial
        revolution. All house types, the medieval
        first-floor halls and hall-houses, the
        sub-medieval farmhouses of the Tudor and
        Stuart period, the gentry houses of the
        renaissance and the cottages of quarrymen and
        smallholder, are described and discussed in
        terms of their plan and construction as well as
        their historical and geographical significance.
        Glossary, general index, index of houses
        mentioned in the text.

Stevens, Joan   740
**Old Jersey houses and those who lived in
them.**
Vol 1: 1500–1700. Jersey: Five Oaks Press, 1965.
255pp. Bibl p 239.
Vol 2: 1700 onwards. London: Phillimore, 1977.
246pp. Bibl p 237.
Volume one records in detail some 200 houses.
Volume two records some 250 houses from 1700
up to the early years of the 20th century. Each
volume includes a glossary and index.

Sutcliffe, Anthony, *editor*   741
**Multi-storey living: the British
working-class experience.** London: Croom Helm,
1974. 249pp. Bibls.
Contributions by various writers on the rise of
flats in Britain from 1750 to the present. Index.

Tarn, John Nelson   742
**Five per cent philanthropy: an account of
housing in urban areas between 1840 and 1914.**
Cambridge: Cambridge University Press, 1973.
211pp. Bibl notes pp 183–196. Bibl pp 197–201.
Deals with the various currents of reform and
the growth of responsible organisations, the
philanthropic trusts, societies and companies
who built the first cheap but sanitary
accommodation for working people in city
centres. Index.

Thompson, A. Hamilton   743
**Military architecture in England during the
middle ages.** London: Henry Frowde, Oxford
University Press, 1912. 384pp. Bibl pp xiii–xxi.
Reprinted, East Ardsley: EP Publishing; Totowa
(New Jersey): Rowman and Littlefield, 1975.
Traces the growth of the general principles of
medieval fortification, with special reference to
castles, from the Anglo-Saxon conquests to the
end of the 15th century. Index.

Tipping, H. Avray   744
English homes. London: Country Life,
1921–37. 10 vols.
From Norman to late Georgian (1066–1820),
these volumes survey, through photographic
illustrations and text, the greater houses and
castles and their gardens of each period. Separate
index in each volume. Brief biographical notes
on the principal architects of each volume.
Continues Charles Latham, *In English homes* (*see*
721).
A new more concise and selective edition of
this work, covering the period 1625–1840 has
been issued in five volumes by Country Life
under the general title *English country houses*, as
follows:

Hill, Oliver and Cornforth, John. *Caroline,
1625–1685*. London. 1966.
Lees-Milne, James. *Baroque, 1685–1715*.
London. 1970.
Hussey, Christopher. *Early Georgian,
1715–1760*. Rev ed. London. 1965.
Hussey, Christopher. *Mid Georgian, 1760–1800*.
Rev ed. London. 1963.
Hussey, Christopher. *Late Georgian, 1800–1840*.
London. 1958.

Toy, Sidney   745
The castles of Great Britain. 3rd ed. London:
Heinemann, 1963. 294pp plus 33 plates. Bibl.
A history of the development of the art of
fortification during the middle ages. Considers
the castle in its military aspect, as a fortress, and
its domestic arrangements in so far as they
influence or are ancillary to its military
functions. Index.

Tranter, Nigel G.   746
The fortified house in Scotland.
Vol 1: South-east Scotland. 1962.
Vol 2: Central Scotland. 1963.
Vol 3: South-west Scotland. 1965.
Vol 4: Aberdeen, Angus and Kincardineshire. 1966.
Vol 5: North and west Scotland and miscellaneous.
1970.
Edinburgh, London: Oliver and Boyd (Vols 1–4), W.
R. Chambers (Vol 5), 1962–70. 5 vols.
Describes briefly the aspect, situation, special
features and history of 530 fortified houses. The
arrangement is by counties.

Turnor, Reginald   747
The smaller English house, 1500–1939.
London: Batsford, 1952. 216pp. Microfiche, London:
Architectural Press.
From the late medieval times until the end of the
19th century. Gives an account of the design,
development and decoration of the smaller
English home, both in the town and in the
country. Index.

Wood, Margaret   748
The English medieval house. London:
Phoenix, 1965. 448pp. Bibl pp 417–429.
A detailed survey of the evolution and growth of
the medieval house as influenced by changing
social conditions. Glossary. Index.

Woodforde, John   749
Georgian houses for all. London: Routledge
and Kegan Paul, 1978. 177pp. Bibl pp 168–170.
Contents: Palladian comfort; five types of house;
living in London; building materials and
economy; the farmhouse; the parsonage;
furnishing and lighting; bedrooms; hygiene; the
sash window; chimneys and fireplaces;

fireplaces;/*continued*
non-classical work; the villas and the end;
archival records; the Georgian tradition revived.
Deals with the smaller Georgian house. The
chapter on archival records is a simple
introduction to the kinds of documents held by
record offices. Index.

Yorke, F. R. S.   750
The modern house in England. London:
Architectural Press, 1937 (since revised). 144pp.
Bibl p 143.
An important book for the second generation of
modern movement architect. Contains plans,
constructional details and photographs of the
most admired contemporary buildings. A sequel
to Yorke's *The modern house* (London:
Architectural Press, 1934) which is important
historically as the first collection of illustrations
of the new domestic architecture presented to
the English public, but which included only
about half a dozen English examples.

For other items relating to this section see items in:

▬▬▬ **7.9**

Building types: ecclesiastical

(Abbeys, cathedrals, chapels, churches, meeting
houses, monasteries, priories, etc)

Addleshaw, G. W. O. and **Etchells**, Frederick   751
**The architectural setting of Anglican
    worship: an inquiry . . . from the reformation to
    the present day.** London: Faber and Faber, 1948.
288pp.
    A standard work.

Allen, Frank James   752
**The great church towers of England, chiefly
    of the perpendicular period: a photographic
    study of all the principal towers, with critical
    notes, record of architectural details, and
    exposition of the principles of tower design.**

7.9 Building types: ecclesiastical

design./*continued*
Cambridge: Cambridge University Press, 1932.
205pp.
> Arranged by county. Index of towers under counties in alphabetical order.

Betjeman, *Sir* John, *editor*   753
**Collins' pocket guide to English parish
    churches.** Rev ed. London: Collins, 1968. 2 vols.
> One volume covers the South, the other the
> North. Each volume contains a long historical
> introduction. The arrangement is alphabetically
> by place names. A glossary of architectural
> terms, an index of architects and artists and an
> index of places is in each volume. In all, about
> 4,000 entries, including 19th and 20th century
> churches. A new edition, *Collins guide to parish
> churches of England and Wales* (London: Collins,
> 1980. 528pp) is now available.

Bond, Francis   754
**Gothic architecture in England: an analysis
    of the origin and development of English church
    architecture from the Norman Conquest to the
    dissolution of the monasteries.** London: Batsford,
    1906. 782pp. Bibl pp viii–xii. Microfiche, London:
    Architectural Press. Reprinted, New York: Arno,
    1972.
> A very full treatise on the subject. Index of
> places. Index to illustrations. Index of subject
> matter. Glossary.

Bond, Francis   755
**An introduction to English church
    architecture, from the eleventh to the sixteenth
    century.** London, New York, etc: Humphrey
    Milford, Oxford University Press, 1913. 2 vols.
    Reprinted, Kennebunkport (Maine): Longwood
    Press, 1979.
> Fully illustrated introduction. Chapters discuss
> differentiation of the parish church from
> cathedrals, churches of monks and canons and
> collegiate churches, the purposes which the
> various portions of the greater churches were
> intended to subserve, the planning of the
> cathedral, monastic and collegiate churches and
> the growth of the English parish church. Much
> of the book is devoted to building construction
> (vaulting, abutment system, walls and arches,
> the pier and its members, windows, doorways
> and porches, roofs, towers and spires). English
> and French glossaries. Indexes of places and
> subjects.

Bowyer, Jack   756
The evolution of church building. London:
    Crosby Lockwood Staples, 1977. 139pp.
> A brief history of the development of the
> tradition of ecclesiastical building in Britain from
> the 9th century to the present. Chapters on the
> greater churches, abbeys and conventual houses,

parish churches, construction of churches,
nonconformist chapels and meeting houses and
church fittings and furniture. An appendix lists,
by geographical area, the buildings described in
the text. Index.

Butler, Lionel and **Given-Wilson**, Chris   75?
Medieval monasteries of Great Britain.
    London: Michael Joseph, 1979. 416pp. Bibl p 408.
> A study of all the main monastic sites still
> surviving in Great Britain. The introduction
> discusses monasticism and the buildings of the
> monastery, and is followed by a gazetteer which
> describes the history and architecture of eighty
> monasteries (sixty-one in England, eleven in
> Scotland, eight in Wales). There is an appendix
> of secondary sites, a glossary and a full index.

Carr, Gerald Lawrence   75?
**The Commissioners' churches of London,
    1818–1837: a study of religious art, architecture
    and patronage in Britain from the formation of
    the Commission to the accession of Victoria.**
    Ann Arbor (Mich), London: University Microfilms
    International, 1979. Facsimile reprint. 3 vols.
    Bibl pp 957–981. Ph D Dissertation: University of
    Michigan, 1976.
> Complements M. H. Port's *Six hundred new
> churches* (*see* 793), which does not deal with the
> Commission's architecture as art to the extent
> that this study does. Appendix III (pp 729–752)
> is a checklist of the Commissioners' churches of
> London, which includes data relating to the
> style, cost and accommodation of a church as
> originally built, names of all architects and
> essential bibliography. No index.

Champneys, Arthur C.   759
**Irish ecclesiastical architecture, with some
    notice of similar or related work in England,
    Scotland and elsewhere.** London: G. Bell and
    Sons; Dublin: Hodges, Figgis, 1910. Reprinted,
    Dublin, 1970. 258pp.
> From primitive architecture to late Irish gothic
> of the 16th century. Index of places. Index of
> subjects and persons.

Chatfield, Mark   760
Churches the Victorians forgot. Ashbourne:
    Moorland Publishing, 1979. 171pp.
> A study, in words and pictures, of 50 churches
> (out of approximately 70) which preserve intact
> the 'prayer-book' interiors of the Anglican
> church between around 1570 and the 1840s.
> About 80 additional churches, some with
> completely unrestored interiors and some with
> prayer-book interiors marred by later alterations,
> are included in the gazetteer. No index.

Child, Mark   761
Discovering church architecture. Aylesbury:
Shire Publications, 1976. 64pp. Bibl pp 62–64.
(Discovering series, no 214).
A dictionary of terms. Illustrated with line
drawings.

Clarke, Basil and **Betjeman**, *Sir* John   762
English churches. London: Vista, 1964.
208pp.
Pictorial survey of English churches from Saxon
times to 1962. Index.

Clifton-Taylor, Alec   763
The cathedrals of England. London: Thames
and Hudson, 1967. 288pp.
A brief history from Norman times to the
present with a section of short summaries
written primarily for those not yet familiar with
the cathedrals of England, indicating which
buildings are most worth seeing and what are the
most memorable features of each. Glossary.
Index.

Cobb, Gerald   764
The old churches of London. London:
Batsford, 1941–42. 116pp.
Mainly churches of the City of London.
Includes a list of churches giving brief details of
when they were built, rebuilt, demolished, etc.
Index.

Cook, G. H.   765
**The English cathedral through the
centuries.** London: Phoenix House, 1957. 384pp.
Bibl p 371.
The cathedral is placed in its historical context.
The chief works carried out in cathedral
churches during the successive periods of
medieval architecture are surveyed in broad
outline. Index.

Cook, G. H.   766
**English collegiate churches of the middle
ages.** London: Phoenix House, 1959. 228pp.
Bibl p 223.
Treats 35 colleges, giving an introduction to the
purpose of these establishments, and of their
constitution and personnel as well as to the
architecture. Index.

Cook, G. H.   767
The English mediaeval parish church.
London: Phoenix House, 1959. 302pp.
Bibl pp 283–284.
An introduction to the historical, ecclesiological
and architectural aspects. Glossary. Index of
places. General index.

Cook, G. H.   768
English monasteries in the middle ages.
London: Phoenix House, 1961. 282pp.
Bibl pp 270–271.
Gives an account of the monastic establishments
in England from the 7th to the 16th century,
concentrating on the planning of monastic
churches and the conventual buildings attached
to them. Index.

Cook, Olive and **Smith**, Edwin   769
English abbeys and priories. London:
Thames and Hudson, 1960. 63pp. Bibl p 61.
An introduction to English abbeys and priories
which does not claim to be comprehensive in
text or illustration and shows only a proportion
of the surviving buildings. Map of localities. No
index.

Cowan, Ian B. and **Easson**, D. E.   770
Medieval religious houses: Scotland. 2nd ed.
London: Longman, 1976. 252pp.
Not a book about architecture but about the
history of religious foundations. The entries,
however, make documentary mention of
buildings. Index of religious houses.

Cruden, Stewart   771
**Scottish abbeys; an introduction to the
medieval abbeys and priories of Scotland.**
Edinburgh: HMSO, 1960. 92pp. Bibl p 88.
Contents: The origins of monasticism; the Celtic
monasteries; the monastic orders; the buildings;
the monastic orders in Scotland; the ancient
monuments. No index.

De Breffny, Brian and **Mott**, George   772
The churches and abbeys of Ireland.
London: Thames and Hudson, 1976. 208pp.
Bibl p 202.
A chronological survey from Celtic times to the
present of about 300 surviving churches and
abbeys. Index of places. Index of personal
names.

Dirsztay, Patricia   773
Church furnishings: a NADFAS guide.
London: Routledge and Kegan Paul, 1978. 246pp.
Bibliographies.
Contents: Architectural terms; books and
bookbinding; brasses, arms and armour;
ceramics; clocks; costume; creatures and
animals; crosses and crucifix; decorative motifs;
flowers, fruit and trees; frames; heraldry;
lettering; memorials and monuments;
metalwork; miscellany; musical instruments;
saints, scenes, signs and symbols; sanctuary;
shapes; stonework; textiles; vestments; wall

wall/*continued*
paintings; wall appendages; windows;
woodwork; guide to English periods and styles;
mouldings. Index. Unfortunately it has serious
omissions and many mistakes.

Dolbey, George W.   774
The architectural expression of Methodism:
the first hundred years. London: Epworth Press,
1964. 195pp plus 24 plates. Bibl pp 183–185.
Concerned with the development of Methodist
church buildings from early spontaneous
18th-century experiments to the large urbane
and monumental structures of the 1830s. Index.

Fenwick, Hubert   775
Scotland's abbeys and cathedrals. London:
Robert Hale, 1978. 288pp.
From pre-Norman times to the gothic revival
and neo-medieval cathedrals of the 19th century.
Includes a glossary and a list of Scottish abbeys
and cathedrals normally open to the public.
Index.

Gilyard-Beer, R.   776
Abbeys: an illustrated guide to the abbeys
of England and Wales. 2nd ed. London: HMSO,
1976. 99pp.
A short introduction to the various Orders and
their daily life and organisation, followed by a
section on the buildings themselves, general
features and examples. Index of English and
Welsh religious houses mentioned in the text and
general index.

Gwynn, Aubrey and **Hadcock**, R. Neville   777
Medieval religious houses: Ireland: with an
appendix to early sites. With a foreword by David
Knowles. Harlow: Longmans, 1970. 479pp.
Not a book about architecture but about the
history of religious foundations. The entries,
however, make documentary mention of
buildings. Index.

Harvey, John   778
Cathedrals of England and Wales. London:
Batsford, 1974. 272pp. Bibl pp 254–259.
Traces the general course of development of
cathedral history and design up to the
renaissance. Includes a section of historical and
descriptive notes on 31 cathedrals, containing a
statement of the main facts about the see and
foundation; dimensions of the building; the chief
building dates; where known, the architects'
names; and ground plans. General index and
index of architects and artists.

Hay, George   779
The architecture of Scottish
post-reformation churches, 1560–1843. Oxford:
Clarendon Press, 1957. 300pp. Bibl pp 283–286.
Traces the development and character of
churches built between the reformation (1560)
and the disruption (1843). Its primary concern is
with buildings erected by the establishment, but
also includes some of other denominations who
made their own contributions to the religious life
of the period. Appendix A (pp 241–278) is an
inventory and index of churches 1560–1843,
arranged by county, then place, then church.
Names of architects or designers are given in
notes, if known. The appendix also serves as an
index to churches mentioned in the text.

Howell, Peter   780
Victorian churches. London: Country Life,
1968. 64pp. Bibl p 64. (RIBA drawings series).
A general survey of the rise of church building in
the 19th century, the reasons behind it, the
architects and other figures involved, the styles
and the buildings. No index.

Ison, Leonora and Walter   781
English church architecture through the
ages. London: Arthur Barker, 1972. 124pp.
A very general survey of England's churches,
cathedrals and monastic buildings from
Romano-British times to the present. Index.

King, R. J.   782
Handbook to the Welsh cathedrals. London:
John Murray, 1887. 334pp.
Covers Llandaff, St Davids, St Asaph and
Bangor. No index.

Knowles, David and **Hadcock**, R. Neville   783
Medieval religious houses, England and
Wales. [New] ed. [Harlow]: Longman, 1971. 565pp.
Lists of houses arranged according to their
order, with historic notes, and alphabetical
index.

Leask, Harold G.   784
Irish churches and monastic buildings.
Vol 1. The first phases and the romanesque. 1955.
173pp.
Vol 2. Gothic architecture to AD 1400. 1958. 162pp.
Vol 3. Medieval gothic: the last phases. 1960. 190pp.
Bibl.
Dundalk: Dundalgen Press.
Indexes in each volume.

Lidbetter, Hubert   785
**The Friends meeting house: an historical
    survey of the places of worship of the Society of
    Friends (Quakers), from the days of their
    founder George Fox, in the 17th century, to the
    present day.** 2nd ed. York: W. Sessions, 1979. 84pp
plus 42 plates.
    A survey of the history, siting, planning,
    construction and architectural character of the
    Friends meeting houses up to the 20th century,
    with examples from Britain, Ireland, Scotland
    and America. Index. Previous edition, 1961.
    The second edition is virtually unaltered except
    for a page of corrigenda.

Lindley, Kenneth   786
Chapels and meeting houses. Written and
    illustrated by Kenneth Lindley; foreword by John
    Piper. London: J. Baker, 1969. 85pp.
    A general survey of nonconformist chapels and
    Friends meeting houses, their architecture and
    particular style. No index.

Lindsay, Ian G.   787
The Scottish parish kirk. Edinburgh:
    St Andrews Press, 1960. 94pp.

Little, Bryan   788
Abbeys and priories in England and Wales.
    London: Batsford, 1979. 216pp. Bibl p 212.
    The first half of the book consists of a general
    survey which includes sections on origins, the
    Norman transformation, life and buildings,
    friars and hospitals, the dissolution, continuance
    and survival, the English revival, Anglican
    communities and the modern scene. The second
    half is an extended gazetteer which provides
    information on the history and surviving
    architecture of the abbeys and priories which in
    the author's view are best worth visiting today.
    Index.

Little, Bryan   789
**Catholic churches since 1623: a study of
    Roman Catholic churches in England and Wales
    from penal times to the present decade.** London:
    Robert Hale, 1966. 256pp. Bibl pp 17–18, bibl notes
    pp 229–243.
    Includes an index.

MacGibbon, D. and **Ross**, T.   790
The ecclesiastical architecture of Scotland.
    Edinburgh: David Douglas, 1896–97. 3 vols.
    A comprehensive survey. Detailed lists of
    contents in each volume and general index to the
    whole work in vol 3.

Muthesius, Hermann   791
**Die neuere kirchliche Baukunst in England:
    Entwicklung, Bedingungen und Grundzüge des
    Kirchenbaues der englischen Staatskirche und
    der Secten.** Berlin: Wilhelm Ernst, 1901. 176pp.
Bibl p xvi.
    A detailed and well-illustrated study of the
    established and nonconformist churches in
    19th-century England. Index of names, places
    and subjects.

Petrie, George   792
**The ecclesiastical architecture of Ireland
    anterior to the Anglo-Norman invasion,
    comprising an essay on the origin and uses of
    the round towers of Ireland.** 2nd ed. Dublin:
Hodges and Smith, 1845. 525pp.
    A study of the round towers from the 5th to the
    13th centuries. Index.

Port, M. H.   793
**Six hundred new churches: a study of the
    Church Building Commission, 1818–56, and its
    church building activities.** London: SPCK, 1961.
208pp. Bibl pp 192–193.
    A detailed history of the Commissioners and
    their work, covering the beginnings of the
    Church Building Movement, how the
    Commission was brought into being and how it
    carried out its functions, the architects and styles
    involved, the relations of the Commissioners
    with the architectural profession, etc. Appendix
    1 (pp 132–173) lists all churches built with the
    aid of parliamentary grants between 1818–56.
    For each church, architect, contractor, cost of
    the actual building, grant, style, date,
    accommodation and other remarks are given.
    Appendix 3 (pp 177–190) lists all architects
    employed on Commissioners' churches, together
    with a list of their churches. Index.

Taylor, H. M. and Joan   794
Anglo-Saxon architecture. Cambridge (Eng):
    Cambridge University Press, 1965–1978. 3 vols.
    Bibl vol 3, pp 1087–1092.
    A catalogue of the Anglo-Saxon fabric surviving
    in the churches of England. The first volume, a
    short introduction, is a survey of pre-Conquest
    architectural features and the reasons for
    designating them as characteristically
    Anglo-Saxon. The second volume is the
    catalogue in which each church is described.
    Arranged in alphabetical order of parish names.
    The third volume is typological, with chapters
    devoted to the study of each principal
    architectural feature. Cumulative index in vol 3.
    Provides extensive visual documentation. An
    indispensable tool for research.

7.9 Building types: ecclesiastical

Whiffen, Marcus   795
**Stuart and Georgian churches: the
architecture of the Church of England outside
London, 1603–1837.** London: Batsford, 1947–48.
118pp. (The British art and building series).
      Provides a list of churches mentioned in the
book, arranged by county. Index.

White, James F.   796
**The Cambridge movement: the
ecclesiologists and the gothic revival.** Cambridge
(Eng): Cambridge University Press, 1962 (reprinted
1980). 272pp. Bibl pp 237–253.
      An account of the work of the Cambridge
Camden Society whose aims were to exercise
vigilance over the design and fittings of new
churches, to preserve and restore existing
medieval churches, and to introduce the spirit of
Catholic worship into the Anglican liturgy. The
bibliography is in two parts, the first a
chronological list of the publications of the
Cambridge Camden Society and its successor,
the Ecclesiological Society, 1839–1864, the
second a selection of related works. Indexes of
persons, places and subjects.

Williams, Glanmor   797
**The Welsh church from conquest to
reformation.** Cardiff: Wales University Press, 1962.
602pp. Bibl.

For other items relating to this section see items in:

7.10

Building types: industrial and commercial

(Arcades, factories, industrial archaeology, shops and stores, warehouses, watermills and windmills, etc)

Artley, Alexandra, editor   798
The golden age of shop design: European shop interiors, 1880–1939. London: Architectural Press, 1975. 128pp. Bibl p 128.
> A collection of photographs of shops and department stores. Includes a chronology of European shop design.

Brockman, H. A. N.   799
The British architect in industry, 1841–1940.
London: Allen and Unwin, 1974. 186pp. Bibl p 177.
> Includes warehouses, factories, power houses, railway stations and mechanically operative buildings. Index.

Brown, R. J.   800
Windmills of England. London: Robert Hale, 1976. 256pp. Bibl p 251.
> Describes the windmill's development in

7.10 Building types: industrial and commercial

development/*continued*
England, its construction and how its machinery
worked and describes preserved windmills and
their history, county by county. Index.

Buchanan, R. A.   801
Industrial archaeology in Britain. 2nd ed.
London: A. Lane, 1980. 475pp. Bibl. pp 437–452.
First published: Harmondsworth: Penguin Books,
1972.
Contents: 1. introduction (definitions and
techniques, historical framework); industrial
categories (coal-mining, metal, engineering,
textile and chemical industries, building,
agriculture, and rural crafts, consumer
industries and urban crafts); 3. power, transport
and public services; 4. the progress of industrial
archaeology (organisation of the subject, the
study of industrial archaeology); 5. regional
survey. Index.

Dan, Horace and **Willmott**, E. C. Morgan   802
**English shop fronts old and new: a series of
examples by leading architects; selected and
specially photographed, together with
descriptive notes and illustrations.** London:
Batsford, 1907. 48 pp plus 52 plates. Microfiche,
London: Architectural Press.

Dean, David   803
**English shop fronts from contemporary
source books, 1792–1840, including Designs for
shop fronts, by I. and J. Taylor, 1792; A series of
designs for shop fronts, by J. Young, 1828;
Designs for shop fronts, by J. Faulkner, 1831;
Shop fronts and exterior doors, by T. King, n.d.;
On the construction and decoration of the shop
fronts of London, by N. Whittock, 1840.** With a
preface by David Dean. London: Tiranti, 1970. 11 pp
plus 77 plates. Bibl p 77.
An annotated collection of illustrations from
pattern books.

De Little, R. J.   804
The windmill, yesterday and today.
London: John Baker, 1972. 101pp. Bibl p 101.
A short account and history of the various types
of windmill. List of about 60 windmills to be
seen. Glossary. Index of windmills.

Farries, K. G.   805
**'Researching a county's windmill history:
Essex'**, in *Transactions of the 4th symposium of The
International Molinological Society, Matlock, England,
1–8 September 1977*. London: Wind and Watermill
Section, The Society for the Protection of Ancient
Buildings for The International Molinological
Society, 1978. pp 75–90.
A review of sources of recorded information and
of their potential for windmill research.

Discusses printed material (journals, local
histories, trade directories, newspaper files, etc),
manuscripts, maps and illustrations. While the
examples cited are specific to Essex, the types of
sources are more widely relevant.

Geist, Johann Friedrich   806
Pasagen: ein Bautyp des 19. Jahrhunderts.
3. ergänzte Aufl. Munich: Prestel, 1979. 560 pp.
Bibl refs.
International study of arcades with many
examples from Britain. Indexes of places and
names.

Lindsey, C. F., *compiler*   807
Windmills: a bibliographical guide.
London: The Author, 1974. 48pp.
A guide to the literature and other sources of
information. The first part consists of an
alphabetical author list of books and pamphlets,
together with a selection of periodical articles.
The rest of the booklet covers other publications
and organisations which can be consulted. There
is an index to the bibliography (places and
subjects) on pp 34–36.

Rees, D. Morgan   808
**Mines, mills and furnaces: an introduction
to industrial archaeology in Wales.** London:
HMSO, 1969. 117pp. Bibl pp 99–105.
History of and guide to important sites. Index.

Reynolds, John   809
Windmills and watermills. London: Hugh
Evelyn, 1970. 196pp. Bibl pp 192–193. (Excursions
into architecture).
Traces the development of mills and milling,
and explains the details of milling machinery.
Index.

Rothery, Sean   810
The shops of Ireland. Dublin: Gill and
Macmillan, 1978. 126pp. Bibl pp 118–119.
A study of the development of Irish shops from
rural converted houses to city planned shops.
Illustrated with drawings by the author. Index.

Syson, Leslie   811
British water-mills. London: Batsford, 1965.
176pp. Bibl. pp 167–171.
Concerned primarily with the technical aspect.
Glossary. Index.

Wailes, Rex   812
The English windmill. 2nd ed. London:
Routledge and Kegan Paul, 1967. 246pp.
Bibl pp 221–223.

Discusses the different types of mills and their variations in different parts of the country, giving a detailed account of their machinery, how they worked and the men who operated and built them. How they should be preserved and recorded is also discussed. Glossary. Index.

Wailes, Rex   813
A source book of windmills and watermills.
London: Ward Lock, 1979. 128pp.
Brief illustrated guide to mills. The first half of the book deals with the various forms of windmill and the essential machinery. The second half is devoted to waterwheels and watermills. Glossary. Brief list of mills open to the public.

For other items relating to this section see items in:

■■■ Selective bibliography

7.11 Building types: recreational

for other items relating to this section/*continued*

■■■ **7.11**

Building types: recreational

(Cinemas, hotels, inns, music halls, piers, pubs, spas, theatres, etc)

Adamson, Simon H.   814
Seaside piers. London: Batsford in association with the Victorian Society, 1977. 116pp.
The social, architectural, technical and financial aspects of the British seaside pier. Appendices provide an annotated list of all piers ever constructed and a similarly annotated list of all surviving piers.

Addison, William   815
English spas. London: Batsford, 1951. 152pp.
A social history of English spas, concentrating mainly on the better-known examples, but does look at some smaller spas. Index.

Girouard, Mark   816
Victorian pubs. London: Studio Vista, 1975. 223pp. Bibl pp 209–210.
Mainly concerned with Victorian pubs in London, but includes a much less deeply researched epilogue on city pubs in the rest of England and in Ireland. Index.

Glasstone, Victor   817
Victorian and Edwardian theatres: an architectural and social survey. London: Thames and Hudson, 1975. 136pp. Bibl p 134.
An illustrated survey of British theatre architecture c 1830–1920. Indexes of architects and designers and of buildings.

Howard, Diana   818
London theatres and music halls, 1850–1950. London: Library Association, 1970. 291pp. Bibl pp 269–276.
A directory, arranged alphabetically by name of theatre (with former or other names indexed). Names of architects, and sometimes decorators and contractors, are supplied. Bibliographical sources and official records (eg plans in the GLC Architects Department) are cited. Supplies dates of operation, capacity, and notes about building alterations. Includes a directory of collections. Names index to buildings, but not to architects.

Leacroft, Richard   819
The development of the English playhouse. London: Eyre Methuen, 1973. 354pp. Bibl pp 338–345.
Presents the architectural development of the English playhouse from its beginnings in the Christian church to the establishment of the picture-frame theatre around 1900. Index.

Lindley, Kenneth   820
Seaside architecture. London: H. Evelyn, 1973. 160pp (Excursions into architecture).
Describes the elements that go to make up the seaside resort, from the railway station down to the front, along the promenade and out to the end. Appendix I: a list of pleasure piers. Appendix II: a list of cliff railways. Index.

Mickleburgh, Timothy J.   821
Guide to British piers. Atherstone: The Author, 1979. 39pp.
A booklet which aims to give a comprehensive account of all piers in the UK. Arranged by area. Brief entries for each pier give date of construction and history. No index.

Richardson, *Sir* A. E. and **Eberlein**,   822
H. Donaldson
The English inn, past and present: a review of its history and social life. London: Batsford, 1925. 308pp. Microfiche, London: Architectural Press. (The old English life series).
The English inn in medieval, Tudor, Georgian and later times.

Richardson, *Sir* A. E.   823
The old inns of England. With a foreword by Sir Edwin Lutyens; illustrated from drawings by Brian Cook. London: Batsford, 1934. 118pp. Microfiche, London: Architectural Press.
A detailed study of the English inn over the last three centuries, with discussion of the social and historical influence. Includes a selected list of notable inns (arranged by county). Index.

Sharp, Dennis   824
The picture palace, and other buildings for the movies. London: Hugh Evelyn, 1969. Bibl pp 220–222. (Excursions into architecture).
A history of the cinema. Includes a selective list of cinemas in Britain from 1900–1966. Index. A new edition is in preparation.

Southern, Richard   825
The Victorian theatre, a pictorial survey.
   Newton Abbot: David and Charles, 1970. 112pp.
   Bibl pp 109–110.
      Describes the character and techniques of the
      Victorian theatre, the stage machinery, methods
      of scene-changing, theatre architecture and
      scene-painting. Index.

Stoddard, Richard   826
Theatre and cinema architecture: a guide to
   information sources. Detroit: Gale Research, 1978.
   368pp. (Performing arts information guide series, 5).
      A bibliography of publications (books, periodical
      articles, theses etc) relating to theatres, cinemas,
      opera houses and dance facilities. Chapter 10
      covers theatre architecture in Great Britain
      (general histories, renaissance, restoration and
      eighteenth century, nineteenth century, and
      twentieth century), and chapter 19 covers
      cinema architecture in Great Britain. There is an
      author index, an index of architects, designers,
      consultants and decorators, a theatre and cinema
      index (see both Great Britain and Ireland, under
      which individual buildings are arranged by
      place) and a subject index.

Taylor, Derek and **Bush**, David   827
The golden age of British hotels. London:
   Northwood, 1974. 170pp. Bibl pp 166 and 170.
      Primarily about the hotel business from
      1837–1974. Index, with names of hotels entered
      under the name of the town.

Tidworth, Simon   828
Theatres: an illustrated history. London: Pall
   Mall, 1973. 224pp. Bibl pp 213–14.
      A general international survey from the Greeks
      to the present. Index.

For other items relating to this section see items in:

7.12 Building types: education and welfare

7.12

Building types: education and welfare

(Almshouses, hospitals, libraries, schools, etc)

Clay, Rotha Mary   829
The mediaeval hospitals of England.
    London: Methuen, 1909. 357pp. Bibl pp 339–342.
    (The Antiquary's books).
        Primarily concerned with the history of these
        ecclesiastical institutions, but includes a section
        on the buildings. Index.

Godfrey, Walter H.   830
**The English almshouse, with some account
    of its predecessor, the medieval hospital.**
    London: Faber and Faber, 1955. 93pp.
        A general introduction to the planning of the
        buildings and their changing architectural
        character. Index.

Robson, E. R.   831
School architecture. With an introduction by
    Malcolm Seaborne. Leicester: Leicester University
    Press, 1972. 440pp. Bibl pp 27–30. (The Victorian
    library). Facsimile reprint of 1874 ed.
        The bibliography lists works on school
        architecture and building published between
        1800 and 1880. Robson was associated with the
        buildings of the London School Board, whose
        first architect he was from 1871 to 1889, after
        which he acted as consultant architect to the
        Education Department in Whitehall. Index.

Seaborne, Malcolm   832
**The English school: its architecture and
    organization.** London: Routledge and Kegan Paul,
    1971–77. 2 vols. Bibl notes in vol 1. Bibl pp 215–225
    in vol 2.
        Vol 1 begins with the background to the
        founding of Winchester College in 1382 and
        ends with the major legislative changes of
        1868–70. Treats the subject from the point of
        view of architectural history, as well as of the
        development of educational ideas and practices.
        Appendix 2: Elementary day schools illustrated
        in *The Builder*, 1843–70. Appendix 3:
        Middle-class schools illustrated in *The Builder*
        before 1870 and middle-class schools illustrated
        in *The Building news* before 1870. Index.
        Vol 2, by Malcolm Seaborne and Roy Lowe,

covers the period 1870–1970, from the Board
School era to the design of post-war schools.
Index.

Thompson, Anthony   833
**Library buildings of Britain and Europe: an
    interpretational study. With examples mainly
    from Britain and some from Europe and
    overseas.** London: Butterworths, 1963. 326pp.
        Mostly about the 20th century, but good
        historical survey (pp 63–75), with its own
        bibliography.

Thompson, John D. and **Goldin**, Grace   834
**The hospital, a social and architectural
    history.** New Haven, London: Yale University
    Press, 1975. 349pp. Bibl pp 339–342.
        Part 1 is a history of hospital ward design in
        Europe and the United States. Part 2 reviews
        contemporary planning problems in the US and
        Great Britain. Index.

For other items relating to this section see items in:

1.   **How to find out: guides to the literature**
      2 *Architectural periodicals index.*
      4 Avery Architectural Library. *Catalog.*
      5 Avery Architectural Library. *An index to
         architectural periodicals.*
    29 Harvard University, Graduate School of Design.
         Catalog of the library.
    45 Royal Institute of British Architects, Library.
         Catalogue.
    46 Royal Institute of British Architects, Library.
         *Comprehensive index to architectural periodicals.
         1956–70.*
    47 Royal Institute of British Architects, Library.
         RIBA Annual review of periodical articles.
    48 Royal Institute of British Architects, Library.
         RIBA Library bulletin.

**2.1 Biographical dictionaries, encyclopaedias,
     directories, surveys and indexes**
    109 Linstrum. *West Yorkshire architects and
         architecture.*

3.   **How to find out about architects and buildings:
     unpublished sources, indexes and catalogues**
    161 British Architectural Library. Classified
         catalogues.
    163 British Architectural Library. Grey books index.
    164 British Architectural Library. Periodicals subject
         index.
    167 British Architectural Library, Drawings
         Collection. Indexes.

4.3 Some of the most important periodicals
    182 *The Architect.*
    183 *The Architects' journal.*
    186 *The British architect.*
    188 *The Builder.*
    189 *Building news.*

7.13

Building types: transport

(Bridges, canal architecture, railway architecture)

Biddle, Gordon   835
Victorian stations: railway stations in England and Wales, 1830–1923. Newton Abbot: David and Charles, 1973. 256pp. Bibl pp 227–230.
> Especially useful for the smaller stations. Glossary. General index and index of stations.

Binney, Marcus and **Pearce**, David, *editors*   836
Railway architecture. Written by members and associates of SAVE Britain's Heritage. London: Orbis, 1979. 256pp. Bibl p 248.
> A survey of the diversity and significance of railway buildings in Britain, which covers not only railway stations but also hotels, goods warehouses, engine sheds, train sheds, locomotive carriage and rolling stock works, bridges and viaducts, signal boxes, stationmasters' houses, railway workers' cottages and model villages. An appendix: Notes on selected stations and associated buildings, covers the main historic stations and a limited number of secondary ones. Index.

British Waterways Board   837
Canal architecture in Britain. London: The Board, 1976. 40pp. Bibl p 40.
> An illustrated general introduction. The British Waterways Board are the custodians of a number of listed buildings and are concerned in part with the restoration and conservation of the canals and their buildings.

De Maré, Eric   838
The bridges of Britain. New ed. London: Batsford, 1975. 136pp.
> Mainly an illustrated survey from medieval to modern times. Includes a gazetteer with a selective list of existing bridges, old and new, in England, Scotland and Wales. No index.

Harris, Robert   839
Canals and their architecture. London: Hugh Evelyn, 1969. 223pp. Bibl pp 217–219. (Excursions into architecture).
> Describes the bridges, locks, aqueducts and tunnels as well as canalside buildings, including tollhouses, canal inns, maintenance yards, wharves and warehouses. Glossary. Index.

Jervoise, Edwin   840
The ancient bridges of the south of England. 1930. **The ancient bridges of the north of England.** 1931. **The ancient bridges of mid and eastern England.** 1932. **The ancient bridges of Wales and western England.** 1936. London: Architectural Press. Reprinted, Wakefield: E.P. Publishing.
> A river-by-river survey of ancient bridges. Each volume includes an index of bridges.

Meeks, Carroll L. V.   841
The railway station: an architectural history. London: Architectural Press; New Haven: Yale University Press, 1957. 203pp. Bibl pp 175–186.
> A chronological and detailed study of the large passenger railway stations of the Western world from 1800–1956. Index.

Public Works, Roads and Transport Congress, 1933   842
British bridges: an illustrated technical and historical record. An introduction by J. Buchan and a paper on bridge development by C. H. Bressey. London: Public Works, Roads and Transport Congress, 1933. 498pp. Bibl p 492.
> Photographs and descriptions of 443 bridges. Index of bridges.

Ruddock, Ted   843
Arch bridges and their builders, 1735–1835.
 Cambridge: Cambridge University Press, 1979.
 254pp. Bibl pp 229–231.
  A history of bridge building in Britain and
  Ireland. Includes a chapter on bridges by
  architects. Index of bridges and general index
  (including names of architects).

For other items relating to this section see items in:

1. **How to find out: guides to the literature**
   2 *Architectural periodicals index.*
   4 Avery Architectural Library. *Catalog.*
   5 Avery Architectural Library. *An index to
     architectural periodicals.*
   10 *The British Transport Historical Records
      collection.*
   13 Cossons. *The BP book of industrial archaeology.*
   18 Department of the Environment Library.
      Catalogues.
   29 Harvard University, Graduate School of Design.
      Catalog of the library.
   32 Hudson. *Industrial archaeology: a new
      introduction.*
   34 *Industrial archaeologists' guide.*
   43 Parris. *British Transport historical records.*
   45 Royal Institute of British Architects, Library.
      Catalogue.
   46 Royal Institute of British Architects, Library.
      *Comprehensive index to architectural periodicals,
      1956–70.*
   47 Royal Institute of British Architects, Library.
      RIBA Annual review of periodical articles.
   49 Royal Institute of British Architects, Library.
      RIBA Library bulletin.

2.1 **Biographical dictionaries, encyclopaedias,
    directories, surveys and indexes**
   102 *The Industrial archaeology of the British Isles,*
       series.
   103 *Industrial archaeology of the British Isles,* series.

3. **How to find out about architects and buildings:
   unpublished sources indexes and catalogues**
   161 British Architectural Library. Classified
       catalogues.
   163 British Architectural Library. Grey books index.
   164 British Architectural Library. Periodicals subject
       index.
   167 British Architectural Library. Drawings
       Collection. Indexes.

4.3 **Some of the most important periodicals**
   188 *The Builder.*
   191 *The Civil engineer and architect's journal.*

5.2 **Guide to societies, institutions and organisations**
   226 Association for Industrial Archaeology.
   236 British Architectural Library.
   237 British Architectural Library. Drawings
       Collection.

243 British Railways Board.
248 British Waterways Board.
275 Departments of the Environment and
    Transport, Library.
296 Greater London Council.
311 Institution of Civil Engineers.
313 Institution of Structural Engineers.
336 National Railway Museum.
337 National Record of Industrial Monuments.
343 Newcomen Society for the History of
    Engineering and Technology.
352 Public Record Office.
353 Public Record Office of Northern Ireland.
356 Railway and Canal Historical Society.
383 Science Museum Library.
387 Scottish Record Office.
388 Scottish Society for Industrial Archaeology.
401 South East Wales Industrial Archaeology
    Society.
409 Transport Trust.
411 Ulster Folk and Transport Museum.

6.2 **Guide to sources of architectural photographs
    and slides**
   437 John Beecham Library.
   462 John R. Hume.
   466 Lucinda Lambton.
   467 Peter Laws.
   487 Douglas Thompson.

7.4 **Nineteenth and twentieth centuries**
   573 Curl. *Victorian architecture.*
   606 Physick. *Marble halls: drawings and models for
       Victorian secular buildings.*
   614 Summerson. *The architecture of Victorian
       London.*

7.5 **Building construction: materials and methods**
   630 *A History of technology.*
   638 Mainstone. *Developments in structural form.*

7.7 **Building types: general**
   685 Pevsner. *A history of building types.*

7.10 **Building types: industrial and commercial**
   799 Brockman. *The British architect in industry,
       1841–1940.*
   801 Buchanan. *Industrial archaeology in Britain.*

7.11 **Building types: recreational**
   820 Lindley. *Seaside architecture.*

7.14

Lighthouses and coast defences

Hague, Douglas B. and **Christie**, Rosemary   844
**Lighthouses: their architecture, history and
   archaeology.** Llandysul: Gomer Press, 1975. 307pp.
   Bibl pp 258–292.
    A survey of the world's lighthouses, old and new
    which is most thorough on the British Isles.
    Glossary. Brief biographies. Index.

Hogg, Ian V.   845
Coast defences of England and Wales,
    1856–1956. Newton Abbot: David and Charles,
    1974. 264pp. Bibl p 255.
        Discusses why they were built and how they
        were built. Appendix gives a complete list in
        alphabetical order of every defensive work of
        significance around the shores of England and
        Wales. Index.

For other items relating to this section see items in:

▬▬ **7.15**

Landscape and planning

(Follies, gardens and garden architecture, garden cities,
model villages, town planning and urban history, street
furniture, etc)

Ashworth, William   846
**The genesis of modern British town
    planning: a study in economic and social history
    of the nineteenth and twentieth centuries.**
    London: Routledge and Kegan Paul, 1954. 259pp.
    Bibl pp 238–252. (International library of sociology
    and social reconstruction).
        The first, and still excellent, general history of
        British planning from the 1830s to the 1947 Act.
        Index of place names and index of persons and
        subjects.

Aston, Michael and **Bond**, James   847
The landscape of towns. London: J. M. Dent,
    1976. 255pp. Bibl pp 221–238. (Archaeology in the
    field).
        An account of how towns have developed from
        the first substantial settlements of pre-Roman
        times to towns and cities of today, showing how
        features such as the layout of streets, the shape
        and size of buildings and the position of the
        market-place contribute to the unique character
        of every town.

Barley, M. W., *editor*   848
**The plans and topography of medieval
    towns in England and Wales.** London: Council for
    British Archaeology, 1976. 92pp. Bibl pp 84–88.
    (CBA Research Report no 14).
        Includes a chapter on sources for urban
        topography: documents, buildings, and
        archaeology, by D. M. Palliser.

Bell, Colin and Rose   849
**City fathers: the early history of town
    planning in Britain.** London: Cresset Press, 1969.
    216pp. Bibl p 214.
        Principally a study of the small, planned
        community tradition in British urban design up
        to the end of the 19th century. Index.

Cherry, Gordon E.   850
The evolution of British town planning.
  Leighton Buzzard: Leonard Hill, 1974. 275pp.
  Bibl refs.
    A commemorative volume on the history of the
    planning profession in general, and of the Royal
    Town Planning Institute from 1914–74 in
    particular, placed in the context of the broader
    development of British planning theory and
    practice. General index and index of place
    names.

Clark, H. F.   851
The English landscape garden. 2nd ed.
  Gloucester: Alan Sutton, 1980. 95pp plus 32 plates.
  Originally published London: Pleides Books,
  1948. Full documentation of Clark's study can
  be found in his article 'Eighteenth-century
  elysiums. The role of "Association" in the
  landscape movement', *Journal of the Warburg
  and Courtauld Institutes*, 6 (1943), pp 165–189,
  reprinted in *England and the Mediterranean
  tradition: studies in art, history and literature*
  (London, 1945).

Creese, Walter L.   852
**The search for environment: the garden
  city: before and after.** New Haven, London: Yale
  University Press, 1966. 340pp. Bibl notes.
    A detailed study of the British new communities
    tradition, from the early model industrial
    villages to the new towns, concentrating on the
    physical environment. Index.

Darley, Gillian   853
Villages of vision. London: Architectural Press,
  1975. 152pp. Bibl pp 149–150.
    Deals with the planned settlements and model
    villages in Britain, from the 18th century to the
    present day, including estate villages, industrial,
    religious and political communities. Gazetteer of
    post-17th-century planned villages in England
    and Wales, Scotland and Ireland. Index of
    people and places.

Dutton, Ralph   854
The English garden. 2nd ed. London:
  Batsford, 1950. 122pp. (British heritage series).
  Covers the period from 1066 to 1900. Index.

The Garden: a celebration of 1,000 years   855
  of British gardening. Edited by John
  Harris; introduction by Hugh Johnson. London:
  Mitchell Beazley in association with New
  Perspectives Publishing, 1979. 192pp.
    Originally produced to accompany an
    exhibition at the Victoria and Albert Museum, it
    contains 28 articles by specialist contributors.

The first 10 chapters cover the history and
development of garden design from medieval
times to the present day. The next chapters deal
with specific garden subjects (flowers, plants and
trees, exotic plants, tools) and on specialist
aspects of gardening (the kitchen garden, physic
and botanic gardens, herb gardens, cottage and
suburban gardens, Scottish gardens). There is a
chapter devoted to English gardening books.

Gruffydd, J. St. Bodfan   856
**Protecting historic landscapes: gardens and
  parks.** [n.p.]: The Author under the auspices of the
  Landscape Institute, 1977. 64pp. Bibl pp 62–64.
  (Leverhulme research studies).
    An argument and proposed methodology for the
    'listing', recording, and grading of historic
    landscapes similar to that for historic buildings.
    The study, however, is concerned primarily
    with Oxfordshire, north of the Thames.

Gutkind, E. A.   857
**Urban development in Western Europe: the
  Netherlands and Great Britain.** New York: Free
  Press; London: Collier-Macmillan, 1971. 512pp.
  Bibl pp 487–504. (International history of city
  development, vol 6).
    More than half of this major work is devoted to
    Great Britain. Index.

Hadfield, Miles   858
A history of British gardening. 3rd ed.
  London: J. Murray, 1979. 509pp. Bibl notes
  pp 455–474.
    A comprehensive introduction to garden history.
    First published in 1960 under the title *Gardening
    in Britain* (Hutchinson), the second edition was
    published in 1969 (London: Spring Books). Now
    extended by an appendix covering the post-war
    years by Susan and Geoffrey Jellicoe. Index and
    index to appendix.

Hunt, John Dixon and **Willis**, Peter, *editors*   859
**The genius of the place: the English
  landscape garden 1620–1820.** London: Paul Elek;
  New York: Harper and Row, 1975. 390pp.
  Bibl pp 381–382.
    An anthology of original texts, plans, and
    illustrations tracing the transformation of the
    English garden from the geometric garden of the
    Tudors and Stuarts into the *jardin anglais*. A
    short essay by the editors precedes each writer.
    Index.

Hunt, Peter, *editor*   860
The book of garden ornament. London:
  J. M. Dent, 1974. 298pp.
    Photographs of the landscaping and
    ornamentation of historic gardens with brief

accompanying text. Part 1, 'Ornaments and decorations' covers statuary, water, vases and other containers, steps, balustrades, screens etc, colonnades and pergolas, gates, sundials, ironwork, treillage, paving, garden furniture, topiary, knots and parterres and rustic adornments. Part 2, 'Gardens buildings' includes gatehouses, garden houses, temples, orangeries, chinoiserie and japonaiserie, aviaries and dovecotes, bridges, and mausoleums and memorials. Index.

Hussey, Christopher   861
English gardens and landscapes, 1700–1750.
   London: Country Life, 1967. 174pp.
      Illustrates the principal gardens and garden architecture attached to country houses. Index.

Hyams, Edward   862
The English garden. London: Thames and
   Hudson, 1964. 288pp. Bibl pp 281–283.
      A general history. List of notable gardens in Britain. Index of people. Index of places.

Jones, Barbara   863
Follies and grottoes. 2nd ed. London:
   Constable, 1974. 459pp. Bibl pp 445–446.
      The first part traces the rise and fall of folly fashions. The second part forms a reference section of over 830 follies which can be found today in England, Ireland, Scotland and Wales, arranged by county. Index.

Platt, Colin   864
The English medieval town. London:
   Paladin, 1979. 272pp. Bibl pp 257–268. Originally published: London: Secker and Warburg, 1976.
      Study of the history and archaeology of the medieval town. The chapter on the urban landscape discusses dominant influences on town plans – markets, defences, castles, abbeys; administrative and social influences, the suburbs; fortification; trading quarters; streets, paving and the prevention of encroachments; tenement plots; the first town houses; the partition of tenement plots and its effect on house plans; houses of right-angle, parallel and courtyard types; lesser town houses; cottages; sanitation; furnishings. Bibl notes. Index.

Strong, Roy   865
The renaissance garden in England.
   London: Thames and Hudson, 1979. 240pp.
   Bibl notes pp 224–233.
      Deals with the garden of the palace and the great house from its inception in the reign of Henry VIII until the outbreak of the Civil War. The illustrations include the surviving visual material in the form of plans, diagrams, views and engravings of the lost gardens of Tudor and Stuart England. Index.

Tait, A. A.   866
The landscape garden in Scotland,
   1735–1835. Edinburgh: Edinburgh University Press, 1980. 283pp. Bibl. notes.
      Shows how the landscape movement worked in Scotland and how distinct both the personalities and ideas were from those in England. Studies all the major gardens of the period and many less well-known examples. Includes a list of gardeners and their work. Index.

Taylor, Nicholas   867
The village in the city. London: Temple
   Smith, 1973. 239pp. (Towards a new society).
      A history of the suburb from the middle ages to the present day. Includes a discussion of planned housing densities and the resulting British house-types. No index.

Teodori, Massimo   868
Architettura e città in Gran Bretagna:
   pianificazione urbanistica e interventi edilizi
   nelle città inglesi degli ultima cento anni.
   Bologna: Cappelli, 1967. 255pp. Bibl pp 227–240.
      A comprehensive study emphasising physical design. Index.

Tipping, H. Avray   869
English gardens. London: Country Life, 1925.
   375pp.
      Illustrates and describes 52 English gardens from the 17th century to the 1920s.

Warren, Geoffrey   870
Vanishing street furniture. Newton Abbot,
   London etc: David and Charles, 1978. 159pp. Bibl pp 153–154.
      Covers the developments of wells, pumps, conduit heads, drinking fountains, cattle, horse and dog troughs, public lavatories, street lighting, pillar boxes, stamp-vending machines, sundials, clocks and clock towers, milestones, duty posts, signposts, bollards, warning signs, street names, house and shop numbers, cabbies' shelters, porters' rests, seats and benches, gratings and covers, mounting blocks, footscrapers and railings. The survey ends about World War I. Index.

For other items relating to this section see items in:

1.   **How to find out: guides to the literature**
     2 *Architectural periodicals index.*
     4 Avery Architectural Library. *Catalog.*
     5 Avery Architectural Library. *An index to architectural periodicals.*
    18 Department of the Environment Library. *Catalogues.*

for other items relating to this section/*continued*

19 Dobai. *Die Kunstliteratur des Klassizismus und der Romantik in England.*
26 Harley. *Historian's guide to ordnance survey maps.*
27 Harley. *Maps for the local historian.*
29 Harvard University, Graduate School of Design. *Catalog of the library.*
45 Royal Institute of British Architects, Library. *Catalogue.*
46 Royal Institute of British Architects, Library. *Comprehensive index to architectural periodicals, 1956–70.*
47 Royal Institute of British Architects, Library. *RIBA Annual review of periodical articles.*
48 Royal Institute of British Architects, Library. *RIBA Booklist.*
49 Royal Institute of British Architects, Library. *RIBA Library bulletin.*
55 Sutcliffe. *The history of modern town planning: a bibliographic guide.*
57 *Urban history yearbook.*

2.1 Biographical dictionaries, encylopaedias, directories, surveys and indexes
69 *Biographical dictionary of British gardeners.*
86 *Directory of official architecture and planning, 1974/75– .*
87 Eden. *Dictionary of land surveyors and local cartographers of Great Britain and Ireland, 1550–1850.*
97 Harris. *Catalogue of British drawings for architecture, decoration, sculpture and landscape gardening 1550–1900 in American collections.*

2.2 Indexes to research and theses
157 University of Birmingham, Centre for Urban and Regional Studies. *A first list of UK students' theses and dissertations on planning and urban and regional studies.*
158 *Urban history yearbook.*

3. How to find out about architects and buildings: unpublished sources, indexes and catalogues
161 British Architectural Library. Classified catalogues.
164 British Architectural Library, Drawings Collection. Indexes.
174 Simo. An index of country houses.

4.3 Some of the most important periodicals
184 *Architectural magazine.*
188 *The Builder.*
192 *Country life.*

5.1 Published directories to societies, institutions and organisations
201 Civic Trust. *Environmental directory.*
205 *The Environment: sources of information for teachers.*
206 *Guide to government departments and other libraries and information bureaux.*

5.2 Guide to societies, institutions and organisations
228 Association for the Protection of Rural Scotland.
236 British Architectural Library.

237 British Architectural Library. Drawings Collection.
260 Civic Trust.
267 Council for the Protection of Rural England.
268 Council for the Protection of Rural Wales.
270 Crown Estate Commissioners.
275 Departments of the Environment and Transport, Library.
278 Department of the Environment for Northern Ireland.
290 The Garden History Society.
296 Greater London Council.
297 Guildhall Library.
298 Hampstead Garden Suburb Archive.
309 Institute of Advanced Architectural Studies, University of York.
322 Landscape Institute (incorporating the Institute of Landscape Architects).
323 London Topographical Society.
331 National Institute for Physical Planning and Construction Research (An Foras Forbartha).
344 North Hertfordshire District Council, Planning Department.
345 North Hertfordshire District Council Museums Services, First Garden City Museum.
346 Ordnance Survey Department Library.
348 Planning History Group.
352 Public Record Office.
353 Public Record Office of Northern Ireland.
355 The Queen's University of Belfast, Architecture and Planning Information Service.
370 Royal Horticultural Society.
374 Royal Institution of Chartered Surveyors.
378 Royal Town Planning Institute.
387 Scottish Record Office.
408 Town and Country Planning Association.

6.2 Guide to sources of architectural photographs and slides
430 Aerofilms Ltd.
431 Malcolm Aird Associates.
447 Denness Collection of Colour Prints.
457 The Iris Hardwick Library of Photographs.
466 Lucinda Lambton.
478 Postal Publicity Photographic Library.
483 Jessica Strang.
490 University of Cambridge, Committee for Aerial Photography.
495 Andy Williams Photographic Library.
496 Woodmansterne Ltd.
497 John and Patricia Woolverton Colour Library.

7.3 Renaissance to neoclassic
549 Burke. *English art, 1714–1800.*
550 Chalklin. *The provincial towns of Georgian England.*
553 Davis. *The gothick taste.*
554 Downes. *English baroque architecture.*
556 Pilcher. *The Regency style, 1800–1830.*
559 Steegman. *The Rule of taste from George I to George IV.*
561 Summerson. *Georgian London.*
562 *Vitruvius Britannicus.*

.4 Nineteenth and twentieth centuries
  569 Burton. *A choice over our heads: a guide to
        architecture and design since 1830.*
  602 Olsen. *The growth of Victorian London.*
  606 Physick. *Marble halls: drawings and models for
        Victorian secular buildings.*

.5 Building construction: materials and methods
  631 Hix. *The glass house.*
  635 Knowles. *A history of building regulation in
        London, 1189–1972.*

.8 Building types: domestic
  688 Automobile Association. *AA guide to stately
        homes, castles and gardens.*
  705 Fleming. *Scottish country houses and gardens open
        to the public.*
  710 Gotch. *The English home from Charles I to
        George IV.*
  714 Harris. *The artist and the country house: a history
        of country house and garden view painting in
        Britain, 1540–1870.*
  717 *Historic houses, castles and gardens in Great
        Britain and Ireland.*
  718 Jackson. *Semi-detached London: suburban
        development, life and transport, 1900–39.*
  719 Jones. *English village homes and country buildings.*
  724 Macartney. *English houses and gardens in the 17th
        and 18th centuries.*
  744 Tipping. *English homes.*

7.13 Building types: transport
  836 Binney. *Railway architecture.*

▬ Index

The index contains entries under authors, editors, organisations, subjects and titles. Title entries are generally made for main entries only. References are to item numbers, except where subjects have been treated extensively within a particular section, wher references are to section numbers. Arrangement is word-by-word.

Additional items relating to a particular section are noted at the end of that section and are therefore not specifically noted in the index.

(p) indicates collection of photographs
(s) indicates collection of slides

C

C

D

D

E

E

F

F

H

H

N

N

O

P

P

Q

R

S

T

U

V

W